NEWSPAPER D
OF THE
Vol. 1: Apr   ber 1, 1775

Armand Francis Lucier

HERITAGE BOOKS, INC.

OTHER HERITAGE BOOKS BY THE AUTHOR:

1767 CHRONICLE (1995)

JOURNAL OF OCCURRENCES, 1768-1769: PATRIOT PROPAGANDA ON THE BRITISH OCCUPATION OF BOSTON (1996)

JOLLY OLD ENGLAND (1996)

*FRENCH AND INDIAN WAR NOTICES
ABSTRACTED FROM COLONIAL NEWSPAPERS:
VOLUME 1: 1754-1755 (1999)
VOLUME 2: 1756-1757 (1999)
VOL. 3: JAN. 1, 1758-SEPT. 17, 1759 (1999)
VOL. 4: SEPT. 17, 1759-DEC. 30, 1760 (1999)
AFTERMATH, VOL. 5: Jan 1, 1761-Jan 17, 1763 (2000)*

*Pontiac's Conspiracy & Other Indian Affairs:
Notices Abstracted from Colonial Newspapers, 1763-1765 (2000)*

PUBLISHED 2001 BY

HERITAGE BOOKS, INC.
1540E POINTER RIDGE PLACE
BOWIE, MARYLAND 20716
1-800-398-7709
WWW.HERITAGEBOOKS.COM

ISBN 0-7884-1805-X

A COMPLETE CATALOG LISTING HUNDREDS OF TITLES
ON HISTORY, GENEALOGY, AND AMERICANA
AVAILABLE FREE UPON REQUEST

FOREWORD

In the year 1775 there were 34 newspapers in the American Provinces with a combined circulation of about 5000 copies a week. *Datelines of the American Revolution* is a collection of articles published in the various cities and towns, arranged chronologically as to each publishing date.

In many cases these weekly newspapers were the only source of information the inhabitants received from outside of their communities.

The root of these articles published came to hand many different ways; authentic accounts, letters, proclamations, speeches, affidavits, and from newspapers exchanged from each of the provinces. At times unconfirmed reports and fabrications were printed.

Volume One begins with the opening volleys at Lexington and Concord, followed by the Battle of Bunker Hill. It also covers other skirmishes and military affairs, up to the siege of St. John's.

These newspapers reported the meeting of the delegates at the Continental Congress in Philadelphia. Imagine the public reaction when the Congress voted to unite the Provinces into one force for the common cause, and chose George Washington to command the united military forces.

At times readers may find some of these letters, commentaries, and speeches lengthy; yet, they are essential in order to understand the sentiments of the American people and their leaders.

Armand Francis Lucier.

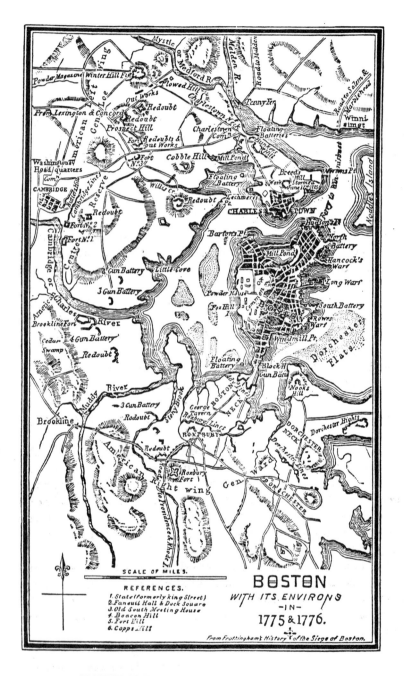

"BOSTON WITH ITS ENVIRONS IN 1775-1776"
From *Library of American History* by Edward S. Ellis.
Jones Brothers Publishing, Cincinnati, Ohio, 1905.

CONTENTS

CONTRIBUTORS

Boston Gazette. Watertown Massachusetts.
Connecticut Courant. Hartford Connecticut.
Essex Gazette. Salem Massachusetts.
Halifax Gazette. Halifax Nova Scotia.
Lloyd's Evening Post. London England.
London Gazette. London England.
Maryland Gazette. Annapolis Maryland.
Massachusetts Gazette. Boston Massachusetts.
Massachusetts Spy. Worcester Massachusetts.
New England Chronicle. Cambridge Massachusetts.
New Hampshire Gazette. Portsmouth New Hampshire.
New Haven Mercury. New Haven Connecticut.
New London Gazette. New London Connecticut.
New York Gazette. New York New York.
New York Journal. New York New York.
New York Mercury. New York New York.
Norfolk Gazette. Norfolk Virginia.
Norfolk Intellegincier. Norfolk Virginia.
North Carolina Gazette. Wilmington N. Carolina.
Norwich Packet. Norwich Connecticut.
Pennsylvania Gazette. Philadelphia Pa.
Providence Gazette. Providence Rhode Island.
South Carolina Gazette. Charlestown S. Carolina.

All articles are presented with no attempt to
correct composition, punctuation, capitalization
or spelling, except where it was thought for
clarity.

APRIL 1775

SALEM April 18. Capt. Collins brings advice, That the Act for restraining the Trade and blocking up all the Ports of New-England, had passed the House of Commons. That Lord Chathan, with a Number of his patriotic Friends, finding their efforts, for saving the Nation from tyranny and the Horrors of a Civil War ineffectual, arose from their Seats, and abruptly left the House of Lords, giving as a Reason for their Conduct, that they would have no farther Concern in a Legislature who were involving the Nation in Blood and Slaughter.

NORWICH April 22. This Evening, a little after 7 o'Clock, Mr. David Nevins, who yesterday forenoon, went Express from this Town, to obtain Intelligence, returned from Providence, with the following important Advices.

On Tuesday Evening last, Advice was received here from Boston that a Detachment of the King's Troops had fired upon and killed a Number of the Inhabitants of Lexington, about Twelve Miles from Boston; in Consequence of which an Engagement had happened.

Upon receiving the alarming Intelligence, the Inhabitants of the Province immediately assembled. The Officers of the Independent Companies and Militia with a Number of Gentlemen of the Town had a Meeting, and two Expresses were dispatched for Lexington to obtain authentic accounts while others were sent in different parts of this Colony and Connecticut.

The Express that went to Lexington returned yesterday Morning, and relate in substance the following.

"On Tuesday Night, the 18th Instant about 1300 Troops very privately embarked at Charlestown ferry, in boats, and after landing at Cambridge,

proceeded towards Concord, in order, as is supposed, to destroy the Provincial Magazine.

"At Lexington, early next Morning they came to
with a small Number of Men, who were performing
the Manual Exercise, and after accosting them
in Language the most prophane and insulting,
ordered them to lay down their Arms and to disperse, which they at first refused to do, but on
being threatened they began to dispurse, and
were immediately fired upon and eight of them
killed.

"The Troops afterwards proceeded to Concord
where they destroyed about 60 Barrels of Flour
and some Gun-cartriges after which they began to
return when about 300 Americans coming up, a
skirmish ensued.

"At Lexington the Troops received a reinforcement of 1000 Men and Two-Field-Pieces, notwithstanding which, the Americans continued to push
them closely, and pursued them about 12 Miles
to Bunker's Hill, in Charlestown, when Night
coming on the firing ceased. Our People, not
thinking it prudent to attack them in so advantageous a Situation without Artillery.

"The Troops immediately entrenched on the Hill,
and the Americans, after placing a strong Guard
to observe their Motions, marched to Cambridge,
at which and other place, large Bodies of Americans have since assembled.

"On Thursday the 20th Instant, about four o'-
Clock in the Afternoon the Troops suddenly de-
camped, embarked on board Boats at Charlestown,
and returned to Boston.

"That of the King's Troops. One Lieutenant,
and about 70 Privates were killed, a considerable Number wounded and about 30 taken Prisoners,
among whom are two Captains: That on the part of
the Americans, about 30 were killed, and 3 or 4
taken Prisoners; not a single wounded man stand
alive. The Troops having, with a Barbarity heretofore unpracticed by British Soldiers, destroyed all they met with: That at Lexington they
burnt Four dwellings and Two Out Houses, an aged
Man whom was found sick in his Bed, was run
through with a Bayonet; and Two aged infirm
persons were shot in another House: That Altho'

the Americans were continually reinforced by small parties, not more than 300 were at any time engaged: That they behaved with the greatest intrepidity; and had they been joined by the main body which assembled at Concord, while waiting to receive the Troops on another Road (which it was expected they would take) it is believed the whole Corps would have been cut off."

After the Troops had returned to Boston, 150 of the Americans marched to Marshfield, in order to engage what Troops they should find there.

This Morning two Gentlemen Members of Rhode-Island Assembly, at Providence, informed Mr. Nevins, That on the Way to the Eastward, they heard a heavy and continued Firing, which they imagined was another Engagement between the Americans and the King's Troops at Marshfield; and added, that they perceived in that Quarter, a Line of Fire, about Half a Mile in Length, which had been much the Appearance of Buildings burning.

PROVIDENCE April 22. The several Independent companies of this and the neighbouring towns, and a body of the militia in all 1000 men, were in readiness, and some of them had begun to march; but on receiving authentic advice that they would be notified by an Express if their assistance should be necessary, one of the companies has since returned here, and the others, we hear were about to return also. The whole of them, however to be in readiness to march at a moment's warning.

The Troops at Marshfield having, it is said, fired on some minute men, and killed two of their number, a large body of Americans, with some of the pieces of cannon, we are told, have marched to attack them.

NEWPORT April 24. We this moment hear the Americans have taken half the soldiers at Marshfield, the other having made their escape into the swamp where they were surrounded, so that it is almost impossible for them to get out without being taken.

NORWICH April 24. Sunday 4. P. M. A Gentleman arrived here this Day, and has favoured us with the following Particulars, which we think proper

3

to communicate to the Public; who may depend,
that the most strenuous Exertion of abilities,
and unremitting assidity of the Publishers,
shall never be wanting to give them Satisfaction.

Concord, April 21. To Col. E. Williams,
Sir,
I have waited on the Committee of the Provincial Congress and it is their Determination to
have a Standing Army of 22,000 Men from New-England Colonies, of which, it is supposed, the
Colony of Connecticut must raise 6,000, and begs
they would be at Cambridge as speedily as possible, with Conveniences; together with provisions, and a sufficiency of Ammunition for their
own use.

The Battle here is much as had been represented, at present, except that there is more killed,
and a Number more taken Prisoner.

The Accounts at present are so confused, that
it is impossible to ascertain the Number exact,
but shall inform you of the proceedings, from
Time to Time, as we have new Occourrances; mean
Time I am, Sir, your humble Servant

Israel Putnam.
further Notice, A True Copy   E. Williams.
Monday Morning, One o'Clock
About Nine o'Clock last Evening the fillowing
Letters were brought here by Express from Wood-
stock.

Gentlemen,
The Accounts I have yet received from the Army
are confused, and no great certainty is yet to
be had of the particular State and Circumstances
of our Forces or those of the Enemy. Thus much,
however may be depended upon; That British Forces are retreated to Boston: That the Siege of
the Town and Castle is determined upon: That the
Number slain of the British Troops far exceeds
that of the Provincials: The proportion, as near
as I collect, is about Five or Six to One.

Among their Slain are some Officers; the Commander of the first Brigade is supposed to be
among the Dead; The Ravages and barbarous Cruelty of the Enemies is almost unparalleled among
the Savage Nations ——— Old Men, Women, and

4

children have not escaped their brutal Rage, but in some Instances have been cut to pieces in a most inhuman Manner.

A Son of the infamous Mundamus Counsellor, Col. Murray, went out with the first Brigade, as their Guide is among the Slain.

More Men will doubtless be wanted; I therefore whish them to be detached and in readiness as soon as possible, but not to march till further Orders.

The Troops from Lyme are not yet arrived here but I hope they will join us this Day. I wish our Provisions to be in readiness as soon as possible, and sent on, unless Accounts are received that we are on Return.

On meeting the Express from Boston, I beg of you to forward Provisions forthwith, with a Further Reinforcement from our Regiment to be ready
Samuel Parsons.
To the Committee of New-London and Lyme.
Woodstock, April 23, 1775.

Thursday 4. P. M.
Mr. David Nevins of this Town, who has been indefatigable to obtain authentic Intelligence, having this Day, and has favoured us with the following Accounts: That his Excellency General Gage has published a Manifesto, forbidding the Troops, under his Command, to injure or insult such of the Inhabitants of Boston as are peaceable, on Pain of Death. That as many of the people of Boston are so inclined, are to have Liberty to leave the Town, this Day, and retire into the Country with their Effects, after the depositing of their Arms in Custody of the Select Men of the Town.

Mr. Nevins has credibly informed, that during the few Days that all the intercourse between Boston and the Country was prohibited, many Inhabitants of the former would have been greatly distressed for the necessaries of Life, if not the General humanely supplied in those that applied to him.

A Gentleman from Newport informs us that on Thursday last, many of the Inhabitants of that place were in motion to assist their Brethren near Boston; information of which being brought on board the Rose Man of War, (then opposite the Town) the Commander immediately got a Spring upon the Cable, and sent an Officer on shore to intimate to the Governor, that at that same Minute a Party of armed Men left the Town, it should be knocked about the Ears of its Inhabitants.

By a Gentleman of veracity just arrived from New-York, we are informed, That News of the Brigade marching out of Boston, &c. was received by an Express at New-York about 6 o'Clock on Sunday Morning: Immediately on which the Committee convened, and at 5 o'Clock in the Afternoon, they were met by a large Body of the Sons of Freedom; who, between 7 and 8 o'Clock went to the Mayor and requested the Keys of the Old City-Hall, in which were deposited the City Arms: He at first refused to comply, but told them, if they would wait till Morning, he would deliver the Keys to them; but they did not chuse to wait till that Time, but immediately went to the hall, and with an Ax began to break the door; on which the Mayor delivered the Keys, and they took out 600 Arms, leaving a Centry of 50 Men to guard the remainder, At 2 o'Clock the next Morning they took the Residue. On Monday Morning the Sons of Freedom went through the City with a Drum for Volunteers, and there immediately appeared about 1500, who engaged to be ready to march on the short-of Notice. On Sunday Evening they set a Guard of 50 Men at the powder House, the same night they unloaded a Sloop (Supposed to be Capt. Burnam's) who had taken in a Load of Flour for the King's Troops at Boston, and put the same in the Store from whence it was taken. The Person who loaded the Vessel, acknowlwdged his Error to the Committee, and promised never to give the like offence again.

The Hon. Assembly of this Colony met Yesterday, at Hartford; many Gentlemen, from the various Towns in the Vicinity, set out this Morning to accommodate the members with the most recent Advices, and be presented at the spirited Resolves, which it is presumed they will make.

Our latest Advices from Providence import, That the Lower House of Rhode-Island Assembly,

voted, That a Body of Men should immediately be
raised to defend the Colony; but the Upper House
rejected the Bill. These transactions coming to
the knowledge of the Inhabitants, they surrounded the Court-House, and exclaimed against the
conduct of the Council. After much Altercation
a Bill passed that 1500 Men should be forthwith
raised and paid by the Colony.
NORWICH April 24. Monday Morning, One o'Clock.
about Nine o'Clock last Evening the following
Letters were brought here by Express from Woodstock. To the Committee of New-London and Lyme.
            Cambridge, Saturday Morning, April 22.
    Gentlemen,
I have waited on the General and several Committees, and they all agree that the Men must
come down to this Place, for we know not when
we shall be attacked in this confused State,
The Troops in Boston are in Motion, and preparing to make an Attack some where; but we have
no News from Boston unless by some few of the
Inhabitants that run the risque of their Lives
by getting out of Town by Stealth, for Boston
is shut up! There is no coming or going out any
other Way! The People of the Town are all Prisoners, and what their Fate will be, God only
known; for the Troops have behaved in a very
cruel and barbarous Manner; going into Houses
and killing sick People, that were not able to
go one step, putting the Muzzle of the Gun into
their Mouths, and blowing their Heads in Pieces.
Some Children had their Brains beat out! several Houses and Barns burned! and, for Miles together not a House or Shop but had their Windows
broke, and hundreds of shot in them! They were
about 40 of our People killed, but rather more
of the Troops, and 30 of the latter taken Prisoners. Enough of that, for this confused State!
Prey let the Men be properly inlisted and officered; let their Teams to bring Provisions,
and further Supply sent immediately after them.
    Take care they be sent in good order.
                                Israel Putnam.
        A True Copy   Hezikiah Bissel.
Tuesday Morning, the following was brought by
express, to Colonel Judidiah Harrington of this

7

Town, Dated at Pomfret on Monday the 20th inst.
3 o'Clock P. M.

Sir,

I am this moment informed, by express from Woodstock, taken from the Mouth of the Express that
arrived there, 2 o'Clock this afternoon, that the
Contest between the first Brigade that marched
to Concord, was still continuing this Morning,
at the town of Lexington, to which said Brigade
had retreated. That another Brigade, said to be
the second, mentioned in the letter of this
Morning, had landed with a Quantity of Artillery, at the place where the first Troops did;
the Provincials were determined to prevent the
two Brigades from joining their Strength if possible, and remain still in the greatest need of
Succours.

N. B. The Regulars, when at Concord, burnt the
Court-House, took two Pieces of Cannon, which
they rendered Useless, and began to take take up
Concord Bridge, on which Capt. Davis, who with
many on both Sides , were killed, then made an
attack upon the King's Troops, on which they
retreated to Lexington.

In haste, I am Sir, Your Most Humble
Servent.   Ebenezer Williams.

To Col. Obadiah Johnson, Canterbury.

P. S. Mr. McFarling, of Plainfield, Merchant,
has just now returned from Boston, by way of
Providence, who conversed with an Express from
Lexington, who further informs that about 4,000
of our People had surrounded the first Brigade
above-mentioned, who were on a hill in Lexington
that the action continued and that there were
about 50 of our people killed and 150 of the Regulars, as near as they could be determined,
when the Express came away.

NEW-YORK April 24. Yesterday Morning we had
Reports in this City from Rhode-Island and New
London, That an Action had happened between the
King's Troops and the Inhabitants of Boston,
which was not credited; but about 12 o'Clock an
Express arrived with the following account, viz.

Watertown, Wednesday Morning near 10 o'Clock
to all Friends of American Liberty, let it be
known,

That this Morning before break of Day, a brigade consisting of about 1000 or 1200 Men Landed at Phip's, at Cambridge, and marched to Lexington, where they found a Company of our Colony Militia in Arms, upon whom they fired without any provocation, and killed 6 Men and wounded 4 others. By Express from Boston we find another Brigade are upon their March from Boston, supposed to be about 1000. The Bearer Israel Bissel is charged to alarm the Country quite so Connectient, and all persons are desired to furnish him with fresh horses, as they may be needed. I have spoken with several who have seen the Dead and Wounded. Pray let the Delegates from the Colony of Connecticut see this: they know Col. Foster, of Brookfield one of our Delegates.

T. Palmer one of the Committee for Safety, a True Copy taken from the Original, per order of the Committee of Correspondence for Worcester April 20, 1775.

SALEM April 25. Last Wednesday, the 19th of April, the Troops of his Britannick Majesty commenced Hostilities upon the People of this Province, attended with circumstances of cruelty not less brutal than with our venerable Ancestors received from the vilest Savages of the wilderness. The Particulars relative to this Interesting Event, by which we are involved in all the Horrors of a civil War, we have endeavoured to collect as well as the present confused State of Affairs will admit.

On Tuesday Evening a Detachment from the Army, consisting it is said of 8 or 900 Men, Commanded by Lieut. Col. Smith, embarked at the Bottom of the Common in Boston, on board a Number of Boats, and landed at Phips's Farm, a little Way up the Charles River, from whence they proceeded with Silence and Expedition, on their Way to Concord, about 18 Miles from Boston. The People were soon alarmed, and began to assemble, in several Towns, before Day-Light, in order to watch the motion of the Troops. At Lexington, 6 Miles from Concord, a Company of Militia, of about 100 Men, mustered near the Meeting-House; the Troops came in sight of them just before Sun-rise; and running within a few Rods of them, the commanding

Officer accosted the Militia in words to this
effect. —— "Disperse you Rebels —— Damn you,
throw down your Arms and Disperse:" Upon which
the Troops huzzad, and immediately one or two
Officers discharged their Pistols, which were
instantly followed by the Firing of 4 or 5 of
the Soldiers, and then there seemed take a general Discharge from the whole body: Eight of our
Men were killed, and nine wounded. In a few Minutes after the Action the Enemy renewed their
March for Concord: at which Place they destroyed
several Carriages, Carriage Wheels, and about
20 Barrels of Flour, all belonging to the Province. Here about 150 Men going towards a Bridge
of which the Enemy were in Possession, the latter fired, and killed 2 of our Men, who then
returned the fire, and obliged the Enemy to retreat back to Lexington, where they met Lord
Percy, with a large Reinforcement, with two
Pieces of Cannon. The Enemy now having a Body
of about 1800 Men, made a Halt, picked up many
of their Dead, and took Care of their wounded.
At Menotomy, a few of our Men attacked a Party
of twelve of the Enemy, (carrying Stores and
Provisions to the Troops) killed one of them,
wounded several, made the rest Prisoners, and
took Possession of all the Arms, Stores, Pro-
vosions, &c. without any loss on our Side. The
Enemy having halted one or two Hours at Lexington, found it necessary to make a second retreat
carrying with them many of their Dead and Wounded, who they put into Chaises and on Horses that
they found standing in the Road. They continued
their Retreat from Lexington to Charlestown
with great Precipitation; and notwithstanding
their Field-Pieces, our People continued the
Pursuit, firing at them till they got to Charlestown Neck, (which they reached a little after
Sunset) over which the Enemy passed, proceeded
to Bunker's Hill, and soon afterwards went into
Town, under the Protection of the Somerset Man
of War. of 64 Guns.

In Lexington the Enemy set Fire to Deacon Joseph Loring's House and Barn, Mrs. Mulliken's
House, and Shop, and Mr. Joshua Bond's House
and Shop, which were all consumed. They also set

Fire to to several Houses, but our People extinguished the Flames. They pillaged almost every House they passed by, breaking and destroying Doors, Windows, Glasses, &c. and carrying off Cloathing and other valuable Effects. It Appeared to be their Design to burn and destroy all before them; and nothing but our rigorous Pursuit prevented their infernal Purposes from being put in Execution. But the savage Barbarity execised upon the Bodies of our unfortunate Brethren who fell is almost incredible: Not content with shooting down the unarmed, aged and infirm, they disregarded the Cries of the wounded, killing them without Mercy, and mangling their Bodies in the most shocking Manner.

We have the Pleasure to say, that, notwithstanding the highest Provocation, given by the Enemy, not one Instance of Cruelty, that we heard of was committed by our victorious Militia; but, listening to the merciful Dictates of the Christian Religion, they "Breached higher Sentiments of Humanity."

The Consternation of the People of Charlestown when our Enemies were entering the Town, is inexpressible; the Troops however behaved tolerably civil, and the People have since nearly all left the Town.

The Public most sincerely sympathize with the Friends and Relitives of our deceased Brethren, who gloriously sacrificed their Lives, in fighting for the Liberties of their Country. By there noble, intrepid Conduct in belonging to defeat the Forces at the ungreatful Tyrant, they have endeared their Memories to the present Generation, who will transmit their Names to posterity with the highest Honours.

NEWPORT April 27. We are assured, that there are thirty thousand men in the province of Pennsylvania, determined to protect the Congress, in case any attempt should be made to dispurse it.

PORTSMOUTH April 28. It is proposed for the Confederation of all America, that the memories of all such noble Persons, who for the Liberties of this Country shall be so unfortunate to fall in Battle, shall be honorably prepretuated to

11

Posterity, that their Families shall be immediately and handsomely provided for, their Widows shall have a fixed Annuity for Life, which shall enable them to live as well as in their Husbands Life time, and that the Children shall be provided for an education at the Public Expence.

MAY 1775

HARTFORD May 1. Extract of a Letter from Cambridge April 24, 1775.

"I understand that General Gage has sent to seize all our vessels, upon the sea coast, and if you have any at New-London, I believe you may expect soon to be visited."

The following is a true Copy of the kill'd, wounded, and prisoners in the late Engagement, taken by Capt. Mason, Provincial Engineer, and said to be in a letter from General Gage to the Navy. 19 Marines, 63 Soldiers, 103 wounded and taken Prisoners.

The Boston and New-York Posts are stopt, and do not perform their usual stages.

New-York May 1. Extract of a Letter received from Weathersfield, April 23, 1775.

"The late frequent Marching and countermarching into the Country, were calculated to conceal the most cruel and inhuman Design, and imagining they had laid Suspicion asleep, they picked on Wednesday Night for the Execution. A Hint being got, two Expresses were sent to alarm the Congress; one of them had the good fortune to arrive, the other (Mr. Revere) is missing, supposed to be Way-laid and slain. In the Night of Tuesday, the Company of Grenadiers and of Light Infantry, from every Regiment, were Transported to Charlestown in Long Boats, and at Day-Break began their march to Lexington, where a Number of the Inhabitants were assembled peaceably without Arms to consult their Safety. The Commander called them Rebels, and bid them all to disperse. On their Refusal, he fired, killed killed and wounded nine. Then proceeded on towards Concord, marching their way with Cruelty and Barbarity never equaled by the Savages of America. In one House a Woman and seven Children

13

were slaughtered (perhaps on their Return) At Concord they seized two Pieces of Cannon, and destroyed two others, with all the Flour, &c.

"By this Time about 400 (no Account make them more than 500) of our Men assembled, and placed themselves so advantageously, without being perceived that when the Enemy were on their return, they received the full fire of our Men. A heavy Engagement ensued, the Enemy retreating and our Men pressing on them with constant reinforcements. At Lexington; they retook their two Pieces of Cannon, seized the Enemy's Waggons and Baggage, and made about 20 Prisoners, continued to press the Regulars close to Charlestown, where they were on the point of giving up (one Account says, this Brigade was almost all cut off) but Reinforcements, under the command of Lord Percy, having been detached that morning from Boston, they joined the first Detachment in the return and retired with it to Bunker's Hill, where they entreanched, and Night parted them. Our Numbers increased, and next Morning would have surrounded the Hill, had it not been for the situation near the Water, where one Side they were exposed to the Fire from a Man of War.

"We lost 30 Men in the Action. The lowest account of the Enemy's loss 150, Lord Percy, Gen. Haldimand, and many of the Officers, are said among the slain. A Gentleman of Veracity assured us, that he numbered without Half a Mile from the Place, where the fight began, 150. The Post confirms the same Account.

"We are in Motion here, and equipt from the Town Yesterday, 100 young Men, who cheerfully offered their Services, 10 Days Provisions and 64 Rounds per Man. They are all well armed and in high spirits, my Brother is gone with them, and others of the first Property. Our Neighbouring Towns are all arming and moving. Men of the first Character and Property, shoulder their Arms and march off for the Field of Action. We shall by Night have several Thousand from this Colony, on their march.

"The Eyes of America are on New-York, the Ministry have certainly been promised by some of your leading Men, that your Province would desert us, but you will be able to form a better judgement when you see how this Intelligence is relished. Take care yourself, we have more than Men enough to block up the Enemy at Boston; and if we are like to fall by Treachery by Heaven we will not fall unrevenged of the Traitors; But if Ball and Broads will reach them, they shall fall with us. It is no Time now to dally, or to be meagerly neutral, he that is not for us, is against us, and ought to feel the first of our Resentment. You must now declare most explicitly, one way or the other; that we may know whether we are to go to Boston or New-York; if you desert, our Men will as cheerfully attack New-York as Boston, for we can but perish, and that we are determined upon, or be free. I have nothing more to add, but I am,

Your Freind and Countryman, &c,"
"P. S. Col. Murray's Son, one of the Tories, undertook to guide the regulars in the march to Concord, and their Retreat was taken Prisoner, but attempting to escape from our People, they shot him, a death to honourable for such a Villain! They have made another of them a Prisoner but I do not recollect his Name; none of ours were taken.

Query. Will Col. Grant believe now that New-England Men dare look Regulars in the Face? —— Eighteen Hundred of their best Men retreating with Loss, before on Third of their Number, —— seems almost incredible, and I think must be called upon to show the world, "That whom our call Fathers did beget us," and that we desire to enjoy the Blessings they purchased for us, with their Lives and Fortunes. We fix on our Standard and Drums, the Colony Arms, with the motto, round it in letters of gold, which we construe thus; God who transplanted us hither, will support us.

Extract of another letter of the same date.
"On Tuesday Night the 18th Instant, as secretly as possible, General Gage Draughted out about 1000 or 1200 the best Troops, which he embarked on a Transport, and landed that Night at Cambridge. Wednesday Morning by Day break they marched up to Lexington, where before breakfast,

as usual, about 30 of the Inhabitants were prac-
ticing the manual Exercise, Upon with the least
Provocation, they fired about 15 Minutes, killed
six Men, and wounded several, without a single
shot from our Men, who retreated as past as possible. Hence they proceed to Concord; on the
Road thither, they fired at, and killed a Man on
Horseback, went to the House where Mr. Hancock
lodged, who, with Mr. Samuel Adams, luckily got
out of their Way, but by the means of a secret
and speedy Intelligence. The House was searched
for them, but when they could not be found, the
inhuman Soldiery killed the Woman of the House
and all the Children, and set Fire to the House.
Mr. Paul Revere was Missing when the Express
came away. In their to Concord, the Regulars
Fired at and killed Hogs, Geese, Cattle and every thing that came in their way, and burnt several Houses.

When they came to Concord they took possession
of the Court-House, destroyed about 100 Barrels
of Flour, and many of Pork, pluged up one Cannon,
and broke another belonging to the Provincials,
after which they matched back towards Boston.
But before they marched far, they were met by
300 Provincials, who received two Fires from the
Regulars before they returned it. On the second
Fire from the Provincials, the Troops began to
retreat Firing regularly, till the came to Cambridge Plains, when the Provincials had now increased the fire of Six Hundred; the Troops then
took to their Heels, and ran helter skelter;
our Men pursuing and killing then, till they
came to a place called Bunken Hill in Charles
Town. General Gage knowing they were attacked,
sent out Reinforcement of about 900, with Waggons of Provisions, this Reinforcement was boldly attacked, by a less number of Provincials;
on which a brisk Skirmish ensued. Our Men had so
much the advantage as to take the Waggons and
Provisions, killed the Commander of them Capt.
Hogskie; and take 8 Prisoners: 10 more clubed
their Muskets and came over to us, and many were
killed on both Sides. The Remainder of the Reinforcement joined the main body, which all retreated together, till they come to Bunken Hill,

16

where they encamped.

Night put an end to the Firing, the Country having been alarmed, the Provincials joined in from every Quarters. When the Express left the Place, he said there could not be less than 30 or 40,000 of our Men under Arms, and more coming very fast. They had surrounded the Regular Troops, and were throwing up an entrenchment to hinder their Retreat on the N. E. side where a Ship of War lies within a Mile of them. Our Men are in high Spirits, no dejected countenance among them, which is not the case with the Regulars. It is supposed 150 of the latter are killed, and among them Lord Percy and General Haldimand, but this is only a conjecture. Of our Men it is supposed we have lost about 30 or 40, but none of note, that we can hear of. The whole Colony is alarmed, and has already marched, and is ready.

This moment an Express is arrived. The Troops Encamped on Thursday Night got to Boston under the Guns of the Ships. Percy is Missing, supposed to be Burned with the other Dead, by the Regular Troops in a Barn. Col. Murray's Son, who was the Pilot out is dead.

NEW-YORK May 1. Since our last we have received the following Particulars relative to the Action that lately happened at Boston, between the King's Troops and the Inhabitants of Massachusetts-Bay, viz.

Wallingford, Monday April 24,
Dear Sir,
Colonel Wadsworth was over in this Place most of Yesterday, and has ordered 20 Men out of each Company in his Regiment, some of which had already set off, and others go this Morning. He brings Accounts, which came to him authenticated from Thursday in the Afternoon. The King's Troops being reinforced a second Time, and joined, and suppose, from what I can learn, by the Party who were intercepted by Col. Gardner, were then encamped on Winter-Hill, and were surrounded by 20,000 of our Men, who were entrenching. Col. Gardner's Ambush proved fatal to Lord Percy, and another General Officer, who were killed on the spot, the first Fire.

17

To Counterbalance this good News, the Story
is that our first Man to command, (who he is I
know not) is also killed. It seem they had lost
many Men on both Sides. Col. Wadsworth had the
account in a Letter from Hartford. The Country
beyond here are all gone, and we expect it will
be impossible to procure Horses for our Waggons,
as they have, and will, in every Place employ
themselves, all their Horses. In this Place they
find a Horse for every 6th Man and pressing them
for that Purpose. I know of no Way but you must
immediately send a couple of suitable Horses who
may overtake us at Hartford possibly; where we
must return Mrs. Noyes's and Meloy's if he holds
out so far. Remember the Horses must be had at
any rate. I am in the greatest Haste, your entire Friend and humble Servant.

James Lockwood.

N. B. Col. Gardner took 9 Prisoners, and 12
clubbed their Firelocks and come over to our
Party. Col. Gardner's Party consisted of 700
and the Regulars 1800 instead of 1200, as we
heard before; they have sent a Vessel up Mystic
River, as far as Temple's Farm, which is about
Half a Mile from Winter Hill. These Accounts
being true, all the King's Forces except 4 or
500 must be encamped at Winter Hill.

At this Instance of the Gentlemen of Fairfield
departed from hence, this is copied Verbatim
from the Original to be forwarded to that Town.

Isaac Beers.
Pierport Edwards.

New-Haven April 24, Half past 9, forenoon.
The above copy, came authenticated from the
several Towns through which it passed, by the
following Gentlemen, viz.

Fairfield, 24th April, 3 o'Clock afternoon
Thadeus Burr, Andrew Rowland, Elijah Abel.

Norwalk, 24th April, 7 o'Clock Afternoon,
John Cannon, Thadeus Burr, Samuel Graman,
Committee.

Stanford 24th April Evening, John Hait jun.
Samuel Hotton, David Waith, Daniel Gray, Jonathan Waring, jun.

Greenwich, April 25, 3 0'Clock Morning, Amos
Mead.

The following Gentlemen write, that in each
Town, they shall hold themselves in Readiness
to march more men immediately, if wanted, and
request their Brethren in the Western Towns and
Governments to do the same, and that all material Intelligence, shall be forwarded with
speed.

Some Accounts mentioned, that the soldiery
had been guilty of some shocking Barbarities,
in wantonly burning Houses and murdering Men,
Women and Children; but on those we shall not
mention Particulars, till the Arrival of more
circumstantial Accounts.

NEW-YORK May 1. We hear they are Letters in
this Town; from Connecticut, which say, That the
Number of Men lately dissembled at Boston, including those from Connecticut and Rhode Island
Amounting to 60,000; that they are mostly returned to their respective Homes, leaving an
Army of about 15,000 to watch General Gage's
Motions, who, we are told, has given the Inhabitants of Boston Permission to leave the Town,
on Condition they left their Arms behind them;
that two Frigates, and three General Officers
were arrived at Boston from England, and a large
Number of Troops hourly expected; and both General Gage and the Inhabitants of Boston, had
sent Expresses to Great-Britain with Accounts
of the late Action at Lexington and Concord.

We are well assured, that the Report of the
Troops and Inhabitants of Marshfield being cut
off, is without Foundation, they having all got
safe to Boston.

We still seem to be in great Suspence about
our Accounts from Boston, the Authenticity of
part of them being doubtless; however we make
not the least doubt there has been a smart Engagement between the King's Troops and the Provincials, in which we hear the former has lost
300 Men, killed, wounded, and taken Prisoners,
and the latter 37; but we do not learn there
was any General Officer lost on either side;
and the regular post being now stopped, between
this Place and Boston, 'tis probable we will
remain somewhat longer in the Dark concerning
this very disagreeable unhappy Transaction.

A Letter from Boston dated last Monday, and received since writing the above Paragraph, says.

"The Communication between this Town and country is entirely stopped up, and not a Soul permitted to go in and out without a Pass. This Day the Governor has disarmed all the Inhabitants, after giving them his Word and Honor that the Soldiers should not molest nor plunder them. Cambridge is the Head Quarters of the Provincials, and they are commanded by General _____, They entrenching themselves at Roxbury, and are erecting Batteries to play on our Lines.

PHILADELPHIA May 2. A Message from the Governor to the Assembly.

Gentlemen.

I have ordered the Secretary to lay before you a resolution entered into the British House of Commons, the Twentieth of February last, relating to the unhappy differences subsisting between our Mother Country and her American Colonies. You will perceive by this resolve, not only a strong disposition manifested by the August body to remove the causes, which have given rise to the discontents and complaints of his Majesty's subjects in the Colonies. And the dreadful impending evils likely to ensue from them, but that they have pointed out the terms, on what they think it just and reasonable a final accommodation should be groundless.

Let me earnestly entreat you, Gentlemen, to weigh and consider this plan of reconciliation held forth and offered by the parent to her children, with that temper, calmness and deliberation that the importance of the subject, and the present criticle situation of the affairs, demand. Give me leave to observe, that the Colonies, amidst all those complaints which a jealousy of their liberties has occasioned towards the burthens of the Mother Country to whose protection and care they owe not only their present opulence, but even their very existence. On the contrary, every state and representation thereof their supposed grievances, that I have seen, avows the propriety of such a measure, and their willingness to comply with it.

The dispute then appears to me to be brought

to the point; Whether the redress of any grievance the Colonist have reason to complain of.
shall precede, or be postponed to, the settlement of that just proportion, which America
should bear towards the common support and defence of the whole British empire.

You have, in the resolution of the House of
Commons, which I have authority to tell you is
entirely approved by his Majesty, a solemn declaration that an exemption from any duty, Tax
or assessment, present or future, except such
duties as may be expedient from the regulation
of commerce, shall be the immediate consequence
of proposal on the part of any of the colony
legislatures, accepting by his Majesty and the
two Houses of Parliament, to make provisions,
according to their respective circumstances,
for contributing their proportion to the common
defence, and the support of the civil government
of each colony.

I will not do you so much injustice, Gentlemen, as to suppose, you can desire a better security for the enviable performance or this
engagement, than the resolve itself, and his
Majesty's approbation of it given you.

As you are the first Assembly on the continent
to whom this resolution has been communicated,
much depends on the moderation and wisdom of
your councils, and you will be deservedly revered to the latest posterity, if by any possible
means, you can be instrumental in restoring the
public tranquility, and rescuing both countries
from the dreadful calamities od a civil war.

May 2, 1775.　　　　John Penn.

WORCESTER May 3. Americans! I forever bear in
mind the Battle of Lexington: where the British
troops, unmolested amd unprovoked, wantonly and
in a most inhuman manner fired upon and killed
a number of our countrymen, the robbed them of
their provisions, ransacked, plundered and burnt
their houses! nor could the tears of the defenceless women, some of whom were in the pains
of childbirth, the cries of the helpless babes,
nor the prayers of the old age, confined to beds
of sickness, appease their thirst for blood. or
divert them from the Design of Murder and Robbery.

The particulars of this alarming event will, we are credibly informed, be soon published by authority, as a committee of the provincial congress have been appointed to make a special enquiry, and to take depositions, on oath, of such as knowing the matter. In the mean time to satisfy the expectations of our readers, we have collected from those whose veracity is unquestionable, the following accounts, viz.

A few days before the battle, the grenadiers and light infantry companies were all drafted from the several regular regiments in Boston, and put under the command of an officer, and it was observed that most of the transports and other boats were put together, and fitted for immediate service. This maneuvre gave rise to a suspicion that some formidable expedition was intended by the soldiery, but what or where the inhabitants could not determine, however, the town watches in Boston, Charlestown, Cambridge &c. were ordered to look well to the landing place. About 10 o'clock on the night of the 18th of April, the troops in Boston were discovered to be on their move in a very secret manner, and it was found they were embarking in boats, (which they privately brought to the place in the evening) at the bottom of the common; expresses set of immediately to alarm the country, that they might be on their guard. When the expresses got about a mile beyond Lexington, they were stopped by about fourteen officers on horseback, who came out of Boston in the afternoon of that day, and were lurking in the bye-places in the country till after dark. One of the expresses immediately fled, and was pursued two miles by an officer, who when he had got up with him presented his pistol, and told him he was a dead man if he did not stop, but he rode on until he came up to a house, when stopping of a sudden his horse threw him off; having the presence of mind to hollow to the people in the house. "Turn out! Turn out! I got one of them!" the officer immediately retreated as fast as he had pursued: the other express after passing through a strict examination, by some means got clear. The body of the troops in the mean time,

22

under the command of Lieut. Colonel Smith, had crossed the river, and landed at Phipp's Farm: The immediately, to the number of 1000 proceeded to Lexington, 6 miles below Concord, with great silence: A company of militia, of about 80 men, mustered near the meeting-house; the troops came in sight of them just before sunrise; the militia upon seeing the troops began to disperse; the troops then set out upon the run, hallowing and huzzaing, and coming within a few rods of them, the commanding officer accosted the militia in words to this effect "disperse you damn'd rebels!, damn you disperse!" Upon which the troops again Huzzaed, and immediately one or two officers discharged their pistols, which were instantly followed by the firing of four or five of the soldiers, and then they seemed to be a general discharge from the whole body; it is to be noticed, they fired upon our people as they were dispersing, agreeable to their command, and that we did not even return the fire: Eight of our men were killed and nine wounded; The troops then laughed and damned the Yankees, and said they could not bear the smell of gunpowder. A little after this the troops renewed their march to Concord into parties, and went directly to several places where the province stores were deposited. Each party was supposed to have a tory pilot. One party went into the goal yard, and spiked up and otherways damaged two cannon belonging to the province, and broke and set fire to the carriages. They then entered a store and rolled out about 100 barrels of flour, which they unheaded, and emptied 40 in the river; at the same time others were entering houses and shops, and unheading barrels, chests, &c. the property of private persons; some took possessions of the town-house to which they set fire, but was extinguished by our people without much hurt. Another party of the troops took possession of the North-Bridge about 150 provincials who mustered upon the alarm, coming towards the bridge, the troops fired upon them without ceremony, and killed two upon the spot! Thus did the troops of Britain's King fired First at two several times upon his loyal American subjects and put a period to ten lives before one gun was fired upon them. Our people then returned the fire, and obliged the troops to retreat, who were soon joined by their other parties, but finding they were still pursued, the whole body retreated back to Lexington, both provincials and troops firing as they went. During this time an express was sent from the troops to General Gage, who thereupon sent out a reinforcementof about 1400 men, under the command of Earl Piercy, with two field pieces. Upon the arrival of the reinforcement at Lexington, just as the retreating party had got there, they made a stand, picked up their dead, and took all the carriages they could find and put their wounded thereon; others of them, to their eternal disgrace be it spoken, were robbing and setting houses on fire, and discharging their cannon at the meeting house. Whilst this was transacting a few of our men at Menotomy, a few miles distant, attacked a party of twelve of the enemy, (carrying stores and provisions to the troops) killed one of them, and took possession of their arms, stores and provisions &c. without any loss on our side. The enemy having halted above an hour at Lexington found it necessary to make a second retreat, carrying with them many of their dead and wounded. They continued their retreat from Lexington to Charlestown with great precipitation our men continued the pursuit, firing till they got to Charlestown Neck. (which they reached a little after sun-set) over which the enemy passed, proceeded up Bunker's Hill, and the next day went into Boston under the protection of the Somerset man of war of 64 guns.

A young man, unarmed, who was taken prisoner by the enemy, and made to assist in carrying off their wounded, says, that he saw a barber who lives in Boston, thought to be one of the Wardens, with the troops, and that he heard them say he was one of the pilots; he likewise saw the said barber fire twice upon our people, and heard Earl Piercy order the troops to fire the houses: He also informs that several officers were among the wounded who were carried in to

Boston, where our informant was dismissed. They took two of our men prisoners in battle who are now confined in Barracks.

Immediately upon return of the troops to Boston all communication to and from the town was stopped by Gen. Gage. The provincials who flew to the assistance of their distressed countrymen are posted in Cambridge, Charlestown, Roxbury, Watertown, &c. and have placed guards on Roxbury Neck, within gun-shot of the enemy; guards are also placed every where in view of the town to observe the motions of the King's troops: The Council of safety and supplies set at Cambridge and the Provincial Congress at Watertown. The troops in Boston are fortifying the place on all sides, and a frigate of war is stationed up Cambridge river, and a 64 gun ship between Boston and Charlestown.

The following is a list of the provincial who was killed or wounded.

Messrs. *Robert Munroe, *Jonas Parker, Samuel Hadley, *Jonathan Brown, *John Rusmand, Nathaniel Wyman, and Judidiah Merice, of Lexington. Messrs. Jason Russel, Jabez Wyman, and John Winship of Menotomy. Deacon Haynes, and Mr. ——— Reed of Sudbury. Capt. James Miles of Concord. Capt. Jonathan Wilson of Bedford, Capt. Davis, ——— Horsmer, and Mr. James Howard of Acton. *Mr. Azeal Porter, Mr. Daniel Thompsom, of Woburn. Mr. James Miller, and Capt. William Barber's son, age 14, of Charlestown. Isaac Gardner, Esq. of Brookline. Mr. John Hicks, of cambridge Mr. Henry Putnam, of Medford. Messrs. Abadage Ramsdell, Danuel Townsend, William Flint, and Thomas Hadley, of Lynn. Messrs. Henry Jacob, Samuel Cook, Ebenezer Goldthwait, George Southwick, Benjamin Doland, jun. Jothan Webb, and Perley Putnam of Danvers. And Mr. Benjamin Pierce of Salem.

Wounded. Messrs. John Robbins, John Tidd, Solomon Pierce, Thomas Winship, Nathaniel Farmer, Joseph Conte, Ebenezer Munroe, Francis Brown, and Prince Easterbrooks (a negroman) of Lexington. Mr. ——— Hemmingway, of Framingham. Nr. John Lane of Bedford. Mr. George Reed, and John Bacon of Woburn. Mr. William Polly, of

Medford. Mr. Jusha Felt, and Timothy Monroe of Lynn, Mr. Nathan Putnam, and Mr. Dennis Wallis, of Danvers. Mr. Samuel Frost, and Mr. Seth Russel of Menotomy.

Those distinguished by [*] mark were killed by the first fire of the enemy.

We have seen an account of the loss of the enemy, said to have come from an officer on one of the men of war, by which it appears that 63 of the regulars, and 49 marines were killed and 103 of both wounded. In all 215. Lieut. Gould of the 4th regiment, who is wounded and Lieut. Potter of the marines, and about thirty soldiers are prisoners.

Mr. James Howard and one of the regulars discharged their pieces at the same instant, and each killed the other.

Last Thursday morning the Hon. John Hancock, Esq; Mr. Samuel Adams, and Robert Treat Paine, escorted by a number of Gentlemen of the town, set out for Philadelphia to meet the Grand Assembly of Congress of which they are members. And in the Afternoon of the same day John Adams, Esq; another member of the Grand Congress passed through the town, also on his way to Philadelphia, Thomas Cushing, we hear is gone by way of Newport.

WORCESTER May 3. The following is a copy of a Letter from a Gentleman in Newport, to the commanding Officer of the Provincial Army at Cambridge,   New-Port, April 26th, 1775.

It is with pleasure that I communicate to you by express, the following important Intelligence by a vessel just arrived here from New-York. We are informed that the news of the engagement between the regulars and provincials, got to New-York on Sunday last, between the fore and afternoon service; that the people of the City immediately arose, disarmed the soldiers and possessed themselves of the forts and magazines, in which they found about fifteen hundred arms, that they unloaded two transports bound for Boston, Capt. Montegue not daring to give them any assistance; that a third transport had sailed while they were seizing the two others, and the people had fitted out a vessel in order

to take her and bring her back; that they had
forbid all the pilots from bringing up any King's
ships; that Capt. Montigue was not able to procure a pilot in the whole city; and that the
inhabitants were preparing to put themselves in
the best posture of defence. The gentleman who
brings this intelligence left Elizabeth-Town
yesterday morning, and tells us, that on Monday
the committee of that town and county met, and
agreed to raise 1000 men immediately, to assist
in the defence of New-York, against any attack
that may be made upon them. I have the honour
to assure that this intelligence may be depended
upon, and I am Sir, your most humble servant.
John Collens, Chairman of the Committee of Boston.

PHILADELPHIA May 3. On Saturday last we had a
meeting in this City of the military associators, when it was determined that each ward
should be formed into one or more companies:
the officers to be chosen in the respective
wards, two troops of light horse are now raising. Two Companies of expert rifle-men, and two
companies of artillery-men are now forming. We
have six pieces of brass artillery, and several
light iron ones. Our provincial arms, powder,
&c. are all secured, Three provincial magazines
are forming. In short Mars has established his
empire in this populous city: and it is not
doubted, but we shall have a few weeks from this
date, 4000 men, well equipped, for our own defence or for assistance of our neighbours.

NORWICH May 4. By several Gentlemen lately
arrived here from the Vicinity of Boston, we are
informed. That great Numbers of the Inhabitants
of that Metropolis had surrendered their Arms,
upon condition of having the Liberty to retire
into the Country; that about 250 Persons obtained a Passport and were suffered to leave
the Town, after which General Gage ordered a
fortification to be closed up, and although the
remaining Multitude had complied with his regulation, he would not permit them to depart.
[Panic Faith was anciently a Proverb.]

A Report is current here, that recent Intelligence has been received from New-York, that
many of its Inhabitants were preparing to storm

Fort George, in that City, and to attempt either to board or sink the Ship of War stationed there. It is also said, that no Business is now transacted at the Custom-Houses of New-York, New-Haven, or New-London, and as the Boston and the New-York Posts, who usually comes into New-London on Wednesday in the Afternoon, were not arrived their at 8 o'Clock this Morning, it is supposed the Post-Office are also shut up.

NEW-YORK May 4. Extract of a letter arrived from Boston Thursday April 19, 1775, (we presume it should have been dated the 20th) to a merchant in this City.

"What I was apprehensive in my last, is now confirmed. Yesterday morning the grenadiers and light infantry of all the regiments in town marched out very unexpectedly, and proceeded to Concord, 21 miles from hence, at which place the provincial congress sat, and where large magazines, belonging to the country were collected, which were totally destroyed. This party consisted of about eight hundred men, under the command of Lieut. Colonel Smith of the 10th regiment; about six hours after those left Boston, a brigade was ordered out, consisting of one thousand men, commanded by Lord Percy: These marched about sixteen miles, to a place called Lexington, where they met the first party returning, and who in their first march up, had killed eight or ten men that opposed the march. Upon the army's return, near Lexington, they were fired on from the woods, which was returned. Thus the engagement became general, and continued for seven hours, during which several lives were lost, and a great number wounded. ——— It is surprizing how soon that the country people mustered, and in vast numbers; so much that the Troops were obliged to retreat near twelve miles, and all this way a constant firing was kept up on both sides; the country people fired all from cover, and, by that means, had much the advantage of the troops. The engagement lasted till night put an end to it. I saw a great part of it from Beacon-Hill. They kept a constant firing until the got to Charlestown. The loss on part of the troops, from the best information, is

about two hundred killed; among which they are
no officers, though many very much wounded.
Lieut. Gould, of the fourth regiment is also
wounded. Major Moneriesse, Capts. Parson, and
Mr. Haines, are safe returned. The loss on the
side of the country must be considerable; at
present there is no coming to any certainty.
From the preparations that are making, I think
it will be soon renewed."

Another account mentioned, That Capt. Parson
of the 10th, Mr. Baldwin of the 47th, Mr. Cox
of the 5th, Capt. Sutherland of the 30th, and
Mr. M'Nigh of the 4th, were wounded, and that
Mr. Gould was since dead.

NEW-York May 4. A corespondents, has sent us
(tho' we know not by what authority) the following return of the killed, wounded, and missing,
of the regulars and provincials, &c. from the
late near Boston,
49 Marines, 43 Soldiers, killed. 103 Wounded
total 215 Killed, wounded, and missing.

Two wagons loaded with provisions, &c. taken
from the regulars and the waggoner killed.
35 Provincials Killed and missing.
4 Houses and one Barn burnt at Lexington.
50 or 60 Barrels of flour destroyed at Concord.
2 Guns carriages burnt.

On the Night of Tuesday April 18th, a body of
Regulars embarked in boats and landed at Cambridge or Watertown, and made a march up to
Lexington Meeting-House, where a number of Provincials were collected, to the amount of 60 or
70 Mem. The Regulars ordered them to lay down
their Arms, but they refused; the Regulars then
advanced fast and in a high tone ordered to
lay doen their Arms, and disperse immediately;
The Provincials sensible they could not defend
themselves retreated, and the Regulars cry'd
out, God damn you we'll hasten you, and killed
six Men and mortally wounded another.

The Troops then proceeded to Concord, dis-
mounted some cannon, destroyed a magazine of
Flour and other stores, and then advanced to
Concord Bridge, where Colonel Pierce and Major
Buttrick met them with about 250 Men; when the
Troops saw the Provincials, they began to pull

up the Bridge, and the Provincials hastened down
towards them but had orders not to fire till the
Regulars began, (not knowing of the men killed
at Lexington.) The Regulars soon fired several
shot over the Country People's head. but they
had orders still not to fire upon the Regulars,
till they were sure they meant to hurt them;
but the Troops soon fired again and killed Capt.
Davis, which was soon followed with a warm fire
from both sides; The Regulars soon retreated to
an eminence, and formed themselves on order of
Battle. The Provincials did not attack, but ran
round to a place of ground that suited them;
when the Troops retreated, The Provincials gave
them a hot fire that threw them into confusion;
they hurried back to Lexington where they were
joined by Earl Percy with 1200 men, and two
Field-Pieces; there they halted some time, and
burnt four Houses, two Shops, and two Barns,
fired a few shot at the Meeting-House, and then
retired towards Boston.

The Country People kept up a furious fire, and
a large number of them entrenched themselves at
Cambridge, to cut off the retreat of the troops,
but fortunately for them they took another route,
and escaped a total overthrow. Those in the
pursuit kept up their fire till night, when the
Regulars drew up in order of battle on a hill
im Charlestown, within reach of the Ships guns,
where they left them, and the next day entered
Boston, with the loss of between 2 and 300 killed,
wounded, and taken prisoners. The loss of the
Country People was about 40 killed and wounded.

PHILADELPHIA May 4. A Message to the Governor
from the Assembly.

May it Please your Honour,
We have taken into our serious consideration
your message of the 2d instant, and "the resolution of the British House of Commons therein
referred to."

Having "weighed and considered this plan with
the temper, calmness and deliberation that the
importance of the subject, and the present critical situation of affairs demand;" We are sincerely sorry, that we cannot "think the terms
pointed out" afford "a just and reasonable ground

for a small accommodation" betweenGreat-Britain and the colonies.

Your Honour observes "That the colonies, amidst all those complaints which a jealousy of their liberties has occasioned, have never denied the justice or equity of their contributing towards the burthens of the country." but your Honour must know, that they have ever unanimously asserted it on their indisputable right, that all aids from them should be their own from and voluntary gifts, not taken by force, not extorting by fear.

Under which these deceptions the plan held forth and offered by the parent to her children" at this time, with its attendant circumstances, deserves to be classed, we chose rather to submit to the determination of your Honour's good sense, that to attempt proving by the enumeration of notorious facts, or the repetition of obvious reasons.

If no other objections plan proposed occurred to us, we should esteem it dishonourable desertion of our sister colonies, connected by in union, founded on just motives and mutual faith and conducted by general councils, for a single colony to adopt a measure, so extensive in consequence, without the advice and consent of those colonies engaged with us by solemn ties in the same common cause.

For we with your Honour to be assured, that we can for no project appearing reasonable to us, of any lasting advantage for Pennsylvania, however agreeable as they may be in the beginning, but what must arise from a communication of rights and prosperity with the other colonies; and that if such a prospect be opened to us, we have too sincere an affection for our brethren, and too strict a regard "for the inviolable performance of" our "engagement," to receive any pleasure from the benefits equally due them, yet confined to ourselves, and which, by generously rejecting them at present, may at length be secured for all.

Your Honour, is pleased to observe, that as we are "the first assembly on the continent, to whom this resolution has been communicated, much depends on the moderation and wisdom of our councils, and we shall be deservedly revered to the latest posterity, if by any possible means" we "can be instrumental in restoring the public tranquility, and rescuing both countries from the dreadful calamities of a civil war.

Your Honour, from your long residence and conversation among us, must be persuaded, that the people we represent are as peaceful and obedient to government, as true and faithful to the sovereign, and as affectionate and dutiful to the superior state as any in the world; and though we are not inattentive to approbation of "posterity" as it might reflect honour upon our country, yet higher motives have taught us upon all occasions to demonstrate, by every testimony, our devotion to our King and parent state.

Still animated by the same principles, and most earnestly desirous of enjoying our former undisturbed condition of dependence and subordination, productive of so many blessings to "both countries" we cannot express the satisfaction we should have "if by any possible means" we could "be instrumental is restoring the public Tranquility;" should such opportunity offer, we shall endeavour the utmost diligence and zeal to improve it, and to convince his Majesty and our mother country, that we shall ever be ready and willing with our lives and fortunes to support the interest of his Majesty and that country, by every effort that can be reasonably expected from the most loyal subjects and most dutiful colonists.

Under Divine Providence shall cause, in the course of his dispensation, such a happy period to arrive, we can only deprecate, and if it be possible, strive, by prudence, to avoid "The Calamities of a civil war," a "dreadful misfortune' indeed! and not to be exceeded but by an utter subversions of the Liberties of America.

      May 4,   Signed by order of the House
      1775.   John Morton, Speaker.

We are well informed that the above Message passed without one dissenting vote.

Saturday last John Sullivan, and John Langdon, Esqs; delegates for New-Hampshire arrived here.

Monday evening the brig Charlestown Packet arrived here from South Carolina, with whom came passengers the Hon. Henry Middleton, Christopher Gadsden, John Rutledge, and Edward Rutledge, Esqrs. delegates for that province. Thomas Lynch, Esq; the other delegate sailed the day before in a schooner.

Yesterday the Hon. Payton Randolph Esq; George Washington, Patrick Henry, Richard Henry Lee, Edward Pendleton, Benjamin Harrison, and Richard Bland Esquires, Delegates for Virginia. Richard Caswell and Joseph Hewes, Esq; Delegates for North Carolina. Samuel Chase, Thomas Johnson, and John Hall, Esquires, Delegates for Maryland, also Ceasor Rodney, and George Reid, Esquires, delegates for the Counties of New Castle, Kent and Sussex, on Delaware.

WILLIAMSBURG May 4. At a council held at the Palace May 2, 1775.

Present his Excellency the Governor, Thomas Nelson, Richard Corbin, William Byrd, Ralph Wormeley junior, Esquires, John Camm, clerk and John Page, Esquire.

The Governor was pleased to address himself to the Board in the fillowing manner.

Gentlemen,

Commotions and insurrections have suddenly been excited among the people, which threaten the very existence of his Majesty's government in this colony; and no other cause is assigned for such dangerous measured that that of gunpowder which had, some time past, been brought from on board one of the King's ships to which it belonged and was deposited in the magazine of this city, hath been removed, which, it is known, was done by my order, I so whom, under the constitutional right of the Crown which I represent, the custody and disposal of all public stores of arms and ammunition alone belong; and whether I acted in this matter (as my indispensable duty required) to anticipate the malevolent designs of the enemies of order and government, or to prevent the attempt of any enterprising Negroes, the powder being still as ready and ready and convenient for being distributed for the defence of the country upon any emergency

33

as it was before; which I have publicly engaged
to do, the expediency of the step I have taken
is equally Manifest; and therefore it must be
evident that the same headstrong and designing
people, who have already but too successfully
deployed their artifices in deluding his Majesty's faithful subjects, and seducing them from
their duty and allegiance, have seized this entirely groundless subject of complaint, only to
inflame afresh, and to precipitate as many as
possible of the unwary, into acts, which involving them in the same guilt, their corruptors
think may bind them to the same plans and schemes
which are unquestionably meditated in this colony, for subverting the present, and erecting a
new form of government.

Induced by an unaffected regard for it's general welfare of the people, when I have had the
honour of governing, as well as actuated by duty
and zeal in the service of his Majesty. I call
upon you, his council in this colony, for your
advice upon this pressing occasion, and I submit
it to you, whether a proclamation should not
issue conformable to what I have now suggested;
and, before our fellow subjects abandon themselves totally to extremities, which must inevitably fraw down an accumulation of every human
misery upon their unhappy country, to warn them
if their danger, to remind them of their sacred
oath of allegiance which they have taken, and
to call up in their breast that loyalty and affection, which upon so many occasions have been
professed by them to their King, their lawful
Sovereign: And further, to urge and exhort, in
particular, those whose criminal proceedings on
this occasion have been, and are obedience to
the laws; and in general, all persons whatsoever
to rely upon the goodness and tenderness of our
most gracious Sovereign to all his Subjects,
equally, and upon the wisdom of his councils,
for a redress of all their real grievances, which
redress can only be obtained by constitutional
applications: and, lately, to enjoin all orders
of the people to submit, as becomes good subjects, to the legal authority of their government, in the protection of which their own

happiness is most interested.

The Council thereupon acquainted his Excellency, that as the matters he had been pleased to communicate to them were of the greatest consequence, they desired time to deliberate thereof till the next day.

WILLIAMSBURG May 5. Later Wednesday night, Col. Carter Brazion, arrived in town, from a Number of armed people, all men of property, led by Patrick Henry, Esq; on their march for this city, from the counties of Hanover, New-Kent, and King William. The news of their coming, we are well assured is the general spread over the country, by the removal of all the gunpowder, from the public magazine, and to secure the treasury from a like catastrophe: as also seize upon the person of his Majesty's Receiver General (there in the city) till either the gunpowder was restored, or a sum of money paid down to its value. Next morning Col. Brazion returned who the honorable Richard Corbin's bill of exchange for 320 Pounds sterling; and at the same time the inhabitants of the city engaging themselves to guard the publick treasury, the gentlemen dispersed yesterday afternoon, and returning to their respective homes, perfectly satisfied with the success of their expedition. They had proceeded as far as Doncastle about 25 miles from town, where encamped to the number of 150 men and upwards, all well accoutred, and had a very martial Appearance.

As soon as his Excellency the Governor received intelligence of the above armed force coming down, he dispatched a messenger to the Fowie, man of war, lying before Yorktown, and by ten o'clock yesterday morning a detachment of 40 sailors and marines belonging to the ship, under the command of Captain Stretch, arrived at the Palace; they did not march through the mainstreet, but were led through the Governor's park.

The town of York, we are well informed, was threatened with a command from his Majesty's ship the Fowie by her commander, If the Inhabitants presumed to molest the troops in their landing, of their march to this city. They are now in the palace; how long they will stay is uncertain.

Upward of 100 citizens last night guarded the public treasury, and patrolled the streets.

This morning a warrant was issued to search certain houses, for arms, suspected to have been taken out of the magazine in this city, a considerable number being missing; but the officer, we hear, has not been able to find any.

PROVIDENCE May 6. The honourable general assembly of this colony have resolved to raise immediately fifteen hundred effective men, for the preservation of the liberties in America. They are to be formed into three regiments, and to defray the expence, the sum of twenty thousand pounds is to be emitted in paper bills.

By the latest accounts from Boston, the inhabitants are at length permitted to come out; but no more than 20 Or 30 waggons allowed to enter the town in a day, for removing their effects.

By Capt. Carpenter, who arrived here on Tuessay from New-York, which place he left on saturday last, we learn, that the inhabitants had not then taken possession of the Fort, as had been reported; but that they had seized the city arms, and appointed a committee of one hundred persons to determine on measures proper to be adopted for the common safety.

The following is an exart Copy of a Letter which was intercepted at Roxbury on Thursday last.   Boston, 4th May, 1775.

Dear Sons,

After my effectnate Love to your Mother, Sisters &c. Inform you that on ye 27th of April I left the Ship took passage on Board a packet sloop on ye 1st Instant in health arrived here, where I expected to Stay till the Rebels are subdued, which I Believe will not be long first as the Ships and Troops are Dayly expected. My greatest fears are you will be Seduced or compeld to take arms with those Deluded people. Dear Sons if those Wicked Siners the rebels intice you believe them not, but die by the Sword rather than be hanged as Rebels, which will certainly be your fate Sooner or latter if you Joyn them or be killed in battle and will be no more than you decarve, I wish you in Boston and all the friends

to Government, the Rebels have proclaimed that
those finds may have Liberty and come in, but as
all their declarations have hether too proved
false I fear this may be to, Let Ruggles know
his father wants him here, you may come by water
from Newport, I here the King will give you provisions & pay you Wages but by expearance you
know your persons nor Estates are not safe in
the Countrey for as soon as you have Raised any
thing thayl Rob you of it, as they are more savage & cruell then Heathens of any other Creture
& it is generaly Thought them Devils, you will
put yourselves out of the power as soon as possible. This is from your effectional Father.

                                  Thos. Gilbert.
     (Addressed)
   To Thomas Peres Gilbert   Bradford.
   P. S. Pagett, Green, and Jack are here, it will
be well if these lines Reach you as all my Letters are intercepted by those Rebels who want
every one to be kept in Dark like themselves,
(Misery Loves Company) DIRECTED TO Major Thomas
Gilbert in Barkley.
   HARTFORD May 8. In Provincial Congress Watertown April 30, 1775.
   Whereas agreement hath been made, between General Gage, and the inhabitants of the town of
Boston, as many may be so disposed, exempting
their fire arms and ammunition, into the country.
   Resolved, That any of the inhabitants of this
colony, who may incline to go into the town of
Boston with effects, fire-arms and ammunition
excepted, have tolleration for that purpose;
and that they be protected from any injury and
insult whatever, in their removal to Boston,
and that this resolve be immediately published.
   P. S. Officers are appointed for the giving
permits for the above purpose, one at the sign
of the Sun in Charlestown, and another at the
House of Mr. John Greaton, jun. at Roxbury.
            Joseph Warren, President, Pro. Tem.
   A true extract from the minutes
                    Samuel Freeman Sec. Pro. Tem.
   NEW-YORK May 8. The 7th of April Capt. Young
spoke with Capt. M'Halvaine in lat. 49, 39,

lon. 15, 51, from Cork for Philadelphia, who informed him, that when he sailed from that port, 22 ships were taking on board several regiments of foot and one of horse, for Boston; and on the 12th following, Capt. Young fell in with, in lat. 15, 39, lon. 35, 23, with six ships and a brig, from Plymouth bound to Boston with troops.

Last Sunday week a number of Provincial troops arrived in this city from the western part of Connecticut also Monday a detachment of the calvary of that province.

WORCESTER May 10. We hear that the Senacas, one of the Six Nations of Indians are determine to support the Americans, against the arbitrary occasions of the British Parliament, and, if desired will lend their help in this day of general distress, expecting if the colonies are subjected, they shall also fall a sacrifice to the relentless fury of Great-Britain.

The General Assembly of the Colony of Connecticut have passed an act for immediately raising and paying 6000 effective men, for the defence of the colony, &c.

The report of an engagement between New-York and an English man of war, we are informed is without foundation.

The Tories in Boston seem in general as desirous of quitting that capital to the whigs, many have embarked in a ship, Capt. Callahan master for London, some have gone to Halifax, and others among who are a number of addressers to the late Governor Hutchingson, chuse rather to put confidence in the people and are returning into the country.

WORCESTER May 10. It is confidently asserted, that several houses in Boston belonging to persons who had removed out of that distressed town, have been plundered of effects left therein, by the soldiery. The Hon. John Hancock, Esqr's, house, we hear was entered by a number of the soldiers, who began to pillage and break down the fences; but upon complaint being made by the select men to Gen. Gage, he ordered the fences to be repaired, and Earl Piercy to take possession of the house.

All accounts agree that five or six hundred

marines, to reinforce the King's troop's arrived at Boston on Saturday last from Halifax.

Our army have begun an entrenchment at Cambridge.

General Gage is making Boston as secure from an attack as he possibly can. However it is now thought by some that the bulwarks are not so strong as to be impregnable.

One Mansfield, a breeces-maker, in Boston, who went out with the troops in the late engagement was in the skirmish fired at by the regulars through mistake, they taking him for one of our men. The ball entered his neck and came out of his mouth. Wretches like him often meet their just reward.

Some officers in the King's army, it is said, have sworn that the Americans fired first. Their method of cheating the Devil, we are told, have been by some means brought out. They procured three or four traitors of their God and country, born among us, and took with them, and they first fired upon their countrymen, which was immediately followed by the regulars. It is also said these wretches were dressed in soldiers cloathing.

When the second brigade marched out of Boston to reinforce the first, nothing was played by the fifes and drums but Yankee Doodle, (which had become their favorite tune ever since that notable exploit, which did such honour to the troops of Britain's King, of tarring and feathering a poor countryman in Boston, and parading with him through the principal streets, under arms with their bayonets fixed:) Upon their return to Boston, one asked his brother officer how he liked the tune now. "Damn them, returned he, they made us dance it till we were tired," since which Yankee Doodle sounds less sweet to their ears.

The commanding officer at Cambridge, has given leave to the regulars who were taken prisoners, either to go to Boston and join their respective regiments, or have liberty to work in the country for those who would employ them. In consequence of which those who was confined in this town, fifteen in number, heartily requested to

be employed by the people, not chusing to return
to their regiments to fight against the American brethren, tho' some of them expressed their
willingness to spill their blood in defence of
their King in a righteous cause. They all set
out yesterday for different towns.

Since our last we received the names of three
more of our brethren who fell in battle, viz.
Mr. James Miller of Charlestown, Mr. Moses
Richardson of Cambridge, and Nathaniel Coolidge
of Watertown, which with those mentioned are
tho't to be the whole of our people who were
killed.

There were not above 400 at most of our people
who pursued and engaged the murdering troops of
Briton's King from Concord to Charlestown.

New-York May 11. We hear from Philadelphia
that on the 5th instant, to the great joy of
that city, Doct. Benj. Franklin arrived there
in 6 weeks from London, and was highly pleased
to find the Americans arming and preparing for
the worst events, against which he thinks our
spirited executions will be the only means, under God to secure us. Acts the ministry seem
determined on our submission to slavery, they
suppose the troops already sent and ordered to
Boston, will be sufficient for reducing that
place, and have therefore ordered 3 or 4 regiments to New-York, where it is expected many
will be glad of their arrival, as the goods with
which the men of war and transports are in a
manner loaded, will there ready to be disposed
of by the agents under whose care they were sent.
The ministry, however, notwithstanding their
haughtiness, and seeming confidence are not a
little anxious for the event of these measures
[as well they may!]

We hear Doct. Franklin has been by an unanimous vote of the assembly of Pennsylvania and
approbation of the people, added to the number
of Delegates to the Continental Congress.

NEW-YORK. On Saturday arrived here from the
eastward, on their way to Philadelphia, to attend the Continental Congress the Hon. John
Hancock, and Thomas Cushing, Esqs; Samuel Adams,
and Robert-Treat Paine, Esqs; Delegates for the

Province of Massachusetts-Bay; and Hon. Elipha-
let Dyer & Roger Sherman, Esqs; and Silas Deane,
Esq; Delegate for the colony of Connecticut:
They were met a few miles out of town by a great
number of principal gentlemen of this place, in
carriages, and on horseback, and escorted into
the city by near a thousand men under arms; the
roads were lined with greater numbers of people
than ever was known on any occasion before,
their arrival was announced by the ringing of
bells, and other demonstrations of joy: They had
double centries placed at the doors of their
lodgings.

PHILADELPHIA May 13. Affidavits and depositions to the commencement of the late hostilities in the province of Massachusetts-Bay, together with addresses from the Provincial Convention of the said province, to the Congress
now sitting in this city, and published by their
order.   Charels Thompson, Sec.

We solomon Brown, Jonathan Loring, and Elijah
Sanderson; all of lawful age of Lexington in the
county of middlesex and colony of Massachusetts
Bay in New-England, do testify and declare, that
on the evening of the eighteenth of April, inst.
being on the road between Concord and Lexington
and all of us mounted on horses: we were about
ten on the clock, suddenly surprized by nine
serjeants, whom we took to be regular officers,
who rode up to us mounted and armed, each having
a pistol in his hand, and after putting pistols
to our breast; and seizing the bridles, of our
horses, they swore that if we stirred another
step, we should be all dead men, upon which we
surrendered ourselves: they detained us until
two the next morning, in which time they searched
and greatly abused us, having first enquired
about the Magazine at Concord, whether any
guards were posted there, and wether the bridges
were up, and said four or five regiments of Regulars, would be in possession of the stores
soon, then they brought us back to Lexington,
cut the horses bridles and turned them loose,
and then left us. Lexington, April 25, 1775.

Solmon Brown, Jonathan Loring, Elijah Sanderson,

41

I Elijah Sanderson, above named, do further
testify, and declare, that I was in Lexington
Common, the morning of the nineteenth of April
aforesaid, having been dismissed by the officers
above mentioned, and saw a large body of the
regular troops advancing towards Lexington company, many of whom were then dispersing. I heard
one of the regulars whom I took to be an officer
say, damn them we will have them, and immediately the regulars shouted aloud, run and fired
on the Lexington company, which did not fire a
gun before the regulars discharged on them.
Eight of the Lexington company were killed while
they were dispersing, and at a considerable
distance from each other, and many wounded,
and although a spectator, I narrowly escaped
with my life.
   Lexington, April 25, 1775. Elijah Sanderson
                  Lexington, April 23, 1775.
I Thomas Price Willard, of lawful age, do
testify & declare, that being in the house of
Daniel Harrington, of said Lexington, on the
nineteenth instant, in the morning, about half
an hour before sunrise, looked out at the window
of said house and saw (as I supposed) about four
hundred of regulars, in one body, coming up the
road, and marched towards the north part of the
common, back of the meeting house of said Lexington, and as soon as the regulars were against
the east end of the meeting house, the commanding officer said something, what I know not, but
upon that the regulars ran till they came within
about eight or nine rods of about an hundred of
the militia of Lexington, who were collected on
said common at which time the militia of Lexington dispersed, then the officers made a huzza,
and the private soldiers succeeded them: Directly after this an officer rode before the regulars, to the other side of the body, and hal-
lowed after the militia of said Lexington, and
said, "lay down your arms." And that there was
not a gun fired till the militia of Lexington
were dispersed; and further said not.
                  Thomas Price Willard.
        Lexington 25th of April 1775.
Simon Winship of Lexington in the county of

Middlesex, and province of Massachusetts-Bay,
New-England; being of lawful age, Testifieth
and saith, that on the nineteenth of april last,
about four o'clock in the morning, as he was
passing the public goal in said Lexington, peaceably and unarmed, about two miles and a half
distant from the meeting-house in Lexington, he
was met by a body of the King's troops, and being stopt by some officers of said regular
troops was commanded to dismount; upon asking
why he must dismount, he was obliged by force
to quit his horse, and ordered to march in the
midst of the body, and being examined whether
he had been warning the minute men, he answered
no, but had been out, and then returning to his
farther's. Said Winship further testifies, that
he marched with said troops until he came within
about half a quarter of a mile of said meeting
house, where an officer commanded the troops to
halt, the then prime and load; this being done,
the said troops marched on till they came within
a few rods of Capt. Parker's company, who were
partly collected on the place of parade; when
said Winship observed an officer at the head of
said troops flourishing his sword, and with a
loud voice giving the word, fire, which was instantly followed by a discharge of arms from
said regular troops; and said Winship is positive and in the most solemn manner declares,
that there was no discharge of arms on either
side till the word fire was given by said officer
as above.   Simon Winship.
                    Lexington April 25, 1775.
    I John Parker of lawful age, and commander of
the militia in Lexington, do testify and declare,
that on the 19th instant, in the morning, about
one on the clock, being informed that there were
a number of regular officers riding up and down
the road, stopping an insulting people as they
passed the road, and also was informed, that a
number of regular troops were on their march
from Boston, in order to take the province stores
at Concord; ordered our militia to meet on the
common in said Lexington, to consult what to do,
and concluded not to be discovered, nor meddle
or make with said regular troops (if they should

43

approach) unless they should insult or molest
us, and upon their sudden approach I immediately ordered our militia to disperse and not fire;
immediately said troops made their appearance
and rushed furiously, fired upon and killed eight
of our party, without receiving any provocation
thereof from us.   John Parker.
                 Lexington, April 24, 1775.
   I John Robins, being of lawful age, do testify
and say, that on the nineteenth instant, the
company under the command of John Parker, being
drawn up, (sometime before sunrise) on the green
or common, and I being in the front rank, there
suddenly appeared a number of the King's troops,
about a thousand, as I thought, at the distance
of about 60 or 70 yards from us huzzaying, and
on a quik pace towards us, with three officers
in their front on horseback, and on full gallop
towards us, the foremost of which cried, "throw
down your arms, you villains, you rebels." upon
which said company dispersed. The foremost of the
three officers ordered their men saying, "fire,
by God fire," at which moment we received a very
heavy and close fire from them, at which instant
being wounded, I fell and several of our men
were shot dead by me; Captain Parker's men, I
believe, had not then fired a gun: and further
this deponent say it not.   John Robins.
   We Benjamin Tidd of Lexington, and Joseph Abbot of Lincoln, in the county of Middlesex, and
colony of Massachusetts-Bay in New-England, of
lawful age, do testify and declare that on the
morning of the nineteenth of April, instant,
about five o'clock being at Lexington common,
and mounted on horses we saw a body of regular
troops marching up to the Lexington company,
which was then dispersed, soon after the regulars fired first a few guns, which we took to be
pistols from some of the regulars that were
mounted on horses, and then the said regulars
fired a volley or two, before any of the guns
were fired by the Lexington company, our horses
immediately started and we rode off, and further
say not.   Benjamin Tidd, Joseph Abbot.
           Lexington April, 25th 1775.
   We Nathaniel Millekin, Philip Russel, Moses

Harrington, jun. Thomas and Daniel Harrington,
William Grimes, William Tidd, Isaac Hastings,
Jonas Stone, jun. James Wyman, Taddeus Harring-
ton, John Chamber, Josua Reed, jun. Joseph Simonds, Phinias Smith, John Chandler, jun. Ruben
Lock, Joel Viles, Nathan Reed, Samuel Tidd,
Benjumin Lock, Thomas Winship, Simeon Snow, John
Smith, Moses Harringyon, the 3d, Joshua Reed,
Ebenezer Parker, John Harrington, Enoch Willington, John Hormer, Isaac Green, Phinias Stearns,
Isaac Durant, and Thomas Headley, jun. all lawful age, and inhabitants of Lexington in the
county of Middlesex, and colony of the Massachusetts-Bay in New-England; do testify and declare, that on the 19th of April instant, about
one or two o'clock in the morning, being informed that several officers of the regulars,
had that evening before been riding up and down
the road, and had detained and insulted the inhabitants passing the same and also understanding that a body of regulars were marching from
Boston towards Concord, with intent (as it was
supposed) to take the stores belonging to the
colony in that town, we were alarmed, having
met at the place of our company's parade were
dismissed by our Captain John Parker, for the
present, which orders to be ready to attend at
the beat of the drum, —— we further testify
and declare that about five o'clock in the morning, hearing our drum beat, we proceeded towards
the parade, and soon found that a large body of
troops were marching towards us, some of our
company were coming up to the parade, and others
had reached it; at which time the company began
to disperse, whilst our backs were turned on the
troops, we were fired on by them and a number
of our men were instantly killed and wounded —
not a gun was fired by any person in our company
on the regulars, to our knowledge, before they
fired on us, and they continued fired firing
until we had all made our escape.
      Signed by each of the above Deposers.
We Nathaniel Carkhurst, John Parker, John
Monroe, jun. John Wunship, Solomon Pierce, John
Murry, Abner Meeds, John Bridge, jun. Ebenezer
Bowman, William Monroe, 3d. Micah Hager, Samuel

Sounderson, Samuel Hastings, and James Brown , of
Lexington in the country of Middlesex, and colony of Massachusetts-Bay in New-England; and all
of lawful age to testify and say, that on the
morning of the nineteenth of April instant about
one or two o'clock being informed that a number
of regular officers had been riding up and down
the road the evening and night preceding, and
some of the inhabitants as they were passing had
been insulted by the officers, and stopped by
them; and being also informed that the regular
troops were on their march from Boston (as it was
said) to take the colony stores, then deposited
at Concord! We met on the parade of our company
in this town; after the company had collected,
we were ordered by Captain John Parker (who commanded us) to disperse for the present, and be
ready to attend the beat of the drum; and accordingly the company went into houses near that
place of parade. We further testify and say,
that about five o'clock in the morning we attended the beat of our drum, and were formed on
the parade, we were faced towards the regulars
then marching up to us, and some of our company
were coming to the parade with their backs towards the troops; and others on the parade began to disperse when the regulars fired on the
company, before a gun was fired by any of our
company on them; they killed eight of our company, and wounded several, and continued their
fire until we had made our escape.
        Signed by each of the above Deposers.
    Lexington April 25, 1775.
    I Timothy Smith of Lexington, in the county
of Middlesex, and colony of Massachusetts-Bay
in New-England; being of lawful age, do testify
and declare, that on the morning of the nineteenth of April inst. being at Lexington common
as a spectator, I saw a large body of regular
troops marching up towards the Lexington company
dispersing, and likewise saw the regular troops
fire on the Lexington company, before the latter
fired a gun; I immediately ran, and a volley
was discharged at me, which put me in imminent
danger of losing my life: I soon returned to the
common, and saw eight of the Lexington men who

were killed, and lay bleeding at a considerable distance from each other; and several were wounded, and further saith not.   Timothy Smith.
Lexington April 25, q775.

We Levy Mead and Levy Harrington, both of Lexington, in the county of Middlesex, and colony of Massachusetts-Bay, in New-England, and of lawful age do testify, and declare, that on the morning of the nineteenth of April, being on Lexington common as spectators, we saw a large body of regular troops marching up towards the Lexington company, and some of the regulars on horses, whom we took to be officers, fired a pistol or two on the Lexington company, which were then dispersing. Those were the first guns that were fired, and they were immediately followed by several vollies from the regulars, by which eight men belonging to said company were killed and seven wounded. Levi Harrington Levi Mead.
Lexington April 25, 1775.

I William Draper of lawful age and inhabitant of Coleraine in the county of Hampshire, and colony of Massachusetts-Bay in New-England, do testify and declare, that being on the parade of said Lexington, April 19th instant, about half an hour before sunrise the king's regular troops appeared at the meeting house of Lexington. Capt. Parker's company who were drawn back the said meeting house on the parade turned from said troops making their escape by dispersing, in the mean time, the regular troops made a huzza and ran towards Capt. Parker's company who were dispersing and immediately after the huzza was made, the commanding officer of the said troops (as I took him) gave the command to the said troops "fire! fire! damn you fire!" and immediately they fired before any of Capt. Parker's company fired, I being within three or rods of said regular troops: and further say not.   William Draper.
Lexington April 23d, 1775.

I Thomas Fessenden, of lawful age, testify and declare that being in a pasture near the meeting house of said Lexington, on Wednesday last, at about half an hour before sun rise, I saw a number of regular troops pass speedily by

said meeting house, to their way towards a company of militia of said Lexington, who were assembled to the number of about one hundred in a company, at the distance of eighteen or twenty rods from said meeting house, and after they had passed by said meeting house, I saw three officers on horse back, advance to the front of said regulars, where one of them being within six rods of the said militia, cried out "Disperse you rebels immediately" on which he brandished his sword over his head three times, mean while the second officer who was about two rods behind him, fired a pistol pointed at said militia, and the regulars kept hazzaying till he had finished brandishing his sword, and when he had thus finished brandishing the sword he pointed it down towards said militia, and immediately on which the said regulars fired a volley at the militia, and then I ran off as fast as I could, while they continued firing till I got out of their reach: I further testify that as soon as ever the officers cryed "disperse you rebels" the said company of militia dispersed every way as fast as they could, and while they were dispersing the regulars kept firing at the incessantly, and further saith not.   Thos. Fessenden.
                              Lincoln, April 23, 1775.
    I John Bateman, belonging to the fifty second regiment, commanded by Colonel Jones on Wednesday morning, on the nineteenth day of April, instant, was in the party marching to Concord, being at Lexington, in the county of Middlesex, being nigh the meeting house in said Lexington, there was a small party of men gathered together in that place, when our said troops march by, and I testify and declare, that I heard the word of command given to the troops to fire, and some of said troops did fire, and I saw one of said small party lay dead on the ground nigh said meeting house; and I testify that I never heard any of the inhabitants so much as fire one gun on said troops.   John Bateman.
                           Lexington, April 23, 1775.
    We John Hoar, John Whitehead, Abraham Garfield, Benjamin Monroe, Isaac Parks, William Hofmer, John Adams, Gregory Stone, all of Lincoln

in the county of Middlesex, Massachusetts-Bay, all lawful age do testify and say, that on wednesday last we were assembled at Concord, in the morning of said day, in consequence of information received, that a brigade of regular troops were on their march to the said town of Concord, who had killed six men at the town of Lexington; about an hour afterwards we saw them approaching, to the number as we apprehended, of about twelve hundred, on which we retreated to a hill about eighty rods back, and the said troops then possession of the hill where we were first posted; presently after this we saw the troops moving towards the North-bridge about one mile from the said Concord meeting-house, we then immediately went before them and passed the bridge just before a party of them, to the number of about two hundred, arrived; that there left about half of their two hundred at the bridge, and proceeded with the rest towards Col. Barret's, about two miles from the said bridge; we then seeing several fires in the town, thought the houses in Concord were in danger, and marching towards the said bridge; and the troops were stationed there, observing our appearance they marched over the bridge and then took up some of the planks; we then hastened our march towards the bridge, and when we got near the bridge they fired on our men, first three guns, one after the other, and then a considerable number more; and then, not before, (having orders from our commanding officers not to fire till we were fired upon) we fired upon the regulars and they retreated. On their retreat through the town of Lexington to Charlestown, they ravaged and destroyed private property, and burnt three houses, one barn and one shop.
Signed by each of the above Deposers.
Lexington April 23, 1775.
We Nathan Barret, Captain Jonathan Farrar, Joseph Butler and Francis Wheeler, Lieutenants, John Barret, Ensign, John Brown, Silas Walker, Ephraim Melvil, Nathan Butbuck, Stephen Husmer, jun. Samuel Barett, thomas Jones, Joseph Chandler, Peter Wheeler, Nathan Peirce and Edward Richardson, all of Concord, in the county of

Middlesex, in the province of Massachusetts-Bay all of lawful age, testify and declare, that on Wednesday, the nineteenth instant, about an hour after sunrise we assembled on a hill near the meeting house in Concord, aforesaid, in consequence of an information, that a number of regular troops had killed six of our countrymen at Lexington, and were an their march to said Concord, at about an hour afterwards we saw them approaching, to the number as we imagined, of about twelve hundred, on which we retreated to a hill about eighty rods back, and the aforesaid troops then took possession of that hill that we were first posted, presently after this we saw them moving towards the North-Bridge about one mile from said meeting house, we then immediately went before them, and passed the bridge just before a party of them to the number of about two hundred arrived; they then left about two hundred at the bridge, and proceeded with the rest towards Col. Barret's, about two miles from the said bridge, we then seeing several fires in the town, thought our houses were in danger, and immediately marched back towards said bridge, and the troops who were stationed there observing our approach marched back over the bridge & then took up some planks; we then hastened our steps towards the bridge, and when we got near the bridge they fired on our men, first three guns, one after the other, & then a considerable number more, upon which, and not before, (having orders from our commanding officer not to fire till we were fired upon) we fired upon the regulars, and they retreated. At Concord and on their retreat through Lexington, they plundered many houses, burnt three at Lexington, together with a shop and barn; and committed damages more or less, to almost every house from Goncord to Charlestown,

Signed by each of the above Deposers.

Concord April 23, 1775.

I Timothy Minot, junior of Concord, on the nineteenth day of this instant, April, after that I heard of the regular troops firing about Lexington men, and fearing that hostilities might be committed at Concord, thought it my

incumbent duty to secure my family; sometime after that returning towards my own dwelling, and finding that the bridge on the northern part of said Concord, was guarded by regular troops: Being a spectator of what had happened at said bridge, declare, that the regular troops stationed on the bridge, after they saw the men who had collected on the westerly side of said Bridge marched toward said bridge, then the troops returned towards the easterly side of said bridge, and formed themselves as I thought for regular fight: after they had fired one gun, then two or three more, before men that were stationed on the westerly part of the bridge fired upon them.   Timothy Minot Junior.
                      Lexington April 23, 1755.

I James Barret of Concord, Colonel of a regiment of militia, in the county of Middlesex, do testify and say that on Wednesday morning last, about day break, I was informed of the approach of a number of the regular troops to the town of Concord, where were some magazines belonging to this province, when they were assembled some of the militia of this and other neighbouring towns, When I ordered them to march to the North Bridge, (so called) which they had passed and were taking up: I ordered said militia to march to said bridge and pass the same, but not to fire on the King's troops unless they were fired first upon. We advanced near said bridge, when the said troops fired upon the militia and killed two men dead on the spot, and wounded several others; which was the first firing of guns in the town of Concord, my detachment then returned the fire, which killed and wounded several of the King's troops.   James Barret.
                      Lexington April 23, 1775.

We Bradberry Robinson, Samuel Spring, Thadeus Bancroft, all of Concord, and James Adams of Lexington, of the county of Middlesex, all of lawful age, do testify and say, that on Wednesday morning last, near ten on the clock, we saw near one hundred regular troops, being inside the town of Concord, at the North-Bridge in said town, (so called) and having passed the same they were taking up said bridge, when about

three hundred of our militia were advancing towards said bridge, when, without saying any thing to us discharged a number of guns on us. which killed two men dead on the spot and wounded several others; when we returned the fire on them killed two of them and wounded several; which was the beginning of hostilities in the town of Concord.   Sign by each of the above Deposers.
Concord April 23, 1775.

I James Marr, of lawful age, testify and say, that on the evening of the eighteenth instant, I received orders from George Hutchingson, and adjutant of the fourth regiment of the regular troops, stationed at Boston, to prepare and march, to which order I attended, and Marched for Concord, where I was ordered by an officer with about one hundred men to guard a certain bridge there; While attending that service a number of people came along us I Suppose to cross said bridge: at which time a number of the regular troops, first fired upon them.

James Marr.

I Edward Thornton Gould, of his Majesty's own regiment of foot, being of lawful age, do testify and declare that on the evening of the 18th instant, under the orders of General Gage, I embarked with the light infantry and grenadiers of the line, commanded by Col. Smith, and landed on the marshes of Cambridge, from whence we proceeded to Lexington. On our arrival at that place, we saw a body of provincial troops armed, to the number of sixty or seventy men, on our approach they dispersed, and soon after firing began, but which party fired first I cannot honestly say, as our troops rushed on shouting and hussaing, previous to the firing, which was continued by our troops, so long as any of the provincials were to be seen. From whence we marched to Concord, on a hill near the entrance of the town, we saw another body of Provincials assembled, the light infantry companies were ordered up the hill to disperse them, and on our approach they retreated towards Concord; the grenadiers continued the road under the hill towards the town. Six companies of light infantry were ordered down to take possession of the bridge which the provincials retreated over; the company I commanded was one, three companies of the above detachment went forwards about two miles, in the meantime the provincial troops returned to the number of about three or four hundred: We drew upon on the Concord side the bridge, the provincials came down upon us, upon which we engaged and gave the first fire; this was the first engagement after the one at Lexington; a continual firimg from both parties lasted through the whole day; I myself was wounded at the attack of the bridge, and am now treated with the greatest humanity, and taken all possible care of by the provincials at Medford.

Medford, April 25, 1775. Edward thornton Gould.
Lieut. King's own Regt.

Province of Massachusetts-Bay, Middlesex County, April 25, 1775.

Lieut. Thornton Gould aforesaid personally made Oath to the truth of the foregoing declaration by him subscribed before us,

Thad. Mason, Joshua Johnson, and Simon Tufts, Justices of the peace for the county aforesaid, Quarum anus.

Province of Massachusetts-Bay Charlestown.

I Nathaniel Gorham, Notary and Tebellion Public, by lawful authority duly admitted and sworn, hereby testify, that all whom it doth or may concern. That Tadeus Mason, Joshua Johnson and Simon Tufts, Esqs; are three of his Majesty's Justice of the Peace (Quarum anus) for the county of Middlesex; and that full Faith and credit is, and ought to be given to their transactions as such, both in court and out. Is witnessed whereof, I have hereonto assigned my name and seal, this twenty-fifth day of April; Anno Domini, one thousand Seven Hundred, and Seventy five.   Nathaniel Gorham
Notary Public   (L.S.)

(All the above Depositions are swore to before Justices of the Peace, and duly attested by Notary Public, in manner of last one.)

NEW-York May 15. "We hear the important passes of Crown Point and Ticonderoga, are taken possession of by a number of Provincials from Connecticut, in order to prevent the Canadians and

Indians making Incursions into the New-England Provinces; but by a Letter from Hartford of the 7th Instant, we hear Governor Carleton had dispatched a Number of Regulars from Canada, and reinforced those Garrisons; however Col. Arnold who commanded the Provincial Party, was determined to proceed at all events, as he expected a reinforcement on his March.

The Martial Spirit through this Province at this juncture is almost beyond Conception; many new Companies have been already raised in this City, and several more are in Contemplation, most of them are in very neat Uniforms; much of their Time spent in perfecting themselves in the Manuel Exercise, and several of them are already so compleat as to vie with the best Veterans.

Col. Philip Shuyler, George Clinton, Esqs; two of our delegates, set out from this City last Friday, in order to attend the Continental Congress; Robert Livingston, jun. Esq; Simon Boerum, Esq; Col. Lewis Morris, and Major Richard Floyd, set out a few Days before for the like Purpose. And we hear the Congress was to be opened with a Sermon by the Revd. Mr. Duché, last Thursday, and that business would then be immediately fallen upon.

The late Seizure of the Powder at the Magagine at Williamsburg, has incenced the Inhabitants of that Province to such a degree against his Excellency Lord Dunmore their Governor, that the Virginia Gazette, or Norfolk Intelligencier of the 4th Instant says, "His Excellency the Governor, we hear with his Family have retired on board his Majesty's Ship Fowey, now lying at York, in consequence of the Disturbances occasioned by the removal of the Powder from the public Magazine in Williamsburg."

We hear from Newark, New-Jersey, that on Monday last, the Boston, Connecticut and New-York Delegates, were received at the Ferry by a number of Gentlemen from this Town. Captain Allen, at the Heaof the Troop of Horses, and Capt, Rutgers, at the Head of his Company of Grenadiers (which were allowed by the Gentlemen present, to be as compleat companions as they had here) The whole proceeded to Newark, where an entertainment was provided, and a Number of patriotic toasts were drank. After Dinner they were escorted to Elizabeth Town, and on their way they were met by Gentlemen and Militia of that place.

WORCESTER May 17. Yesterday Col. James Easton, of Pittsfield, passed through this town on his way to the Hon. the Provincial Congress, with the important intelligence of the reduction of Ticonderoga to the American forces, on the 10th instant. A corespondent, whose veracity may be depended upon, that sent us the following account of this interesting affair, viz.

"Col. James Easton, and Col. Ethan Allan, Having raised about 150 men for the purpose, agreeable to a plan formed in Connecticut, detached a party of about thirty men to go to Scheensborough and take into custody Major Scheen, and his party of regular soldiers, and with the remainder having crossed the Lake in boats in the night, landed about half a mile from said fortress, immediately marched with a great silence to the gate of the fortress, and at break of day, May 10th, made the assault with great intrepidity: Our men darting like lightning upon the guards gave them but just time to snap two guns at our men before they took them prisoners. This was immediately followed by the reduction of the fort and its dependencies. About 40 of the King's troops are taken prisoners, (including one captain, one lieutenant and inferior officers) with a number of women and children belonging to the soldiery, at this garrison; Major Scheen and the whole of his party are also taken. The prisoners are now under a guard on their way to Hartford, where it is probable they will arrived the latter end of the week. Those who took an account of the ordinance, warlike stores, &c. judged it amounted to no less than 3000,000 pounds in value. A party was immediately detached to take possession of Crown-Point, where no great opposition is expected would be made, as the possession of this place affords us to enter all of Canada, and may be of infinite importance for us in the future, it must rejoice the hearts of all the lovers of their country that so noble an acquisition was made without the loss of one life, and is certainly an encomium upon the wisdom and valour of the New-Englanders, however some tories would fain insinuate that they will not fight, nor encounter danger."

What do you thing of the Yankees now?

We are told there are above 100 pieces cannon from 6 to 14 pounders, at Ticonderoga.

CAMBRIDGE May 18. Saturday Col. Easton arrived at the provincial congress at Watertown from Ticonderoga, and brings the glorious news of the taking that place by the American forces, without the loss of a man: of which interesting event we have collected the following particulars, viz. Last Thursday se'nnight, about 240 men from Connecticut and this province, under Col. Allen and Col. Easton, arrived at the lake near Ticonderoga, 80 of them crossed it, and came to the fort about dawn of day. The centry was much surprized at seeing such a body of men, and snapped his piece at them; our men however immediately rushed forward, seized and confined the centry, pushed through the covered way, and all got safe upon the parade, while the garrison were sleeping in their beds. They immediately formed a hollow square, and gave three Huzzas, which brought out the garrison; an inconsiderable skirmish, with cutlasses or bayonets, insued, in which a small number of the enemy received some wounds. The commanding officer soon came forth: Col. Easton clapped him on the shoulder, told him he was his prisoner, and demanded, in the name of America, an instant surrender of the fort, with all its contents, to the American forces. The officer was in great confusion, and expressed himself to this effect --- Damn you, what, -- what -- does all this mean? ----- Col. Easton again told him, that he and his garrison were prisoners: The officer said, that he hoped he should be treated with honour: Col. Easton replied, he should be treated with much more honour than our people had met with the British troops. The officer then said, he was all submission and immediately ordered his soldiers

56

to deliver up all their arms, in number of 100 stands. As they gave up their arms the prisoners were secured in the hollow square. The American forces having thus providently got Possession of one hundred pieces of cannon, several mortars, and a considerable quantity of shot, stores and some powder. After this acquisition, a detachment of our troops was dispatched to take possession of Crown-Point, where there is a considerable number of cannon. Another detachment was sent to Skenesborough, where they took Major Schene, and his family, with a number of soldiers, and several small pieces of cannon.

Last Wednesday Capt. Andrews arrived at Marblehead from Halifax, and we hear he brings intelligence that 20 tons of hay, being about to be shipped from thence for the use of the ministerial army in Boston, the people found means to set it on fire, by which it was near all happily consumed.

NORWICH May 18. Copy of a letter to his excellency General Gage, from the Honourable Jonathan Trumbull, Esq; Governor of his Majesty's Colony of Connecticut, in behalf of the General assembly of said Colony,

Sir,   Dated Hartford April 28, 1775.
The alarming situation of public affairs in this country, and the late unfortunate transactions in the province of Massachusetts-Bay, have induced the General Assembly of this colony, now sitting in this place, to appoint a committee of their body to wait upon your Excellency, and to desire me, in their name, to write to you relative to these very interesting matters.

The Inhabitants of this colony are intimately connected with the people of your province, and esteem themselves bound by the strongest ties of friendship, as well as of concern for them. You will not therefore be surprised that your first arrival at Boston, with a body of his Majesty's Troops, for the declared purpose of carrying into execution certain acts of Parliament, which, in their apprehension, were unconstitutional and oppressive, should have given the people of the colony a very just and general alarm; your subsequent proceedings in fortifying

the town of Boston, and other military preparations, greatly increased that apprehensions for
the safety of the friends and brethren; they
could not be unconcerned spectators of their
suffering in that which they seemed the common
cause of this country; but the late hostile and
secret inroads of some of the troops under your
command into the heart of the country, and the
violence they have committed, have driven them
almost into a state of desperation. They feel
not only for their friends, but for themselves,
and their dearest interests and connection. We
wish not to exaggerate, we are not sure of every part of our information; but by the best
intelligence that we have yet been able to obtain, the late transaction was a most unprovoked
attack upon the lives anf property of his Majesty's subjects; and it is represented to us,
that such outrages have been committed as would
disgrace even barbarians, much more Britons, so
highly famed for humanity as well as bravery:
It is feared therefore that we are devoted to
destruction, and that you have it in command and
intention to ravage and desolate the country.
If this is not the case, permit us to ask, why
have these outrages been committed? Why is the
town of Boston now shut up? And to what end are
all the hostile preparations that are daily making, and why do we continually hear of fresh
destinations of troops for this country? The
people of this colony, you may rely upon it,
abhor the idea of taking arms against the troops
of their Sovereign, and dread nothing so much
as the horrors of civil war; but at the same
time we beg leave to assure your Excellency,
that as they apprehend themselves justified by
the principle of self defence, so they are most
firmly resolved to defend their rights and privileges to the last extremity; nor will they be
restrained from giving aid to their brethren,
if any unjustifiable attack is made upon them.
Be so good, therefore, as to explain yourself
upon this most important subject, as far as is
consistent with your duty to our common Sovereign. Is there no way to prevent this unhappy
dispute from coming to extremities? Is there no

alternative but absolute submission, or the desolation of war? by that humanity which constitutes so amiable a part of your character, for the honour of your Sovereign, and by the glory of the British Empire, we entreat you to prevent it, if it be possible; surely it is to be hoped that the temperate wisdom of the empire might, even yet, find expedient to restore peace, that so all parts of the empire may enjoy their particular rights, honours and immunities: Certainly this is an event most devoutly to be wished for; and will it not be consistent with your duty, to suspend the operations of war on pour part, and enable us on ours to quiet the minds of the people, at least, till the result of some farther deliberations may be known? The importance of the occasion will, we doubt not, sufficiently apologize for the earnestness with which we address you, and any seeming improprieties which may attend it, as well as induce you to give us the most explicit and favourable answer, in your power.

    I am, with the great esteem and respect,
    in behalf of the General Assembly, Sir,
(Signed)   J. Trumbull.
    <u>To his Excellency Thomas Gage Esq;</u>

His Excellency General Gage's Answer to the foregoing Letter.

Sir,   Dated Boston, May 3d, 1775.
I Am to acknowledge the receipt of your letter of the 28th of April last, in behalf of the General Assembly of your colony, relative to the alarming situation of public affairs in this colony, and the late transactions in this province: That this situation is greatly alarming, and that these transactions are truly unfortunate, are truths to be regretted by every friend of America, and by every well wisher for the peace, prosperity and happiness of this province, cannot fail of inducing the former to interpose their good offices, to convince the latter of their impropriety of their past conduct, and to persuade them to return to their allegiance, and to seek redress of any supposed grievances, in those decent and constitutional methods in which one can hope to be successful.

That troops should be employed for the purpose
of protecting the magistrates in the execution
of their duty, when opposed with violence, it is
not a new thing in the English or any other government: That any acts of the British Parliament are unconstitutional or opposite, I am not
to suppose; if any such they are, in the apprehension of the people of this province, it had
been happy for them if they had sought relief
only in the way which the constitution, their
reason, and their interest, pointed out.

You cannot wander at any fortifying the town
of Boston, or making any other military preparations; when you are assured, that previous to
my taking these steps, such was open threats,
and such the war like preparations throughout
the province, as rendered it my indisputable,
duty to take every precaution in any power, for
the protection of his Majesty's troops under my
command, against all hostile attempts. The intelligence you seem to have received, relative
to the late excursion of a body of troops into
the country, is altogether injurious, and contrary to the true state of facts; the troops
disclaim, with indignation, the barbarous outrages of which they are accused, so contrary to
their known humanity. I have taken the greatest
pains to discover if any were committed, and
have found examples of their tenderness both to
the young and the old, but no vestige of cruelty
or barbarity: It is possible that in firing into houses, from whence they were fired upon,
that old people, women or children, may have
suffered, but if any such thing has happened,
it was in their defence, and undesigned. I have
no command to ravage and desolate the country,
and were it my intention, I have had pretence
to begin it, upon the sea ports, who are at the
mercy of the fleet; For your better information,
I inclose you a narrative of that affair, taken
from gentlemen of indisputable honour and vora-
city, who were eye-witnesses of all the transactions of that day, the leaders here have taken
pains to prevent any account of this affair getting abroad, but such as they have thought proper to publish themselves; and to that end the

post has been stopped, the mails broken open, and letters taken out; and by these means the most injurious and inflammatory accounts have been spread throughout the continent, which have served to deceive and inflame the minds of the people.

When the resolves of the Provincial Congress breathed nothing but war, when those two great and effectual prerogatives of the King, the levying of troops, and disposing of the public monies, were wrested from him, and when magazines were forming by an assembly of men, unknown to the constitution, for the declared purpose of levying war against the King, you must acknowledge it was my duty, and it was the dictate of humanity, to prevent, if possible, the calamity of civil war, by destroying such magazines. This and this alone, I attempted. You ask why is the town of Boston now shut up, I can only refer you, for an answer, to those bodies of armed men, who now surround the town, and prevent all access to it. The hostile preparation you mention; are such as the conduct of the people of this province has rendered it prudent to make for the defence of those under my command.

You assure me the people of your colony abhor the idea of taking arms against the troops of their Sovereign. I wish the people of this province, for their own sakes, could make the same declaration. You enquire, is there no way to prevent this unhappy dispute from coming to extremities? Is there no alternative, but absolute submission, on the desolations of war? I answer, I hope there is; the King and Parliament seem to hold out terms of reconciliation, consistent with the honour and interest of Great-Britain, and the rights and privileges of the colonies; they have mutually declared their readiness to avoid any real grievances of the colonies, and to afford them every just and reasonable indulgence, which shall, in a dutiful and constitutional manner be laid before them; and his Majesty adds, it is his ardent wish, that his disposition may have a happy effect on the temper and conduct of his subjects in America: I must add likewise the resolution of the 27th February,

on the grand dispute of taxation and revenue,
leaving it to the colonies to tax themselves,
under certain conditions; here is surely a foundation for an accommodation, to people who wish
a reconciliation rather than a destructive war,
between countries so nearly connected, by the
ties of blood and interest; but I fear that the
leaders of this province have been, and still
are, intent only on shedding blood.

It is reported that the friends to the American
cause, that is, those who were known as such,
before the late Association was set on foot,
keep a strict watch over the new converts to
liberty Principles and measures the new sons of
Liberty being uncommonly assiduous in forming
themselves into companies, and in learning the
military art, to strengthen, as they say the
hands of opposition.   I am Sir, &c.
      (Signed)   T. Gage.
To his Honour Governor Trumbull.

NORWICH May 18. Last Tuesday Afternoon Accounts received here, that a Body of Men, known
by the Appellation of the Green Mountain boys,
had surprized the garrison and taken the Forts
at Ticonderoga and Crown Point, in which they
found near 300 pieces of cannon, many of them
Brass, a great quantity of small Arms, 20 Barrels of Gun-Powder, and upwards of a ton of Musket Balls. It is said the Captors found in the
Fort warelike Stores, &c. to the ammount of
500,000 Pounds Sterling.

The Intelligence respecting the Particulars of
this Transaction varies; the most credible we
have been able to obtain is, that two seperate
Parties engaged in the Expedition, and that one
Party got possession of what boats were to be
found, and took the Fort before the others could
cross the lake, that after they had joined, a
dispute arose about the Booty; however they
agreed that it should be equally divided between
the two Colonies to which the Adventurers belonged. The Troops taken in the Forts, viz. 60
private Men and e Commissioned Officers, at
Ticonderoga, and 8 Men and an Officer at Crown-
Point, are made prisoners; and it is reported,
are now confined in Albany Goal, No Blood was

spilt upon the Occasion, only one centinal, who made some resistance, received a deep wound on the Cheek with a Broad Sword.

By a private letter from Philadelphia, we are informed, that Dr. Franklin has been invited to assist at the Deliberations of the Continental Congress, and that he has taken a Seat among the Members of that August Body; That Col. Washington, of Virginia, has intimated to the Congress, that he can, upon very short Notice, raise an army of 15,000 brave Virginians, completely equipped, and will march them to any part of the Continent where they may be wanted.

We hear that six Transports from England, with Troops to reinforce General Gage at Boston, on Monday last.

PROVIDENCE May 20. Sunday last two transports arrived at Boston from England with about 300 soldiers and we hear four others have since arrived having on board 600 troops, as a further reinforcement to General Gage.

We hear, that two small vessels having been lately seized by the men of war at Newport, and fitted out as cruisers, for the purpose of robbing and plundering the sea coast, in order to supply their fellow-ruffians at Boston with fresh provisions, the inhabitants of Dartmouth dispatched an armed sloop to take them, which was soon accomplished; one of them struck without making any resistance, the other was taken after a short contest, wherein one of our people and three of the enemy were wounded. The prisoners (except the wounded) about 17 in number were sent to Taunton.

Capt, William Chace, from Baltimore-Town in Maryland, advises, that an account of the late engagement with the King's troops was received there by land in six days, when the inhabitants immediately took possession of the provincial magazine, with 1500 small-arms, and secured all the military stores that could be found in private hands. The worthy inhabitants of Maryland and Virginia were ready with their lives and fortunes to defend the common cause of America.

Capt. Chace likewise informs, that the Governor of Virginia had fled on board a man of war, to avoid the resentment of the people, on account of the part he took in a late seizure of powder at Williamsburg, and that it was thought he would go to Boston.

WATERTOWN May 22. Provincial Congress.

Whereas a number of men, some of whom have in times past, by the good people of this province as been raised to the highest places of honour and trust, have become inimical to this colony, and merely on principals of avarice, have in conjunction with the late Governor Hutchinson, been trying to reduce all Americans to the most abject state of slavery: And, as well to avoid the just indignation of the people, as to pursue their diabolical plan, have fled to Boston and other places of refuge:

Therefore Resolved, That those persons, among whom are the mandamus counsellors, are guilty of such atrocious and unnatural crimes, against their country, that every friend of mankind ought to foresake and detest them, until they shall evidence a sincere repentance, by action worthy of men and christains; and that no person within this colony shall take any deed, lease or conveyance whatsoever, of the land, houses or estates of such persons.

And it is hereby recommended of the committee of inspection, in every town in this colony, to see this resolve fully enforced, unless in such cases as the Congress shall otherways direct.

Joseph Warren, President P.T.

Attest   Samuel Freeman, Secr'y P.T.

In Provincial Congress, Watertown, May 25, 1775

Where as applications hath been made to this Congress, by some of the Officers of the army, that some effectual method may be taken for the return of absconding soldiers, or such that might tarry beyond the time limited by furlow. Therefor.

Resolve, That it be, and it is hereby recommended in the Committee of Correspondence, in the several towns and districts in this colony, or to the Selectmen, where no such Committee are appointed, that they take effectual care that such absconding or delinquent soldiers be immediately sent back to their respective

64

Regements.

Joseph Warren, President P.T.
Attest, Samuel Freeman, Secr'y. P.T.
HARTFORD May 22. In the Provincial Congress,
Water-town, April 26, 1775. (Massachusetts-Bay)
To the Inhabitants of Great-Britain.
Friends and fellow-Subjects,
Hostilities are at length commenced in this colony, by the troops under the command of General
Gage, and it being of the greatest importance,
that an early, true and authentic account of
this inhuman proceeding should be known to you,
the Congress of this Colony have transmitted
the same, and from want of a session of the Honorable Constitutional Congress, think it proper
to address you on the alarming occasion.
By the clearest depositions relative to this
transaction, it will appear, that on the night
proceeding the nineteenth of April instant a
body of King's troops, under command of Colonel
Smith, were secretly landed at Cambridge, with
an apparent design to take and destroy the military and other stores provided for the defence
of this Colony, and deposited at Concord; that
some inhabitants of the Colony on the night
aforesaid, whilst traveling peaceably on the
road between Boston and Concord were seized and
greatly abused by armed men, who appeared to be
officers of General Gage's army; that the town
of Lexington by these means was alarmed, and a
company of the inhabitants mustered on the Occasion; that the regular troops on their way to
Concord marched into the said town of Lexington,
and said company on their approach began to disperse; that notwithstanding this, the regulars
rushed on with great violence, and first began
hostilities by firing on said Lexington Company,
whereby they killed eight and wounded several
others; that the regulars continued their fire,
until those of the said company who were neither killed or wounded, had made their escape;
that Colonel Smith with the detachment, then
marched to Concord, where a number of provincials were again fired on by the troops, two
of them killed and several wounded, before the
provincials fired at them; and that those hostile

measures of the troops produced an engagement
that lasted through the day, in which many of
the provincials and more of the regular troops
were killed or wounded.

To give a particular account of the ravages
of the troops, would be very difficult, if not
impracticable; let it suffice to say, a great
number of houses on the road were plundered, and
rendered unfit for use; several were burnt, Wom-
en in child-bed driven by the soldiers naked
into the streets; old men peaceably in their
houses were shot dead; and such scenes exhibited
as would disgrace the annals of the most un-
civilized nations.

These, brethren, are marks of ministerial vengeance, against this colony, for refusing with
her sister colonies, a submission to slavery;
but they have not yet detached us from our Royal
Sovereign. We profess to his loyal and dutiful
subjects, and so hardly dealt with as we have
been, are still ready, with our lives and fortunes, to defend his person, family, crown and
dignity. Nevertheless to the persecution and
tyranny of his cruel ministry we will not tamely
submit, appealing to Heaven for the justness of
our cause, we determine to die or be free.

We cannot think that the honor, wisdom, and
valour of Britons will suffer them to be longer
inactive spectators of measures in which they
themselves are so deeply interested, measures
pursued in opposition to the solemn protest of
many noble Lords, and express sense of conspic-
uous Commoners, whose knowledge and virtue has
long characterized then as some of the greatest
men in the nation, measures executing contrary
to the interest, petitions and resolves of the
many large and respectable opulent counties,
cities, and boroughs in Great-Britain, measures
highly incompatible with justice, but still pursued with a specious pretence of easing the nation of its burthen, measures which if successful, must end in the ruin and slavery of Britain.
as well as the persecuted American colonies.

We surely hope, that the Great Sovereign of
the universe, who hath also often appeared for
the English nation, will support you in every

rational and manly exertion with these colonies for saving it from ruin, and that in a constitutional connection with the mother country, we shall soon be altogether a free and happy people.   Per Order.
              Joseph Warren. President Pro. Tem.
   HARTFORD May 22. Extract of a Letter from a Gentleman at Cambridge, to his Correspondent in this place, dated May 15, 1775.
   "Yesterday two or three ships arrived in Boston, it is said by some, with marines, if so, they must be part of the expected fleet ---- by orders it is said they came with part of the 29th regiment from Pensacola, I rather think the latter account is the true one, however, we must prepare for the worst."
   Authentic Account of the taking the fortress of Ticonderoga and Crown-Point, by a party of forces from this Colony.
   On Saturday the 29th of April Captain Edward Mott of Lyme, Capt, Noah Phelps of Sinsbury, with a small number of the gentlemen, set out from this place in order to take possession of the important fortresses of Ticonderoga and Crown-Point. They marched very privately unarmed till they came to Pittsfield when they informed Col. Easton and John Brown Esq; of their business, and requested their assistance; they likewise immediately dispatched an express to the intrepid Col. Ethan Allen, of Bennington desiring him to be ready to join them with a party of his valiant Green Mountain Boys. These Gentlemen, with the greatest cheerfulness joined Capts. Mott and Phelps, with a number of men sufficient to carry into Execution the important enterprize, and proceeded as directed by them. Col. Allen commanding the soldiery, on Wednesday Morning they surprized and took possession of the fortress making prisoners of the Commandant and his party. The next Day a party under the command of Seth Warner, took Possession of Crown Point, with the ordinance stores, consisting of upwards of 200 pieces of cannon 5 Mortars sundry hawitzers, 50 swivels, 28 barrels of powder, &c. On the 9th inst. they took into custody Major Scheene, at Skeensborough, who immediately

set out for, and arrived at this place on Thursday last.

The prisoners taken at Ticonderoga, to the number of 47; were put under the command of Epaphras Bull of this place, who arrived in this town on Saturday night last. The prisoners he left under guard at New-Hartford, on Saturday, but are expected in town this day.

The officers and soldiers in this important expedition, behaved with the greatest intrepidity and good conduct, and therefore merit the highest applause of their grateful country.

We hear that six Regiments of Volunteers, ordered to be raised by the General Assembly of this Colony, for the Defence of the same, are all filled, and wait only for marching orders. The greatest part of those destined for Boston, are now on their March for the Head Quarters at Cambridge. The Company from Farmington, under the Command of Capt. Noadiah Hooker, passed through this Town for that place on Thursday last; and on Saturday, a Company from Middletown, commanded by Maj. ----- Meigs; and Col. Samuel Wylly's Company, of this place, are ordered to march Thursday next. May God preserve them and make them Victorious.

NEWPORT May 22. The following is taken from a manuscript account of the fire that happened in Boston last Wednesday night.

The fire began in the barracks under the arch formerly improved by Benjamin Davis, half after eight o'clock, 17 May. The soldiers were receiving some cartridges, by which means one took fire, and communicated many more, which immediately set fire to the room.

The following is a list of stores burnt, with the owners names prefixed.

John Hancock, a store and shed, Thomas Fairweather, 1 store, Benjamin Andres, 1 dotto: Edward Gray, 1 ditto, Joseph Barrel, 1 ditto, John Head, 1 ditto; John Williams, 1 ditto, with 50 barrels of flour, donation; Hyslop & Burtow, 1 ditto, Andrew Black, 1 ditto, Nathaniel Carey, 1 ditto and shed; Alexander Hill, 1 ditto and shed, James Russel, Impost-Office; John Scoley, 1 store, John Sweetser, 1 dotto, 3 ditto at the

town dock; six stores and a cooper's shop owned
by Eliakin Hutchinson, adjoiming the town-dock
improved for barracks; 1 store opened by Elias
Thomas sail-Maker, a store leading down to the
barracks, improved by Grant Webster and William
Blair. Thomas Brattle's shed pulled down to stop
the fire. Total 27 stores, 1 cooper's shop, 4
sheds burnt, but not one dwelling house.

Instead of ringing the bells as usual, the
soldiers beat to arms, by which means the people were in great confusion not being used to
such signals in time of fire.

NEW-YORK May 22. Friday Night last Capt. Reynolds arrived here from Porthmouth, in New-Hampshire: Last Monday off Cape Anne, he was boarded
by Capt. Graves, in a Tender, who had come out
of Boston the Day before, and informed him that
three Transports arrive the 6th Instant, from
England, with Troops, and that many more were
hourly expected; the several Vessels were then
in sight, which he imagined was part of the
Fleet, and several guns had been heard in the
offing.

Thursday Capt. Reynolds spoke with Capt. Lynd-
say, in the Falcon Sloop of war, who acquainted
him, that having advice that a Sloop lay on a
Place called Sandwich, that had carried some
provisions to Providence, &c. for the use of the
Boston Provincials, he dispatched his Lieutenant, with his Tender and 20 Men, and two other
Officers to take Possession of her; which they
accordingly did: But, before they could carry
her off, she was retaken, as also the Tender,
by four Boats from the Country, and they say the
Lieutenant lost an Arm, the Gunner was wounded
in the Head, and the Doctor's Mate in one of his
Legs. The Seamen were sent Prisoners into the
Country.

By a letter that arrived here from Cambridge,
we learn, that the Troops in the Provincial Camp
at Boston, consisted of about 7000 Men, but that
they were daily increasing from New-Hampshire,
Rhode-Island and Connecticut; were high in spirits, and abounded with provisions.

PHILADELPHIA May 24. On Wednesday evening last
arrived, John Brown, Esq; from Ticonderoga,

express to the General Congress. Mr. Brown has brought intercepted letters from Lieut. Malcom Fraser, to his friend in New-England, from whom it appears, that General Carleton has almost unlimited power, civil and military, and has issued orders for raising a Canadian regiment, in which Mr. Fraser observes, the officers find difficulty, as the common people are by no means fond of the service. He likewise remarks, that all the King's European subjects are dissatisfied at the partial preference given to the late converts to loyalty as he phrases it, to their utter exclusion from all considerance on even common civility. Matters are indeed in such a situation that many, if not most of the merchants talk of leaving the province.

Mr. Brown also relates, that two regular officers of the 26th regiment, now in Canada, applied to two Indians, one a head warrior of the Caughanaiwaga tribe, to go out with them on a hunt, to the south and east of the rivers St. Lawrence and Surell, and pressing the Indians farther and farther on said course, they at length arrived at Cohass, where the Indians say they were stopt and interrogated by the Inhabitants, to whom they pretended they were only on a hunt, which the inhabitants (as the Indians told Mr. Brown) replied must be false, as no hunters used silver (bright) barrelled guns. However the Cohass people dismissed them all; and when they returned into the woods, the Indian warrior insisted on knowing what their real intentions was, and they told him, that it was to reconnoitre the woods, to find a passage for an army to march to the assistance of the King's Friends in Boston. The Indians asked Where they would get the army? They answered Canada, and that the Indians in the upper castles would join them. —— The Chief, on this, expressed resentment, that he, being one of the head men of the Caughanaiwaga tribe, should never have been consulted in the affair. But Mr. Brown presumes the aversion of this honest fellow and his friends to their schemes, was the reason of being kept from their knowledge.

The conductors of this grand expedition are to

70

be Monsieurs St. Luke le Corne, the villain who let loose the Indians on the prisoners at Fort William Henry, and one of his associates.

CAMBRIDGE May 25. About half after 8 o'clock on Wednesday evening, last week, a fire broke out in a barrack on Treat's wharf, in Boston. It was occasioned by the soldiers receiving a number of cartridges, one of which took fire, and communicated it to many more, which immediately set fire to the room, and soon catched the adjoining buildings. All the stores on the south side of the dock are destroyed, except that at the head of the wharf, occupied by Mr. Samuel Eliot. All the stores from Mr. Eliot's to Ellis Gray's, which make the north corner of Spear's wharf, excepting that occupied at the Commissary's office, are also destroyed. The fire raged with great fury all night. The following letter contains an account of the transaction, of the military at the fire; and will give the public some idea of the present wretched policy of that once well-governed town.

Extract of a letter from Boston.

"I propose to give you a circumstantial account of the late fire, previous to which please to observe, that for ten days past, a report have been propagated, that the liberty party intended to set fire to the town in different places as soon as the greatest part of them had got out. The General took the alarm, and took the engines under guard, and appointed new Captains; the late engine men took umbrage at it; but to the point. I being informed the barracks was on fire, ran through the street crying fire, (as no bell rung) but was stopped by a man who told me it was the officer's order not to cry fire, one having threatened to beat the man's brains out that did. The drums all this time beating to arms. When I came to the fire I found no engine there. Applying to one of the late engine men to know the reason, was informed that he had applied for the engine, but the bayonet was pointed at him, and he was told that he must apply to some officer for an order before he could have it. After this fatal delay the engines appeared with the new appointed Captain

and military firewards, and a miserable figure
they cut, the former not knowing how to obey it,
lhe latter had known how to command. Upon the
whole, it appears to me plain as the meridian
sun, had the engines been on the old footing,
the fire would have been put out and *twenty
thousand pounds sterling loss prevented. Let
that be as it may, I will venture to say, had
the fire broke out in the center of the town it
would had laid it to ashes, in the direction it
took to the water. May God preserve this second
Sodom from the fate of the first!"
    *The whole loss is thought to be 40,000 pounds
Sterling.
    CAMBRIDGE May 25. Last Sabbath about 10 o'clock
A. M. an express arrived at General Thomas's
quarters at Roxbury, informing him four sloops
(two of them armed) were sailed from Boston, to
the south shore of the bay, and that a number
of soldiers were landing at Weymouth. General
Thomas ordered three companies to march to the
support of the inhabitants. When arrived they
found the soldiers had not attempted to land at
Weymouth; but had landed on Grape-Island, from
whence they were carrying off hay on board the
sloops. The people of Weymouth assembled on a
point of land next to Grape-Island, the distance
from Weymouth shore to said island, was to great
for small arms to do execution; nevertheless,
our people frequently fired. The fire was returned from one of the vessels with swivel guns,
but the shot passed over our heads, and did no
mischief. Matters continued in this state for
several hours, the soldiers polling the hay down
to the water side, our people firing at the vessel, and they now and then discharging a swivel-
gun. The tide was now come in and several light-
ers which were aground, were got afloat, upon
which our people, who were ardent for battle,
got on board, hoisted sail, and bore directly
down upon the nearest point of the island. The
soldiers and sailors immediately left the barn,
and made for their boats, and put off from one
end of the island, whilst our people landed on
the other. The sloops hoisted sail with all possible expedition, whilst our people set fire to

72

the Barn, and burnt 70 or 80 tons of hay, then
fired several tons which had been polled down
to the water-side, and brought off the cattle.
As the vessels passed Horse Neck, a sort of
promontory which extended from Germantown, they
fired their swivels and small arms at our people
pretty briskly but without effect, though one of
the bullets from their small arms, which passed
over our people, struck against a stone with
such force as to take off a large part of the
bullet. Whether any of the enemy were wounded,
is uncertain, though it is reported three of
them were, It is thought that they did not carry
off more than one or two tons of hay.

NORWICH May 25. We hear, that the Provincial
Convention of New-York having requested Instructions from the Continental Congress, how to proceed, in Case the Troops, soon expected from
Great-Britain, should arrive at that city, received for an answer, "It is the Opinion of the
Congress that the Troops should be suffered to
land, and take possession of the Barracks, unmolested; but if they should attempt to erect
Fortifications, or throw up Intrenchments, they
ought to be immediately opposed."

It is reported that the Troops taken by the
New-England Forces, at the Reduction of Ticon-
daroga and Crown-Point, were brought to Hartford
on tuesday last, and now under confinement there.

On Tuesday last, Major Durkge's Company of
this Colony Troops, consisting of 100 well appointed, and disciplined men, marched from this
town, under the Command of Lieutenant Joshua
Huntington, to join Brigadier Putnam's Regiment
now assembling at the American Army's Head-Quarters, near Boston.

Last Evening, a Company of able bodied, well
armed Soldiers, Part of Colonel Parson's Regiment, arrived here from Saybrook, on their way
to the Camp: And, this Day Capt. Coit's Company,
of the latest mentioned Regiment, marched from
hence for the Army.

NORWICH May 25. From the New-England Chronicle, &c. published in Cambridge.

[in our last we inserted a curiosity, an infamous, lying letter from General Gage, in answer

to a very sensible polite one he received from
Governor Trumbull. The following is (we suppose)
the narrative of the late engagement taken (as
the General says) "From gentlemen of indisputable hounor and veracity." to which he refers
the Governor; and which we now insert (with some
remarks) as another specimen of the detestable
principals of the barbarity committed.]

On Tuesday the 18th of April about half past
10 at night Lieutenant Colonel Smith of the 10th
regiment, embarked from the common at Boston,
with the grenadiers and light infantry of the
troops there, and landed on the opposite side,
from whence he began to march towards Concord,
where he was ordered to destroy a magazine of
military stores, deposited there for the use of
an army to be assembled, in order to act against
his Majesty and his government. --- [this magazine of stores was honestly provided for use of
the people, not for the purpose of acting against
legal government, but in order to unable them
to preserve their just rights and privileges,
most villainously invaded by a desperate administration; and the seize and destruction of such
stores was nothing more nor less than absolute
robbery: Therefore, General Gage or any other
man (let his private character have been ever
so amiable) who effected, or even attempted the
destruction of property procure for such virtuous purposes, ought immediately to have been
killed upon the spot, as an infamous public
robber.] ------ The Colonel called his officers
together, and gave orders, that the troops should
not fire, unless fired upon; and after marching
a few miles, detached six companies of light
infantry, under the command of Major Pitcairn,
to take possession of the two bridges on the
other side of Concord, soon after they heard
many Signal guns, and the ringing of alarm bells
repeatedly, which convinced them, that the country was rising to oppose them, and that it was
a preconcerted scheme to oppose the King's
troops, whenever there should be a favorable
opportunity for it ----- [The "King's Troops"
have been, for many years past, converted into
instruments of tyranny: and their being suffered

to remain among us, in that character redounds
not much: the honour of a free and spirited people. That it has been predetermine, or "preconcerted," to oppose the "King's Troops" or any
other body of men, rather than submit to the
oppressive edicts (and thereby become slaves)
of a corrupt British Parliament, or rather the
vessels of a Jacobitish, tory ministry in an
incontrovertible, acknowledging, a truth -----
in which every good man ought to glory: And our
not opposing these engines of oppression, the
"King's Troops," till the 19th of April, must
ever be considered as a criminal neglect of a
most important duty, which can admit of no pal-
liation but by supposing that day to be the first
"favourable opportunity for it."] ----- About 3
o'clock the next morning, the troops being advanced within two miles of Lexington, intelligence was received that about 500 men in arms,
were assembled, and determined to oppose the
King's troops;* and on Major Pitcairn's Galloping up to the head of the advanced companies
two officers informed him that a man (advanced
from those that were assembled) had presented
his musket and attempted to shoot them, but the
piece flashed in the pan: On this the Major gave
directions to the troops to move forward, but
on no account to fire, nor even to attempt it,
without orders. When they arrived at the end of
the village, they observed about 200 armed men,
drawn up on a green, and when the troops came
within a hundred yards of them they began to
file off towards some stone walls, on the right
flank: The light infantry observing this, ran
after them; The Major instantly called to the
soldiers not to fire, but to surround and disarm
them; some of them had jumped over a wall, then
fired four or five shot at the troops, wounded
a man in the 10th regiment, and the Major's
horse in two places, and at the same time several shot were fired from the meeting-house on
the left: Upon this, without any order or regularity, the light infantry began a scattered
fire, and killed several of the country people;
but were silenced as soon as the authority of
those officers could make them.

[As the true narration of the late engagement, and a just representation of the severe barbarity of our enemies, are prepared or preparing by proper authority, it is necessary here particularly to expose the gross misrepresentations, and contradict the many lies contained in this "circumstantial account" The remainder of the notoriously false narrative will therefore be inserted without any further remarks at this time.]

+After this Colonel Smith marched up with the remainder of the detachment, and the whole body proceeded to Concord, where they arrived about 9 o'clock, without any thing further happening; but vast numbers of armed people were seen assembling on all the heights: while Colonel Smith with the grenadiers, and part of the light infantry remained at Concord, to search for cannon, &c. there: he detached Captain Parson with six light companies to secure a bridge at some distance from Concord, and to proceed from thence to certain houses, where it was supposed there was cannon and ammunitions, Captain Parsons, in pursuance of these orders, posted three companies at the bridge, and on some heights, near it, under command of Capt. Laurie of the 43d regiment and with the remainder went to destroy some cannon, wheels, powder, and ball; the people still continued increasing on the heights; and in about an hour after, a large body of them began to move towards the bridge, the light companies of the 4th and 10th then descended, and joined Captain Laurie, the people continued to advance in great numbers; and fired upon the King's troops, killed three men, wounded four officers, one serjeant, and four private men, upon which (after returning the fire) Captain Laurie and his officers, thought it prudent to retreat to the main body at Concord, and were soon joined by two companies of grenadiers; when Captain Parson returned with the three companies over the bridge, they observed three soldiers on the ground, one of then scalped, his head mangled, and his ears cut off, though not quite dead; a sight which struck the soldiers with horror; Captain Parson marched on and joined the

76

Main body, who were only waiting for his coming up, to march back to Boston; Colonel Smith had executed his orders, without opposition, by destroying all the military stores he could find; both the Colonel and Major Pitcairn, having taken all possible pains to convince the inhabitants that no injury was intended them, and that if the opened their doors when requested, to search for said stores, not a slight of mischief should be done; neither had any of the people the least occasion to complain, but they were sulky, and one of them even struck Major Pitcairn. Except, upon Capt. Laurie, at the bridge, no hostilities happened from the affair at Lexington, till the troops began their march back. As soon as the troops had got out the town of Concord, they received a heavy fire from all sides, from walls, fences, houses, trees, barns, &c. which continued without intermission, till they met the first brigade, with two field pieces, near Lexington; ordered out under the command of Lord Percy to support them: (advice having been received about seven o'clock the next morning, that signals had been made and expresses gone out to alarm the country, and that the people were raising to attack the troops under Colonel Smith.) Upon the firing of the field pieces, the people's fire was for a while silenced, but as they still continued to increase greatly in numbers, they fired again as before, from all places where they could find cover, upon the whole body, and continued so doing for the space of Fifteen miles: notwithstanding their numbers they did not attack openly during the whole day, but kept under cover on all occasions. The troops were very much fatigued, the greater part of the men having been under arms all night, and made a march of upwards of forty miles before they arrived at Charlestown, from whence they were ferryed over to Boston.

The troops had about 60 killed, and many more wounded: Reports are various about the loss sustained by the country people, some make it very considerable, others not so much.

That this unfortunate affair has happened

through the rashness and imprudence of a few people, who began firing on the troops at Lexington.

+Notwithstanding the fire from the meeting-House, Colonel Smith and Major Pitcairn, with the greatest difficulty kept the soldiers from forcing into the meeting-house, and putting all those in it to death.

PHILADELPHIA May 25. It is proposed by the Field Officers of the City and Liberties of philadelphia, to review the three Battalions under their Command, on Monday next at Five o'Clock in the Morning.

CAMBRIDGE May 26. Last Sunday 3 or 4 schooners and sloops with several boats, were sent from Boston to Leverett's Island near Weymouth, about 10 or 12 miles below Boston, in order to get a quantity of hay and cattle, they arrived at low water, which gave the people time to collect, who wounded three of the enemy, and drove them off. They had got a ton and a half of the hay on board, some more they had collected near the water, was burnt by the people.

We hear Gen. Gage blamed the Admiral for sending vessels, that were so small on this enterprize.

Lieut. Gold, who was taken by the Provincials in the engagement of the 19th ult. was a few days since exchanged for an old man named Breed, who has a large family, he was taken by the regulars in the same engagement. Lieut. Gold has a fortune of 1900 pounds per annum. 'Tis said, when first taken, that he offered 2000 pounds for his ransom.

We learn that the regular officers in Boston of Gen. Putnam's acquaintance, have frequently of late sent to him, begging for fresh provisions, which the humane General has as often sent them, without pay.

Two regular soldiers were blown up at a fire in Boston, and killed. It seems Gen. Gage has some time before taken possession of the engine, and appointed new officers over them, who were unskilled, this (together with the time spent in procuring a permit from the General) occasioned the fire's getting a great head.

CAMBRIDGE May 28. Yesterday a party of the United American Army was ordered to take the cattle, hay, &c. from Noodle's and Hog Insland. While executing their orders were attacked by a number of the King's troops from Boston, in an armed schooner, a sloop, and eight or ten boats belonging to the men of war: a brisk fire began about four o'clock P. M. and continued much of the night, then ceased a little, and at dawn of day was renewed, by which time Capt. Foster, with two field pieces from this camp, joined our troops, when a heavy fire from shore on the armed vessels put them into great distress. The schooner's deck were soon cleared, and she drifted on the ferry-way at Winesimet, where our people set fire to her, and she was soon blown up, and destroyed. Sixteen four-pounders, and six swivels, were taken out of her by our people. The sloop was disabled and obliged to be towed off by the men of war's boats, the remaining of them are returned to their den. Our people had none killed, three wounded, but none of them dangerously. The number of killed and wounded of the enemy not known.

HARTFORD May 29. Extract of a letter from the Camp at Cambridge, dated May 18, 1775.

"We hear from Halifax, that the people have at last, shown they have spirit ——— it seems the agents for procuring forage for the expected regiment of Dragoons had taken without the consent of the owner, and were shipping for Boston a great quantity of hay, on which the people set fire to, and wholly destroyed it; and when that work was finished, they attempted the like with the King's magazine, which they several times fired, but they were extinguished by the people from the ships of war lying there, who made a brisk fire on the people, and prevented them from effecting their design. The fugitives from Boston are gone for Halifax, but the people say, no damned tories shall be allowed to breath in their air, for that these poor devils can't find a resting place there, which was the only place on the continent that they were ever dared and hope they might stay in.

"The plan of continually harassing the troops

79

in Boston is still continued; last Saturday all
the men on duty in this camp, about 2500 marched
in Charlestown, down to the ferry-ways, and then
countermarched, and came back again, being within a short musquet shot of the Somerset, which
lays in the ferry-way, and in fair shot of several of their batteries; they all turned out in
town, were amazed at their numbers, they swore
there were at least 10000 men, and some said
15000, so much did their fear magnified our numbers, they swore we were impudent fellows, and
it was a damned insult on them: When on the Ferry-way, one of our Men, a Paddy, hail'd the ship
with "What do you think of the Congress now?"
At the same Time the Troops at Roxbury, about
1500 of them, marched down to Dorchester Neck,
and paraded round there, and about 400 from here
made their appearances on Lechemere's Farm, that
they were under the most fearful Apprehensions
for their own Safety --- they were more surprized
being told that the army had all broke up and
gone home, but they found the Tories had deceived
them in that, as in every Thing else.
  HARTFORD May 29. From Worcester dated April
26, 1775.
                Province of Massachusetts-Bay.
  Hannah Bradish of that part of Cambridge, that
is called Menotomy, and daughter of Mr. Timothy
Paine, of Worcester, in the country of Worcester county, esq; of lawful age, testify and
says, That about five o'clock on Wednesday after
noon, being in his bed chamber, with her infant
child, about 8 days old, she was surprized by
the firing of the King's troops and our people,
on their return from Concord. She being weak
and unable to go out of her house, in order to
secure herself and family, they all retired into the kitchen, in the back part of the house.
She soon found the house surrounded with the
King's troops; that upon observation made, at
least seventy bullets were shot into the front
part of the house; several bullets were lodged
in the kitchen where she was, & passed thro' an
easy chair she had just gone from. The door of
the front part of the house was broke open; she
did not see any soldiers in the house, but

supposed by the noise, they were in the front part. After the troops had gone off, she missed the following things, which she verily believes were taken out of the house by the KIng's Troops, viz. one rich brocaded gown, called a negligee, one lutestring gown, of white quilt, one pair of brocade shoes, three shifts, light white aprons, three caps, one case if ivory knives and forks, and several other small articles.

Hannah Bradish.

Worcester, April 26, 1775.

Privince of Massachusetts'Bay.

Worcester, ff. April 26, 1775.

Mrs. Hannah Bradish, the deponent, maketh, oath before us, the subscribers, two of his Majesty's Justices of the Peace for the county of Worcester, and of the quorum, that the above deposition, according to her best recollection, is the truth. Which is taken in perpetuam reimemorium.

Thomas Steel.

Timothy Paine.

HARTFORD May 29. Extract of a Letter from Ticonderoga, dated May 23, 1775.

"I shall endeavour to give you a very concise Journal of matters here since the 12th instant.

"May 12. We set sail from Skeenesborough, in a Schooner belong to Major Scheene, which we christened Liberty.

"Sunday 13. Arrived at Ticonderoga, from whence after some preparations, we set sail for Crown-Point.

"Monday 14. Contrary winds retarded our voyage, and the day drew to a close when we anchored at Crown-Point.

"Tuesday 15. Contrary winds. Col. Arnold with thirty men took the boat, and proceeded on for St. John's, leaving to Capt. Slo-- the command of the vessel with the sailors; and to me the command of the soldiers on board: About twelve o'clock, while beating down, we espied a boat, sent out our Coxwain to bring her in, it proved to be the French post from Montreal, with Ensign Moland on board, we examined the mail, and among other things found an exact list of the regular troops in the northern department, amounting to upward of seven hundred.

"Wednesday, 16, a fair gale, we overtook Col. Arnold in the boat, took him on board, and at night arrived within thirty miles of St. John's, when the wind fell, and the vessel was becalmed. We immediately armed our two boats, maned them with thirty five men, and determined by dint of rowing to fetch St. John's, and take the place and the King's sloop by surprize at break of day.

"Thursday, 17. After rowing hard all night we arrived within half a mile of the place at sunrise, sent a man to bring us information, and in a small creek, infested with numberless swams of gnats and muskutoes, waited with impatience for his return.

"The man returning informed us they were surprized of our coming, though they had feared of the taking of Ticonderoga and Crown-Point. We directly pushed for shore, and landed at about sixty rods distance from the barracks; the men had their arms, but upon our briskly marching up to their faces, they retired inside the barracks, left their arms, and resigned themselves into our hands.

"We took fourteen prisoners, fourteen stands of arms, and some small boats. We also took the King's sloop, two fine brass field pieces & four boats. We destroyed five boats more lest they should be used against us. Just at the completion of our business, a fine gale arose from the north; We directly hoisted sail, and returned in triumph. About six miles from St. John's we met Col. Allen with four boats and ninety men, who determined to proceed and maintain the ground. The scheme Col. Arnold thought inpracticable, as Montreal was near, with plenty of men and every necessary of war: Nevertheless, Col. Allen proceeded, and encamped on the opposite side of the lake (or river as it is there called) the next morning he was attacked by two hundred regulars, was obliged to decamp and retreat.

"Friday, 18. Returned to Crown-Point, and from thence to Ticonderoga.

"Saturday, 19, Encamped at Ticonderoga. Since that time, nothing material has happened. It is Col. Arnold's present design, that the sloop

Enterprize (as she is called) and the schooner Liberty shall cruize on the lake, and defend our frontiers, 'till men, provisions and ammunition are furnished to carry on the war."

NEW-YORK May 29. Saturday Morning an Express arrived here from Ticonderoga in 3 Days; by him we learn; Major Arnold dispatched Mr. Oswell and 33 Men, in a schooner and some battoes, to take possession of a sloop that lay in St. John's; at the same time Capt. Ethan Allan set out with 30 Men to facilitate the undertaking, and stopped on the way for reinforcement of 20 more; but Mr. Oswell perceived the scheme; and took possession of the vessel that lay in St. John's, with all the battoes, and made 24 Soldiers and six Seamen Prisoners of war, before Capt. Allen came up; but the latter contrary to advice, proceeded to St. John's where he unluckily fell in with 150 Regulars that were dispatched to the succour of Crown-Point and Ticonderoga, and after entrenching a field shot made a good retreat with the loss of 3 Men only.

NEW-YORK May 29. In Provincial Congress at the City of New-York May 25, 1775.

Whereas the enemies of American liberty are indefatigable in their endeavours to disunite these colonies; and in prosecuting this measure, evil-minded persons may insinuate that the northern colonies have hostile intentions against our fellow-subjects in Canada.

Resolve. That this Congress do most earnestly recommend it to all persons whatsoever, not to commit any hostilities against people of that country, and do hereby declare to the world, that we do consider every such step as infamous and highly inimicle to all the colonies.

Ordered that the above resolution be published.
A true copy of the minutes,
Robert Benson Secry.

NEW-YORK May 29. Friday Morning last, his Majesty's Ship Asia, George Vandeput, Esq; Commander, arrived here from Boston, after a passage of 16 Days.

When the Ship left Boston no Transports nor Troops had then arrived there from England, or Ireland; but two Days after Capt. Vandeput, came out, he fell in with 6 Transports from England with Troops on board.

Major Wooster, an experience Officer, was to march from New-Haven for Greenwich, within about 12 Miles of this Province, with 2500 Men, last Friday; there to encamp during the Summer Season, in order to be at hand to support the City of New-York in case some Assistance should be wanted.

Last Wednesday the Hon. Payton Randolph, Esq; set off for Philadelphia for Virginia, to attend his Place as Speaker of the House of Burgesses of that Province; when the Hon. John Hancock, Esq; was appointed President of the Continental Congress in his room.

WORCESTER May 31. A correspondent, at Cambridge, has favoured us with the following authentic account of the skirmish on Hog and Noodle Islands in Boston Harbour, viz.

"On the 27th inst. a party of the Massachusetts forces, under the command of Col. Nixon, together with a party of the New-Hampshire force, joined by Col. Putnam, in all about 600, were ordered to drive off the sheep and other stock on Hog-Island; whilst this was compleating, a party of the King's troops came out of a barn on Noodle-Island and were driving off a number of horses from thence; between Hog-Island and aforesaid barn on Noodle-Island, there is a level marsh of about half a mile in length, surrounded with water, and entirely open to the view of the enemy; notwithstanding this about six of the provincial forces, animated with that spirit which is natural to Americans, landed on Noodle Island, and although the marsh was void of any cover, and the enemy might securely fire upon them from the barn, and a stone wall adjacent to it, they marched up in open view, and without the loss of a man dispersed the enemy who fled with precipitation; they then recovered the horses which the enemy were driving off. About this time an armed schooner, with a number of barges came up the creek, keeping up a constant fire upon our men at Winnisimet-ferry and parts adjacent: About 20 or 30 of the provincials had now landed on Noodle-Island to support the aforesaid party of six. As the schooner had arrived along side the marsh, and our people found it impossible to carry off the stock on Noodle-Island, they were obliged to kill eleven horses and brought off only one or two horned cattle, the schooner together with the barges armed with swivels, immediately fired grape shot at our party on the marsh, and although the party were entirely exposed to their fire without any cover, the schooner was not more than fifty rods distant, they providentially neither killed or wounded a man, but the party regained Hog-Island in safety, secured only by the fire of 12 provincials on an eminence who obliged 100 of the King's troops to retreat. About this time a party of regulars to the number of 50, supported by two other bodies appeared bringing about 200 in each, came upon Noodle-Island. The former, party of 50 advanced platoons upon a number of Provincials who were on guard on the marsh on Hog-Island, a very brisk fire immediately commenced from the said party, and from the provincials on the summit of Hog-Island, likewise from the regular bodies that supported the fifty, and from the schooner and barge: This lasted till about sun-down, when the schooner and barges fell down the creek, keeping a continued fire. After this the wind dying away, the barges towed her back to Winnisimet, our people put in a heave fire of small arms upon the barges, and two three-pounders coming up to our assistance began to play upon them, and after two or three hours engagement obliged the barges to quit her, and carry off the crew: After which our people set fire to her, and notwithstanding all attempts to prevent it by the barges she was burnt on the ways of Winnisimet-ferry. Through the kind inteposition of divine providence, we have not lost a single life in this engagement which was very hot from the armed schooner which mounted four 6-pounders and 12 swivels, and also from an armed sloop that lay within reach of small arms and from two twelve pounders on Noodle-Island, and from one or two of the men of war in the harbour; only four of the provincials were wounded, but neither of them mortally.

what number of the enemy were killed and wounded
we cannot ascertain, but it is thought their
loss is very considerable. Our people have got
in possession the cannon and every thing else
on board the schooner which was not destroyed
by the fire.

CAMBRIDGE June 1. To the Inhabitants of Massachusetts-Bay.

Friends and Fellow Countrymen,

With great satisfaction we bear publick testimony Of your Disposition to save the glorious
Cause in which America is now engaged, Evidenced
by your readiness to supply, on the Credit of
the Colony, many necessary Articles for the use
of the Army, and in various other ways, by which
you have given convincing Proof that you are
heartily disposed to maintain the publick liberty.

The Cause, we have not the least doubt, if you
condone to exert yourselves in conjunction with
our sister Colonies, will finally prevail.

This Congress have opened a Subscription for
One Hundred Thousand Pounds, lawful Money, for
which the Receiver-General is directed to issue
Notes on Interest, at the Rate of Six per Cent.
per Annum, payable in June 1777; and it is of
the utmost Importance that the Money be immediately obtained, that the publick credit may not
suffer, we most earnestly recommend to such of
you as have cash in your Hands, which you can
spare from the necessary Supplies of your Families, that you will put it in our power to carry into Effect the Measures undertaken for the
Salvation of the Country.

That the Army should be well supplied with
every Article necessary for the most effectual
military Operations, you must all be sensible;
and that if we should fail herein it may prove
ruinous and destructive to the Community, whose
Safety, under God, depends upon their vigorous
Exertions.

As you have already, in many Instances, nobly
exerted yourselves, this Congress have not the

smallest Doubt but that you will, with great
Cheerfulness, crown all by furnishing as much
cash as will be necessary for the good Purposes
aforementioned, especially when it is considered
that they are now no ways of Improving money in
Trade and that there is the greatest probability
to other Colonies will give a ready Currency to
the Notes, which will render them in one respect,
at least, on a better footing than any Notes
heretofore used in this Colony.

If you should furnish the Money that is now
needed, you will perform a meritorious Service
for your Country, and prove yourselves sincerely
attached to its Interest; but if undue Caution
should prevent your doing this effectual Service; the Colony, the total Loss, both of your
Liberties and the very Property which you, by
retaining it, affect to save, may be the unhappy
Consequence, it being past all Controversy that
the Destruction of Individuals must be involved
in that of the Publick.

                    Joseph Warren President P. T.
    Attest.   Samuel Freeman, Secr'y P. T.
    CAMBRIDGE June 1. We are well informed that a
few Days after the Battle of Lexington, the Regular Troops stole away all the Cattle, Sheep,
Hay, 7c. from Governor's Island and Thompson
Island in Boston Harbour.

On the 27th ult. as a Party of the Massachusetts Forces, together with a party of the New-
Hampshire Forces in all 600 were attempting to
bring off the stock upon Hog Island, about 30
Men upon Noodle Island were doing the same, when
a hundred Regulars landed upon the last mentioned
Island, and pursued our Men till they had got
safely back to Hog Island: Then the Regulars
began to fire very briskly by Platoons upon our
Men. In the meantime, an armed Schooner with a
Number of Barges, came up to Hog-Island to prevent our People's leaving said Island, which she
could not effect; after that, several Barges
were towing her back to her Station, as there
was little Wind, and flood Tide: Our People got
in a heavy fire of small Arms upon the Barges,
and two 3-Pounders coming up for assistance,
began to play upon them, and soon obliged the

Barges to quiet her, and to carry off her Crew:
After which the People set Fire to her although
the Barges exerted themselves very vigorously
to prevent it. She was burnt upon the Ways at
Winnisinet-Ferry.

We have not lost a single Life, although the
Engagement was very warm from the armed Schooner
(which mounted four 6-Pounders and 12 Swivels)
an armed Sloop that lay within reach of the small
Arms, from one or two 12-Pounders upon Noodle
Island, and from the Barges, which were all
fixed with swivels.

Hog-Island was stript of the Stock, and some
was taken from Noodle's Island.

Two or three Persons only of our Men were
wounded, but none mortally. How many of the enemy we killed and wounded we cannot ascertain.

We have in our Hands all in the Schooner that
was not destroyed by the fire.

We have to inform our Friends that since the
above Attempts to remove the live Stock from the
Islands, it has been actually done: Five or six
hundred Sheep, and Lambs, upwards of 20 Head of
Cattle and a Number of Horses, have been removed
to the main Land.

Perhaps History cannot furnish us with a more
miraculous Interposition of Divine Province:
Although our Enemies kept a warm Fire, both from
the Cannon and Small Arms, yet we have but three
Men Wounded, two of which received from our Men:
none of them supposed to be mortal. By way of
Caution, we would inform the Public, that one
of the Captains that was killed in the Engagement at Concord, was killed by his own Countrymen. That was the unhappy consequence of firing
at to great a Distance.

We still beg the most earnest and constant
Prayers of our pious Friends, that our Heads may
always be covered in the Day of Battle. The Lord
is a man of War, let Salvation be ascribed to
the Lord.

Our Enemies in Boston, we are informed, are
very confident of having various Accounts of the
Number of our Men whom they killed and wounded;
some of them are so moderate as to mention only
2 or 300; others of them make our loss amount

to 600.

We are informed, that in the Caberus Frigate, Capt. Chads, who arrived at Boston last Thursday from England, came passengers, Major-General Howe, Clinton, and Burgoyne.

NORWICH June 1. A gentleman in town favoured us with the following Copies of Letters from the Commanding Officers of Crown-Point, and Ticonderoga.

Gentlemen,   Crown-Point May 19, 1775.

I wrote you the 14th instant by Mr. Romans, which I make no doubt you have received: the afternoon of the same day, I left Ticonderoga, with Captains Brown, Oswold, and fifty men, in a small schooner; arrived at Skenesborough and proceeded for St. John's marched two small Batteaux, with 35 men, and at 6 the next morning arrived there, and surprized a serjeant and his party of 12 men, took the King's sloop, about 70 tons, a brass 6-pounder, and 7 men, without any loss on either side.

The Captain was hourly expected from Montreal, with a large detachment of men, some guns and carriages for the sloop; as was a Captain and 40 men from Chamblee, at 12 miles distance from St. John's so the providence seems to have smiled upon us, in arriving so fortunate an hour; for had we been six hours later, in all possibility we would have miscarried in our design. The wind proving favorable, in two hours after our arrival, we got on board all the stores, provisions, &c. and weighed anchor for this place, with the sloop and five large batteaux, which we seized, having destroyed five others, and arrived here ten this morning, not leaving any one craft of any kind behind, that the enemy can cross the lake in, if they have any such intentions. I must here observe, that in my return, some distance this side of St. John's, I met Col. Allen with 90 or 100 of his men, in a starving condition, and supplied him with provisions. ---- He informed me of his intention of proceeding on to St. John's, and keeping possession there. It appears to me a wild, expensive, impracticable scheme; and provided it could be carried into execution of no consequence, so long as we are

90

masters of the lake, and that I make no doubt
we shall be, as I am determined to arm the sloop
and schooner immediately. For particulars must
beg leave to refer you to Capt. Osworld, who has
been very active and serviceable and is a prudent good officer.   B. Arnold.
   P. S. By return sent to General Gage last
week, I find there are in the 7th and 26th regiment now in Canada, 717 men, including 70 we
have taken Prisoners.
   Sir,   Ticonderoga May 21, 1775.
   Col. Allen and the party just arrived from St.
John's, where they were attacked the next morning after I came away (the 19th inst.) by above
200 regulars, with 6 field pieces, and were
obliged to make a precipitate retreat, with the
loss of three men missing. They have returned
without provisions and much fatigued. Pray send
on all the provisions you have immediately, and
those men who will engage for the summer. I have
here, exclusive of Col. Allen's men, 120 men,
and have the sloop and schooner in as good order
as possible for the time. I shall immediately
proceed to Crown-Point, and make a stand, in
order to secure the cannon at that place. I am
under no apprehension from the enemy at present,
as we are masters of the lake. Do not fail to
send down powder, without loss time, as we have
only a few rounds. I am &c.
                       B. Arnold Commander.
   P. S. Send this forward to Albany, to hurry
the provisions.
         To Captain John Stephens.
   A true copy,   Samuel Stringer, Chairman
            of Committee,   Albany, May 23, 1775.
   Sir,   Fort-George, May 22, 9 o'clock 1775.
   You will see by the inclosed that the troops
in Canada are proceeding against us. Col. Arnold
charged the bearer of the inclosed, Mr. Lyman,
that it signify, that his desire is, that the
contents of the inclosed be forwarded to the
different colonies, and to the Continental
Congress by express.
              Yours, J. Stephens Commander.
   P. S. You will see, Gentlemen, by the inclosed,
that the troops are in want of powder, and that

I have not now more than 25 lb. at present; so that I cannot afford them any considerable assistance at present.

To the Chairman of the Committee at Albany.

A true copy, Samuel Stringer, Chairman of the Committee at Albany.

NEW-YORK June 1. Provincial Congress New-York May 31, 1775.

Resolve, That it be recommended to the inhabitants of this Colony in general, immediately to furnish themselves with necessary arms and ammunition, to use all diligence to perfect themselves in the military art; and if necessary form themselves into companies for that purpose, until the further order of Congress.

Robert Benson Secretary.

PORTHSMOUTH (New-Hampshire) June 2. Last Tuesday about 30 or 40 Men, from on board the Scarborough man of war now in this Harbour, came on shore at Fort William and Mary, and have torn down great part if the breast work of said fort, and did other damage.

They say before the attempt, the Scarborough took two provision vessels, loaded with Corn, Pork, Flour, Rye, &c. coming in from Long-Island; which were for the relief of this place; as the inhabitants are in great want of provisions; and notwithstanding the most prudent application of the principal gentlemen of this town, the Captain refused to release them.

O shocking situation. Upon this refusal. it was apprehended the most violent outrage and insult of the people would immediately follow this detention of their provisions, the consequences of which would be most probably very fatal to his Majesty's subjects by bringing into the most imminent danger the lives and properties of his said subjects, which ought by all means to be prevented if possible.

Upon this unimaginable transaction, the inhabitants of this and neighbouring towns, were greatly alarmed; and the next morning between 5 and 600 men in arms, went down to the battery called Jerry's Point and brought off eight cannon 14 and 32 pounders, being the whole that were there; and brought them up to town. While

92

they were taking off the above cannon, the Canceaux, with a tender, set full sail with the two provision vessels for Boston. The next day the town was full of men from the country in arms.

This uncommon exertion of arbitrary power, immediately alarmed the inhabitants, and the committee of safety having met, a memorial was by approbation presented to the Governor and council, who took every prudent method in their power to pacify the people, and to obtain a release of the captures. His Excellency repaired on board the Scarbourough, and informed the Captain that the provisions were the property of some of the inhabitants, who had before contracted for the same, but the only answer he could obtain was "That Admiral Graves and the General had forwarded orders to take every provision vessel that should be met with, on every station, and to send them forthwith to Boston for the supply of the army and navy." Captain Barkley, the commander of the Scarborough, informed two of the committee at Fort William Mary, that his orders were such that he must even take all vessels with salt and molasses, they being a species of provisions, and send them all to Boston.

NEW-LONDON June 2. Lieut. Dewey in a tender, bound from Boston to Newport, was brought too by a Man of War in Boston Bay, on board of which were the Generals Burgoyne, Clinton, and Howe who asked him what Number the Provincials and Regular Armies consisted of? He replied, the Provincials consisted of about 10,000, and the Regulars between 4 and 5000. They said they did not understand how so large a Number of Regular Troops could be blocked up by such a Number of Peasants, and added, let us but get in, and we'll soon find Elbow-Room.

PHILADELPHIA June 2. In Congress, June 2 1775. Upon Motion resolved,

That no Bill of Exchange, draught, or order of any officer in the army, or navy, their agents or contractors, be received, or negotiated, or any money supplied to them by any person in America. That no provisions or necessaries of any kind be furnished, or supplied to, or for the use of the British army or navy in the colony of Massachusetts-Bay, and that no vessel employ in transporting British troops to america, or from any part of North-America to another, or warlike stores, or provisions for said troops, be freighted, or forwarded with provisions or any necessaries, until further orders from this Congress.

A true Copy from the Minutes,
Charles Thompson, Secr'y.

PROVIDENCE June 3. A number of the inhabitants of Plymouth, we learn, went a few days ago to Nantucket in whale boats, and took from there 800 barrels of flour, the property of a merchant at Dartmouth, and which it is supposed was intended to be smuggled into Boston, for the supplying of the ministerial army.

Last week the company of the Train or Artillery, lately raised here, all well accounted, with four excellent field pieces marched to join the American army near Boston; they made a very military appearance, and are, without exception; as complete a body of men as any in the King's dominions.

The other companies raised here, and in the adjacent towns, as also several from the south counties, all able bodied men, and well armed, have marched to the American camp.

HARTFORD June 5. We hear from Albany that the General Committee for that city, have resolved to raise 800 Men for the Defence of American Liberty, and that as soon as said Resolve was made public, three Companies were immediately enlisted, who have since marched for the defence of the important Fortress of Ticonderoga and Crown-Point.

Last Week the 4th Regiment of Troops raised by the Colony, under the Command of Col. Benjamin Hinman, marched for their station assigned station at Ticonderoga.

WATERTOWN June 5. Joseph Warren Esq; was chosen President and Mr. Samuel Freeman, jun. secretary of the Provincial Congress.

General Putnam hath received a Letter from one of the Indian Nations in Canada, by which they testify their Friendship for him and the glorious cause in which he and the American Patriots are engaged.

It is said the Governor of Canada has wrote General Gage he can get Officers there, to act against New-England, but no Privates, the people in general declaring they will not fight against these Colonies.

WARTERTOWN June 5. The New-York Provincial Congress have desired the General Assembly of the Colony of Connecticut to send sufficient Forces to hold the important Fortresses of Ticonderoga and Crown-Point, until the Province can raise Troops for the Purpose, and they will reimburse the Expence. Those Fortresses being within the Limits of that Province.

We hear that five Tons of good Gun-Powder has within a few Weeks past been made at Philadelphia.

NEWPORT June 5. Last Saturday George Rome, having bought a quantity of Flour, &c. put it in some Stores on the point, supposed for the Use of the Enemy of this Country, a Number of People collected together, and insisted in having the Flour given up, which was accomplished before Sunset, notwithstanding said Rome had the Effrontery to insult the Town by getting a Number of Marines on shore, from the Mem of War in the Harbour. The Flour, being 84 Barrels, was lodged in the Brick Market.

Newport June 5. Extract of a letter from Philadelphia, of a late date.

"We have, in this city 3 battalions consisting of about 600 men each, who have made such rapid progress in military discipline, to be able to go through all the necessaries Maneuvers with great ease and quickness. This is not to be wondered of; when we consider, that for near a month past they have been under arms 6 hours every day Saturday and Sunday excempted. Besides these, there is a large company well trained to the artillery; and a company of about 100 rifle men. This last company I hear have the extraordinary rule with regard to the admission of every man among them —— When a person offers to avail himself among them, he is examined whether he can hit a circle of about 6 inches in diameter, 5 times out of 6, at the distance

95

of 150 Yards, if he cannot be is put by until, by practice, he is enable to do it. What not a company this qualified be able to effect? Every county in our province are entering their forces.

HARTFORD June 5, The following Extract from several Letters from the Soldiery in Boston, may serve to show the importance of the Action, and the Pains taken by their Superiors to have it thought that the Provincials began the fire, and behaved with savage Barbarity during the Action.

Boston April 28, 1775.

"I am well all but a Wound I received through the Leg with a Ball from one of the Bostonians. At the time I wrote you from Quebec. I had the strongest assurance of going home, but laying the Tax on the New-England People caused us to be ordered for Boston, where we remained in peace with the Inhabitants, till the Night of the 18th of April, twenty one Companies of Grenadiers and Light-Infantry were ordered into the country about 18 Miles; where, between 4 and 5 o'Clock in the Morning, we met an incredible Number of the People of the Country in arms against us. Col. Smith of the 10th Regiment ordered us to rush on them with our Bayonets fixed; at which Time some of the People Fired on us, and our Men returning the Fire, the Engagement begun; they did not fight us like a regular Army, only like Savages, behind Trees and Stone Walls, and out of the Woods and Houses, where in the latter we killed a Number of them, as well as in the Woods and Fields. The Engagement began between 4 and 5 in the morning, and lasted till 8 at Night. I can't be sure when you'll get another letter from me, as the extensive Continent is all in Arms against us; The People are very numerous, and full as bad as the Indians for scalping and cutting the dead Men's Ears and Noses off and these they get alive, that are wounded and can't get off the Ground."

"The Grenadiers, and light Infantry marched for Concord where were Powder and Ball, Arms, and Cannon mounted on Carriages, but before we could destroy them all, we were fire on by the country people, who are not brought up in our military way as ourselves, were surrounded

always in the woods, the Firing was very hot on
both Sides; about 2 in the Afternoon the 2d brigade came up, which was 4 Regiments and part of
the Artillery, which were of no Use to us, as
the Enemy were in the woods, and when we found
they fired from Houses, we set them on Fire, and
they then ran to the woods like Devils. We were
obliged to retreat to Boston again, over the
Charles-River, our Ammunition being all fired
away. We had 150 wounded and killed, and some
taken Prisoners; we were forced to leave some
behind, who were wounded. We got back to Boston
about 2 o'Clock the next Morning, and them that
we were able to walk were forced to mount Guards
and lie in the Field. I never broke any Fast for
48 Hours, for we carried no Provisions and we
thought to be back next Morning. I had my hat
shot off my Head 3 Times, 2 balls went through
my coat, and carried away my bayonet by my Side,
and near being killed. The People of Boston are
in great Trouble, for G. Gage will not let the
People out. Direct for me to Chatham's Division
of Marines."
    "Honour'd Mother,   April 25, 1775.
    "The Rebels, when we came to Concord, burnt
their Stores, fired upon the King's Troops, and
a small Engagement ensued. About two o'Clock
our Brigade came up to them, we engaged and continued fighting and retreating towards Boston.
The Rebels were monstrous numerous, and surrounded us on every Side, when the come up we
gave them a smart Fire, but they never would
engage us properly. We killed some Hundreds and
burnt some of their Houses. I received a Wound
in my Head. The Troops are in Boston, and surrounded on the Land Side by the Rebels, who are
very numerous, and fully determined to lose
their Lives and Fortunes, rather than be Taxed
by England. We had 34 killed and wounded. I supposed the King's Troops in all 160. In Case they
should take Boston the Troops shall retire on
board the Men of War, and then the Men of War
will burn the Town and remain till more Troops
come from England, and then conquer them, so
their Estates and Lives will be forfeited. There
is only 4000 Soldiers, and about 50 or 60,000

97

of them."

"Loving Brothers and Sisters,   May 2, 1775.
My Husband is now lying in one of the Hospitals,
at a place called Cambridge, and there is now
40 or 50,000 of them gathered together, and we
are not 4000 at most. It is very troublesome
Times, for we are expecting the Town to be burnt
down every Day, and I believe are sold, and I
hear my Husband's leg is broke, and my Heart is
almost broke."

CHARLESTOWN S. Carolina June 6, 1775.
                    Association.
Unanimously agree to the Provincial Congress
of South Carolina, on Saturday 3d June 1775.

The actual Commencement by the British Troops,
in the bloody scene on the 19th of April last,
near Boston ——— the increase of arbitrary impositions from a wicked and despotick ministry,
and the dread of instigated insurrections in the
Colonies are causes sufficient to drive an oppressed people to the rise of arms: We therefore, the subscribers, inhabitants of South
Carolina, holding ourselves in bound, by the
most sacred of all obligations, the duty of good
citizens towards an injured country and thoroughly convinced, that, under our present distressed circumstances, we shall be justified
before God and Man, in resisting force by Force;
Do Unite ourselves, under every tie of religion
and honour, and associate as a hand in her defence against every Foe: ——— Hereby solemnly
engaging that, wherever one Continental of Provincial Councils shall decree it necessary, we
will go forth, and be ready to sacrifice our
lives and fortunes to secure her freedom and
safety. This obligation to continue in full
force until a reconciliation shall take place
between Great-Britain and America, whose Constitutional Principles; and events which we most
ardently desire. And we will hold all those persons, unamicable to the Liberties of the Colonies, who shall refuse to subscribe to the Association.

        Subscribed by every Member present, on
the 4th day of June 1775.
        Certified by Henry Laurens, President.

WORCESTER June 7.   (Massachusetts Spy)
I. Thomas beg leave to inform the Public, That
he has engaged two Riders, one to go from hence
to Cambridge and Salem, the other one to Providence and Newport. The great advantage that will
arise to the Public from their going to and returning from, the places abovementioned, is well
known, especially with regard to fresh and authentic intelligence. He begs the assistance of
the public to support this undertaking, by promoting the circulation of New-Papers, and helping the Riders to such business as they may be
thought capable of transacting.
PHILADELPHIA June 7. An Account of the commencement of Hostilities between Great-Britain
and America, in the Province of Massachusetts-
Bay by the Rev. Mr. William Gordon of Roxbury
in a Letter to a Gentleman in England (Published
by the consent of the author.)
My Dear Sir,
I Shall now give you a letter upon the public
affairs. This colony, judging itself possessed
of an undoubted right to the charter'd privileges which had been granted by our glorious de-
liverer King William III and finding that the continent was roused by the measures and principles
of administration, was determined upon providing
the necessary requisites for full defence, in
case there should be an attempt to support the
late unconstitutional acts by the point of the
sword, and upon making that resistance which
the laws of God and nature justified, and the
circumstances of the people would admit, and so
to leave it with the righteous judge of the
world to settle the dispute. Accordingly the
Provincial Congress, substituted by the inhabitants in lieu of the General Assembly, which
could not convene but by call of the Governor,
prepared a quantity of stores for the service
of an army, whenever the same might be brought
into the field. These stores were deposited in
various places; many of them at Concord, about
20 miles from Charlestown, which lies on the
other side of the river, opposite Boston, answering to Southwark, but without the advantage
of a bridge, it was apprehended by numbers, from

99

the attempt made to surprise some cannon at Salem on February 26, that these would be something of a like kind in other places, and many
were uneasy, after the resolution of the Parliament were known, that any quantity of stores
was within so small a distance of Boston, while
there were no regular force established for the
defence of them. Several were desirous of raising an army instantly upon hearing what had been
determined at home, but it was judged best upon
the whole not to do it, as that step might be
immediately construed to the disadvantage of the
colony by the enemies of it, and might not meet
with the unanimous approbation of the Continental Congress. Here I must break off for a few
minutes, to inform you, by way of episode, that
on the 30th of March the Governor ordered out
about 1100 men, to parade it for the distance
of five miles to Jamaica Plains, and surround
the way of Dorchester back again; in performing
which military exploits, they did considerable
damage to the stone fences, which occasioned a
Committee's being formed, and waiting upon the
Provincial Congress, then at Concord, on the
point of adjourning, which prevented their ad-
journment, and lengthened out the session till
the news of what Parliament had done reached
them on April 2d, by a vessel from Falmouth,
which brought the account before the Governor
had received his dispatches, so that obnoxious
persons took the advantage of withdrawing from
Boston, or keeping away, that they might not be
caught by the General, were ordered for that
given from home, as there is much reason to suppose was the case, from a hint in an intercepted letter of Mr. Manduit's to Commissioner Mr.
Hollowell, and from subsequent intelligence.
The tories had been for a long while filling
the officers and soldiers, with the idea, that
the Yankees would not fight, but would certainly run from it, wherever there was an appearance
of hostilities on the part of the regulars.
They had repeated the story the story so often,
that they themselves really believed it, and
the military were persuaded to think the same,
in general, so that they held the country people

100

in the most contempt. The officers had discovered, especially since the warlike feat of tarring and feathering, a disposition to quarrel, and to provoke the people to begin, that they might have some colour for hostilities. This cast of mind was much increased upon the news of what Parliament had resolved upon; the people however bore insults politely, being determined that they would not be the aggressors. At length the General was fixed, upon sending a detachment to Concord to destroy the stores, having been, I apprehend, worried into it by the native tories that were about him, and confirmed in his design by the opinion of his officers, about ten of whom, on the 18th of April, passed over to Charlestown ferry, and by way of the Neck through Roxbury, armed with swords and pistols, and placed themselves on different parts of the road in the night to prevent all intelligence, and the country's being alarmed; They stopped various persons, threatening to blow brains out, ordering them to dismount, &c. The grenadiers and light infantry companies had been taking off duty some days, under pretence of learning a new exercise, which made the Bostoneans jealous; one and another were confirmed in their suspicions by what they saw and heard on the 18th, for that expresses were forwarded to alarm the country, some of whom were secured by the officers on the road; the last had not got out of town more than about five minutes, when the order arrived to stop all persons from leaving the town. An Alarm was spread in many places (to some of the number of officers on the road to Concord proved an alarm) however, as there had been repeated false ones, the country was at a loss what to judge. One of the first of the night, when it was very dark, the detachment, consisting of all the grenadiers and light infantry, that the flower of the army, to the amount of 800, or better, officers included, the companies having been filled up, and several of the inimical torified natives repaired to the boats, and got into them just as the moon rose, crossed the water, landed at Cambridge side, took through a private way to avoid discovery,

and therefore had to go through some places up
to their thighs in water. They then made a quick
march of it to Lexington, about 13 miles from
Charlestown, and got there by half an hour after four. Here I must pause again, to acquaint
you that in the morning of the 19th, before we
had breakfasted, between eight and nine, the
whole neighbourhood, was in alarm; the minute
men (so called from their having agreed to turn
out at a minute's warning) were collecting together; we had an account that the regulars had
killed six of our men at Lexington; the country
was in an uproar, another detachment was coming
out of Boston; and I was desired to take care
of myself and partner.

I concluded that the brigade was intended to
support the grenadiers and light infantry, and
to cover their retreat, in which I was not mistaken. The brigade took out two cannon, the detachment had none. Having sent off my books,
which I had finished packing up the day before,
conjecturing what was coming on from the moment
I had heard of the resolution of Parliament,
tho' I did not expect it till the reinforcement,
arrived, we got into our chaise, and went to
Dedham. At night we had it confirmed to us, that
the regulars had been roughly handled by the
Yankees, a term of reproach for the New-Englanders, when applied by the regulars. The Brigade
under Lord Percy marched out, playing, by way
of contempt, Yankee Doodle; they were Afterwards
told, they had been made to dance to it. Soon
after the affair, knowing what untruths are propagated by each party in matters of nature, I
concluded that I would ride to Concord, enquire
for myself, and not rest upon the depositions
that might be taken by others; accordingly I
went the last week. The Provincial Congress
have taken depositions, which they have forwarded to Great-Britain; but the Ministry and
pretended friends to government will cry them
down, as been evidence from party persons and
rebels; the like may be objected against the
present account, as it will materially contradict what has been published in Boston, though
not expressly, yet as is commonly supposed, by

authority; however with the impartial world, and three who will not imagine me capable of sacrificing honesty to the old, at present heretical, principles of the revolution, it may have some weight. Before Major Pitcairn arrived at Lexington signal guns had been fired, and the bells had been rang to give the alarm; but let not the sound of bells lead you to think a ring of bells like what you hear in England; for they are only small fixed bells, one in a parish, just sufficient to notify the people the time for attending worship &c. Lexington now being alarmed, the trainband or militia, and the alarm men (consisting of the aged and other exempted from turning out, excepting upon an alarm) repaired in general to the common, close in with the Meeting-house, the usual place of parade; and these were present when the roll was called over about one hundred and thirty of both, as I was told by Mr. Daniel Harrington, Clerk to the company, who further said, that the night being chilly, so as to make it uncomfortable being upon the parade, they having received no certain intelligence of the regulars being upon their march, and being waiting for the same, the men were dismissed, to appear again at the beat of drum. Some who lived near went home, others to the public house at the corner of the common. Upon information being received about half an hour after, that the troops were not far off, the remains of the company who were at hand collected together, to the amount of about 60 or 70, by the time regulars appeared, but were chiefly in a confused state, only a few of them being drawn up, which accounts for other witnesses making the number less, about 30. There were present, as spectators, about 40 more, scarce any who had arms. The printed account tells us, indeed, that they observed about 200 armed men. Possibly the intelligence they had before received had frightened those that gave to account to the General, so that they saw more than double. The said account, which has little truth in it, says, that Major Pitcairn, galloping up to the head of the advanced companies, two officers informed him that a man (advanced

from those that assembled) had presented his
musket, and attempted to shot them, but the piece
flashed in the pan. The simple truth I take to
be this, which I received from one of the prisoners at Concord in free conversation, one John
Marr, a native of Aberdeen in Scotland, of the
4th regiment, who was upon the advanced guard,
consisting of six, besides a serjeant and corporal. They were met by three men on horse-back
before they got to the meeting-house a good way;
an officer bid them stop; to which it was answered, you had better turn back, for you shall
not enter town; when the said three persons rode
back again, and at some distance one of them
offered to fire, but the piece flashed in the
pan, without going off. I asked Marr, whether he
could tell if the piece was designed at the soldiers, or to give an alarm? he could not say
which. The said Marr further declared, that when
they and the others advanced, Major Pitcairn
said to the Lexington company, (which by the by,
was the only one there) stop you rebels! and he
supposed that the design was to take away their
arms; but upon seeing the regulars they dispersed, and a firing commenced but who fired
first he could not say. The said Marr, together
with Evans Davies, of the 23d, George Cooper of
the 23d, and William M'Donald, of the 38th, re-
spectfully assured me in each others presence,
that being in the room where John Bateman, of
the 52d was (he was in an adjoining room, too
ill to admit of my conversing with him) they
heard the said Bateman say, that the regulars
fired first, and saw him go thro' the formality
of confirming the same by an oath on the Bible.
Emanuel Lee, a private in the 18th regiment,
Royal Irish, acquainted me, that it was the talk
among the soldiers that Major Pitcairn fired his
pistol, then drew his sword and ordered them to
fire; which agreed with what Levi Harrington, a
youth of 14 last November, told us, that being
upon the common, and hearing the regulars were
coming up, he went to the meeting-house, and saw
them down the road, on which he returned to the
Lexington company —— that a person on horseback rode round the meeting-house, and came

towards the company that way, said some thing
loud, but could not tell what, rode a little further, then stopt and fired a pistol, then 3 or 4
regulars fired their guns, upon which, hearing
the bullets whistling he ran off, and saw no
more of the affairs.

Mr. Paul Revere, who was sent express, was
taken and detained some time by the officers,
being afterwards upon the spot, and finding the
regulars at hand; passed through the Lexington
company with another, having between them a box
of papers belonging to Mr. Hancock, and went
down a cross road, till there was a house so between him and the company, as that he could not
see the latter; he told me likewise, that he had
not gone half a gun shot from them before the
regulars appeared; that they halted about three
seconds; that upon hearing the report of a pistol or gun, he looked round, and saw the smoke
from the regulars, our people being out of view
because of the house; then the regulars huzza'd
and fired; first two more guns, then the advanced
guard, and so the whole body; the bullets flying thich about him, and he having nothing to
defend himself, ran into a wood where he halted,
and heard the firing for about a quarter of an
hour. Francis Brown, one of the Lexington militia, informed me, that he was upon the common,
that two pistols were fired from the party of
the soldiers towards the militia men, as they
were getting over the wall to be out of the way,
and that immediately upon it the soldiers began
to fire their guns; that being got over the wall,
and seeing the soldiers fire pretty freely, he
fired upon them and some others did the same.
Simon Winship, of Lexington declared, that being
upon the road about 4 o'clock, two miles and a
half on the side of the meeting house, he was
stopt by the regulars and commanded by some of
the officers to march with the said troops until he came within about half or quarter of a
mile of the said meeting house, when an officer
commanded the troops to halt, and then prime and
load, which being done, the troops marched on
till they came a few rods of Capt. Palmer's
Lexington company who were partly collected on

the place of parade, when said Winship observed
an officer at the head of said troops flourishing his sword round his head in the air, and
with a loud voice giving the word fire; the said
Winship is positive that there were no discharge
on either side, until the word fire was given
by the said officer above.

I shall not trouble you with motre particulars, but give you the substance as it lies in
my own mind, collected from the persons whom I
examined for my own satisfaction. The Lexington
company, upon seeing the troops, and being of
themselves so unequal a match for them, were
deliberating, for a few moments what they should
do, when several dispersing of their own head,
the Captain soon ordered the rest to disperse
for their own safety. Before the order was given,
three or four of the regular officers, seeing
the company as they came up on the rising ground
on this side of the meeting-house, leaving it on
the right hand, and so came upon them that way,
upon coming up, one cry'd out, "you damn'd rebels lay down your arms;" another, "stop you rebels;" a third "Disperse you rebels," &c. Major
Pitcairn, I supposed, thinking himself satisfied
by parliamentary authority to consider then as
rebels, perceived that they did not actually
lay down their arms, observing that the generality were getting off while a few continued in
their military positions, and apprehending they
could be no great huff in killing a few such
Yankees, which might probably, according to the
notion that had been instilled him by the tory
party, of the Americans being poltroons, on all
the contest, gave the command to fire, then fired
his own pistol, and so set the whole affair a
going. The printed account say very different,
but whatever the General may have sent home in
support of that account, the public have nothing
but bare affections, and I have such valid evidence of the falsehood of the matters therein
contained, that with me it has very little weight.
The same account tells that several shots were
fired from a meeting house on the left, of which
I heard not a single syllable either from the
prisoners or others and the mention of which

it could have been almost impossible to have
avoided, had it been so, by one or another among
the numbers with whom I freely and familiary
conversed. —— There is a curious not at the
bottom of the account, telling us, that notwithstanding the fire from the meeting-house, Col.
Smith and Major Pitcairn with the greatest difficulty kept the soldiers from forcing into the
meeting-house, and putting all those in it to
their death. Would you not suppose that there
was a great number in the meeting-house, while
the regulars were upon the common on the right
of it, between that and the Lexington company?
without doubt. And who do you imagine they were?
One Joshua Simonds, who happened to be getting
powder there as the troops arrived; besides whom
I believe there were not two, if so much as one,
for by reason of the position of the meeting-
house, none would have remained in it through
choice, but fools and madmen. However if Col.
Smith and Major Pitcairn's humanity prevented
the soldiers putting all those persons to death,
their military skill should certainly have made
some of them prisoners, and the account should
have given us their names. To what I have wrote
respecting Major Pitcairn, I am sensible his
general character may be objected. But character
must not be allowed to overthrow positive evidence when good, and the conclusions fairly de-
ducted therefrom. Besides such hearings from Mr.
Jones in what shameful abusive manner, with
oaths and curses, he was treated by the Major
at Concord, for shutting the doors of his tavern
against the troops, and in order to terrify him
to make discoveries of stores, and the manner
the Major crow'd over the two four and twenty
pounders found in the yard, as a mighty acquisition, worthy the expedition on which the detachment was employed, I have no such great
opinion of the Major's character, though when he
found that nothing could be done of any great
importance, by bullying, mastering and threat-
ning, he could alter his tone, begin to coax,
and offer a reward.
It may be said Jones was a goaler, Yet, and
such a goaler as I would give credit to, sooner

than the generality of those officers, that will degrade the British army, by employing their swords in taking away the rights of a free people when they ought to be devoted to a good cause only. There were killed at Lexington eight persons; one Parker, of the same name with the captain of the company, and two or three more, on the common; the rest on the other side of the walls and fences while dispersing. The soldiers fired at persons who had no arms. Eight hundred of the best British troops in America having then nobly vanquished a company of non resisting Yankees whole dispersing, and slaughtered a few of then by way of experiment, marched forward in the greatest of their might to Concord. The Concord people had received the alarm, and had drawn themselves up in order for defence; upon a messenger's coming and telling them the regulars were three times their number, they prudently changed their situation, determining to wait for reinforcements from the neighbouring towns, which were now alarmed, but as to the vast number of armed people seen assembling in all the heights, as related in the account, 'tis mostly fiction.

The Concord company retired over the North Bridge, and when strengthened returned to it, with a view of dislodging Capt. Laurie, and seizing it for themselves. They knew not what happened at Lexington, and therefore orders were given by the commander not to give the first fire; they boldly marched towards it, though not in great numbers (as Told in the Account) and were fired upon by the regulars, by which fire a Captain belonging to Acton was killed and I think a private. The Rev. Mr. Emerson of Concord, living in the neighbourhood of the bridge, who gave me the acedant, went near enough to see it, and was nearest the regulars than the killed. He was very uneasy till he found that the fire was returned, and continued till the regulars were driven off. Lieut. Gould, who was at the bridge, was wounded and taken prisoner, has deposed, that their regulars gave first fire there, though the private narrative asserts the contrary; and the soldiers, that knew any thing of the

matter, with whom I conversed, made no scruple
of owning the same that Mr. Gould deposed. After
the engagement began, the whole detachment collected together as fast as it could. The narrative tell us that as Captain Parsons returned
with his three companies over the bridge, they
observed there soldiers on the ground, one of
them scalped, his head was much mangled, and his
ears cut off, though not yet dead; all this is
not fiction, though the most is. The Rev. Emerson informed me how the matter was, with great
concern for it having happened.

A Young fellow coming over the bridge in order
to join the country people, and seeing the soldier wounded and attempting to get up, not being
under the feeling of humanity, very barbarously
broke his scull and let out his brains, with a
small axe (apprehend of a small tomahawk I had)
but as to his being scalped and having his ears
cut off, there was nothing to it. The poor object
lived an hour or two before he expired. The Detachment, when joined by Captain Parsons, made
a hasty retreat, finding by woful experience
that the Yankees would fight, and that their
numbers would be continually increasing. The
regulars were pushed with vigour by the country
people, who took the advantage of walls, fences,
&c. but those that could get up to engage, were
not on equal terms with the regulars in point
of number, and part of the day, though the country was collecting together from all quarters,
and there been two hours more for it, would
probably have cut off each detachment and brigade, or made them prisoners. The soldiers being to obliged to retreat with haste to Lexington
had no time to do considerable mischief. But a
little on this side of Lexington meeting-house,
where they met by the brigade with cannon under
Lord Percy, the scheme changed. The inhabitants
had quitted their houses in general upon the
road, leaving almost every thing behind them,
and thinking themselves well off escaping with
their lives. The soldiers, burnt in Lexington
three houses, one barn and two shops, one of
which joined the house, and a still house adjoining to the barn: Other houses and buildings

were attempted to be burnt all narrowly escaped.
You would have been shock'd at the destruction
which has been made by the regulars from Boston,
as they are miscalled, had you been present with
me to have beheld it. Many houses were plundered
of every thing valuable that could be taken away,
and what could not be carried off was destroyed:
looking glasses, pots, pans, &c. were broken
all to pieces; doors when not fastened, sashes
and windows wantonly destroyed. The people say
that the soldiers are worse than the Indians,
in flight, they have given the country such an
early specimen of their brutality, as well make
the inhabitants dread submission to the power
of the British ministry, and determine then to
fight desperately rather than to have such cruel
masters to hold it over them. —— The troops at
length reached Charlestown, where there was no
attacking them with safety to the town, and the
night and next day crossed over in boats to
Boston, where they continue to be shut up; for
people poured down in to amazing a manner from
all parts, for hours of miles round, even the
grey headed came, to assist their countrymen,
the General was obliged to see about in fortifying the town immediately at all points and
places. The proceeding of April 19th has united
the colony and continent and brought in new-York
to act vigorously as any other place whatsoever;
and has raised an army in an instant, which are
lodged in the several houses of the towns round
Boston till their tents are finished, which will
be soon. All that is attended to, besides plow-
ing, and planting, &c. is making ready for
fighting. The new importations and non Exportations will now take place from necessity, and
trifles give place to war. We have a fine spring,
prospects of great plenty; their was scarce ever known such a good sale of lands; we are in no
danger of starving tho' the cruel acts against
the New-England government; and the men who had
been used to the colony, a hardy generation of
people, laid North has undesignedly kept in the
country to give strength to our military operations, and to assist as occasions may require:
Thanks to a superior wisdom, for his blunders.

The General by expecting reinforcements, but few have yet arrived as yet; the winds, contrary to the common run of this season, instead of being easterly, have been mostly reverse. When the reinforcement arrive, and is recovered of the voyage, the General will be obliged in humour, to attempt dislodging the people, and and penetrating into the country; both soldiers and the inhabitants are in want of fresh provisions, and will be like to suffer much, should the provincial army is able to keep the town shut up on all sides exempting the water, as at present.

The General engaged with the Select-men of Boston, that if the town's people would deliver up their arms, into his custody, those that chuse it should be allowed to go out with their effects; some townsmen complied, and the General forfeited his word, for which there will be as accounting, should they ever have it in their power to call him to account. A few have been allowed to come out with many of their effects; numbers are not permitted to come out, and the chief of these who have been, obliged to leave their merchandize and goods (linen and household stuff, with all plate excepted) behind them. yet must look back to the origin of the united provinces that you may have an idea of the resolutions of this people. May the present struggle end as happily in favor of the Ameirican Liberty, without proving the destruction of Great-Britain. We are upon a second addition of King Charles the First's reign engaged ——— May the dispute be adjusted, before the times are too tragical to admit of it. Both officers and privates have altered their opinion of the Yankees very much since the 19th of April.

The detachment, while at Concord dissembled two 24 pounders, destroying their two carriages, and seven wheels for the same with their limbers; sixteen wheels for brass 9 pounders, and two carriages, with limbers and wheels for two four pounders; 300 pounds of balls thrown into the river, wells and other places about 66 barrels of flour, half of which was saved. Estimates of the number that were killed. Apprehend upon the whole, the regulars had more than 200 killed and 230 wounded, besides 50 taken prisoner. The country people had about 50 killed, 7 or 8 taken prisoners, and a few wounded.

N. B. I never saw the printed account till Monday, so that I was not directed by it in any of my enquiries when at Lexington and Concord. The General. I am persuaded gave positive orders to the detachment not to fire first, or I am wholly mistaken in my opinion of him. The prisoners at Worcester, Concord and Lexington, all agree to their being exceedingly being well used. The policy of the people would determine berate, if their humanity did not.

May 17, 1775.

CAMBRIDGE June 8. In Provincial Congress, in Watertown, june 6, 1775.

Whereas the provisions already made for the removal of the poor of Boston, suffering by the cruel hands of arbitrary power, has not answered the salutary Purposes intended, and it becomes necessary that further Provisions be made:

Therefore Resolved, That such suffering Poor shall be allowed to remove into any Town or District in the Colony, other than such Towns or Districts as are already ordered to provide for and receive the number of said Poor to them assigned.

And every Town and District in the Colony, that shall receive and provide necessary support for such suffering poor, shall be indemnified in every Respect, as fully as any other Town or District in the Colony, provided they observe and comply with the directions already given relative to said poor.

And whereas in the present distress Circumstances and Confusion of the Town of Boston, some of the poor have or may remove of said Town without a proper certificate from the committee of donation, and the Town to whom such persons remove may refuse to receive them for Want of the same.

Resolve, That it is recommended to the Select men of the several Towns and Districts in this Colony, to which such Persons may remove, that such provisions be made as is necessary to prevent their suffering, until such certificates

can be provided, they observing the directions
to said poor, and such Persons shall be considered as a part of the Arangement.

And whereas it is found extremely difficult
for the Committee at Charlestown and Roxbury to
remove the said poor to the several Towns and
Districts to which they are destined, for want
of of teams to get such a distance as is necessary in many cases. It is further recommended
to the Selectmen of each Town and District in
this Colony, that they assist in removing said
poor upon every necessary occasion, when it is
in their power, to the several Places of their
Assignment, keeping a particular Account of
their Trouble and Expence, and the Names of the
Persons they assist, and they shall be paid in
Manner as is before provided.

And the Committee at Charlestown and Roxbury
(who were appointed by the Congress to make provisions for such poor as might come out of the
Town of Boston) are desired to procure a List
of said poor from the committee of Donations
for further Use; and also to take the Advantage
of the Terms that may come from the Westward,
for the Removal of said poor, by every Opportunity in their Power. A True Copy of the Minutes.
                     Samuel Freeman, Secr'y.

CAMBRIDGE June 8. Tuesday last being the Day
agreed for the Exchange of Prisoners, between
12 and 1 o'Clock, Dr. Warren and Brigadier General Putnam in a place on together with Major
Dunbar, and Lieut. Hamilton of the 64th on Horseback; Lieut Potter of the Marines, in a Chaise;
John Tyne, Samuel Marcy, Thomas Parry, and Thomas
Sharp, of the Marines wounded Men, in two Carts:
the whole escorted by Wheathersfield Company
under the command of Capt. Chester, entered the
Town of Charlestown, and marching slowly through
it halted at the Ferry, where, upon a signal
being given, Major Moncrief landed from the
Lively, in order to receive the Prisoners, and
see old Friend General Putnam; Their meeting was
truly cordial and affectionate. The wounded
Privates were soon set on board the Lively; but
Major Moncrief and the other Officers, returned
with General Putnam and Dr. Warren, to the house

of Dr. Foster, where an entertainment was provided for them. About 3 o'Clock a signal was
made by the Lively, that they were ready to deliver up our Prisoners; upon which General Putnam and Major Moncrief went to the Ferry; where
they received Messrs. John Peck; James Hews;
James Brewer and Daniel Preston, of Boston;
Messrs. Samuel Frost and Seth Russel of Cambridge; Mr. Joseph Bell of Danver, Mr. Elijah
Seaver of Roxbury, and Caeser Augustus a Negro
Servant to Mr. Tileston of Dorchester, who were
conducted on to the House Of Capt. Foster, and
there refreshed; after which the General and
Major returned to their Company, and spent an
Hour or two in a very agreeable Manner. Between
5 and 6 o'Clock Major Moncrief, with the officers that had been delivered to him, were conducted to the ferry, where the Lively's Barge
was received them: after which General Putnam,
with the Prisoners who had been delivered to
him, &c. returned to Cambridge, escorted in the
same manner as before. The whole was executed
with the utmost Decency and great Humour, and
the Wheathersfield Company did honour to themselves, their Officers, and Country. The Regular
Officers expressed themselves as highly pleased;
those who had been Prisoners politely acknowledged the general, kind treatment they had received from their Captures; the privates, who
were all wounded men, expressed in the strongest terms, their grateful Sense of the treatment
which had bee shewn them in their miserable
situation; some of them could do it only by their
tears. It would have been to the Honour of the
British Arms, if the Prisoners taken from us
could with justice made the same Acknowledgement. I cannot be surprised that any officer of
Rank or Common Humanity, were knowing to the
repeated cruel: such that were offered them; but
it may be amiss to hint to the Upstarts concerned, two Truths, of which they seem to be
totally ignorant, viz. That Compassion is as
effectual a Part of the Character of a truly
brave Man as daring; and that Insult offered to
a Person entire's in the Power of the Insulter,
smell as strong as Cowardice as it does of

Cruelty.

Last Wednesday s'nnight a Number of Provincials under the command of Col. Robinson, made an acquisition of about 500 Sheep, and 30 Head of Cattle from Patrick's Island.

And on Friday Night last the Provincial troops made another acquisition of about 800 Sheep and Lambs from Deer Island, together with a number of Cattle. Major Creaton, who commanded the Party, also took a Barge belonging to one of the Men of War, together with 4 or 5 Prisoners.

CAMBRIDGE June 8. A correspondent have favvoured us with the following etymology of the word Yankee.

"When the New-England colonies were first settled, the inhabitants were obliged to fight their way against many nations of Indians. They found but little difficulty in subdoing them all, except one tribe who were known by the name of the Yankees, which signified invincible. After the waste of much blood and treasure, the Yankees were at last Subdued by the New-England men. The remains of the nation (agreeable to the Indian custon) transferred their name on their conquerors. For a whill they were called Yenkoos; but in corruption to names in all languages, they got through time the name Yankee. A name which we hope will soon be equal to that of the Roman, or an Ancient Englishman.

NEW-York June 8. A circumstantial account of the late Battle at Chelsea, Hog Island, &c.

On Saturday last, a party of the American army at Cambridge, to the number between 2 and 300 men, had orders to drive off the live stock from Hog and Noodle's Islands, which lie near chelsea and Winnesimmet, on the N. E. side of Boston Harbour. From Chelsea to hog Island, at low water, it is about knee high, and from that to Noodle's Island about the same. The stock on the former belonged to Mr. Oliver Wendall, at Boston, and Mr. Jonathan Jackson, at Newburyport, that on Noodle;s Island was owned by Mr. ———— Williams, of Boston, who hired the Island.

At 11 o'clock A. M. between 20 or 40 men went from Chelsea to Hog Island, and from thence to noodle's Island, to drive off the stock which

115

was there, but were interrupted by a schooner
and a sloop, dispatched from the fleet in Boston
harbour, and 40 Marines, who had been stationed
on the Island to protect the live stock. However
they sent off 2 fine English stallions, 2 colts
and 3 cows; killed 15 horses, 8 colts, and 3
cows, burnt a large barn, full of salt hay, and
an old farm house. By this time they were fired
on from the schooner and sloop, and a large number of marines in boats, sent from the several
men of war; upon which they retreated to a ditch
on the marshes, and kept themselves undiscovered,
till they had an opportunity to fire on the Marines, when they shot down two dead, and wounded
two more, one of whom died short after. They
then retreated to Hog-Island, where they were
joined by the remainder of their party from
Chelsea, and drove off all the stock thereon.
viz. between 3 and 400 sheep and lambs, some
cows and horses, &c.

During this there were firing between the provincials and the schooner, sloop, boats and marines on the other island. Having cleared Hog
Island, the provincials drew upon Chelsea Neck,
and sent for a reinforcement of 300 men, and 2
pieces of cannon [4 pounders] which arrived after which, General Putnam went down and hailed
the schooner, and told the people that, if they
would submit, they should have good quarters,
which the schooner returned with a cannon shot,
this was immediately answered with 2 cannon from
the provincials: Upon this a very heavy fire ensued from both sides, which lasted till eleven
o'clock at night, when the fire from the schooner
ceased, the fire from the shore being so hot,
that her people were obliged to quit her, and
take to the boats, a great number of which had
been from the ships to their assistance, and
also a large reinforcement of marines sent to
Noodle's Island, with 2 twelve pounders.

The schooner being thus left, drove ashore,
where about break of day, the provincials carried some hay under her stern, and set her on
fire the sloop keeping up a small fire upon us
then; at which time a heavy cannonading was begun at Noodle's Island Hill, with 12 pounders

upon the provincials; also General Putnam kept
a heavy fire upon the sloop, which disabled her
much, and killed many of her men, so that her
men found that she was obliged to be tow'd off
by the boats when the firing ceased, excepting
a few shot which were exchanged between the party at Chelsea, and the marines on Noodle's Island. Thus ended this long action, without the
loss of one provincial, and only four wounded
by the busting of his own gun, another only lost
his little finger. The loss of the enemy amounted to 30 killed and 50 wounded. The provincials
took out of the schooner 4 double fortified 4
pounders, twelve swivels, chief of her rigging
and sails, many clothes, some money, &c. which
the sailors and marines left behind, they having
quited in haste.

A Gentleman from Boston informs, that on Sunday last, at Providence, he saw the Express from
Cambridge, who brought advice that the Stock-
borough Man of War of 20 and a sloop of 14 Guns
had been taken at Portsmouth, by the provincials
assisted by the press men on board, without the
lost of a Man.

NORWICH June 8. Extract of a Letter from a
Gentleman in shaftsbury, to his friend in this
Town.

"A bad Accident lately happened at Ticondroga.
A Demoniac being left in a room, in which were
18 loaded Muskets snatched up one of then presented it to a Man then with him, and desired
him to leave the Place on Pain of Death, his
desire was instantly complied with; but another
Man entering the Room soon after, was shot through
the Body; he then dropped his Piece seized another, and shot the wounded Man through the
Calves of his Legs; two Men then rushed in, and
without taking his Arms, led him round the Corner the Barracks; but the mischievous Biped
disengaged himself, fired upon a Man at the Window and shot him through the knee, then drawing
his sword he almost cut off an arm of one of his
attendants, upon which the People present, without further Ceremony shot him dead."

NEW-LONDON June 9. We learn that all the Men
of War which were in the Harbours near Boston

have been called to that Place, and that every method taken to strengthen the Town. The entrenchment at the fortification is now extended quite across the Neck, by which the Town is become an Island. Gen. Gage, by all his late conduct, appears to be greatly alarmed.

While the Provincials were clearing Noodle and Hog Island of their stock, one of the largest Men of War kept a constant fire on them; but at so great a distance as not to do them the least injury. Our People picked up a number of their shot on those Islands. The troops in Boston at the same time were under review on the common.

Last Saturday, Col. Clover, and the Sons of the late worthy Col. Lee of Marblehead, brought to Head Quarters at Cambridge, from Marblehead, a bag of Letters, arrived there from London, in a Schooner of the late Col. Lee's taken by administration to bring them. She sail'd the 12th or 14th of April. In the Bag are Letters from Administration to General Gage, the Admiral, and to the Tories in Boston. Those Letters were under Inspection at the Camp, when our last account came from thence.

WILLIAMSBURG June 10. In the night of Saturday the 3d instant some young men got into the public magazine of this city, intending to furnish themselves with arms, but were presently after surprized by the report of a gun which was so artfully placed (said to be contrived by Lord Dunmore) that upon touching a string which was in their way, it went off and wounded three present, but not mortally; one of them is terribly hurt by several small balls that entered his arm and shoulder; another, by the lost of two fingers of his right hand, rendered incapable of following his profession for subsistence; the other wounded very slightly. There were two guns prepared for this horrible purpose, one of which was brought out next morning, and found to be double charged. On Monday a committee was appointed in the House of Burgesses to examine the state of the magazine who have planted a guard over it, till measures shall be collected for a better security.

BOSTON June 12. By his Excellency The Hon.

Thomas Gage Esq; Governor and Commander in chief
in and over his Malesty's Province of Massachusetts-Bay, and Vice Admiral of the same.

A PROCLAMATION

Whereas the infatuated Multitudes, who have
long suffered themselves to be conducted by certain well known incendiaries and Traitors, in a
fatal Progression of Crime, against the constitutional authority of the state, have at length
proceeded to avowed Rebellion & the good effects which were expected to arise from the Patience and Lenity of the King's Government, have
been often frustrated, and are now rendered
hopeless, by the Influence of the same evil council; it only remains for those who are intrusted
with the supreme rule, as well for the Punishment of the guilty as the protection of the well
affected, to prove they do not hear the Sword
in vain.

The infringements which have been committed
upon the most sacred Rights of the Crown and
People of Great-Britain, are too many to enumerate on one side, and are all too atrocious to be
palliated on the other. All unprejudiced People
who have been Witnesses of the late Transactions,
in this and the neighbouring Provinces, will
find upon a transient, Marks of Premeditation
and Conspiracy that would justify the Fullness
of Chastisement: And even those who are least
acquainted with Facts, cannot fail to receive a
just Impression of their Enormity in Proportion
as they discover the Arts and Assiduity, by
which they have falsified or concealed. The
Authors of the present unnatural Revolt never
daring to trust their Cause or their Actions,
to the Judgement of an impartial Public, or even
to the dispassionate Reflection of their followers, have uniformly placed their chief Confidence in the Suppression of Truth: And while
indefatigable and shameless Pains have been
taken to obstruct every appeal to the real interest of the People of America; the grossest
Forgeries, Calumnies and Absurdities that ever
insulted human understanding, have been impressed upon their Credulity. The Press, that Distinguished Appendage of public Liberty, and when

fairly and impartially employed its best support, but been invariably prostituted to the
the most contrary purpose: The animated Language
of ancient and virtuous Times, calculated to
vindicate and promote the just Rights, and Interest of Mankind, have been applied to countenance the most abandoned Violation of those
sacred Blessings; and not only from the flagitious Prints, but from the popular Haragues of
the Times, Men have been thought to depend upon
Activity to Treason, for the Security of their
Person, and Properties; 'till for compleat the
horrid Profanation of Terms, and of Ideas, the
Name of God, has been introduced in the Pulpits
to excite and Justify Devastation and Massacre.
Yhe Minds of Men having been thus gradually
prepared for the worst Extremities, A Number of
armed Persons, to the Amount of many Thousands,
assembled on the 19th of April last, and from
behind Walls, and lurking Holes, attacked a Detachment of the King's Troops who were not expecting so consummate an Act of Phrenzy, unpre-
pared for Vengeance, and willing to decline it,
made use of their Arms only in their own defence.
Since that Period the Rebels delving Confidence
from Impunity fired upon the King's Ships and
Subjects, with cannon and small arms, have possessed the Roads, and other Communications,
which the Town of Boston was supplied with Provisions; and with a preposterous Parade of Military Arrangements, they affect to hold the Army
besieged; while Part of their Body make daily
and idiferiminate Invasions upon private Properties, and with a Wantoness of Cruelty ever
incident to lawless Tumults, carry Depredations
and Distress wherever they turn their steps.
The Action of the 19th of April are of such Notoriety, as much best all Attempts to contradict them, and the Flames of Buildings and other
Property from the Islands, & adjacent Country,
for some Weeks past, spread a melancholy Con-
firmation of the subsequent Assertion.
In This Emergency of complicated Calamities,
I avail myself of the late effect within the
Bounds of my Duty to spare the effusion of Blood;
to offer, and I do hereby in his Majesty's Name,

offer and promise, his most gracious Pardon to all Persons who shall forthwith lay down their Arms, and return to the Duties of peaceable subjects, excepting only from the benefit of such Pardon, Samuel Adams and John Hancock, who offences are of too flagitious a Nature to admit of any other Consideration than that of condign Punishment.

And to the end that no Person within the Limits of this proffered Mercy, may plead Ignorance of the Consequences of refusing it. I by these presents proclaim not only the Persons above-named an example, but also all their, Adherent, associates, and Abettors, meaning to comprehend in those Terms, all and every Person, and Persons of what Class, Denomination or Description soever, who have appeared in Arms against the King's Government, and shall not lay down the same above-Mentioned; and likewise all such as shall so take Arms against the King's Government, and shall not lay down the same above-mentioned: and likewise all such as shall so take Arms after the date hereof, or who shall any-wise protect or conceal such Offenders, or assist them with Money, Provisions, Cattle, Arms, Ammunition, Carriages, or any other necessity for Subsistence of Offence; or shall hold secret Correspondence with them by Letter, Message, Signal or otherwise, to be Rebels and Traitors, and as such be treated.

And Whereas during the Continuance of the present unnatural Rebellion, Justice cannot be administered by the Common Law of the Land, the Course whereof has, for a long Time past, been violently impended, and wholly interrupted; from whence results a Necessary for using and exercising of the Law Martial, within and throughout this Province, for so long Time as the present unhappy Occasion shall necessarily require; whereof all Persons are hereby required to take Notice, and govern themselves, as well to maintain Order and Regularity among the peaceable Inhabitants of the Province, as to resist, encounters and subdue the Rebels and Traitors above-discribed by such as shall be called upon those purposes.

To these inevitable, but I trust salutary measures, it is a far more pleasing Part of my Duty, to add the assurance of Protection and Support, to all who in to trying a Crisis, shall manifest their diligence to the King, and affection to the Parent State. In that such Persons as may have been intimidated to quit that Inhabitation in the Course of the Alarm, may return to their respective Callings and Professions; and stand distinct and separate from the Parricides of the Constitution, till God in his Mercy shall restore to his Creatures, in this distracted land, that System of Happiness for which they have been seduced, the Religion of Peace, and Liberty founded upon Law.

Given at Boston, this Twelft Day of June, in the Fifteenth Year of the Reign of his Majesty George the Third, by the Grace of God of Great-Britain, France and Ireland, King, Defender of the Faith, &c.   Anne que Domini,
       1775.   Tho's Gage.
By His Excellency's Command.
  Tho's Flucker, Secr'y,
            God Save rhe King.
WATERTOWN June 12. It has been reported, that the honorable the Continental Congress has voted Seventy Thousand Men for the common defence of the Rights and Liberties of the American Colonies. ―――― Also the Sum of Three Million Lawful Money for their Support.

We have the Pleasure to inform the public that the Grand American Army is nearly compleated. Great Numbers of the Connecticut, New-Hampshire and Rhode-Island Troops are arrived; among the latter a fine Company of Artillery, with four excellent Field Pieces. Many large Pieces of battery Cannon are expected soon, from different Places, twelve Pieces, 18 and 24 Pounders, with a Quantity of Ordinance Stores, we are informed are already arrived from Providence.

        Extract of a Letter from Connecticut.
"Our men enter into service with great ardor, most of the Captains have enlisted more than their complement, and some who came too late have brought in, rather than be disappointed of a share in the service."

122

We hear from Boston, that on Monday last, Gage attended by principal Refugees, and Officers of his Clan, met at the Town House for the purpose of drowning their Sorrows in Bumpers; but before the solemn and loyal Rites were begun, a most dreadful Gun Powder Plot presented itself to their gloomy Imagination; Immediately my Lord high Constable received express Command to take Assistance, if necessary, and make the strictest Search after this horrible Magazine, which was supposed to lay concealed in the Cellars beneath the Fabrick (undoubtedly designed by the Rebels to destroy the truly pious, just and humane General, and his virtuous Attendants assembled above) in Consequence of which, Application was made (by him) for the keys, belonging to the same; but not being able through Impatience to contain them, a Bayonet, together with his suspicious countenance, and a Centry penetrated these otherwise impregnable Vaults, and give full scope to a most thorough Examination of the contents; when after overturning & reoverturning all that could conceal the awful Combustibles, without discovering any Thing capable of being acted by Fire, except a few empty Powdering tubs, except a half famished Rat or two, the mighty Consternation began to subside, and the Gentry aloft to enter fully into the business of the day. Whether the same tremor took Possession of the Troops (posted in Kingstreet on the Occasion) as of their Matters, we cannot precisely inform our Readers; but this is certain, no sooner was the word present given, that a most hideous and irregular popping was heard through their whole Ranks, which sounded neither like Gun, Drum, Trumpet, Blunderbuss or Thunder. This frightful Noise, was once or twice heard to the no small Astonishment of many Eyes and Ears Winesses to the whole

HARTFORD June 12.　　(Connecticut Courant)
New-Milford May 29, 1775

Mr. Watson,

The committee of observation from this town, having daily notifies Zackeriah Ferris, Joseph Ferris, jun. James Oborne, Danial Taylor, Nathanial Taylor and Hezakeah Steven, jun. all of this town, to appear this day, (if they saw Cause) before said committee, to give reasons (if any were) why they should not be advertised as foe to the rights of British Americans, and said Zaheriah Farris, Joseph Ferris, jun. James Osborne, Nathaniel Taylor, and Hezakiah Steven, jun. having neglected to appear, and give any satisfaction to said committee, and said Daniel Taylor having appear'd and declared his opposition to the doings of the Congress, and said committee having fully deliberated upon, and finding said persons obstinately fixed, in their inimical opposition to the doings of the congress, and the now bleeding cause of America, think itself in duty bound, agreeable to the 11th article of the association, entered into the Continental Congress, to make this publication, that each of said persons be universally neglected, and treated as incorrigible Enemies to the rights of British Americans, according to said article of said association.

By Order of the Committee,
Samuel Canfield Clerk.

N. B. Five other persons being notified to appear as above, have signified a recantation of their principles, and a compliance in full with the doings of the Congress to the satisfaction of the Committee.

NEW-YORK June 12. A Gentleman that left Boston about six Days ago, assures for Fact, that he saw landed on the Long Wharf, at that Place, out of one boat alone, no less than 64 dead Men that had been killed by the Provincials at the late Attack at Noodle's and Hog Islands, as mentioned in our last.

On Tuesday the regular soldiers stationed in the barracks here about 50 embarked on board boats belonging to the Asia Man of War. The inhabitants took from them their spare arms, about 90, and some ammunition.

CHARLESTOWN S. Carolina June 12. The Officers of Regular Regiments now raising in this Province tho' they have not possessed their Commissions more than a Fortnight, have been so successful as to enlist upwards of one hundred recruits in that short Space of Time: The Mode of

Exercise they are learning, we hear, is to be adopted by all the other detached Companies, as well as the Militia in general, in which, at present, there is much Difference: The Recruits are lodged in the Barracks where the Serjeants and Drill-Masters are indefatigable to instruct them their Duty.

The association signed by the Provincial Congress, and recommended by them as a proper Instrument to be subscribed to, at this juncture, by Persons of all persuasions, was in a few Days, with the greatest Avidity and Cheerfulness, signed also by almost every Man in this Town: In short, such is here the Spirit for Liberty and Freedom, that of the very few who objected, there was only two who was hardy enough to insult or treat it with Contempt, viz. Lauglin Martin and John Dealy, on which account they drew on themselves the resentment of the Populous, who, on Thursday last, furnished each of them with a suit of Cloating, of the American Manufacture, made of Mr. Foot humourously calls a Thickset composed of Tar and Feathers; thus garbed, they were carted through the pricipal Streets, after which, as Rebels to the State to which they belong, they were conveyed, without any other Injury to their Persons, on board a ship bound to Britain: But Martin's Recantation, and subscription with his own Hands, together with the Intercession of his Friends, We hear has revoked the latter part of the Sentence, and that he will be permitted to pursue his business as usual; Dealy was not even suffered to come on shore, but actually sailed this morning, in the Ship Liberty, Capt. Lasley, bound for the above-mentioned Port.

The Militia Companies continue to patrol the Town and Neighbourhood every Night, the salutary Consequence of which are every Day more apparent: that nightly Meetings and Riots of the Negroes are entirely suppressed, and those Depredations and Robberies with which we had used to be so frequently alarmed are now no more.

HARTFORD June 14. Deserted from the service of the Colony of Connecticut, on the 8th of June instant, from Sheffield, a soldier named Thomas

Clark, belonging to the 7th company in the 6th
regiment, he is of a middling stature, light
complexion pitted with the snall pox, and pimp-
ly face, about 30 years of age, had on a light
coloured sustain coat, callico waistcoat, and a
pair of drab breeches, white stackings, and un-
derstands the manual exercise well, he faloni-
ously took and carried away two silver watches
when he deserted. Whoever will take up said deserter, and return him to the commanding Officer of said regiment at New-London or to me
the commander at Ticonderoga, shall have Twenty
Dollars reward, and all necessary charges paid
by me.   Edward Mott, Comm.
   CAMBRIDGE June 15, Extract of a Letter from a
member of the Continental Congress.
   "The Congress are as firm as a Rock; they are
firmly united in all their Resolutions."
   The 2000 Men, voted to be raised by the New-
Hampshire Congress are all inlisted and many of
them have already joined the American Army. They
are commanded by General Nathaniel Fulson.
   Whithin 2 or 3 Days past, we are informed, 20
or 30 Transports have arrived in Boston from
England with Troops, military Stores, Horses,
&c. as a Reinforcement to Thomas Gage, in order
to enable him to prosecute his rebellious design
of subverting the legal Constitution of this
Government.
   It is said the Number of Troops arrived at
Boston, with those expected, amount to about
3 or 4000.
   Saturday last the Provincial Troops set fire
to the Stores at Noodle's Island, which was entirely consumed, no building being now left
standing on said Island.
   NORWICH June 15. The Reports of the Day, which
is presumed is very incredited are,
   That last Monday Afternoon two Transports arrived at Boston from England, having on board
Part of Preston's Light Dragoons, with their
horse. It is said they sailed the 28th of April
in a fleet consisting of 30 Vessels which were
embarked 9 British Regiments. They were separated by a gale od Wind, on the Banks of Newfound-
land. In one of these arrived, 16 Horses died

126

on the passage.

To this we shall add the Intelligence brought Yesterday by a Gentleman from New-London. viz. Mr. Shaw, of that place, Merchant, has received a letter, by a boat in a short Passage from New York informing him that a Vessel from London bound for Quebec, with 50 chests of Arms on board, had (on Account of an irreconcilable difference which happened between the Vessel and her Gunner, who at Sea) put into Philadelphia. In the Vessel came Passengers Major Skene and a Captain of the Army; they were both examined by the Continental Congress and desired to deliver up their Papers, which they complied with. The Vessel was not unloaded when these advices were forwarded, but it was generally believed, that a Quantity of Gun Powder would be found on board.

Our Intelligence further intimate, that Mr. Shaw read the above mentioned Letter to them, and said that the authenticity of it might be depended upon.

NEW-YORK June 15. On Tuesday arrived the Ship Mary and Susanna, Capt. Thompson reports in 5 Weeks and 3 Days from Cock in Ireland. Captain Thompsom reports, that when he left there, having on board three Regiments of Soldiers, that another Regiment at the same place were preparing to embark, and that four were immediately to sail for New-York, where they may be every Day expected.

Last Monday Morning a quantity of military stores were taken from what are called the King's stores at Turtle Bay, and carried clear off.

Yesterday one M'Donald, who is said had been privately inlisting men to serve under General Gage, against their country, was taken into custody, and conducted by a party of the City Grenadiers before the Provincial Congress then sitting, where he was examined, and returned in custody. We hear some important discoveries were made.

PHILADELPHIA June 16. Extract of a letter from Charlestown, South Carolina, dated May 12, 1775.

"Our Committee have resolved no provisions be exported from hence, but that goes in vessels

that had began to load the 24th inst. from which
presume all trade will soon cease here and from
being a town of trade shall become a garrison
town by provincials, as most are determined, and
preparing to defend themselves."

Extract from a letter from Newport, in Rhode-
Island, June 7, 1775.

"We inform you the exportations of provisions
is stopped by an embargo laid on by act of Government."

Extract of a letter from Baltimore, June 13.

"A gentleman who last night came here from
Williamsburg, which place he left on Friday last,
brings an account of Lord Dunmore having the Day
before gone on board a man of war, at York, with
his family. The Assembly sent a deputation to
invite him to return, and assured him protection, but he refused, and pretends to be afraid
of being assassinated."

WATERTOWN June 19. On Friday last, the 19th
Instant, a Detachment of two Captains, eight
Subalterns, and two hundred men of the Corps of
Light Infantry, under the command of Captain
Souter of the Marines landed on Noodle's Island,
near 6 o'Clock in the Morning, for the purpose
of bringing off Hay, which was effected without
any loss. Advanced Parties took possession of
the Heights, and were most scandalously abused
by the people from the opposite shore. The troops
noticed them not, though fired at them if they
shewed their heads. The Detachment did not fire
a shot. [An infamous Lie extracted from good
Madam Draper's last Thursday Gazette.]

Friday Night last a Number of Provincials entrenched on Bunker-Hill in Charlestown; and on
Saturday about Noon a large Number of Regulars
from Boston came across Charle's River, and
landed a little below the Battery near the point,
when a bloody battle commenced, (many being
killed and wounded on both sides.) The very
heavy fire from the shipping, the Battery on
Cop's-Hill, Boston, together with the train of
the Enemy, obliged the Provincials to retreat a
little this side of Charlestown Neck about sunset, when the Enemy took possession of our entrenchments; after which they set the Town of

Charlestown on Fire, beginning with the Meeting House, and we hear they have not left one building unconsumed. The Engagement continues at this publication, 9 o'Clock, with Intermissions. The Confusion of the Town render it impracticable to give a particular Account of what has already occurred, but hope to give a good one in our next. The Provincials are in high spirits.

WATERTOWN June 19. In Provincial Congress, of June 15, 1775.

Whereas it is necessary that the Colony be Provided with a Magazine of Arms, which are good and sufficient: Therefore,

Resolve, That any Person or Persons who may have such to sell, shall receive so much for them, as the Selectmen of the Towns or districts in which he or they may dwell, shall appraise said Arms at; upon delivery of the same to the Committee of Supply in Watertown, and exhibiting a Certificate of said Appraisement, attested by said Selectmen to the Committee aforesaid, provided said delivery be made within one Month from the date hereof.

A true Copy from the Minutes
    Attest.   Samuel Freeman, Sec'ry.

NEWPORT June 19. Last Thursday one of the providence packets, which had been arbitrarily seized by and detained as a tender to, the man of war in this harbour, was sent up the Bay, 'tis supposed, to take a vessel which 'twas reported had gone to the backside of Connecticut; but unluckily she met with two arm'd vessels which fired upon her so warmly that she was obliged to turn tail, but not being able to get off, the people struck her ashore on the north end of Connecticut and left her; she was immediately got off, and carried away, most probably to be delivered to her proper owners. This happened just before sunset.

Last Friday evening when the men of war in our harbour was shifting their watches, a number of musket balls were fired into the town, one of which entered a closet window of a house on Gravelly point, just to the northward of Long-wharf, went through the closet door, and made a considerable dent in a door in the opposite

129

corner of the room adjoining the closet; by which one or two persons narrowly escaped being killed or wounded.

Last Saturday it being reported that 3 American vessels of force, were lying in Narraganset Bay, Capt. Wallace of the Ship Rose, Captain Ascaugh, of the Swan, and a Tender, came to sail and first beat out within about 2 miles of the Light house, where they bore away, ran up the river, as far as Connecticut point, and took a peep down Narraganset Bay; but not discovering any vessels, they returned to their station in this harbour; while they were on this short and unsuccessful cruise, a number of people boarded and carried off 5 vessels, which these men of war had taken, and left riding in the road.

NEWPORT June 19. (East Greenwich, June 14.)

Sir,

Long have the good people of this colony been oppressed by your conduct, in interrupting their lawful trade, and preventing the importation of provisions necessary for their subsistence. The acts of the British Parliament; already filled with restrictions of trade, oppressive in the highest degree, seem by you to be thought too lenient. Not controlled by those you affect to call your masters, you have detained the persons and taken away the properties of his Majesty's American subjects, without any warrant from the acts of trade; by which you have greatly impeded the intercourse between the different parts of this colony. The inhabitants expecting the interposition of the lawful authority of the colony, have born these outrages with patience almost criminal. The legislature have heard their complaints: and in consequence of an act passed by the General Assembly this day, I demand of you to reason your conduct towards the inhabitants of this colony, in stopping and detaining their vessels; and I also demand of you that you immediately restore the two packets belonging to some inhabitants of the town of Providence, and all other vessels belonging to the inhabitants of this colony, which you have taken or unjustly detained. So long as you remain in the colony, and demean yourself as becomes your office, you may depend upon the protection of the law, and every assistance for promoting the public service in manpower. And you may also be assured that the whole power of the colony will be exerted to secure The Persons and properties of the inhabitants against every lawless invader. An immediate answer is requested to this letter.

I am Sir, your most humble servant,

Nicholas Cooke, Dep. Gov.

To James Wallace, Esq; Commander of his Majesty's Ship Rose, at Newport.

His Majesty's Ship Rose, Rhode Island June 15.

Sir,

I Have received your letter of the 14th inst. Although I am unacquainted with you, or what station you act in ——— suppose you write in behalf of some body of people; therefore, previous to my giving an answer, I must desire to know, whether or not you, or the people on whose behalf you write, are not in open rebellion to your lawful sovereign, and the acts, of the British legislature.

I am Sir, your most humble and obedient Service

James Wallace.

Nicholas Cook, Esq;

Colony of Rhode Island, &c.

The above contains a true copy of a letter from his Honour the Deputy Governor, to Captain Wallace, and of his answer; which are published by order of the General Assembly.

Witness   Henry Ward, Sec'ry.

NORWICH June 19. In one of our late papers, a Captain of the Militia was said to be killed in the Battle of Concord by our own People, owing to the firing at too great a Distance. We are since well assured, by a person who was very near him at the Time, that the said Captain was killed by the Regulars, before a Gun was discharge on our Side. However as Accident of that kind may happen, it is hoped the Caution against firing at too great a distance, in any future Engagement, will be duly observed.

THe patriotic Ladies of the Town of Concord are desired to accept the unfeigned Thanks of the Public for their Care and Kindness in the

collecting and sending to the Hospital a Chest
of old linen Rags, &c. This Instance of their
Humanity and public Spirit does Honour to the
Town, and will we hope induce others to imitate
so good an Example.

We hear that Colonel Gardner of the Americans,
had received a Wound which it was feared would
prove mortal.

The People here are in great Anxiety to learn
the Particulars and Event of the above-mentioned
momentous Action. As Express from Head Quarters
is this Day expected here, and the printers hereof shall be ready to communicate to the Public,
with all possible Dispatch, such authentic Advices as they are able to obtain.

Five Companies of Colonel Parson's Regiment,
that have some Time past been encamped at New-
London, Are this Day expected in Town, they having received orders to join the American Army
with the greatest Expedition. Several Gentlemen
here, and in our Vicinity, are voluntarily equip-
ping themselves for the same purpose.

HARTFORD June 19. By a letter from Albany, to
a gentleman in this town we are informed, that
three Sachems had been at that place and declared their intentions of befriending the people of this country, in their military movements, provided they did not interfere with the
safety of Col. Johnson and Capt. Close, whom
they meant to defend, in duty to their Father-
in-Law, General Johnson. Said letter also mentions, that Col. Johnson with his family, 14
battoes and 13 waggons, loaded with goods and
household furniture, were gone to Fort-Stanwix;
and that Col. Johnson had summoned the Indians
far and near, to meet him in general Congress
at Oswego.

Capt. Edward Motte's company, being insulted
by a couple of rascally tories, as they passed
through the town of Litchfield, the two offenders found it necessary to extinguish the flames
of resentment they had kindled, by eating a
hearty meal of what is vulgarly called Humble
Pie.

NEW-YORK June 19. Friday last the Mercury frigate, Capt. M'Carthy, arrived at Sandy Hook in 14

Days from Boston; He was dispatched from thence by General Gage to order whatever Troops might arrive here from England or Ireland, for Boston; and last Wednesday he luckily fell in with a Transport from Cork with part of the 44th Regiment bound for this Place, but she soon stood to the Eastward, and Capt. M'Carthy now waits at the Hook to give the like Orders to the rest of the Fleet that may arrive here.

NEWPORT June 21. On Thursday last, by one of the packets mentioned in his Honor's letter, which he had been piratically seized and detained by Capt. Wallace, was cruising as a tender, in the Narragansett bay, in quest of plunder, as usual, she spoke with an armed sloop, fitted out by the colony for the protection of the trade whose commander not answering in a tone sufficiently submissive, was fired upon by the Tender: the compliment was returned with such effects as to put the pirate into some confusion, and they endeavoured to make off, but were prevented by an armed packet boat, in the service of the colony, that had by the same time come up; the pirate finding they could not escape ran the vessel on shore on Connecticut, and went off with much precipitation. The firing on both sides continued some minutes, though none of our people were hurt, and but one of the pirates wounded.

PHILADELPHIA June 21. Yesterday Morning the three Battalions of the City and Liberties, together with the Artillery Company, a Troop of Light-Horse, several Companies of Light Infantry with Rangers, and Rifle-men in the whole about 2000, marched out to the Commons, and, having joined in Brigades, were reviewed by General Washington who is appointed Commander in Chief of all the North American Forces by the honourable Continental Congress, where they went through the Manual Excise, Firing and maneuvres, with great Dexterity and Exactness.

CAMBRIDGE June 22. Last Night a Detachment from our Army began an Intrenchment on the Eminence being Bunker-Hill, about a mile to the Northward of the center of the Town of Charlestown. The enemy appeared to be much alarmed on

Saturday Morning, when they discovered our operation, and immediately begun a heavy Cannonading from a battery on Corps Hill, Boston, and from the Ships in the Harbour. Our People, with little Loss, continued to carry on their works till 10 o'Clock, p. m. on Saturday, when they discovered a large Body of the Enemy crossing the Charles River from Boston. They landed on a Point of Land about a Mile eastward of our Intrenchment, and immediately disposed their Army for an Attack, previous to which they set fire to the Town of Charlestown. It is supposed the Enemy intended to attack us under Cover of the Smoke from the burning Houses, the Wind favoured them in such a design; while on the other Side, their Army was extending Northward towards Mistick-River, with an apparent Design of surrounding our men within the Works, & of cutting off any Assistance intended for their Relief. They were however, in some measure, counteracted in their Design, and drew their Army into closer Order. As the Enemy approached, our Men were not only exposed to the Attack of the numerous Musketry, but to the heavy Fire of the Battery on Corps Hill, 4 or 5 Men of War, several armed Boats and floating Batteries in Mistick-River, and a Number of Field Pieces: Notwithstanding which, our Troops within the Intrenchment, under a Breast Work without, sustained the Enemy's Attack with real Bravery and Resolution, killed and wounded great Numbers, and repulsed them several Times; and after bearing, for about 2 Hours, in severe and heavy a Fire as perhaps ever was known, and many have fired away all their Ammunition, they were overpowered by Numbers, and obliged to leave the Intrenchment, retreating about Sunset, to a small Distance over Charlestown Neck.

Our Loss not exceed 50 killed, and 20 or 30 taken Prisoners.

The Town of Charlestown, supposed to contain about 300 Dwelling Houses, a great many of which were large and elegant, besides 150 or 200 Buildings, are almost all laid to Ashes by the barbarity and wanton Cruelty of the infernal Villain, Thomas Gage.

The Enemy yet remains in Possession of Charlestown, and has erected Works for the Defence on
Bunker-Hill. It is said they have brought over
from Boston Part of the Light-Horse.

Our Troops continue the high Spirits. They are
fortifying a very high Hill, about a Mile and a
half from this Town. and within cannon shot of
the Enemy on Bunker-Hill.

The following is a Copy of a Letter from a
Person of Credit, and is thought by many judi-
cious Persons it contains Accounts not far from
Truth.

Hinghan, June, 19, 1775.

"Yesterday I came out of Boston at 2 o'Clock
P. M. I heard the Officers and Soldiers say that
they were sure that they had a Thousand or more
killed and wounded; that they were carrying the
wounded Men from 4 o'Clock on Saturday until I
came away. General Howe commanded the Troops.
They buried their Dead at Charlestown. Among the
Dead was Major Pitcairn. A great many other Officers are dead. There were 5000 Soldiers went
from Boston. The Soldiers and Officers exult
very much upon taking our Lines."

The Account of the Number of Troops which came
from Boston, and mentioned in the above Letter,
is coroberated by the observation of a Gentleman
at Chelsea, who saw them in Boats, and judged
the Number to be near 5000.

It is reported that one of the Enemy's General
Officers is among the slain, said to be Howe or
Burgoyne.

CAMBRIDGE June 22. Extract of a printed half
sheet of the proceedings of the Honourable Provincial Congress of the Colony of New-Jersey,
dated at Trenton the 3d of June instant, that
came to late for this paper. viz.

That the cruel and arbitrary measured of the
British Parliament and Ministry, to enslave the
American Colonies, having made it necessary to
arm and discipline the inhabitants, in defence
of their rights and freedom, and that persons
in whom they can confide, should be chosen to
Command in the Militia, it is recommended and
advised, that one or more companies, consisting
of 80 men (aged from 16 to 50) each, be formed

in each Township or Corporation. That each of
these companies, meet and choose from among themselves 1 Captain, 2 Lieutenants, and 1 Ensign:
which officers, of each company, shall choose
their Serjeants, Corporals and Drummers. That
each Captain provide a muster roll, with every
one at inlisting is to subscribe and according
as the proper officer shall direct, meet, for
improvement in military discipline, the whole
companies at least once a month, and at a general muster, or review of the whole regiment as
often as the field officers shall appoint. Each
person inlisted, to be equipped as soon as possible,with arms and ammunition, &c.

Companies already formed, to be continued,
and completed.

NEW-YORK June 22. We hear that on Monday last
the Connecticut Forces in the Neighbourhood of
Greenwich were reviewed by General Wooster; They
are an exceeding fine Body of Men, and performed
the Exercise and Evaluation with Spirit and Exactness, much to the satisfaction of the Officers, a great number of Gentlemen and Ladies and
a predigious Concourse of the Inhabitants from
that Province as well as from New-York.

Saturday last an Express from Watertown, passed
thro' this City, in his Way to the Continental
Congress: He left the Camp last Monday, and said
some of the Transports were arrived at Boston,
from Cork; and that the Grenadiers and Light
Infantry of General Gage's Army appeared to be
in motion.

We hear there are letters in town advising,
that Col. Guy Johnson having been suspected of
endeavouring to stir up the Indians against the
Colonies, had incurred the resentment of the
people near him, and that fearing the effects
of it, he had retired into Indian country.

Tuesday night a vessel arrived in a short passage from New-London; we have the following Important intelligence, in a letter from a gentleman at Norwich, to his friend in New-York.

Norwich 19th June, 1775.
Sir,
I Understand by David Trumbull, That by an Ex-
press from Cambridge, his Honour our Governor,

136

has advice, that our people attenping to take possession of Bunker's Hill, and Dorchester Point, they were attacked by the regulars, Shipping, &c. Five men of war haul'd up at Charlestown, cover'd the landing of a body of men who drove our people from Bunker's Hill: That three Colonels in our service were wounded, Colonel Gardner mortally; how many are slain on either side is uncertain.

This happened on Saturday about noon at Charlestown when the post came away, our people kept their ground and made a stand, how they have fared at Dorchester, we do not hear; General Putnam was safe when the Express came off; preparations were making for a general attack. Col. Tyler must be on the march as soon as possible, without confusion; I shall procure them as soon as I can and have them to take in his baggage. Col. John Huntington desires I would dispatch an Express immediately to have the troops forwarded; he sent orders in writing yesterday.

The following resolution was reported to have passed in the Continental Congress at Philadelphia, viz. immediately to strike a continental currency of two million dollars. To raise 15,000 more men, 5000 whom to be stationed at New-York. That Colonel Washington was appointed commander in chief of the American forces, and was going to Boston with 1000 rifle men.

PHILADELPHIA June 22.

My Lord,

Altho' I can by no means subscribe to the opinion of diverse people in the world, that an officer in half pay is to be considered in the service; yet I think it a point of delicacy to pay a deference to this opinion erroneous and absurb as it is. I therefore apprise your Lordship in the most public and Solemn manner, that I do renounce my half pay, from the date hereof. At the same time I beg leave to assure your Lordship, that whenever it shall please his Majesty to call me forth to any honourable service against the natural hereditary enemies of our country, or in defence of his just rights and dignity, no man will obey the righteous summons with more zeal and alacrity than myself; but the

137

present measures seem to me so absolutely subversive the rights and liberties of every individual subject, so destructive to the whole empire at large, and ultimately so ruinous to his
Majesty's own people, dignity, and family, that
I think myself obliged in conscience as a citizen, Englishman, and soldier of a free state,
to exert my utmost to defeat them. I must devoutly pray to Almighty God to Direct his Majesty into measures more consonant to his Interest and humour, and more conductive to the Happiness and glory of his people.

I am my Lord
Your most humble servant
Charles Lee.

To the Right Honourable Lord Viscount
<u>Barrington, his Majesty's Secretary of War.</u>
CHARLESTON So. Carolina June 23. In Provincial
Congress.   Wednesday June 21, 1775.
Ordered,
That the Hon. William Henry Drayton, the Hon.
Capt. Bernard Elliot, Col. Charles Pickney, Col.
James Parsons, Col. Isaac Motte, Col. Stephen
Bull, Col. William Moultrie, Major Owen Roberts,
Capt. Thomas Savage, Capt. John Huger, Miles
Brewton, THomas Fergerson, and Gabriel Capres,
Esqs. be a Deputation to present to his Excel-
lency the Governor the Address of this Congress.

To his Excellency the Right Lord William Campbell, Governor and Commander in Chief in and
over the Province of South Carolina.

The humble Address and Declaration of the
Provincial Congress.

May it please your Excellency,
We his Majesty's loyal subjects, the Representatives of the people of this colony in Congress
assembled, beg leave to disclose to your excellency the true cause of our proceeding; not only
that upon your arrival among us, you may receive
no unfavourable impression of our conduct, but
that we may stand justified to the world.

When the ordinary modes of Application for redress of grievances, and the usual means of defence against arbitrary impositions have failed,
mankind generally had have recourse to those
that are extraordinary. Hence the origin of the

Continental Congress, and hence the present rep-
resentatation of the people of this colony.

It is unnecessary to enumerate the grievance
of America; they have been so often represented
that your Excellency cannot be a stranger to
them. Let it therefore suffice to say that the
hands of his Majesty's ministers have long lain
heavy, and now press Us with intolerable weight.
We declare that no love of innovation, no desire
of altering the constitution of Government, no
lust of independence, has had the least influence upon our councils: But, alarmed and roused
by a long succession of arbitrary proceedings
by wicked administration, impressed with the
greatest apprehension of instigated, insurrection, and deeply affected by the commencement
of hostilities by British troops against this
continent, solely for the preservation and in
defence of our lives, liberty, and property, we
have been impelled to associate and to take up
arms.

We firmly deplore those slanderous informa-
tions, and wicked councels, by which his Majesty
has been led into measures, which if persisted
in, must inevitably involve America in all the
calamities of civil war, and rend the British
empire. We only desire the secure enjoyment of
our invaluable rights, and we wish for nothing
more ardently, than a speedy reconciliation with
our mother country, upon constitutional principles.

Conscious of the justice of our cause, and the
integrity of our views we readily profess our
loyal attachment to our Sovereign, his crown and
dignity: And trusting the event of Providence,
we prefer Death to Slavery.

These things we thought it our duty to declare,
that your Excellency, and thro' you, our August
Sovereign, our fellow subjects, and the whole
world, may cleary understand that our taking up
arms, is the result of dire necessity, and in
compliance with the first law of nature.

We intreat and trust, that your Excellency
will make such representation of the state of
this colony, and of our true motive, as to assure his Majesty, that, in the midst of all our

complicated distresses, he has no subjects in
her dominions, who more sincerely desired to
testify their loyalty and affection, or who
would be more willing to devote their lives and
fortunes in his real service.

By order of the Provincial Congress, met at
Charlestown, So. Carolina June 20th, 1775.

Henry Laurens, President.

The deputation being returned, the Honourable
Mr. Draton reported, that they have delivered
the address to the Governor, his Excellency was
pleased to make the following answer:

Gentlemen,

I know of no representative of the People of
this Province, except those constitutionally
convened in General Assembly, and an incompetent
to judge of the Dispute which at present unhappily subsist between Great-Britain and the American Colonies.

It is impossible, during the short interval
since my arrival, that I should have acquired
such a knowledge of the State of the Province,
as to be at present able to make any Representation thereupon to his Majesty, but you may be
assured to no Representation shall ever be made
by me, but what shall be consistent with the
Truth, and with an earnest Endeavour to promote
the real Happines and Prosperity of the Province.

Wm. Campbell.

Published by order of the Congress

Peter Timothy, Secretary June 21st 1775.

NEW-YORK June 24. Last Night Arrived an Express from the Provincial Camp near Boston, with
the following Interesting Account of an Engagement, at Charlestown, between about Three Thousand of the King's Regular Forces and about half
the number of the Provincials on Saturday the
17th Instant. *

On Friday night, June 17th* 1500 of the provincials went to Bunkers Hill, in order to entrench there, and continued intrenching till
Saturday 10 o'clock, when two thousand regulars
marched out of Boston, landed in Charlestown,
and plundering it of all its valuable effects,
set fire to it in 10 different places at once;
then dividing their Army, one part of it marched

up in the front of the provincial's intrenchment, and began to attack the provincials at long
shot: the other part of the Army marched round
the town of Charlestown, under cover of the smoak
occasioned by the fire of the town. The provincial Sentries discovered the regulars marching
upon their left wing. Upon notice of this, given
by the sentry to the Connecticut forces posted
on the wing, Captain Molton of Ashford, with
400 of said forces, immediately repaired to, and
pulled up a post and rail fence, and carrying
the post and rail to another fence, put them together for a breast work. Capt. Multon gave orders to the men, not to fire until the enemy
were got within 15 rods, and then not till the
word was given. At the word's being given the
enemy fell surprisingly. It was thought by spectators who stood at a distance, that our nem did
great execution. The action continued about two
hours, when the regulars on the right wing were
put into confusion, and gave way. The Connecticut troops closely pursued them, and were on the
point of pushing their bayonets; when orders
were received from General Pomeroy, for those
who had been in the action two hours to fall back,
and their places to be supplied by fresh forces.
These orders being mistaken for a direction to
retreat, our troops on the right wing began a
general retreat, which was handed to the left,
the principal place of the action, where Captains
Molton, Chester, Clarke, and Putnam had forced
the enemy to give way and retire before them,
for some considerable distance; and being warmly pursuing the enemy, were with difficulty persuaded to retire. But the right wing, by mistak-
ing the orders, having already retired, the left,
to avoid being encircled, were obliged to retreat also with the main body. They retreated
with precipitation on across the causeway to
Winter-Hill, in which they were exposed to the
fire of the enemy, from their shipping and floating batteries.

We sustained our principal loss in passing the
causeway. The enemy pursued our troops to Winter
Hill, where the provincials being reinforced by
General Putnam, renewed the battle with great

spirit, repulsed the enemy with great slaughter, and pursued them till they got under cover of their cannon from the shipping, when the enemy retreated to Bunkers's Hill, and the provincials to Winter Hill; where, after entrenching and erecting batteries, they on Monday began to fire upon the regulars on Bunker's Hill, and on the ships and floating batteries in the Harbour, when the Express came away. The number of the provincial's killed is between 40 and 70, 140 wounded; of the Connecticut troops 16 were killed, no officers among them was either killed or wounded, except Lieut. Grovesnor, who is wounded in the Hand. A Colonel or Lieut. Col. of the New-Hampshire forces, among the dead. It is also said Doct. Warren is undoubtedly among the slain. The provincials took 3 iron six pounders, some entrenching tools and Knapsacks.

The number of regulars that first attacked the provincials on Bunker's Hill was not less than 2000. The number of provincials was about 1500 who it is supposed would have gained a compleat victory, had not been for the unhappy mistake already mentioned. The regulars were afterwards reinforced with 1000 men. It is uncertain how great a number of the enemy were killed or wounded; but it was supposed by spectators, who saw the whole action, that there could not be less than 500 killed. Mr. Gardner who got out of Boston on Sunday evening says that there were 500 wounded men brought into that place, the morning before he came out. *Date, publisher's error.

The account was taken from Capt. Elijah Hide, of Lebanan, who was a Spectator on Winter-Hill, during the whole action.

WATERTOWN June 24. A Letter from Machias was this Day laid before the Provincial Congress, containing Advices that in Consequence of an Application to that Place from Icabod and Stephen Jones of Boston, and Casco-Bay, for Lumber to supply the Navy and Army, the last mentioned person was arrested by the inhabitants, and put under Guard while the other had made his escape in the Woods. That the Captain of a Tender sent to protect two Sloops which the Traitors aforesaid intended to have loaded, put springs to his

Cables and threatened to burn the Town unless
the prisoners were released: That an engagement
between the People on Shore and the crew on board
the Tender took Place, and the latter was obliged
to put to Sea. The Inhabitants immediately Maned
two Sloops, and arming themselves with Fire Arms,
Swords, Axes and Spears, came up with the Tender
& engaged a second time: That an obstinate Resistance was made, but the Tender was obliged
to yield: The Captain of the Tender was mortally wounded and died the next Morning; five of
the Crew were wounded, and one Marine killed;
two of our men were killed, and five wounded.

Mr. Robert Avery of Norwich, in Connecticut,
who was on board the Tender, a prisoner, was
unhappily killed.

PROVIDENCE June 24. At a meeting of the committee of Inspection, for the towns of Taverton
and Little Compton, held at the dwelling house
of Gidion Wilcox. Esq; on Saturday June 17th.

Nathaniel Searle, jun, Esq; in the Chair.
Information being given to these Committees,
that Abiel Cook, of Little Compton had violated
the seventh article of the Constitutional Congress Association, and was thereby endeavouring
to feed and support the enemies, of American
liberty, by selling some of his sheep to go on
board the Swan man of war at Newport; the sheep
being stopped at Forkland ferry and said Cook
ordered to attend the committee, he attended
accordingly this day, and had the effrontery to
insult the Committee and his country, by declaring, that he had sold the sheep to go on board
the man of war, and would do it again, when any
opportunity should offer.

Voted, That the above sheep be sent as a present to the American Army, near Boston.

Ordered, That the above be printed in the Newport Mercury, that all friends to American liberty may break off all dealings with said Cook,
and treat him as an enemy to his country, and
the liberties of America.

A true copy, by order of the Committee,
William Ladd, Clerk for the Day.

PHILADELPHIA June 24. Last Tuesday evening
Thomas Jefferson, Esq; arrived here from Virginia

to attend the Congress, agreeable to his election, in the room of the Hon. Peyton Randolph, Esq; He was attended by Dr. M'clury.

WILLAMSBURG June 24. Last Thursday a joint address of the Hon. the Council and House of Burgesses was transmitted to the Governor, on board the Fowey man of war, of which the following is a copy. It is said his Excellency intendeds to take up his residence at Portsmouth, and that Lady Dunmore, and the rest of his Lordship's family, will sail tomorrow for England.

To his Excellency the Right Hon. John Earl of Dunmore, his Majesty's Lieutenant Governor, General, and Commander in Chief of the Colony and Dominion of Virginia, and Vice Admiral of the same: The joint Address of the Council and House of Representatives.

My Lord,
We his Majesty's dutiful and loyal subjects the Council and House of Burgesses of Virginia, have received your Lordship's answer to our joint address, by which we represented to your excellency how very insecure we thought the public arms in the Palace since your Lordship's removal from thence, and requested that your Lordship would be pleased to order them to be stored in the public magazine, judging this a repository of much greater security.

You are pleased to tell us, that experience hath shewn the insecurity of the magazine, and that as the Palace hath hitherto been respected, you thought it improper to give any other orders that the arms belonging to the King, which have for so many years been lodged, may still remain in the Palace, and that they may, on no account be touched without your express permission. Though these arms, my Lord, may be considered, in some sort, as belonging to his Majesty's as the supreme head of this government, and that they are properly under your Lordship's directions; yet we humbly conceive that they were originally provided, and have been preserved for the use of the country in cases of emergency.

We would not wish to interfere with your Lordship's authority, of this disposition we presume our former address afforded the strongest testimony; but the reflection that the arms are so much exposed that they may easily be made the most improper and destructive use of, is, to us, entirely alarming.

The Palace, my Lord, hath indeed been hitherto much respected, but not so much out of regard to the building, as to the residence of his majesty's representative. Had your Lordship thought fit to remain there, we should have had no apprehension of danger; but, considering these arms at present exposed to your servants, and every rude invader, the security formerly derived from your Lordship's presence cannot now be relied on.

In your Lordship's answer to an address of the House of Burgesses, you are pleased to say, that experience has demonstrated to you that the city of Williamsburg is an improper place for the residence of our Governor, and give it as a reason for not returning the powder, according to your own voluntary promise, made to the House, that you could not attend to its preservation, nor depend on its security, if returned to the magazine. We should suppose, my Lord, that your Excellency's attention to the arms would be equally necessary for their security, as you know the Palace standing on the edge of the city, and we should, for this reason, imagine it more likely to be rifled than the magazine in the midst of it; besides, should it be thought necessary, a proper guard might be kept at the magazine, which we did not think so decent to propose for your Lordship's Palace. Our apprehensions, my Lord have been not a little increased by considering the several depositions taken by order of the House of Burgeses; we decline commenting upon them, but submit to the world from whereon the unhappy disturbances of this colony took their rise. We must my Lord, once more entreat your Excellency to order arms to be removed to the public magazine.

We cannot, my Lord, decline representing to you, that the important business of this assembly hath been much impeded by your Excellency's removal from the Palace. This step hath deprived us of the necessary and free acceess to your

Lordship, which we conceive the constitution in titles us to. There are several bills of the last importance to this country now ready to be presented to your Excellency for your assent.

We have hitherto, my Lord, in hopes of preserving that harmony which we wish ever to subsist between all the branches of our legislature, submitting to the great to the great inconveniece of sending our members twelve miles to wait on your Excellency on board one of his Majesty's ship of war, to present our several addresses; but we think it would be highly improper, and to great a departure from the contitutional and accustomed mode of transacting the business of the Assembly, to met your excellency at any other place than the Capital, to present such bills as have there been agreed to by the Council and House of Burgesses. We must therefore beseech your Excellency to return to us; and as the advanced season of the year requires our presence in our several counties, we hope your Lordship will be pleased to favour us with your speedy and ultimate answer, that we may certainly know what to depend upon.

His Excellency's Answer.

I have already declared my intentions in regard to the arms at the Palace, and I conceive the council and House of Burgesses are intefering in a matter which does not belong to them. I would be glad to be informed who they design by the terms rude invaders which they have made use of.

The disorders in Williamsburg, and the other parts of the country, drove me to the necessity of changing my place of residence, and if any inconvenience has arisen to the assembly on that account, I am not chargeable with it, but they have not been deprived of any necessary, nor free access to me. The constitution vest me with an undoubted power to call the Assembly for the business of, to any place in, the Colony, exigency may require.

Not having been acquainted with the whole proceedings of the Assembly, I know of no bills of importance, which, if I were included to risk my person again among the people, the assembly

have to present to me, nor whether they be such
as I could assent to.

CAMBRIDGE June 25. Within 2 or 3 days past, we
are informed, 20 or 30 transports have arrived
at Boston from England, with troops, military
stores, horses, &c. as reinforcements to Thomas
Gage, in order to enable him to prosecute his
rebellious design of subverting the legal Constitution of this Government.

It is said the number of troops arrived in
Boston, with these expected, amount to about 3
or 4000.

Saturday last came to town from Philadelphia,
escorted from thence under guard to General
Wooster at Horse Neck, Ensign Moland, lately
taken prisoner by Col. Arnold, on Lake Champlain.

WATERTOWN june 26. In Provincial Congress at
Watertown, June 21, 1775.

Whereas a Number of our inveterate Enemies,
have taken Shelter under the Protection of Gen.
Gage, and his Troops and have left a Considerable Interest, whereby it becomes necessary that
Provisions should be made for the Disposal of
the same; therefore,

Resolve, That the Select Men and Committees
of Correspondence of the several Towns and Districts of this Colony be directed to take under
their Care, the Effects and Estates of the several Persons, who have fled for Protection to
Boston or elsewhere, and to improve the same to
the best Advantage, and render a true Account
of the Profits arising therefrom, to the Congress, or some future House of Representatives
of this Colony, they being allowed a reasonable
Consideration for their Trouble.

JA. Warren, President.
A true Copy from the Minutes,
Attest.   Sam. Freeman, Secr'y.

WATERTOWN June 26. By many Persons of undoubted Veracity, who was in Boston during the late
battle at Charlestown, and were soon after in
the Field of action, we learn, That the Enemy
sustained a greater loss then was at first apprehended. The Ministerial Troops, about 5000
in Number, were commanded by Lord Howe, and by
the most favorable Account, were 1000 of them,

amongst whom were 84 Officers, were killed and wounded; but their loss is generally believed to be much greater. The Work-house, Alms house, and Manufacturing houses were improved for the wounded Regulars, who were removing the whole of the Night, and Sabbath Day succeeding the Battle. Col. Pitcairn, and many other Officers whom they highly esteemed are dead. The Welch Fuzileers were nearly all cut off, and one Captain only remains alive of that Regiment. The Enemy retreated twice before they carried the entrenchments, which were the Work of a Night, and at best imperfect. About 700 Americans fought the Battle, the Residue of the Army from Cambridge not having yet recovered Bunker's Hill timely enough to reinforce our brave Men. The loss on our Side is not yet ascertained, but at the most is supposed to be from 150 to 200 killed & wounded. Major General Warren, late President of the Provincial Congress, was amongst the slain, Col. Parker of Chelmsford, and 27 Privates from different Towns, are Prisoners in Boston Goal. The Officers of the Regulars acknowledge that they have dearly purchased the Hill, and say that the Rebels fought more like Devils than Men. Charlestown containing about 300 Dwelling Houses, and 150 or 200 other Buildings was laid in Ashes by our humane adversaries.

Since our last there have been about 16 or 20 Regulars killed at Charlestown Guard, and we have lost but two Men.

The 8th Instant, one of the Newport Packets which had been seized by the Enemy and fitted out for the Protection of the Colony. On board the Packet were found 8 swivel's, 17 Stands of Arms, and a Number of Pistols, Cutlasses, Catouch-Boxes, &c.

NEW-YORK June 26. Saturday Evening last an Express arrived here from Albany, with Advice, that the Cughnawaga Indians of Canada, had actually taken up the Hatchet; and 'tis supposed they intended to use against the Colonies.

Yesterday Mr. Paul Revere passed through this City in his way to the Continental Congress; and we hear he carried attested accounts, that the Regulars, in the late Action lost 1000 Men and the Provincials 200.

PHILADELPHIA June 26. The following is a list of Field Officers, appointed for the three Battalions of the Philadelphia Militia.

First battalion John Dickenson Esq; Colonel, John Chavalier Lieut. Colonel, Jacob Morgan, and William Coats, Majors.

Second Battalion Daniel Roberdeau Esq; Colonel, Joseph Reed, Esq; Lieut. Colonel, D. John Cox, and John Bayard, Majors.

Third Battalion, John Calwallader, Esq; Colonel, John Nixon, Lieut. Colonel, Thomas Miffin, and Samuel Meridith, Esqs. Major.

NEW-YORK June 29. On Saturday arrived from Philadelphia, in their Way for the Camp at Boston, his Excellency General Washington, appointed by the Hon. the Continental Congress Commander and Chief of the Provincial Troops in North America, attended by General Lee and Schuyler: They were escourted by a Party of Light Horse: The General landed at the Seat of Col. Lipnard about 4 o'Clock on Sunday Afternoon, from whence they were conducted by 9 Companies of Foot, in their Uniforms, and a great number of the principal Inhabitants of this City.

A letter dated in Roxbury June 22 informs on June 21 our advanced party at Dorchester fired into a boat that was sounding, and killed 4 on which they went off. Capt. Coit had 20 of his men wounded, 2 dangerously. We are fortifying here, and hope to give them a warm reception when they come out, we expect another visit on the arrival of the forces which they daily expect. Col. W. Saybrooke, Says, that at the time our people left the ground we had much the better of the enemy, and only retired for want of powder.

NEW-YOPK June 29. The Address of the Provincial Congress of the Colony of New-York.

To his Excellency George Washington, Generalissimo of all the Forces raised, and to be raised in the Confederated Colonies of America.

May it Please your Excellency,
At a time when the most loyal of his Majesty's subjects, from a regard to the laws and constitution, by which he sits on the throne, feel

themselves reduced to the unhappy necessity of taking up arms, to defend their dearest rights and privileges; while we deplore the calamities of this divided Empire, we rejoice in the appointment of a Gentleman from whose abilities and virtue, we are thought to expect both security and peace.

Confiding in you, Sir, and in the worthy Generals, immediately under your Command, we have the most flattering hopes of success, in the glorious struggle for American Liberty, and the fullest assurance that whenever this important contest shall be decided, by that fondest wish of each American soul, an accommodation with our Mother Country you will cheerfully resign the Important Deposit, committed into your hands, and re assure the Character of our worthiest Citizen.

By Order,
P. V. B. Livingston, President, June 26.
His Excellency's Answer.

Gentleman,

At the same time that with you, I deplore the unhappy necessity of such an appointment, as that with which I am now honoured, I cannot but field sentiments of the highest gratitude, for this affecting instance of distinction.

May your warmest wishes be realized in the success of America, at this important and interesting period; and be assured, that every exertion of my worthy colleagues and myself will be equally extended to the reestablishment of peace and harmony, between the Mother Country and these Colonies: As to the fatal, but necessary operations of War ———— when we assumed the Soldiers, we did not lay aside the Citizen, and we shall most sincerely rejoice with you in that happy hour, when the establishment of American Liberty, on the most firm and Solid foundations, shall enable us to return to our private stations in the bosom of a free, peaceful, and happy Country. George Washington.

JULY 1775

WILLIAMSBURG July 1. The General Assembly have adjourned themselves to the 12th of October next, and the delegates are summond to meet in convention, at the town of Richmond, on the 17th instant.

At a meeting of the inhabitants last Tuesday, at the court-house, it was agreed upon to represent to the delegates in the convention, the expediency of a reinforcement of men from the adjacent counties, to be stationed here with the city company, on account of the late alarming report of troops being destined for this colony, from Great-Britain. The number thought required at present 250. It is generally believed this number will be approved in the convention, and that the towns below this will be provided in like manner, so that, in case of emergency, the whole can unite upon the shortest notice, and aid in opposition to any attempt that may be made by British Troops towards the destruction of public liberty in this colony.

From Princess Anne, we hear, that on the eastern shore of that county, lately drifted there several parts of a wreck, quantities of hay, a drummer's uniform, and some other military habits, which make it probable that one of the transports has been lost near the shore.

PROVIDENCE July 2. Wednesday last the honourable General Assembly of this colony met here, pursuent of a warrant issued by his honour the Deputy-Governor.

The house have ordered an additional number of 360 men to be immediately raised for the common defence, and one quarter of militia throughout the colony to be inlisted as minutemen.

WATERTOWN July 3. Since the battle of the 17th instant, a considerable body of the army, have

151

been employed in fortifying Prospect-Hill, Winter-Hill, and other eminences near Charlestown. The former of which is a very fine station, and is full view of the enemy on Bunker-Hill, is said to be now rendered almost impregnable. The lines of Winter Hill are carrying on with great vigour and it is proposed, we are informed, to extend them to those on Prospect-Hill. Similar works are carrying on at Roxbury: Breastworks, within a short half a mile of the enemy's lines, have been thrown up nearest the main street in that town. On a very high hill, a little distant from the meeting house, is erecting a strong fortification within cannon shot of Boston. The above works have been constructed to prevent any excursions the enemy might attempt to make into the country, previous to nearer approaches that may be made for rescuing that unfortunate capital out of our hands of its present unjust tyrannical invaders.

PHILADELPHIA July 3. Extract of a letter from a gentleman in the township of Rygate on Connecticut River, to his father in New-Jersey, dated june 10 1775.

"The Indians and Canadian war is all vanished, We have had positive accounts from many of the Indian tribes, who are certainly applied to by Governor Carleton, to distress the settlements, but they say they have received no offence from the people, so will not make war with them. The French say it is a war of our own raising, and they will have no part of it."

Extract of a letter from a gentleman at Stockbridge (Massachusetts-Bay) to a gentleman of the Congress, dated June 20.

"A firm foundation now turns up to view; the Six Nations, and matters stand well with the Canadian Indians. If I had time, I would relate to you every particular of what betel the messengers of our Indians to the Six Nations, and the Canadians Indians. To be short, they were taken and bound by the regulars, and carried into Montreal, where, by a court-Martial they were condemned to be hanged, for a slight suspicion that they were sent to engage the Indians to fall on the regulars. This event turned much to our advantage, and has fully fixed the minds of the Indians there against the regulars. High threatening words passed between the General and the Indian Sachems, who were raised for and near on the occasion, and a wonderful spirit of benevolence appeared towards the young men that were taken by the Indians there. They told them, in the strongest terms. That they would take their place, they would die for them. The whole story is very effective. The Indian Sachems told the General. You have afforded us money to fight for you, but we would not take it, as we would have nothing to do with your quarrel, but now we shall know who are our enemies. If you think it best to hang these brethren, that came a great way to see us, do it, but remember we shall not forget it. Upon these threatenings, they thought it best to let the prisoners go, who got away with some difficulties. The Canadian Indians further told our Indians, That if they did fight at all, they would fight against the Regulars, for they did not ask them."

BALTIMORE July 3. Extract from the proceedings of the committee for Baltimore County, 3d July.

A Letter from Henry Lloyd, agent for the contractors for supplying the troops at Boston, to Doctor John Stevenson, being fallen into the hands of the committee, was read, and is as follows.

Sir,   Boston 17th May 1775.
The stoppage of provisions from the southern governments for the use of his Majesty's troops, makes it necessary to endeavour to get a supply by concealing from the public eye the destination of provisions shipped for that purpose. I shall therefore propose for your consideration the following method of doing it. Contract a vessel be freighted with flour for the West-Indies? Commanded by a person you can console in who will exact your orders to him, to come into the part and deliver his cargo here, instead of going to the West-Indies, you may take up a vessel as large as 200 tons and give her a full freight. I shall send you bills on the contracts to execute this place, or advise you to draught for the amount of what you may ship to me in this

way, but the negotiation of such bill might mis-
cover your plan and defeat it, so that I should
be glad you would advise me of some friend of
yours, when I am made acquainted with his name,
and the sum you shall draw for, will send to him
from hence my bills on the contractors for the
amount you advise me of: you will please likewise to give the contractors timely advice that
they may insure their interest if they think
proper, and inform me the name of the vessel and
Master you engage, that I may lodge a permit at
the light-house in the harbour, for admission
to come up to town, and discharge her cargo here.
Pray let the flour you purchase will be such as
will keep over the summer and let the casks be
good, well hooped an the heads, well secured with
lining hoops, you will be careful to write me by
a conveyance, that your letter may not fall into
the hands of the provincials.   I an Sir,
                         Your most humble Servant.
    Dr. John Stevenson,   Henry Lloyd.
    The Committee sent for Mr. Stevenson, and hav-
ing shown him the letter, he made the declaration following.
    "I believe the within letter to be Mr, Henry
Lloyd's writing, and I declare that I never received any copy of it, or any other letter to
that purport, and I further declare, that if
this letter had come to my hands, I would not
have executed the order, nor will I execute any
order of that kind from any person whatsoever,
contrary to the Resolve of the Continental Congress, or Provincial Convention.
                         John Stevenson."
    On Motion, Resolved, That Henry Lloyd of Bos-
ton, has knowingly and willfully violated the
Association of the American Congress, by endeavouring to supply the enemies of this country
with provisions; and, that agreeable to the resolution of the said Congress, it is the duty of
us and of all our constituents from hence further to have any commercial intercourse with him
and it is recommended that an inviolable regard
be paid to this resolution.
          (a copy)   William Lux, Secretary.
    Worcester July 5. At the meeting of the standing

Committee, for the County of Worcester, this 30th of June, 1775.

VOTED

That in the present critical situation of our public affairs, when the province is about assuming government, and many persons by undue methods, may be seeking offices for profit and honour: We would offer for the consideration of the respective towns in this county, whether it would not be expedient to instruct their several Members to be very vigilant, and inquire into the Characters of such as may be nominated for Councellors, and also that they pick on proper persons to recommend as respectable to fill up the respective executive and military officers, and that the substance of this vote be inserted in the Worcester Paper.

Joshua Bigelow, Chairman.

PHILADELPHIA July 5. In assembly june 30 1775.

The House taking into consideration, that many of the good people of this Province are conscientiously scrupulous of bearing arms, do hereby earnestly recommend to the association for the defence of their country, and others, that they bear a tender and brotherly regard towards this class of their fellow-subjects and countrymen, and to these conscientious people it is also recommended, that they cheerfully with in proportion to their abilities, such persons as cannots spend both time and substance in the service of their country without great injury to themselves and Families.

Resolved that the sum of Twenty Pounds be paid for every hundred weight of good merchantable salt-petre, that shall be made and manufactured in this Province, and delivered to the unded mentioned Committee, within the space of three months from this time; and that the sum of Fifty Pounds be paid for every hundred weight of good merchantable salt-petre, that shall be made and manufactured in the province and delivered to said Committee within three months next following, and so in proportion for any greater of lesser quantity.

COMMITTEE.

John Dickinson, Michael Swoope, George Gray,

William Thompson, John Montgomery, Thomas Willing, Henry Winkoop, Edward Biddle, Benjamin
Franklin, Anthony Wayne, William Edwards, Daniel
Roberdeau, Benjamin Barthoemew, Bernard Dougher-
ty, John Cadewallender, George Ross, Samuel
Hunter, Andrew Allen, Owen Biddle, Francis Johnson, Richard Reily, Samuel Morris, jun. Robert
Morris, Thomas Wharten, jun. Robert White.
            Extract from the Journal.
            Charles Moore, Clerk of Assembly.
    PHILADELPHIA July 5. Extract of a letter from
an American gentleman at Paris, dated May 2 1775.
    "I find the French are extremely attentive to
our American politics and to a man strongly in
favour of us. Whether mostly from ill will to
Britain, or friendship to the Colonies, may be
matter of doubt; but they profess it to be upon
principle of humanity, and the regard to the
natural rights of mankind. They say that the
Americans will be either revered, or detested
by all Europe, according to the conduct at the
approaching crisis; they will have no middle
character; for in proportion as their virtue and
perseverance will render them a glorious, their
tame submission will make them a despicable
people."
    CAMBRIDGE July 6. None of the men who have been
raised by this and other Colonies, are, in future, to be distinguished as the Troops of any
particular Colony, but as the forces of "The
United Colonies of North America." into whose
joint service they have been taken by Continental Congress, and are to be paid and supported
accordingly.
    The Enemy early in the morning of last Sab-
bath, in Return for some Cannon Shot they received from one of our Fortresses the Afternoon
before, began, and continued for several hours,
a heavy fire upon the Town of Roxbury both from
their Cannon and Mortars. They set one House on
Fire, which was consumed; but did little other
Damage.
    Last Monday died of the Wounds he received in
the Battle of the 17th ult. the amiable the Gallant Col. Thomas Gardner of this Place.
    The following is thought to contain a true

Account of the Loss of the Enemy including those who died of their Wounds; taken June 19, 1775.

Returned of the Killed at Charlestown the 17th June, taken from an orderly Serjeant in Boston.

Commissioned Officers 92. Serjeants 102, Corporals 100, Rank and File 753, total of killed 1047. Wounded 445. total killed and wounded 1492.

CAMBRIDGE July 6. Last Sabbath came to Town from Philadelphia, his Excellency George Washington Esq; appointed, by the Continental Congress, General and Commander in Chief of the American Forces, and was received with every Testimony of Respect due to a Gentleman of his real Worth and elevated Dignity. His Excellency was accompanied by the Hon. Charles Lee, Esq; and a Number of other Gentlemen.

The Continental Congress have also appointed Artemas Ward, Charles Lee, Philip Schuyler, and Israel Putnam, Esquires, Major-Generals, and Huratio Gates Esq; Adjutant-General of the American Army.

THe followinf Address have been presented to his Excellency George Washington and to Major General Lee.

To his Excellency George Washington Esq; General and Commander in Chief of the Continental Army.

May it please your Excellency,
The Congress of the Massachusetts Colony, impressed with every Sentiment of Gratitude and respect, beg leave to congratulate you on your safe arrival: and to wish you all imaginable Happiness and Success, in the Execution of the important duties of your elevated Station. While we applaud that Attention to the public Good, manifested to your Appointment, we equally admire that disinterested Virtue, and distinguished Patriotism, which alone could call you from the Enjoyment of domestic Life, which a sublime and manly Taste, joined with a most affluent Fortune, can afford, to hazard your Life, and to endure the Fatigues of War in the Defence of the Rights of Mankind, and the good of your Country.

The laudable Zeal for the common Cause of America, and Compassion for the Distresses of this Colony, exhibited by late great dispatches made in your journey hither, fully the universal satisfaction we have, with Pleasure, observed on this Occasion; and we are promising presages that the great Expectation formed from your personal Character, and military Abilities, are well founded.

We wish you have found such Regularity and Discipline already established in the Army, as may be agreeable to your expectations. The Hurry with which it was collected, and the many disadvantages, arising from a Suspension of Government, under which we have raised, and endeavoured to regulate the Forces of this Colony, have rendered it a Work of Time. And though in great measure effected, the Completion of so difficult, and at the same Time so necessary a Task is reserved to your Excellency; and we Doubt not will be properly considered and attended to.

We would not presume to prescribe to your Excellency, but supposing you would choose to be informed of the general Character of the Soldiers who compose this Army, beg leave to represent, that the greatest Part of them have not before seen Service. And although naturally brave, and of good understanding, yet for want of experience in military Life, have but little Knowledge of divers Things most essential to the preservation of Health, and even of Life. The Youth in the Army are not possessed of the absolute necessity of Cleanliness in their Dress, and Lodging, continual Exercise, and strict Temperance, to preserve them from Diseases frequently prevailing in Camps; especially among those, who, from their Childhood, have been used to a Laborious Life.

We beg Leave to assure you, that this Congress will, at all Times, be ready to attend to such Requisitions as you may have Occasion to make to us; and to contribute all the Aid in our power, to the Cause of America, and your Happiness and Ease, in the Discharge of the Duties of your exalted Office.

We must fervently implore Almighty God, that the Blessing of Divine Providence may rest on you: that your Head may be covered in the day

of Battle; That every necessary Assistance may
be afforded; and that you may be long continued
in Life and Health, a Blessing to Mankind.

His Excellency's Answer.

Gentlemen,

Your kind Congratulations on my Appointment,
and Arrival, demand my warmest Acknowledgement.
and will ever be retained in grateful Remembrance.

In exchanging the Enjoyments of Domestic Life
for the Duties of my present honourable, but
arduous Station, I only emulate the Virtue and
publick Spirit of the whole Province of Massachusetts-Bay, which with a Firmness, and Patriotism without Example in modern History, has
sacrificed all the comforts and social Life, in
support of the Rights of Mankind, and the Welfare
of our common Country. My highest Ambition is to
be the happy Instrument of vindicating those
Rights, and to see this devoted Province again
restored to Peace, Liberty and Safety.

The short Space of Time which elapsed since my
Arrival does not permit me to decide upon the
State of the Army. The Course of human Affairs
forbids an Expectation that Troops formed under
such Circumstances, should at once possess the
Order, Regularity and Discipline of Veterans.
Whatever discrepancies there may be, will I doubt
not, soon be made up by activity and Zeal of the
Officers, and the Docility and Obedience of the
Men. These Qualities united with their native
Bravery and Spirit will afford a happy presage
to Success, and put a final Period to those
Distresses which now overwhelm this once happy
Country.

I most sincerely thank you, Gentlemen, for
your Declaration of Readiness at all Times to
assist me in the Discharge of the Duties of my
Station: they are so complicated, and extended,
that I shall need the Assistance of every good
Man, and Lover of his Country; I therefore repose the utmost Confidence in your Aids. In return for your affectionate Whishes to myself,
permit me to say, that I earnestly implore that
Divine Being in whose Hands are all human Events,
make you and your Constituents, as Distinguished

in private and public Happiness, as you have
been by ministerial Opposition, by private and
public Distress.   George Washington.

To the Honourable Charles Lee, Esq; Major-
General of the Continental Army.

Sir,
The Congress of the Massachusetts Colony possessed of the fullest Evidence of your attachment to the Rights of Mankind, and regard to the
Distress which America in general, and this
Colony in particular, are involved in by the
impolitic, wicked and tyrannic System, adopted
by Administration, and pursued with relentless
and savage Fury, do, with pleasure, embrace this
Opportunity to express the great Satisfaction
and Gratitude they feel on your appointment as
a Major-General in the American Army.

We sincerely congratulate you on your safe Arrival here, and wish you all possible happiness
and success in the Execution of so important a
Trust. We admire and respect the Character of a
Man who, disregarding the Allurements of Profit
and Distinction on his Merit might procure, engages in the cause of Mankind, in Defence of the
Injured, and Relief of the Oppressed. From your
Character, from your great Abilities and military Experience, united with those of the Commander and Chief, under the Smiles of Providence,
we flatter ourselves with the Prospect of Discipline and Order, Success and Victory.

Be assured, Sir, that it is will give us great
Pleasure to be able to contribute to your Happiness. May Favours and Blessings of Heaven attend you. May divine Providence guard and protect
you, conduct you in the Path of Honour and Virtue, grant you the Reward of the Brave and Virtuous, the Applauses of Mankind, and the Approbation of your own Conscience, and eternal
Happiness hereafter.

His Honour's Adjutant.

To the Gentlemen of the Provincial Congress
of Massachusetts-Bay.

Gentlemen,
Nothing can be so flattering to me as the good
Opinion and Approbation of the Delegates of a
free and uncorrupt People. I was educated in the

highest Reverence for the Right of Mankind, and
have acquired by a long Acquaintance a most particular Regard for the People of America. You
may depend therefore, Gentlemen, on my Zeal and
Integrity. I can promise you nothing from any
Abilities. God Almighty grants us success equal
to the Righteousness of the Cause. I thank you,
Gentlemen for an Address which does me so much
Honour, and shall labour to deserve it.

WATERTOWN July 6. In Provincial Congress July 1.
Whereas the distressed circumstances of the
inhabitants of the town of Charlestown, calls
for the charitable aid of this colony therefore,

Resolve, That such of those inhabitants who
are unable to remove or support themselves, be
removed to the several towns in the County of
Worcester hereto annexed.

And it is further Recommended, To the Selectmen of the aforesaid towns, to provide for, and
employ said inhabitants in the best and prudent
manner that may be, and render their accounts
to this or some future Congress, or House of
Representatives; which reasonable accounts shall
be paid out of the public Treasury of said
Colony.

And it is further resolved. That the Deacon
Cheever, Capt. Brown, and Major Fuller, of New-
town be a committee to agree with teamsters not
exceeding the rate of nine pence per ton, per
mile, for transporting such inhabitants as are
unable to travel with their effects, and give
certificate to such Teamsters expressing that
they are the poor of the town of Charlestown,
and the sum he is to receive for such service;
and upon said Teamsters producing said certificate by the committee of Supplies endorsed with
the rest of the Selectmen of the towns where
such poor and their effects are lodged, that
said Teamster has done service agreed for per
said certificate. The committee of supplies are
hereby directed to draw on the receiver General
of said colony for the payment of said Teamster,
and the said Receiver General is hereby ordered
to pay the same.

A true copy from the minutes,
Attest.   Samuel Freeman, Sec'y.

Lancaster	30	Oakham	6
Mendon	30	Hutchinson	20
Brookfield	20	New Braintree	15
Oxford	15	Southborough	6
Charlton	10	Westborough	20
Sutton	30	Northborough	10
Leicester	12	Shewsbury	10
Spencer	10	Fitchburg	10
Paxton	7	Uxbridge	10
Rutland	18		

NEW-York July 6. Extract of a letter from an Officer of rank and character to a Gentleman in this City, dated Camp at Cambridge, June 27, 1775.

"The rate of the battle at Bunker's Hill is 179 killed, missing and wounded, on our our side; about 50 killed, 30 wounded and prisoners, the remainder wounded and with us, not many dangerously. On the part of the enemy, 1000 men killed on the spot and dead out of their hospitals, before last Wednesday, and 700 remaining wounded, many of the dangerously. General Gage cannot afford to purchase many trenches of us at such price.

"Last Sunday General Clinton sent from his camp at Bunker's Hill a Flag to ours on Prospect Hill, (within reach of a 24 pounder of each other) with letters from our prisoners, informing they had lost of their number, of the wounds, and that they are treated tenderly, and taken care of by army or town surgeons, or both as they choose, a means of communication on like occasion, settled between the two armies, both of which are throwing up works to secure themselves against each other.

"There have been no skirmishes on this side, since the 17th; at Roxbury there has. Last Saturday the enemy cannonaded Roxbury and endeavoured to set it on fire, but did not succeed; and yeaterday afternoon some shot were exchanged between the enemy on the neck, and our people at Roxbury. General Howe says he never saw men behave better than ours did at the breast works."

New-York July 6. From Savannah in Georgia, we hear, that the Account of the Battle of Lexington was received there on the 10th of May, and have given Business a great Shock: The Torries were much chagrined of our Success, and the Friends of Liberty were of elating for the preservations of their Rights; they had seized about 1200 Weight of Powder that was deposited in the Magazine and secured it for the common defence. A great Majority of the Inhabitants of that Province are Friends to Liberties of America. Large Quantities of English Goods are arrived there in the last Ships.

PHILADELPHIA July 6. Declarations by the Representatives of the United Colonies of North America now met in General Congress at Philadelphia, setting forth the Cause and Necessity of their taking up Arms.

If it was possible for men, who exercise their reason to believe that the Divine Author of our existence intended a part of the human race to hold an absolute in, and an unbounded power over others, marked out by his infinite goodness and wisdom, as the object of legal domination, never rightfully resistable, however severe and oppressive, the Inhabitants of these Colonies might at least require from the Parliament of Great-Britain, some evidence, that this dreadful authority over them has been granted to that body. But a reverence for our great Creator, principles of humanity, and the dictates of common sense, must convince all those who reflect upon the subject that government was instituted to promote the welfare of mankind, and ought to be administered for the attainment of that end. The legislature of Great-Britain, however stimulated by an inordinate passion for a power not only unjustifiable, but which they know to be peculiarly reprobated by the very constitution of that kingdom, and desperate of success in any mode of contest where regard should be had to truth, law, or right, have at length deserting those, attempted to effect their cruel and impolitic purpose of enslaving these Colonies by violence, and have thereby rendered it necessary for us to close with the last appeal from reason to Arms. ———— Yet however blinded the assembly may be, by their intemperate rage for unlimited domination, so to slight justice and the opinion of mankind, we esteem ourselves bound by obligation of respect to the rest of the world, to make known the justice of our cause.

Our forefathers, inhabitants of the Island of Great-Britain, left their native land, to seek on these shores a residence for civil and religious freedom. At the expence of their blood, at the hazard of their fortunes, without the least charge to the country from which they removed, by unceasing labor and unconquerable spirit, they effected settlements in the distant inhospitable wilds of America, then filled with numerous & war-like nations of barbarians. Societies of governments, nested with perfect legislatures, were formed under charters from the crown, and an harmonious intercourse was established between the colonies & the Kingdom from which they derived their origin. The Mutual benefits of this union became in a short time so extraordinary, as to excite astonishment. It is universally confessed, that the amazing of the wealth, strength and navigation of the realm, arose from this source; and the minister who so wisely and forcefully directed the measures of Great Britain in the last war, publicly declared, that these colonies enabled her to triumph over her enemies. Towards the conclusion of that war, it pleased our Sovereign to make a change in his counsels. From that fatal moment, the affairs of the British empire began to fall into confusion, and gradually sliding from the summit of glorious prosperity to which they had been advanced by the virtues and abilities of one man, are at length distracted by the convulsions, that now shake it to its deepest foundations. The new ministry sending the brave foe of Britain though frequently defeated, yet still contending, took up the unfortunate idea of granting a hasty peace, and of them subduing her faithful Friends.

These devoted colonies were judged to be in such a state, as to present victories without blood-shed, and all the easy emoluments of statuteable plunder. The uninterrupted tenor of their peaceable and respectful behaviour from the beginning of colonization, their dutiful,

Zealous, and useful service during the war, though so recently and amply acknowledged in the most honorable manner by his Majesty, by the late king, and by the Parliament, could not save them from the mediated innovation. Parliament was influenced to adopt the pernicious project, and assuming a new power over them, have in the course of eleven Years given such decisive specimens of the spirit and consequences attending this power, as to leave no doubt concerning the effects of Acquiescence under it. They have undertaken to give and grant our money without our consent, though we have ever exercised an exclusive right to dispose of our own peoperty; statures have been passed for extending the justification of courts of Admiralty and Vice-Admiralty beyond this ancient limits: for depriving us of the accustomed and inestimable privilege of a trial by jury in cases affecting both life and property, for suspending the legislature of one of the colonies; for interdicting all commerce of another; and for altering fundamentally the form of government established by charter, and secured by acts of its own legislature solemnly confirmed by the crown; for excepting the "murderers" of colonists from legal trial, and in effect, from punishment; for erecting in a neighbouring, acquired by the joint arms of Great-Britain and America a despotism dangerous to our very existence; and for quartering soldiers upon the colonists in time of profound peace. It has also been resolved in Parliament, that colonists charged with committing certain offences, shall be transported to England to be tried.

But why should we enumerate our injuries in detail? By one stature it is declared, that the Parliament can "of right make laws to bind us In All Cases Whatsoever." What is to defend us against so enormous, so unlimited a power? not a single man of those who assume it, is chosen by us; or is subject to our controul or influence: but on the contrary, they are all of them exempt from the opinion of such laws, and an American revenue, if not directed from the ostensible purpose for which it is raised, would actually lighten their own burdens in proportion, as they increase ours. We saw the misery to which such despotism would reduce us. We for ten years incessantly and ineffectually besieged the Throne as supplicants; we reasoned, we remonstrated with parliament in the most mild and decent language. But Administration sensible that we should regard these oppressive measures as freemen ought to do, sent over fleets and armies to enforce them. The indignation of the Americans was roused it is true; but it was the indignation of a virtuous loyal, and affectionate people. A Congress of Delegates from the united colonies was assembled at Philadelphia, on the fifth day of last September. We resolved again to offer on humble and dutiful petition to the King, and also addressed our fellow subjects of Great-Britain. We have pursued every temperate, every respectful measure, we have even proceeded to break off our commercial intercourse with our fellow subjects, as the last peaceable admonition, that our attachment to no nation upon earth should supplant our attachment to liberty. This, we flattered ourselves, was the ultimate step of the controversy: But subsequent events, have shewn, how vain was this hope of finding moderation in our enemies.

Several threatening expressions against the colonies were inserted in his Majesty's speech; our petition, though we were told it was a decent one, that his Majesty had been pleased to receive it graciously, and promise laying it before his Parliament, was huddled into both houses amongst a bundle of American papers, and there neglected. The Lords and Commons in the address, in the month of February said, that "a rebellion at the time actually exist within the province of Massachusetts-Bay, and that those concerned in it, had been countenanced and encouraged by unlawful combinations and engagements, entered into by his Majesty's subjects in several of the other colonies; and therefore they besought his Majesty, that he could take the most effective measures to inforce due obedience to the law and authority of the supreme legislature." Soon after all the commercial

intercourse on whole colonies, with foreign
countries and each other was cut off by an act
of Parliament: by another, several of them in
the seas near their coasts, on which always depended for their sustenance; and large reinforcement of ships and troops were immediately
sent over to General Gage.

Fruitless were all the entreaties, arguments
and eloquence of an illustrious band of the most
distinguished Peers and Commoners, who nobly and
strenuously supported the justice of our cause,
to stay or even to mitigate the heedless fury
with which these accumulated and unexampled outrages were hurried on. Equally fruitless was the
interference of the City of London, of Bristol,
and many other respectable towns in our favour.
Parliament adopted an insidious manoeuvre calculated to divide us, to establish a perpetual
auction of taxations where colony should bid
against colony, all of them uninformed what ransom would redeem their lives, and thus to extort
from us at the point of the bayonet, the unknown
sum that should be sufficient to gratify, if
possible, to gratify, ministerial rapacity, with
the miserable indulgence lost to us of raising
in our own mode the prescribe tribute. What
terms more rigid and humiliating could have been
dictated by remorseless victor to conquered
enemies? In our circumstances to except them
would be to deserve them.

Soon after the intelligence of those proceedings arrived on the continent General Gage who
in the course of the last year, had taken possession of the town of Boston, in the province
of Massachusetts-Bay, and still occupied it as
a garrison, on the 19th day of April, set out
from that place a large detachment of his army,
who made an unprovoked assault on the inhabitants of the said province at the town of Lexington, as appears by the affidavits of a great
number of persons, some of whom were officers
and soldiers of that detachment, murdered eight
of the inhabitants, and wounded many of them.
From thence the troops proceeded in war-like
array to the town of Concord, where they set
upon another party of the inhabitants of the

Same province, killed several and wounding more, until compelled to retreat by the country people suddenly assembled to repel this cruel aggression. Hostilities thus commenced by the British troops, have been since prosecuted by them without regard to faith or reputation. The Inhabitants of Boston being confined within that town by the general their Governor, and having in order to procure this dismission, entered into a treaty with him, it was stipulated that the said inhabitants having deposited their arms with their own magistrates, should have liberty to depart, taking with them their other effects. They accordingly delivered up their arms, but in open violation of honor, in defiance of the obligation of Treaties, which even savage nations esteem sacred, the Governor ordered the arms deposited as aforesaid, that they might be preserved for their owners to be seized by a body of soldiers; detained the greatest part of the inhabitants in the town, and compelled the few who were permitted to retire, to leave their effects behind.

By this peridy wives were separated from their husbands, children from their parents, the aged and the sick from their relations and friends, who wish to attend and comfort them; and those who have been used to live in plenty, and even elegance, were reduced to deplorable distress.

The General further emulating his ministerial masters, by a proclamation bering the date on the 12th of June after venting the grossest falsehoods and colimnies against the good people of these colonies, proceeds to "declare them all either by name or description to be rebels and traitors, to supersede the course of the common law, and instead therefore to publish and order the use and exercise of law Martial." His troops have butchered our countrymen, have wantonly burnt Charles-Town, besides a considerable number of houses in other places; our ships and vessels are seized; the necessary supplies of provisions are interrupted, and he is exerting his utmost power to spread destruction and devastation around him.

We have received certain intelligence, that

General Carleton, the Governor of Canada, is in-
stigating the people of that province and the
Indians, to fall upon us; and we have but too
much reason to apprehend that schemes have been
formed to excite domestic enemies against us.
In brief a part of the colonies now feels, and
all of them are sure of feeling, as far as the
vengeance of administration can inflict them,
the complicated calamities of fire, sword and
famine. We are reduced to the alternative of
chusing an unconditional submission to the tyranny of irritated ministers, or resistance by
force. The latter is our choice. We have counted
the cost of the contest, and find nothing so
dreadful as voluntary slavery. Honor, justice
and humanity forbid us tamely to surrender that
freedom which we received from our gallant ancestors, and which our innocent posterity have
a right to receive from us. We cannot endure the
infamy and guilt of resigning succeeding generations to the wretchedness which inevitably
await them, if we basely entail hereditary bond-
age upon them.

Our cause is just. Our union is perfect. Our
internal resources are great, and if necessary,
foreign assistance is undoubtedly attainable.

We gratefully acknowledge, as signal instances
of the Divine savior towards us, that his Providence would not permit us to be called into
this severe controversy, until we were grown up
to our present strength, had been previously
exercised in war-like operations, & possessed
of the means of defending ourselves. With hearts
fortified with these animating reflections, we
most solemnly, before God and the world declare,
that, exerting the most energy of those powers,
which our beneficent Creator hath generously
bestowed upon us, the army we have been compelled by our enemies to assume, we will, in
defiance of every hazard, with unabating firmness and perseverance, employ for the preservation of our liberties, being with one mind resolved to dye Free-men rather than live slaves.

Lest this declaration should disquiet the
minds of our friends and fellow subjects in any
part of the empire, we assure them that we mean

not to dissolve that Union which has so long and
so happily subsisted between us, and which we
sincerely wish to see restored. Necessity has
not yet driven us into the desperate measure,
or induced us to excite any other nation to war
against them. We have not raised armies with
ambitious designs of separating from Great-
Britain, and establishing independent states.
We fight not for glory or conquest. We exhibit
to mankind the remarkable spectacle of a people
attacked by unprovoked enemies, without any imputation, or even suspicion, of offence.

They boast of their privileges and civiliza-
tion, and yet proffer no milder condition than
servitude or death.

In our own native land, in defence of the freedom that is our birthright, and which we ever
enjoyed till the late violation of it ―――― for
the protection of our property, acquired solely
by the honest industry of our fore-fathers and
ourselves, against violence actually offered,
we have taken up arms. We shall lay them down
when hostilities shall cease to the part of the
aggressors, and all danger of their being renewed shall be removed, and not before.

With a humble confidence in the mercies of the
supreme and impartial Judge and Ruler of the
universe, we most devoutly implore his divine
goodness to conduct us happily through this great
conflict, to dispose our adversaries to reconciliation on reasonable terms, and thereby to
relieve the empire from the calamities of civil
war.

by Order of Congress,
John Hancock, President,
Attested   Charles Thonpson, Sec'y,
Philadelphia, July 6, 1775.

Cambridge July 10. Instructions for the officers of the several Regiments of the Massachusetts-Bay Forces, who are immediately to go upon
the recruiting Service.

You are not to enlist any deserters from the
Ministerial Army, nor any Stroller, Negro, or
Vagabond, or persons suspected of being an Ene-
my to the Liberty of America, not any under 18
Years of age.

As the cause is the best that can engage Men of Courage and principle to take up Arms; so it is expected that none but such will be accepted by the Recruiting Officers: The Pay, Provisions, &c. being ample, it is not doubted but the Officers sent upon this service, will without Delay compleat the respective Corps, and march the Men fortwith to Camp.

You are not to enlist any Person who is not an American-born, unless such person has a Wife and Family, and is a settled Resident in this Country.

The Persons you enlist, must be provided with good and compleat Arms.

Given at the Head Quarters at Cambridge, this 10th day of July 1775.

Horatio Gates Adjutant General.

WATERTOWN July 10. In Provincial Congress met at Watertown July 7, 1775.

Whereas complaints has been made to this Congress, of the inhabitants of some of the far part towns frequently supplying our enemies with butter and cheese, fresh provisions, &c. Also, suspecting intelligence had bee given them.

Therefore Resolved, That it be, and it is hereby recommended to the committee of safety, correspondence, and inspection, and where there are no such committee, to the select-men of the sea port town and districts in this colony, that they forthwith exert themselves to prevent any person or persons from supplying our enemies with any kind of provisions whatsoever, or Intelligence, And it is further recommended to the committees or select-men of aforesaid, of each town not to suffer any vessel, or vessels of any size whatsoever, in the service of our enemies, without first obtaining a permit in writing of the committee, or select-men aforementioned, for that purpose; and that no boats be suffered to land from men of war, traders, or any other vessels, employed to distress the sea coasts and trade of this country, without permit obtained as aforesaid.

By Order of Congress,

Attest,   James Warren, President.

A true Copy.   Samuel Freeman, Sec'ry.

WATERTOWN July 10. Deserted from Capt. Sander's Company, of Col. Serjeant's Regiment, John Gardner, and Archibald Smith. —— if they will return within ten Days from this Date, they will be received; if not 3 Dollars will be paid for each, upon their delivery to Capt. Sanders, at Cambridge.

NEWPORT July 10. Wednesday morning the Kingfisher sloop of war, Capt. Montague, was towed into this harbour, and immediately after coming to anchor, she was thrown upon a very rank temper, by which 'twas supposed she had met with some misfortune the night before, and this was seen up the sound, and many cannon were heard in the night; and we are assured a certain Doctor in this town, went on board said ship sevral times from her arrival till Friday to take care of some of the wounded men.

HARTFORD July 10. (Connecticut Courant)

Mr. Watson,

Please to give the following a place in your News.

To Thomas Gage, Governor and Commander in Chief, of all the Dogs of War, and Sons of Tyranny, in the Province of Massachusetts-Bay, under Commission of the Prince of Darkness, to trample upon the most feared Rights of Mankind: and Vice-Admiral of the same.

As you are an inveterate, and perhaps incorrigible enemy of all good beings, and as such an object of universal hatred, I think it suitable to address you in the language of contempt: and to that purpose shall retort upon you the words of part of our unanimous Proclamation, in a direct opposite sense, which will at the same time, most effectually serve as a mirrour, to exhibit to you and the world, an image, as large as life, of him whose characteristic features are. He was a murderer from the beginning, and abode not in the truth.

Whereas our unhappy King, who has long suffered himself to be conducted by certain well known incendiaries and traitors in a fatal progression of crimes, against the constitutional authority of the state, has at length proceeded to brutal force, against the American colonies;

172

and the good effects which were hoped; and even
expected to a rise from the justice of the King's
government, have been often frustrated, and are
now rendered hopeless, by the influence of the
same evil counsels; it only remains for the people, from whom (under God) originated all civil
power, as well for the punishment of the guilty,
as for the protection of the rights, to prove
they do not bear the sword in vain.

The infringement which have been made upon the
most sacred rights of the people of Great-Britain
and the colonies, it was needless to repeat on
the one side, and are all atrocious to be palliated on witnesses of the late transaction,
towards the Massachusetts-Bay and the neighbouring colonies, will find upon a transient review,
marks of premeditation and papal jacobite con-
piracy, that have merited the full vials of the
wrath of God; and even those who are least acquainted with the facts, cannot fail to receive
a just impression of their enormity, in proportion as they discover the art and assiduity by
which they have been coloured or concealed.

The authors of the present bloody measures,
never daring to trust their cause of their actions to the judgement of an impartial public.
(unless a bribed parliament may be so called)
or even the dispassionate of their own followers,
have uniformly placed their chief confidence in
the suppression of truth and evidence: and while
indefatigable and shameless pains have been tak-
en to obstruct every appeal to the real interest
to the people of America; the greatest forgeries, calumnies, and absurdities, that ever insulted human understanding, have been imposed
upon credulity of the public: and this because
they have repeatedly been beaten out of the field
of argument.

The press, that distinguished appendage of
public liberty, and when fairly and impartially
employed its best support, has by some villians,
brought by administration, been prostituted to
the most contrary purposes. Language, which was
originally designed to vindicate the just rights
and interests of mankind, has been applied to
countenance the most abandoned violation of

those sacred blessings. And not only from the
lying Gazette, but from the harangues and intrigues of some hign flying Jacobite priests,
many have been taught to betray the interests
of British empire, for the security of their
private persons, and augmentation of their properties. But as for possible to compensate for
this horrid profanation of terms and of Ideas,
the generality of the clergy (to their honor be
it spoken) have introduced, explained, and un-
answerably vindicated principles originating
from benevolence and the public good, upon which
our excellent constitution founded in the direct
opposition to devastation and massacre.

The minds of men having this been prepared for
the greatest extremities, on the 19th of April
last, a detachment of upwards of 1000 of the
King's troops, upon excursion into the country,
for the express and acknowledged purpose of
plunder, with a wontonnest of cruelty ever incident to the troops of a tyrant, having fired
upon a number of innocent to the troops of a
Tyrant, having fired upon a number of innocent
and innofensive person at Lexington, who were
assembled for the simple purpose of guarding
their country's rights, and killed several of
them —— were soon after victiriously and bravely attacked by about 300 of the provincials,
and not expecting so consummate an act of hero-
ism from those whom they had ever been taught
to look upon as cowards, we so desconcerted as
to be unable to resist their vengeance, and with
the utmpst precipitation retreated within their
walls and lurking holes, as only recourse left
to save themselves from the just indignation of
their incensed persuers.

Since that perion, the Americans actuated by
the inherent law of self preservation, and animated by every consideration that can warm the
generous breast, have posted themselves in sufficient numbers near the town of Boston, and in
such manner as effectually to prevent all depredations of the like nature in future; and they
are not only to be justified in their attempts
to distress the King's troops, particularly in
their several attacks, upon them, which, under

the direction of heaven, have generally been attended with surprising success: but could they exterpate you and your banditti of murders from the face of the earth, their names must be celebrated with distinguishing marks of honor in the annals of fame.

The actions of the 19th of April are of such notoriety as must baffle all your milicious attenpts to contredict them, and the flames of buildings, and other property, discovered from the island and adjecent country, are but a very inadiquate retaliation, for the conflagaration inkindled by the troops at Lexington.

This being the true state of facts, it is as evident as the sun, that thus far, your proclamation is a series of misrepresentations and falsehoods; the rest is replete with the most consumate impudence. With what face can you, the greatest rebel in America, and as eager for the blood as a canabal, talk of sparing the effusion of blood? What impudence, for you who have forfeited your life into the hands of every good man in the kingdom, to assume to yourself airs of importance, in offering pardon, upon certain conditions, to those who are contending for the constitution of their country? let me tell you we scorn your pardon, we are not yet brought to humiliating a condition, as to feel willing to accept a pardon, for imputed crimes, from the hands of a ruffian. Would not such a proffer as this, have come from you with a better grace, were our lives and fortunes under your absolute comtrol? what conquest have you gained? What lawrels have you won? It is true you have got possession of the town of Boston, and have fortified it for yourself, but how did you obtain it? Did you do it by feats of arms? No, that you never could have done, you did it by the same arts of dissimulation and lying, by which the arch deceiver of mankind got possession of paradise. Are we not therefore warranted to say. You and your father devil, and the lusts of your father you will do? But what if paradise is lost, are you certain it will never be regained? Be you sure that the strong man armed will not be ousted of his possession by him that is stronger than he? But you have laid Charlestown in Ashes? yes, and without the least real advantage to yourself, and to the great detrement of the nation; for which your name will be branded with indelible marks of infemy, so long as America has a being: and for what? why for the satisfaction, that a mind devoid of all benevelence can take in desolating the earth. There is no doubt when you saw the smoke and flames of that beautiful and apulent town ascending to the clouds, you looked on with the satisfaction of a devil, and grinned bearily a ghastly smile. But you have forced our lines; true, with 5000 regular troops, and with the loss of near one fifth killed and wounded, you have got possession of a half compleated intrenchment, defended only by 1500 Americans, and with an inconsiderate loss on their side. It is thus you bring America to an uncostitutional subjection at the feet of Lord North, such is the rapid progress you make with formidable fleets and armies, towaeds enforcing obedience to acts of parliament, throughout this extensive continent; but before you have finished your rout from one end of the continent to the other, far other vengeance expect to feel from America's vindictive hand, though urged on by Britain's King and all the boasted omnipotence of parliament. What remains therefore, is for you to relingquish your pretensions to the heaven-defended America, no longer to contaminate her pure air with the noxious breath of a Tyrant, but leave her to grow up under the divine smiles and benidiction, to a widely extended empire for glory and for beauty the envy and admiration of the whole earth.

Connecticutensis.

HARTFORD July 10. Friday last the General Assembly of this colony ended the business of the special session of this place. They have ordered two more regiments to be immediately raised in the colony to consist of 700 men each, exclusive of officers, who are to join the force of the United Colonies of North America, in defence of our common and violated rights.

PHILADELPHIA July 10. By advice from Montreal, of June 2d, we are informed, that about 25 sail of vessels had arrived at Quebec from England, with dry goods (chiefly Indian commodities, with a great quantity of gun powder) that one transport from Boston had also arrived at Quebec to get forage for the light horse, and was expected to sail again for Boston about the first inst.

Philadelphia July 10. We are informed that the people called the Quakers, at a meeting in this city a few days since have agreed to recommend it to their brethren, in their several meetings in this province and New-Jersey, to promote subcreptions to raise money for the relief necessitous of all religions or denomonations, who are reduced to losses and distress in this time of public calamity, to be distributed among them by a committee of their brethren in New-England and a comittee for the same purpose here.

Extract from a letter from North Carolina, dated June 7, 1775.

"We are much alarmed with the intentions of Administration, and unless affairs take a turn in our favour very shortly, we shall expect the worst efforts of its villainy ―― thay of spiriting up an enemy among ourselves, from whose barbarity is roused, the most dreadful consequences will follow. Our Governor has sent his family to New-York and being greatly disgusted with the people of Newbern, has taken up his residence in Fort Johnson, at the mouth of Cape Fear river, where he has chosen this as a place of retreat from popular complaints: Our brethren in the colonies may be assured that we never shall be bribed by the benefit of an excessive trade to desert the common cause."

NEW-Haven July 12. Last Saturday afternoon, a cruize sloop of war, said to be the Lively, having chaced and fired several shot at an inward bound vessel, belonging to connecticut river, she was boarded by two armed boats, from the man of war, (having run aground on Say-Brook-Bar) who after a short examination, left her. The report of the guns having alarmed the inhabitants, a number of them assembled on the shore armed, and exchanged done random shot with the boats.

PHILADELPHIA July 12. Extract of a letter from Salem, June 24, 1775.

"Long before this reaches you, you will have an account of the action on the 17th. The destruction of Charlestown is a most melancholy affair, and three quarters of the inhabitants have lost their all; for although many of the people had removed their effects, yet there was considerable of value in the town; likewise a great quantity of goods belonging to the people of Boston, which had been brought out and were waiting for an opportunity of being transported into the country.

"Since the martial law has taken place in Boston, the people dare not open their mouths, poor Shrimpton Hunt, your late neighbour, only saying on Saturday, that he hoped our people would get the better, is taken up and confine, its said, in gaol.

"July 1. A person from Boston says, James Lovel is confined in the dungeon of the gaol, for nobody knows what. ——— The inhabitants have no wood. An account has been taken of those that are still in Boston, which amount to 5000. ——— There is a military watch kept by the friends of government. Martin Gay is one of the Captains."

PHILADELPHIA July 12. Extract of a letter from Charles-Town, South-Carolina, June 27, 1775.

"We enclose you extracts of letters from Georgia and Augusta, by which you may judge on our present state, relative to Indian affairs. It seems General Gage has corresponded with the superintendent here on that subject, and he with his deputy in the Cherokee nation. Mr. Stuart finding the matter suspected, left Charlestown, and went to Georgia about the time of the setting of the Congress. Matters taking a turn in Georgia, he found himself obliged to produce his letters, since which he escaped to Florida, and thereby confirmed the suspicion of the intended Indian war. The other extract shews you the present state of the Indian nation."

Extract of a letter from John Wilson, of Augusta, to Misrs. Cambell and Son, dated June 15.

"All the Cherokee traders are come down but two, and have the pleasure to inform you, that they have overpaid their fall cargoes. There is at present but very little indifferent talk with

178

in that nation. They have lately killed two Virginians that had gone up there express, which, I am afraid, will be the cause of a war. Should that be the case, I shall be badly off, having little powder in the fort. I am informed, that one of our traders was stopped by the Indians, in order to bring a Talk down."

Extract of a letter from John Stuart to Mr. Cameron.

"I have received information from General Gage, that certain persons at the northward have been tampering with the Six Nations, and endeavouring to alienate their affections from his Majesty. I mention this to caution you, and that you will use your influence to dispose those people to act in defence of his Majesty and government, if found necessary."

Mr. Cameren's Answer.

"That Mr. Stuart's interest with the Indians was much better, and that he was more beloved by them than any other man; and that he (cameron) had the vanity to think, that he could head any number he thought proper, whenever called upon in support of his Majesty and government;"

"Cameron is Stuart's principal Deputy."

PHILADELPHIA July 12. Extract of a letter from Cambridge, dated Monday July 3, 1775.

"The greatest civility and attention was paid to the Generals on their arrival at the Camp, which was on Sunday about noon. When they were within 20 miles of the Camp, they received an Express that the Parliamentary troops had on Saturday morning about six o'clock begun a very heavy cannonading on the town of Roxbury, when continued better than two hours, without intermission, though with little or no loss, on the side of the Provincials, and that they expected a general attack on Sunday about two o'clock, at the time of high water, this we have confirmed, and I believe was prevented by a heavy rain, which began at half past twelve, and continued till late at night. The Generals have spent this whole day, in reviewing the troops, lines, fortifications, &c. they find the troops to be in good order as could be expected; the regulars have been sounding the shore all this afternoon, and we are in some sort of expectation of a visit at the next high water. Our men are all in good spirits, and wish they may come out; the best account we can get of the late engagement is, that the regulars lost more than 300 in the field, and 700 wounded.

"Among the slain are Colonel Williams, Major Pitcairn and Major Sheriff, it remains a matter of doubt whether or not General Burgoyne in among the dead.

"This we are certain of, General Howe commanded the first division of 1700, and General Burgoyne the second of 1300, and since the battle he has not been seen in Boston "tis given out that he has gone to England; the Provincials had not more than 700 in the action: the Welsh Fuzileers, the best regiment in the English army, carried from the field no more than 17 privates and one Captain; it is also certain Gage lost 84 officers.

Tuesday morning, 6 o'clock. Four horses of Preston's regiment fell into the hands of our centries this morning, which was owing to the regulars calling in all their centries, as they expected a general attack from the provincials, which, we suppose, was owing to our viewing all their lines yesterday evening; we went so near as to make them apprehensive we were reconnoitering, in order to find some place fit to begin an attack. The loss of the Provincials, as by the return made to General Washington this morning, is 138 killed, 301 wounded, and 7 missing."

Norfolk (Virginia) July 12. On Monday arrived in the road the Mercury man of war, of 24 guns, full of men, to relieve the Fowey, which is sailed for Halifax to heave down and refit.

We just now hear of the arrival of the Boston man of war in the road & that the Magdelin armed schooner had put back in distress; so that we have now 4 men of war, an armed schooner for our "Protection and defence!" In consequence of which it is said, 2000 man are to be raised and stationed at Williamsburg and York.

CAMBRIDGE July 13. Printed by Samuel and Ebenezer Hall, at their Office in Stoughton-Hall, Harvard-College. (New-England Chronicle)

In Provincial Congress, Watertown, July 3,
This Congress having taken into consideration
the Difficulties and Troubles which have, and
daily are arising in our Camps by Reasons of divers evil minded Persons selling of spirituous
Liquors, by which Means it is not in the power
of the Officers, although a constant Exertion
has been hetherto made, to prevent the same, is
ordered to keep that steady Government in Camp
so absolutely necessary: Therefore,

Resolve, That if any licenced Person shall
after the 13th Instant presume to sell any spirituous Liquors to any Soldier, without a permit
from the Captain or Commanding Officer of the
Company he belongs to, specifying the Quantity,
shall for the first offence forfeit his Licence;
and for the second, suffer such punishment as
shall be inflicted on him, or her, by a court-
Martial: And any Person who is not a licenced
person, or whose Licence is without the Limits
of said Camps, shall presume to retail any spirituous Liquors to any of the Troops, shall suf-
fur for the first Offence the penalties inflicted
by the Court-Martial. This Resolve not to extend
to any Person who shall have a Licence or Permit
from the General or Commanding Officer.

By Order of Congress,
A true Copy,   James Warren, President.
Attst. Samuel Freeman, Secretary.

CAMBRIDGE July 13. Wednesday se'nnight a Trum-
perter came from the Enemy's Army, with a letter
from General Burgoyne to General Lee, and was
conducted, blindfolded, by our Guards, to Head
Quarters in the town. After delivering the Letter he was permitted to return. The contents of
this Letter has occasioned much Speculation,
and variously reported, but we hear the Substance of it is nothing mere than this: That
General Burgoyne laments his being obliged to
act in opposition to a Gentleman, for whom he
formerly entertained a great Veneration; but
that his Conduct proceeds from the Principle,
and doubt not General Lee is actuated by the
same Motives, that he wishes Affairs might be
accommodated, and desires to have a Conference
with General Lee. We are informed General Lee

181

has returned an answer, in which he declined complying with General Burgoyne's Desire of holding the proposed Conference.

Governor Wentworth, a Native of New-Hampshire has rendered himself so justly obnozious to his Countrymen, by promoting the arbitrary Measures of the British King and Ministry, that he has thought it prudent to repair on board a Man of War for protection.

Since last arrived here from Philadelphia, John Sullivan, Esq; appointed by the Hon. Continental Congress, a Brigadier General of the American Army.

NEW-YORK July 13. The people of Virginia and from other American colonies, continue to be much embarrassed between their respect to the ancient forms of government, and officers which according to those forms were appointed to the administration of public affairs; and their regard to their own freedom, and most important rights and privileges of human nature, which it has long been the avowed business of those forms, and officers to take away and abolish. Instead of trying and punishing those officers, as traitors against the conditions, the most horrid of all traitors, the respect shewn them, and the attempts made to reconcile natural inconsistencies, are truly ridiculous, at the same time that they obstruct and have the most pernicious effect on public affairs.

Lord Dunsmore still continues to injure and insult the people of Virginia, with impunity.

NEW-YORK July 13. Wednesday our Provincial Congress being informed by a number of Freeholders of the City, that our Corporation had prepar'd and intended to present an address to Governor Tryon, congratulating him on his return to his Government, the Congress unanimously voted, that they disapproved the same, and ordered that the Secretary serve a Copy of the above vote on the Mayor, with which was done accordingly.

WILLIAMSBURG July 13. General Lee has lately wrote to the Right Hon. Lord Viscount Barrington Secretary of War, expressly declaring that he would no longer receive his half pay dated from the 22d ult. This great man, at the same time, assured his Lordship, that whenever it shall please his Majesty to call him forth to any honourable service against the natural hereditary enemies of his country, or defence of his just rights and dignity, no subject will obey the righteous summons with more alacrity than himself.

July 15. Arrived in this city several companies of volunteers from the counties of Spotsylvania, King George, Albamarle, James City, Surry, Louise, and Stanford. A party of troops were marched from hence last Tuesday, are now encamped near Yorktown.

WILLIAMSBURG July 14. We have not been able to learn where, Lord Dunmore intends fixing his residence; some say at Portsmouth, but we only mention it as a report.

All his Lordship's domestics have now left the Palace, and are gone, bag and baggage, to his farm at Porto Bello, about six miles from town.

Extract of a letter from General Washington, dated the 20th of June, at Philadelphia, to the Independent Companies of fairfax, Prince william, Fauquier, Spotsylvania, and Richmond.

"Gentlemen,

"I am now about to bid adieu to the companies under your respective commands, at least for a while. I have launched into a wide and extensive field, too boundless for my abilities, as far, very far, beyond my experience. I am called, by the unanimous voice of the colonies to the command of the continental army; an honour I did not aspire to, an honour I was solicitous to avoid, upon a full conviction of my inadequacy to the importance of the service. The partiality of the Congress, however, assisted by a political motive, rendered my reasons unavailing. And I shall, tomorrow, set out for the camp near Boston. I have only to beg you, therefore, before I go (especially as you did me the honour to put your companies under my direction, and know not how soon) you may be called upon in Virginia for an exertion of your military skill) by no means to relax in the discipline of your respective companies."

NEW-LONDON July 14. Last-Lord's Day afternoon a Barge was sent with two swivel and a number of small Arms from the King Fisher man of war, (which was laying in the Sound off the Mouth of the Connecticut River) in chase of a Schooner belonging to Rocky-Hill, who was bound into the River; the Schooner grounding on Say-Brook Bar, she was boarded by the People from the Barge, who attempted to get her afloat, but seeing they could not, left her. On sight of the Barge, Numbers of arm'd People immediately collected on the Points each side of the River, when a number of shots were exchanged on both sides. Our People received no damage, what damage was done to the People on the Barge we don't know, but upon receiving our Fire they immediately rowed in great haste further from shore.

CHARLESTOWN S. Carolina July 14. We have certain accounts that the inhabitants of Georgia now adopted the association of the Continental Congress, and have entered heartily into the American Confederacy for maintaining their just rights. John Houston, Archibald Bulloth, Lyman Hall, Noble Wimberly Jones, Esquires, and the Rev. Dr. Zably, are elected Delegates to represent the colony in the Congress now sitting at Philadelphia; and those gentlemen were to proceed for that city immediately.

WATERTOWN July 17. List of the Enemy killed and wounded at the Battle of Charlestown.

WOUNDED

4th Regiment. Captains Balfour and West. Lieutenants Batton and Brown.

5th Reg. Major Machell, Captain Jackson, and Mariden. Lieutenants Croker and M'Clintock, Ensigns Charlwton and Balequire.

10th Reg. Captains Fitzgerald and Parsons, Lieutenants Pettigrew, Hamilton and Vernon.

14th Reg. Ensign Hasket.

18th Rwg. Lieutenant Righardson.

23d Reg. Capt. Blakeesey, Lieuts, Cochran, Rechwich and Leuthall.

35th Reg. Capt. Drew. Lieuts. Campbell and Sweney, Quarter-Master Mitchell, Ensign Sergent.

43d Reg. Major Spendlove, Lieuts Roberson and Dalrimple.

47th Reg. Malor Smelt. Capts. England, Craig,
and Alcock. Lieut. England.
52d Reg. Capts. Nelson, thompson & Crawford,
Ensigns Chalwund and Grame.
59th Reg. Lieut. Haynes.
63d Reg. Capts. Horsford and Fuller.
65th Reg. Capt. Sinclair, Lieuts. Paxton,
Smith and Hales.
Marines. Capts Lemoige, Hudlasten, Logan,
chandleigh and Johnson. Lieuts. Plicairn, Shutworth, Cambell, Brishain, Arverot, Ray and Dyer,
Engineer Page, Lieut Jardin, Secretary of Gen.
Howe.

KILLED

5th Reg. Capt. Downes.
14th Reg. Lieut. Btuere.
22d Reg. Lieut. Col. Abecrombie.
35th Reg. Capt. Lyon. Lieut Bard.
38th Reg. Lieut. Dutton.
43d Reg. Capt. M'Kennie.
47th Reg. Lieuts. Gould, Willard & Hyllyer.
52d Reg. Major Williams, Captains Addison,
Davison, Smith and Higgins.
63d Reg. Lieut. Dalrymple.
65th Reg. Capt. Hudson.
67th Ewg. Capt. Sharyst, Aid da Camp to Gen.
Howe.
Marines Major Pitecairn, Capts, Campbell and
Elils, Lieuts. Finney, Gardner & Shea.
Major Spendlove, lieuts, Verner and Jardin,
Secretaries to Gen. Howe with many others, we
hear have already died of their Wounds: ————
and a great part of those who are still alive,
are mortally wounded.
We have undoubted Intelligence that General
Gage's Troops are much dispirited: that they are
very sickly, and was heartily disposed to have
off dancing any more to the tune Yankee Doodle.
We have Intelligence from Boston, that the
Enemy are much pleased with the thought of hav-
ing killed many of our Men when we drove them
within their lines, & burst the Guard House.
Major General Lee has appointed William Palfrey
Esq; late of Boston, to be one of the Aides de
Camp.
Last Saturday se'nnight, before Day light, a

185

Party of our men marched towards the Enemy's
advanced Guard on Boston Neck, drove them within
their Lines, burnt the Guard House (formerly
the Dwelling House of Mr. Brown) with several
contiguous Buildings, took two Guns, a Halbert,
and a Drum. Not one of our men was either killed
or wounded, notwithstanding a heavy Fire from
the Enemy's Lines, which were within a quarter
of a mile of the Buildings we set on Fire. It
is thought several of the Enemy were killed and
wounded.

Last Tuesday Night a Party of Men was sent
from Roxbury Camp to Long-Island, in Boston Harbour, from whence they brought off 15 of the
Enemy Prisoners, between 20 and 30 horned Cattle,
and about 100 Sheep. The Prisoners were brought
to Head Quarters on Wednesday, and soon after
sent to Concord.

HARTFORD July 17. Yesterday an express passed
through this town from Crown-Point, with dispatches of importance to his Honour Governor
Trumbull at Lebanon. The Express Left Crown-Point
last Thursday.

We hear the camp distemper rages in the regular army in Boston, as also among the distressed
inhabitants who are confined in that town by order of Tom. Gage; in open violation of his most
solemn engagement. It is to be hoped he will
meet the same Pharaods of old, whose example be
so exactly follows.

We hear Gen. Gage has requested of our army
to send necessaries for the poor distressed poor,
occasioned in Boston.

PHILADELPHIA July 17. Whereas I have spoken
disrespectfully of the General Congress, as well
as those Military Gentlemen who have associated
for the defence of Liberty of America: —— I now
take this opportunity of declaiming that my conduct proceeded from the most contracted notions
of the British constitution, and of the right of
human nature. I am sorry for my guilt, and also
my folly. I now believe all assemblies to be
legal and constitutional, which are formed by
the united sufferance of a free people; and am
convinced, that no soldiers are so respectable,
as those Citizens who take up arms in defence

of Liberty. I believe, that Kings are no longer to be feared or obeyed, then while they execute just laws; and that a corrupt British Ministry, with a venal Parliament at their heels, are attempting to reduce the American Colonies to the lowest degree of slavery. I must sincerely wish that the councils of Congress may always be directed with wisdom, and that the arms of America may always be crowned with success. And I pray, that every man in America, who behaves as I have formerly done, may be obliged to expiate his crime in a more ignominious manner.

Philadelphia July 27.   Mordecai Levy.

WORCESTER July 19. The Committee of Safety, dated 13th July 1775.

Whereas some evil minded persons, taking advantage of the confusions occasioned by the battle of Lexington and Charlestown, have plundered and carried off into several parts of this and the neighbouring colonies, sundry goods and household furniture, belonging to some of the unhappy sufferers of Boston and Charlestown:

Therefore, Resolved, That the Selectmen and Committee of Correspondence in the several towns and districts within this colony; and also the town officers in the neighbouring colonies, be, and they hereby are, severally and earnestly requested to inspect their several towns and districts, and if they shall discover any such goods, or household furniture, such officers are desired to send all such effects to the office of Mr. Pearse Palmer, Quarter-Master General in Cambridge, for the benefit of the true and rightful proprietor.

William Cooper, Sec'ry.

By the Honourable Nicholas Cooke, Esq; Deputy-Governor and Lieutenant Governor of and over the English colony of Rhode-Island and Providence Plantation in New-England in America.

A PROCLAMATION.

Whereas the General Assembly of the colony aforesaid, at their session held at Providence on Wednesday the 28th of June last, taking into consideration the present alarming situation of the colonies, and the necessities of putting this colony into a posture of defence, passed an act requesting me to issue this proclamation, hereby commanding every man in the colony, able to bear arms, immediately to equip himself with arms and ammunition according to the law upon the penalty of the law in such cases provided.

Given under my hand, and the seal of the colony, Providence, the twelth day of July, in the year of our Lord one thousand seven hundred and seventy-five, and fifteenth of the reign of his Majesty George the third, by the grace of God, King of Great-Britain, &c.

Nicholas Cooke.

By his honours's Command,
Henry Ward, , Sec'ry.

God save the King.

PHILADELPHIA July 19. Extract of a letter from Charlestown South-Carolina, June 20, 1775.

"Our place has more the appearance of a garrison town than a mart of trade; one company keeps guard all day, and two every night, in our situation we cannot be too watchful and may require much strength, for our Negroes have all a high notion of their liberty, and we lately learn by intercepted letters and other ways, that there has been endeavoured to set the Indians on us. Mr. Stuart, the Superintendent of Indian affairs, is accused of being the person who has forwarded this wicked design, and he is fled for safety.

"The torries in Georgia are now no more, the province is almost universally on the right side, and are about to choose delegates to send to the Congress."

PHILADELPHIA July 19. Extract of a letter from the Camp at Cambridge, July 8, 1775.

"Yesterday our troops set fire to the ministerial troop's guard house on the Neck, which they affected in the following manner: The night before, a number of our brave troops brought down two field pieces from Roxbury to the Neck; a few concealed themselves in the grass, not far from the house, which combustibles ready, whenever the signal was given, to execute their part, (which was on firing the field pieces) A little before day our people discharged the cannon, and shot through the guard house; upon which the guard came out; our people who lay in Ambush ran in, set it on fire, and went off with 2 muskets, two bayonets, and a halbert. —— The Regulars perceiving the house on fire, returned to extinguish it, but in vain, the few who concerted this scheme got a reinforcement, and plied them with small arms, till the house was consumed."

Extract of a letter from the Camp at Cambridge dated July 9, 1775.

"Yesterday morning at half past two o'clock we were called up, and informed the enemy had attacked our lines at Roxbury; we heard distinctly a firing of small arms and artillery on Roxbury Neck, and soon discovered a great fire in that quarter; but two hours elapsed before we knew the cause, which were as follows:

Two hundred volunteers, from the Rhode-Island and Massachusetts Forces undertook to burn a guard house of the regulars on the Neck, within 300 yards of the enemy's principal works; they detached 6 men about 10 o'clock in the evening, with orders to cross on the marsh up to the rear of the guard house, and there to watch an opportunity to fire it; the remainder of the volunteers scattered themselves in the marsh on each side of the Neck, about 200 yards from the house; two pieces of brass artillery were drawn up softly on the marsh within 300 yards (and upon a signal from the advanced party of 6 men) two rounds of cannon shot were fired through the guard house; Immediately the regulars, who formed a guard of 45, or 50 men, quitted the house, and were then fired on by the musketry, who drove them with precipitation into their lines; the 6 men passed near the house, set fire to it, and burnt it to the ground; after they burnt another house nearer the enemy without losing a man, they took two muskets, and accoutrements, a Halbert, &c. all which were bloody, and shewed evident marks of loss on the part of the regulars; the houses had been a long while made use of by the regulars as an advanced post, and gave them an opportunity of discovering our operations at Roxbury."

PHILADELPHIA July 19. Extract of a letter from the Camp at Cambridge July 11, 1774.

"The General's Express, that ought to have left four days ago, is not yet gone. I therefore sit down to give you some description of our situation here, and that of the enemy. The enemy are situated on Bunker's and Breed's Hills, both on the Peninsula where the late town of Charlestown stood, and within reach and under the cover of the guns, from the ships in the harbour and of a number of floating batteries, which they have built, that carry two guns on their bows, two in their sterns, and one on each side. Our people are situated from Charles-River about 200 rods below the College, where we have a redoubt, which begins the line, then about 60 rods from that another redoubt, and lines continued near 100 rods; then at Charlestown road on the west side of the road at the foot of prospect Hill, another redoubt and strong fortification; then on Prospect Hill, is Putnam's post, a very strong fortification: then between that and Winter Hill a strong citadel, and lines, over Charlestown road to Mistick; than in Mr. Temple's pasture, a strong redoubt, that commands to Mistick River, to that we have a complete line of circumvallation from Charles River to Mistick River; our main fortress on Prospect Hill; the enemy's main fortress on Bunker's Hill, within cannon shot of each other; a hill between these two posts, a little to the eastward of Prospect Hill, called Cobble Hill. I expect will soon cost us a squable, which shall have it, our people or theirs; nor do I expect it will be many days before it begins, which will probably bring on a general engagement; if they let is alone four or five days more, we shall be well prepared, and shan't care how soon they come, the sooner the better. At Roxbury side the enemy have dug across the Neck and let the water through, and our people in turn, have entrenched across the other end of the Neck, and are strongly fortified there, and on the hill by the Meeting House, so strong, that I believe every man in Boston; at Bunker's and Breed's Hills must fall before they could force a passage that way into the country.

General Burgoyne sent a Trumpet yesterday
with a letter to General Lee, wishing a composition of the unhappy differences, &c. and says
the parliament will certainly give up all rights
or pretence of taxation, if that will do, and
wishes a conference: This letter is sent to the
Congress, for their opinions, and for them to
appoint a person whom they can confide in to
attend the conference, and hear what passes, if
they judge it best to have another conference."
A Virginia Paper of the 7th instant says,
"Captain Morgan and Stinson marched from our
frontiers the 29th of June, with two hundred
riflemen, which were desired by Washington."
NEW-YORK July 20. The following Gentlemen appointed Captains, by the Provincial Congress,
for the inlistment of volunteers, to enter into
service for the defence of the liberties of
America, in the first Battalion to be raised in
the city of New-York, under the command of the
Colonels M'Dougal, and Ritzema, have thought
proper to make public, the following places of
rendezvous, and encouragement to volunteers.
Captain John Weissenvelt, and Captain Gershorn
Mott, at Mr. Foster Lewis's innholder near Berk-
man's slip. Captain Willet at Mr. Abraham Van
Dyck's innholder in the Broadway. Captain Jacob
Cheesman at John Rutter's in Cherry street. Captain Samuel Broome at Mr. Foster Lewis's. Captain John Quakenbos, at Mr. Abraham Van Dyck's.
Mr. Edward Bardin's Chapel street, innholder,
and Foster Lewis's, Captain John Johnson at Edward Bardin's. Captain William Goforth, at Abraham Van Dyck's. Lieutenant John Copp, acting in
absence of Captain Richard Varich, private secretary to General Shuyler at Captain Joshua
Banks, in Little Dock street, near the Exchange,
and at William Mariner's in Horse and Cart street
innholder, Captain Van Wyck, at Mr. Abraham Van
Dyck's.
Volunteers from the time of their inlistment,
to enter into an immediate pay, at one shilling
and eleven pence per day; and also to receive
one dollar per week, until they are encamped,
in order to enable them to support themselves
in the immediate time; and they are likewise

to be provided with a suit of regimental cloth-
ing, a firelock, ammunition, accoutrements and
every other article necessary for the equipment
of American Soldiers.

God save the Congress.

NEW-YORK July 20. For these few Days past, a
report has circulated in Town respecting the Mohawk Indians who, it is said, have thrown off
the Connection with Col. Guy Johnson, and engaged in support to the measures of the Continental Congress. We must defer inserting a more
circumstantial Account of the Affair, until it
be properly confirmed.

The Morrow being the Day recommended by the
Continental Congress to be kept as a Day of
fasting, Humiliation, and Prayer, throughout
the British Colonies, we have on that account
published this Paper, one day before the usual
Time.

ANNAPOLIS July 20. The ship Totness, Captain
Harding, belonging to Mr. Gildard, of Liverpool,
having on board a cargo of salt and dry goods,
in coming up the Bay ran aground near the islands at the mouth of West River; upon this the
committee immediately met, and after consideration, determined she should proceed on to Baltimore, her intended port, but before she could
get off, highly resenting so daring an infringement of the Constitutional Association, a Number
of people met, went on board, and set her on
fire.

CAMBRIDGE July 21. Last Saturday, the several
Regiments quartered in this town being assembled
upon the Parade, The Rev. Dr. Langdon, President
of the College, read to them "A Declaration by
the Representatives of the United Colonies of
North America, now met in general Congress at
Philadelphia, setting forth the causes and Necessities of their taking up arms. It was received with great Applause, and the Approbation
of the Army, with that of a great number of other People, was immediately announced by three
Huzzas —— His Excellency the General, with
several other General Officers, &c. were present
on the Occasion.

A Gentleman has favoured us with the following

Account of the Declaration being read upon Prospect Hill.

Last Tuesday Morning, according to Orders issued the Day before, By Major General Putnam, all the Continental Troops under his immediate Command assembled on Prospect-Hill, when a Declaration of the Continental Congress was read, after which an animated and pathetic Address to the Army was made Rev. Mr. Leonard, Chaplain to General Putnam's Regiment and succeeded by a pertinent Prayer; when General Putnam gave a signal, and the whole Army shouted their loud Amen by three cheers; immediately upon which a cannon was fired from the Fort, and the standard lately sent to General Putnam was exhibited flourishing in the Air, having on one side this Motto, An Appeal to Heaven —— and on the other side Qui Transtulit Sustinet. The whole was conducted with the utmost Decency, good Order, and Regularity, and to the universal Acceptance of all present, and to the Philistines on Bunker's Hill —— heard the Shouts of the Israelites, and being very fearful, paraded themselves in Battle Array.

CAMBRIDGE July 21. A Genuine Copy of General Lee's Letter to General Burgoyne upon his arrival in Boston [General Lee served in Portugal under General Burgoyne last war]

Philadelphia June 1775.

My Dear Sir,
We have had twenty different accounts of your arrival at Boston, which have been regularly contradicted the next morning; but as I now find it certain that you are arrived, I shall not delay a single instant addressing myself to you. It is a duty I owe to the friendship I have long and sincerely professed for you; an friendship to which you have the strongest claims from the first moment of our acquaintance. There is no man from whom I have received so many testimonies of esteem and affection; there is no man whose esteem and affection, could in my opinion, have done me greater honour. I entreat and conjure you therefore, my dear Sir, to impute these lines not to a petulant itch of scribbling, but to the most unfeigned solicitude for the future

tranquility of your mind, and for your reputation. I sincerely lament the infatuation of the times, when men of such Stamp as Mr. Burgoyne and Mr. Howe can be seduced into impious and nefarious a service by the artifice of a wicked and insidious court and cabinet. You, Sir, must be sensible that these epithets are not unjustly severe. You have yourself experienced the wickedness and treachery of the court and cabinet. You cannot but recollect their maneuvers in your own select committee, and the treatment yourself as president received from these abandoned men. You cannot but recollect the black business of St. Vincents, by the opposition to which you acquired the highest and most deserved honour. I shall not trouble you with my opinion of the right of taxing America without her consent, as I have seen your speeches, that you have already formed your creed up on this article; but I will boldly affirm, had this right been established by a thousand statutes, had America admitted it from time immemorial, it would be the duty of every good Englishman to exert his utmost to divert Parliament of this right, as it must inevitably work the subversion of the whole empire. The malady under which the state labours, is indisputably derived from the inadequated representation of the subject, and the vast pecuniary, influence of the crown. To add to this pecuniary instance and incompetency of representation is to insure and precipitates our destruction. To wish any addition can scarcely enter the heart of a citizen who has the last spark of public virtue, and who is at the same time capable of seeing consequences the most immediate. I appeal, Sir, to your own conscience, to your experience and knowledge of our court and parliament; and I request you to lay your hand upon your heart, and then answer with your usual integrity and frankness, whether, on the supposition America should be abject enough to submit to the terms imposed, you think a single Guinea raised upon her would be applied to the purpose (as it is ostentatiously held out to deceive the people at home) of easing the Mother country? Or whether you are not convinced that the whole they could extract would be applied solely to heap up still further the enormous fund for corruption which the crown already possesses, and of which a most diabolical use is made. On these principles I say, Sir, every good Englishman, abstracted of all good regard for America, must oppose her being taxed by the British Parliament; for my own part I am convinced that no argument (not totally abhorrent from the spirit of liberty and the British constitution) can be produced to support of this right. But it would be produced to support of this right. But it would be important to trouble you upon a subject which has been simply, and, in my opinion, so fully discussed, I find by a speech given as your's in the public paper, that it was by the King's positive command you embarked on this service. I am somewhat pleased that it is not an office of your seeking, though, at the same time, I must confess that it is very alarming to every virtuous citizen, when he sees men of sense and integrity, (because of a certain profession) lay it down as a rule implicitly to obey the mandate of a court, be they ever so flagitious. It furnishes in my opinion, the best argument for the total reduction of the army. But I am running into a tedious essay, whereas I ought to confine myself to the main design and purpose of this letter, which is to guard you and your colleagues from the prejudices which the same miscreants, who have infatuated General Gage, and still surround him with labour to instill into you against the brave loyal, and most deserving people. The avenues of truth will be shut to you. I insert, Sir, that even General Gage will deceive you as he has deceived himself: I do not say he will do so designedly. I do not think him capable; but his mind is so totally poisoned, and his understanding is so totally blinded by the society of fools and knaves, that he no longer is capable of discerning facts as manifest as the noon-day sun. I assert, Sir, that he is ignorant, that he has from the beginning been consummately ignorant of the principle, temper, disposition, and force of the colonies. I assert, Sir, that his letters to the ministry, at least such as the public have seen, are one continued issue of misrepresentation, injustice and tortured inferences from misstated facts. I affirm, Sir, that he has taken no pains to inform himself of the truth, that he has never conversed with a man who has had courage or honesty to tell him the truth.

I am apprehensive that you and your colleagues may fall into the same trap, and it is the apprehension that you may be inconsiderately hurried by the vigours and activity you possess, into measures which may be fatal to many innocent individuals, may hereafter wound your own feeling, which cannot possibly serve the cause of those who sent you, that has prompted me to address these lines to you. I must devoutly wish, that your industry, valour, and military talents, may be reserved for a more honorable and virtuous service, against the natural enemy of your country (to whom our court are so basely complacent) and not to be wasted in ineffectual attempts to reduce to the wretchedest state of servitude. I say, Sir, that any attempts to accomplish this purpose must be ineffectual. You cannot possibly succeed. No man is better acquainted with the state of the continent than myself. I have ran through almost the whole colonies from the north to the south, and from the first estate gentlemen to the lowest Planters and farmers, and can assure you that the same spirit animates in the whole. Not less than an hundred and fifty thousand gentlemen, yeomen, and farmers, are now in arms determined to preserve their liberties or perish. As to the idea that the Americans are deficient of courage, it is too ridiculous glaringly false to deserve a serious resutation. I never could conceive upon when this notion was founded. I served several campaigns in America last war, and cannot recollect a single instance of ill behaviour in the provincials, where the regulars acquitted themselves well. Indeed we well remember of some instances of the reverse, particularly when the late Colonel Grant, (he who lately pledged himself for the general cowardice of America) ran away with a large body of his own regiments,

and was saved from destruction by the valour of
a few Virginians. Such preposterous argument are
only proper for the Rigby's and Sandwich's from
whose mouths issued, and to whose breast, truth
and decency are utter strangers. You will much
oblige me in communication this letter to General Howe, to whom I could wish it should be considered in some measure addressed, as well as
yourself. Mr. Howe is a man for whom I have ever
had the highest love and reverence. I have honoured him for his own connection, but above all
for his admirable talents and good qualities. I
have courted his acquaintance and friendship,
not only as a pleasure, but as an ornament: I
flatter myself that I had obtained it. Gracious
God made it possible that Mr. Howe should be
provided upon to accept of such an office! That
the brother of him, to whose memory the much
injured people of Boston erected a monument,
should be employed as one of the instruments of
their destruction! But the fashion of the times
it seems is such, as rendered it impossible that
he should avoid it. The commands of our most
gracious Sovereign, are to cancel all the moral
obligations, to sanctify every action, even
those that the Satarp of an eastern despot would
start at. I shall now beg leave to say a few
words with respect to myself and the part I act.
I was bred up from my infancy in the highest
veneration for the liberties of mankind in general. What I have seen in Courts and Princes
convinced me, that power cannot be lodged in
worse hands than in theirs; and of all accounts
I am persuaded that ours is the most corrupt
and hostile to the rights of humanity. I am convinced that a regular plan has been laid (indeed
every act since the present accession evinces
it) to abolish even the shadow of liberty from
among us. It was not the demolition of the tea,
it was not any other particular act of the Bostoneans, or the other provinces which constituted
their crimes. But it is the noble spirit of
liberty manifestly pervading the whole continent,
which has rendered them the objects of ministerial vengeance. Had they been notoriouly of another disposition, and had they been hemines ad

servitdinim paratos, they might have made as
free with the property of the East-India Tea
company and the felonious North himself, with
impunity. But the Lords of St. James's and their
mercenaries of St. Stephen's, well known, that
as long as the free spirit of this great continent remains unsubdued, the progress they can
make in their scheme of universal despositism,
will be but trifling. Hence it is that they wage
inexpiable war against America. In short this
is the asylum of persecuted liberty. Here should
the machinations fury of her enemies prevail,
that bright goddess must fly off from the face
of the earth, and leave not a trace behind.
These, Sir, are my principles; this is my per-
suasion, and consequently I am determined to
act. I have now sir, only to entreat that whatever measures you pursue, whether those which
your real friends (myself amongst them) would
with, or unfortunately, those which our accursed
ministers shall dictate, you will still believe
me to be personally, with the greatest sincerity
and affection.

Your's, &c.   C. Lee.

ALBANY JU1Y 22. Last Sunday se'nnight, about
one o'Clock, P. M. Major General Schuyler arrived here from New-York; he was received upon
his landing by the members of the General Committee for the city and county, and by the City
Troop of Horse, under the command of Captain
Ten Brock, and the Association Company, commanded by Captain Blecher.

The Address of the Committee of Safety, Correspondence and Protection of the city and coun-
of Albany.

Permit us, Sir, to express our fullest appre-
ciation on the appointment, by which your country
has raised you to the chief military command in
this colony. While we deplore as the greatest
misfortune the necessity of such an appointment,
we have the utmost confidence, that you have
accepted of power for the glorious purpose of
executing it for the re-establishment of the
liberties, of America, at present unnaturally
invaded by a deluded and despotic ministry.

CHARLESTOWN June 23. Whereas a Number of Men

belonging to Hubbardston, Rutland & Paxton that have inlisted into the Company that are absent from Camp; it is therefore desired that the Selectmen of each of these before mentioned Towns would send their Men as soon as possible, according to general Orders. Adam Wheeler, Capt.

ADVERTISEMENT.

Several Fire-Arms were borrowed on the day of the last Engagement of the Men belonging to Captain Trevett's Company of Artillery, which are not returned. Those who have them in Possession are requested to return them to Col. Glover's Regiment, now quartered at John Vessel's House in this Town. One of the persons who borrowed them is named Thomas Cartwright.

Deserted from Capt. Putnam's Company, in Col. Mansfield's Regiment, George Douglas, who had on a short blue coat, with white metal Buttons, long white Trowsers, and round Hat; and William Gould, who had on a wond Jacket, long white trowsers, striped linen Shirt, and an old round Hat. It is desired that they may be taken up, and brought to head Quarters in Cambridge.

NEW-YORK July 23. Extract of a Letter from Philadelphia, July 20. 1775.

"This Morning came to Town James Habersham, Esq; Lieut. Governor of Georgia. He came in a Vessel bound to the Northward, and got into a Pilot Boat at our Capes. He is come here for his health. By him there are Letters which inform, that the People of Georgia are become quite hearty in the Common Cause, and have chosen five Delegates, which are expected in a few days.

Capt. Maitland, from London arrived there, and had on Board 13000 Weight of Powder; the inhabitants boarded her, and took all the Powder into their Possession.

NORWICH July 24. The Cambridge Post, who arrived here on Saturday Evening last, informs us that he met with a Company of Rifle-men from Virginia, &c. that Morning on their Way to Join the United American Army near Boston.

WORCESTER July 26. By a person of undoubted veracity, who came out of Boston, last Thursday se'nnight by permission of Gen. Gage, we learn that 1500 and upwards of the regulars force

were killed, wounded and missing, at the battle
on Bumker's-Hill; that 5550 of the inhabitants
were still in Boston, according to Gen. Gage's
account, who had ordered the people to be numbered; that Mr. James Lovell, and Mr. John Leach,
school-masters, Mr. ——— Hunt, and some others
were confined to gaol, That salt Beef sold for
1s, sterling the pound, salt butter 1s, id. and
a small calf fore twenty dollars; a press gang
impressed 100 men on the 7th of June, but they
were mostly released; the refugees are but little noticed by either party, some of them are
employed in Gage's service, and do duty in the
night; it has been very sickly among the King's
troops, between 15 and 30 have died in a day;
several of the tories have caught the distemper
from the troops and died, among whom it is said
are Euson, Wilson, Hutchinson and Colson; the
inhabitants are allowed to be out until 10 o'-
clock at night, and are not much ill-used, in
general, unless they speak with soldiers; Information is given to General Gage, of matters in
our army, &c. but persons in women's cloathing,
who or what they were, was not known to our informant; Gage's army was thought to be 9000
strong, but greatly intimidated; the regiments
arrived last at Boston, were as follows, viz.
Light Dragoon 17th, Col. George Preston, 120
men: Foot 35th, Col. Henry Campbell: 49th, Alexander Maitland: 63d, Francis Grant; 420 men
each. Regiments destined for New-York, but ordered to Boston by Gage, 22d, Gen. Tho. Gage:
40th, Sir Robert Hamilton: 44th, James Abecrom-
by (killed at Bunker's Hill;) 55th. William
Haviland; ; 420 men each. The whole number of
the King's troops lately arrived at Boston 3060.
    It is said General Burgoyne is delirious about
his time; General Gage is often out of his head;
whether or not it is the same distemper that
infects both, is not certainly known.
    WORCESTER July 26. To the Printers.
THe Printers of the Public Papers in America,
are desired to insert the following, as it shews
the methods our blood-thirsty enemies at Boston
(the King's troops and their accursed abettors)
take to furnish themselves with Provisions. it

is hoped a constant and strict watch will be kept, and every vessel thoroughly examined, for whatever is found assisting them with their comforts and luxuries of life, while they are inhumanly butchering our brethren, deserve to suffer the pains of death.

PHILADELPHIA July 26. Extract of a letter from Cambridge, july 13, 1775.

"The day before yesterday we went to Chelsea, summons for the battle of Noodle-Island near to it; while we were on Powder Horn Hill, back of Chelsea, we saw a skirmish between a party of our people, (120 in number) who went in whale boats, to an island about 12 miles from Boston, and burnt a large quantity of hay, which was put into bundles by the Regulars, and intended to be sent Boston for their horses. A great number of Marines, in schooners, men of war boats, and two ships of war kept up a constant fire on our men, while they remained on the island, but this did not prevent them from destroying the hay. The Schooner and boats endeavoured to cut off their retreat, which brought on a very warm engagement, in which we had one killed and two wounded. The loss of the Regulars not known, but supposed to be considerable, as they were drove off from them, and would have not been the case, if they had not lost some men."

"A Gentleman that got out of Boston, Monday, July 10, says, that the inhabitants were numbered, and amounted to 6573. The soldiers numbered, woman and childre to 13600. 300 Tories are chosen to patrol the streets, 49 at night. Very sickly, from 10 to 30 in a day, and no bells allowed to toll. Master Lovell taken up and put in goal, which in consequence of some letters found in Dr. Warren's packet, and Master Leach also. Released out of goal 4. Mr. Hunt saying, that he wished the Americans might kill them all, was confined in goal. 11 dead of the wounded prisoners at Charlestown. Col. Parker dead, he having declared at his last hour, if he got well he would do the same. THe officers say, damn the rebels, that they would not flinch. A great number of floating batteries are building, and five transports and three sloops are sailed for hay and wood to the eastward.

"This Gentlemen also says, the officers and soldiers triumph very much at the death of Doctor Warren, saying it is better to them than 500 men."

CAMBRIDGE July 27. Last Wednesday se'nnight embarked from Dorchester Neck, Col, Greaton, with 96 Men in ten Whale Boats, for Long Island, in order to remove from thence some Stock and Hay. On his way he was fired upon by the Man of War lying near said Island, but notwithstanding the very heavy fire from the ships, he proceeded, when not finding any stock on the Island, he fired the Barns, in which was a quantity of hay, he not being able to remove it; as he perceived several Barges, Cutters, and arm'd Schooners coming upon him, having executed his design, so far as to deprive our enemies of the Advantage they might have received from the Hay, &c. which he destroyed, he retreated; and when on board he found himself beset by the Savage Enemy, who perhaps would have taken some of the hindmost Boats, had it not been for the good conduct of the Commander, and a Party from Squantum, posted on the shore, who by a warm fire drove off the Enemy; they killed one of our Men on the shore, and it is asserted by one in a Boat that there were two of the Enemy Killed. The House catched fire from the Barns and was consumed.

Last Tuesday came to Town from Philadelphia, and joined our Army of the United Colonies, a company of 106 Rifle Men. Many Hundreds more are daily expected. The following Paragraph, from one of the Philadelphia Papers, will give the public an Idea of their peculiar Skill as Marksmen.

"A correspondent informs us that one of the gentlemen appointed to command a company of Rifle Men, to be raised in one of our frontier counties, had so many applications from the people in his neighbourhood, to be enrolled for the service, that a greater number presented than his instructions permitted him to engage, and being unwilling to give offence to any, thought of the following expedient, viz. He with a piece of chalk, drew on a board the figure of a nose

of the common face, which he placed at a distance
of one hundred and fifty yards, declaring that
those who should come nearest the mark should
be enlisted, when sixty odd hit the object, —
General Gage take care of your nose."

CAMBRIDGE July 27. Since our last Major Vose
and Major Loring have returned from Nantasket,
and brought off about 1000 Bushels of Barley,
which they cut. After they had secured the Barley and straw, they went and burnt the Light-
House, and took three Boats with four Men belonging to Boston, which were fishing, brought
off three Casks of oil, and about 50 lb. Powder
from the Light-House; they then burnt the Barn
and Hay upon the Brewsters. Notwithstanding an
almost incessant fire from the Men of War and
Tenders, we had only two Men slightly wounded.

NEW-YORK July 27. On the 18th the Continental
Congress passed sundry resolutions recommending
to all the colonies, that all able bodied men
from 16 to 50 form themselves into regular, militia companies, regiments, &c. one 4th of whom
to be minute men, all to perfect themselves in
the military art, and be provided with arms,
ammunition, and accoutrements.

It is said that the Hon. Continental Congress
will in a few days be adjourned, and that their
next meeting will be at Hartford in Connecticut.

Morgan Lewis, Esq; is appointed Major of Brigade to Major General Shuyler.

On Tuesday and Wednesday a large detachment
from the camp at Harlaem, consisting of about
1000 men, under the command of Col. Waterbury,
marched for Albany: It is said they are intended
as a reinforcement of Ticonderoga, where Major
General Shuyler commands.

PROVIDENCE July 29. A Gentleman from Cambridge
informs, that Advice has been received there by
several regular Soldiers who have deserted, that
it had been determined to attack the Lines of
the American Army on Sunday last; but that no
more than on Quarter of the Troops desired for
the Attack could be prevailed to come out, the
others declaring they would much rather die
within their own Lines than to turn out to be
slaughtered; and that General Gage has been in

consequence, obliged to lay aside the Project.
Some movements made at Bunker's Hill, and the
landing of a number of Troops at Charlestown,
on Sunday, corroborate this Intelligence.

A Beacon in now erecting on a very high hill
in this Town by Order of the Honourable General
Assembly, to alarm the Colony of any sudden emergency. A Watch is likewise kept on Tower Hill,
in case of any attempt by Water from our savage
Enemies.

HARTFORD July 31. (Connecticut Courant)

Mr. Watson,
Mention has been made in the New-London papers
of the gallant and intrepid behaviour of Capt.
Knowlton, Captain Coit, and Lieutenant Dana and
Hide, in the late engagement ot Bunker's Hill.
I think it highly reacheable that the names of
all those officers who, by real and solid merit
distinguished themselves in the action, should
be recorded with honour, and had in everlasting
remembrance by their countrymen; this is a tribute which a proper regard to merit, the dictates
of justice and self preservation seem to require.
I shall therefore proceed to mention a few persons (whose names I have obtained) that signal-
ized themselves on this occasion, and whose
conduct in the battle aforesaid, has not been
publickly noticed, hoping some friend to his
country will do justice to all as soon as they
are known. In this list of heroes it is needless
to expatiate on the character and bravery of
Major General Putnam, whose capacity to form and
execute great designs is known through Europe,
and whose undaunted courage and marshal abilities, strike terror through all the hosts Midi-
anites, and has raised him to an incredible
height in the esteem and friendship of his American brethren; it is sufficient to say, that he
seems to be inspired by God Almighty with a
military genius, and formed to work wonders in
sight of those uncircumcised Philistines at
Boston and Bunker's Hill, who attempt to ravage
this country, and defies the armies of the living God. Major John Chester of Weathersfield,
now Captain of a company in General Spencer's
regiment, and Lieut. Samuel Webb, who marched

up to the lines with their men, and reinforced the troops by their undaunted behaviour, timely and vigorous assistance, it is universally agreed are justly entitled to the grateful acknowledgement of their country ⸺ Capt. John Kyes of Ashford, who is first Lieut in Capt. Knowlton's company, and who on the left wing with him during the action, fought with spirit and invincible resolution, for the truth of this fact I appeal to Capt. Knowlton himself who was on the same wing, an eye witness to his marshal spirit, animating and heroic behaviour. Lieut. Thomas Grovesnor of Pomfret, also merits tribute of thanks for his valiant conduct in charging the enemy closely, and maintaining his ground like a hero, till disabled for action and force to retire by reason of a wound received in one of his hamds. Nor can I without manifest Injustice, pass over in silence the spirited and heroics of Lieut. Dingham of Norwich, and Ensign Bill of Lebanon, who gave full proof of their courage and Marshal spirit on that important day. These with many other officers perhaps, whose names are not yet publickly known, together with the soldiery under their command, beyond all question, acquitted themselves with honour, and fought manfully for their country and the cities of God.   A Friend of Truth.

Hartford July 31. Yesterday Major Clerk's company of volunteers passed through the town, to join the American Army in Cambridge. They are the first company of the last recruits raised by the colony, that have marched for their station, are provided with excellent fire arms, and warlike accoutrements, made in the town of farmington, to which they belong.

Having by accident seen a paper (titled the American Oracle of May 24th) the paragraph relating to the taking of Ticonderoga by Colonel Easton, and being the commanding officer at that time, think, I cannot, in justice to myself, do less than contradict the many particulars therein contained, knowing them to be totally void of truth. Indeed I am quite at a loss to conjecture what could incline this same Col. Easton, to publish a conversation said to be had with

me, except he knowing that I was a prisoner, and
restricted from giving any account at all of
this affair, took the advantage of my situation,
in order to answer his own purpose at the total
expence of his veracity! for I solemnly declare
I never saw Col. Easton, at the same time the
fort was surprised nor has he and I any conversation whatsoever, relating thereto, then, or
at any other time since.

Hartford July 28, 1775.   William Delaplace.

NEW-YORK July 31. Mr. Gaine, Printer and Book-
seller, at New-York.

I the Widow of Joseph Adrian de Keyser, Esq;
one of his Majesty's pensioners and provider
for the Military and other Hospital of the Kingdom, do hereby Certify, to all who it may concern. That Boxes of Anti-Venereal Pills now
sent, are verily of my composition; in truth
of which, and to satisfy all those who may require it, I have given this Certificate, sealed
with my seal of Arms, at Paris, the 1st of
August 1773.

      (seal)   W.Keyser.

CAMBRIDGE Aug. 1. Deserted from the Camp at Cambridge, about the 26th of June last, two inlisted Soldiers, belonging to Captain Seth Murray's Company, named Asa and Robert Perkins, Brothers, 6 feet high, well looking Men. They profess the forgery Business. One of them had on when he went away, a light coloured Coat, the other a brown outside Garment, with a pair of Trowsers. Whoever will take up said Men, and to convey them back to the above said Camp, or contain them so they may be had, shall have Six Dollars Reward, or Four Dollars for either, with all necessary Charges paid; and all committees or Selectmen are desired to do the same.

Camp. at Cambridge, August 1, 1775.

Seth Murray Captain.

NORFOLK Aug. 2. THis town and neighbourhood have been much disturbed lately with the elopement of their Negroes, owing to the mistaken notion, which has unhappily spread among them, of finding shelter on board the men of war in the harbour, notwithstanding the assurances given by the commanding officers that not the least encouragement should be shewn them.

On Friday last a deputation from the commonhall of this borough waited upon the Captain Macartney and Squires of the men of war now lying near, with the thanks of the Corporation for their conduct, in discountenancing the runaway slaves that have made applications for service on board.

On Monday last arrived here from St. Agustine about 60 soldiers, on board a sloop Tender, some time since belonging to Mr. Bowdoin of the Eastern shore. These, with about 40 more are hourly expected, and to compose a body guard for his Excellency our Governor, at his intended place of residence, on board the Ship Willian. The troops above-mentioned are under the command of a Captain and two Lieutenants; the Ensign, it is said, is on his way over land.

CAMBRIDGE Aug. 3. A Copy of General Burgoune's Answer to General Lee, dated July 8th, 1775.

Dear Sir,

When we were last together in service, I should not have thought it within the vicissitude of human affairs, that we should meet at any time, or in any sense, as foes. The letter you have honoured me with, and my own feelings, combine to prove we are still far from being personally such.

I claim not to merit from the attention you so kindly remember in the early periods of our acquaintance, but as they manifest how much it was my pride to be known for your friend; nor have I departed from the duties of that character, when, I will not scruple to say, it has been almost general offence to maintain it: I mean since the violent part you have taken in the commotions of the colonies.

I would exceed the limit and the propriety of our present correspondence to argue at full the great cause in which we are engaged. But Anxious to preserve a consistent and ingenuous character and jealous I confess of having the part I sustained imputed to such motives as you intimate, I will state to you as concisely as I can the principles upon which, not voluntarily, but most conscientiously I under took it.

I have like you, entertained from infancy a veneration for public liberty. I have likewise regarded the British Constitution as the best safeguard of that blessing to be found in the history of mankind.

The vital principle of the constitution, in which it moves and has its being, in the supremacy of the King in parliament ——— a compound, indefinite, indefensible power, coeval with the origin of the empire and co-extensive over its parts.

I am no stranger to the doctrines of Mr. Locke, and the others of the best advocates for the rights of mankind, upon the compact as always implied between the governing and the governed, and the right of resistance in the letter when the compact shall be so violated as to have no other means of redress. I look with reverence almost mounting to Idolatry upon the immoral Whigs who adopted and applied such doctrine during part of the reign of Charles the 1st, and in that of James IId.

Should corruption pervade the three estates of this realm so as to prevent the great ends for which they were instituted, and make the power vested in them for the good of the whole people operate like an abuse of the Prerogative of the crown to generate oppression. I am ready to acknowledge that the same doctrine of resistance applies as forcibly amonst the Abusers of the collective body of Power, and against those or the crown or either of the other competent branches, separatively: Still always understood that no other means of redress can be obtained: A case I contend much more difficult to oppose when it relates to Parts.

But in all cases that have existed or can be conceived, I hold that resistance, to be justifiable, must be directed against the usurpation or undue exercise of power, and that it is not criminal when directed against any power itself inherent in the constitution.

And here you will immediately discern why I draw a line in the allusion I made above to the reign of Charles 1. towards the close of it the true principle of resistance was changed and a new system of Government projected accordingly. The patrons previous to the long Parliament and during a great part of it, as well as the glorious revolutionist of 1688, resisted to vindicate and restore the constitution; the republicans resisted to subvert it.

Now Sir. In your hand upon your heart as you have enjoyed me to do on mine & tell me to which of these purposes do the proceedings of America tend?

In the Weight of taxes imposed, and the impossibility of relief after a due representation of her burthen, that has induced her to take up Arms? Or is it a denial of the Right of British

legislation to impose them and consequently a
struggle for total Indipendence? For the idea of
of power that can tax externally, and not inter-
nally, and all the sophistry that attends it,
tho' it may catch the weakness and prejudice of
the multitude in a speech, or pamphlet, it is to
preposterous to weigh seriously with a Man of
your understanding; and I am confident you will
admit the case to be fairly put. Is it then from
a relief of taxes, or from the controul of Parliament "In all cases whatsoever" we are in war?
If the former, the quarrel is at an end. There
is not a Man of sense and information in America
who does not know it is in the power of the Colonies to put an end to the exercise of taxation
immediately, and forever, I boldly assert it,
because sense and information will also suggest
to every man, that it can never be the interest
of Britain, after her late Experience to make
another trial.
But if the other ground is taken, and it is
intended to wretch from Great-Britain a link of
that substantial and I hope perpetual, chain by
which the empire holds ———— think it not a ministerial mandate; think it not a mere profes-
sional ardour; think it not a prejudice against
part of our fellow subjects, that induces men of
integrity, and among such you have done me the
honour to class me, to act with vigour; but be
assured it is a conviction that the whole of our
political system depends upon the preservation
of the great and essential Part distinctly, and
no part so great and essential as supremacy of
legislature. It is a conviction, that a King of
England never appears in so glorious a light as
when he employs the Executive powers of the
state to maintain the laws, so in the present
execution of that power, his Majesty is particularly entitle to our zeal and grateful obedience, not only as soldiers but as citizens.
These principles, depend upon it, actuate the
army and fleet throughout: And let me at the
same time add, they are few, if any gentlemen
among us who would have drawn his sword in the
cause of Slavery.
But why do I bind myself to the navy and army?

The sentiments I have touched are those of the great bulk of the nation. I appeal to the landed men who have so long borne burthen for America; I appeal to those trading towns who are suffered by the dispute and the city of London at the head of them, notwithstanding the petition & remonstrances which the arts of party and faction have extorted from some individuals, and last, because least in your favour, I appeal to the majorities in the Houses of Parliament upon American Questions this session. The licentious news-writers want assurance to call these majorities ministerial; much less will you give them that name when you impartially examine the characters that compose them. Men of the most independent principles & fortitude, and many of them professedly in opposition to the court in the general line of their conduct.

Among other supporters of the British rights against American claims, I will not speak positive, but I firmly believe, I may name the man of whose integrity you have the highest opinion, and whose friendship is nearest to your heart. I mean Lord Thanet, from whom my aid de camp has a letter for you, and also one from Sir Charles Davers: I do not enclose them, because the writers, little imagining how difficult your conduct would render our intercourse, desire they might be delivered to your own hands.

For this purpose as well as to renew "the rights of friendship," I wish to see you; and above all, I should find an interview happy if it should induce such explanations as might tend in their consequence to peace. I feel in common with all around me, for the unhappy bulk of this country; they forsee not the distress that is impending over them. I know Great-Britain is ready to open her arms upon the first overture of accommodation; I know she is equally resolute to maintain her original rights; and if the war proceeds, your one hundred and fifty thousand men will be no match for her power.

The place I would propose for our meeting is the house upon Boston Neck, just within our advanced centries, called Brown's House. I will obtain authority to give my parole of honour for your safe return. I shall expect the same on your part that no insult be offered to me. If this plan is agreeable to you, name your day and hour. at all events, accept a sincere return of the assurance with which you honour me, and believe me in all personal consideration, affectionately yours.

P. S. I obey your command to General Howe and Clinton. I also communicate your letter and my answer to Lord Percy. They all join me in Compliments, and authorize me to assure you they do the same in principal.

Cambridge, Head-Quarters July 12, 1775.

General Lee's Compliment to General Burgoyne. Would be extremely happy in the inteview he so kindly proposed. But as he perceives that General Burgoyne, has already made up his Mind on the great Subject; and as it is impossible that he [Gen. Lee] should come after his opinion, he is apprehensive that the interview might create those jealousies and Suspicions, so natural to a People struggling in the dearest of the cause, that of their Liberties, Properties, wives children and therefore, defer the happiness of embracing a Man who he most sincerely loves until the Subversion of the present tyrannous Ministry and system, which he is pursuing must be in a few months, as he knows Great-Britain cannot stand the Contest. He begs General Burgoyne will send the Letters which his Aide de Camp has for him. If Gardiner is his Aide de Camp, he desires his love for him.

CAMBRIDGE Aug. 3. We hear that the Enemy are about dismantling Castle William.

Last Monday Morning about 800 Men, went from Roxbury to the spot where the Light-House lately stood, where they found 40 of the Enemy, twenty eight Soldiers and twelve tory Carpenters and Laboures, who were sent from Boston to erect a building for fixing up a Light. Our people before they surrounded, killed four of them (among whom, it is said, was a Lieutenant) and took the Prisoners, bringing 24 regulars, and the twelve workers, with the loss of one man on our side. The same Day the whole Number was brought to Head Quarters in this Town, and the day after sent off to Worcester.

N. B. On their return from the Light-House they were pursued by a number of the Enemy's Barges, when Major Crane who commanded the artillery fired a 24 pounder which killed a Lieutenant, a Soldier, and sunk the Boat; after which the enemy tho't prudent not to pursue any further.

CAMBRIDGE Aug. 3. Some very late intelligence hath been received at Head-Quarters this week from Canada, the substance of which is, that the Canadians and Indians cannot be persuaded by Governor Carleton to join his forces, but are determined to remain neuter: That they are but 500 regulars in Canada, and near all those stationed at St. John's, in Order to make a Stand against the provincials expected down the Lake; and that consequently Quebec and Montreal have been left quite bare of troops, except a small guard at each place.

NEW-YORK Aug. 3. To Benedict Arnold, Esq; Colonel of the Massachusetts regiment, and commander in chief on an expedition to Lake Champlain, for taking the fortress on said Lake, and the armed vessels thereto, into the possession and protection of the American Arms.

We the subscribers, the principal inhabitants on the said lake, in behalf of ourselves, and on behalf of all the inhabitants contiguous thereon, amounting in number to about six hundred families; deeply impressed with a sense of your merit, and the weighty obligations which we lie under to you, in your military capacity, think it our duty to address you in this public manner, to testify our gratitude and thankfulness for the uncommon vigilence, vigour and spirit, with which you have atchieved those important conquests, so essentially necessary for our preservation and safety from the threatned, and much dreaded incursions of an inveterate enemy.

The humanity and benevolence which you have exercised towards the inhabitants of these parts, most immediately affected by the present convulsions, by supplying them with provisions in their distress, render you no less worthy our administration, than your tenderness and polite treatment, of such prisoners as have fallen into your hands, entitle you to the most favourable opinion of some of the regular officers, whose grateful sentiments thereon, you have already received: so you are likewise in a peculiar manner, entitled to our warmest thanks; since you have thereby, and by the proofs they have had of your prudence and valour, been the means of keeping our enemies and their scouting parties, at a distance from us, to which your vigilance in constantly employing such a number of boats, on the north part of this lake, hath not a little contributed.

The humane and polite manner with which you treated your prisoners, insure to you applause of all; you have thereby shewn your adversaries a bright example of of the elevation and generosity of soul, which nothing less than real magnanimity, and innate virtue could inspire.

By your vigilance and conduct, we have been, under providence preserved from the incursions and ravages of an enraged enemy, to whose declared vengeance we cannot help expressing our sorrow, at the approaching period of your removal from us.

Convinced your competency to the undertaking of protecting us, we cannot help lamenting our situation, on the thoughts of losing you, ignorant of the experience or abilities of the gentleman appointed to succeed you. We sincerely wish you rewards adequate to your merit, and are with the utmost gratitude, regards and esteem.

Sir, Your most obliged,
and most obedient Servants,
(Signed by a number of the principal Inhabitants, on behalf of themselves and the rest.)

Lake Champlain, July 3, 1775.
To the very respectable Inhabitants on Lake Champlain.

Gentlemen,
Permit me to return you my most hearty thanks for the polite and obliging Addresses you have been pleased to present me this day, which as it convinces me of your esteem and approbation of my conduct in a military capacity, is more than an adequate recompence for the poor service

214

and protection I have been happy enough to render you, which both duty and humanity requires of me. I am much pleased to have in my power in this public manner, to return you my sincere thanks for your support, vigilance and spirited conduct in the public cause, and cannot express deeply the necessity of leaving you so soon. I heartily wish you the protection of that and Providence which has so generously interposed in your favour heretofore; at all times, be happy in hearing of the welfare of all the inhabitants on Lake Champlain, but of my friends in particular ———and am with the greatest respect and esteem,

Gentlemen your most obedient,

Humble Servant,   Benedict Arnold.

Crown-Point July 4, 1775.

NEW-YORK Aug. 3. (New-York Journal)

Mr. Holt,
the following erroneous account of the reduction of Ticonderoga, was published in Mr. Thomas's Oracle of Liberty the 24th of May last, and as the writer of the account which follows it, had no opportunity of seeing it, till very lately he being up at the forts, ever since they were taken, he could not contradict it sooner. I beg therefore you'll republish it in your next Journal, together with the account that follows it, which may be depended on.

I am Sir your's &c.

"Cambridge, May 18. Yesterday Col. Easton arrived at the Provincial Congress in Watertown, from Ticonderoga, and brings the glorious news of taking the place by the American forces, without the loss of a man; of which interesting event we have collected the following particulars, viz. Last Tuesday se-nnight about 240 men from Connecticut and this province, under Col. Allem, and Easton arrived at the Lake near Ticonderoga, 80 of them cross'd it, and came to the fort about the dawn of day. The centry was much surprized at seeing such a body of men, and snapped his piece at them; our men however rushed forward, seized and confin'd the centry, pushed through the covered way, and all got safe upon the parade, while the garrison were sleeping in

in their beds. They immediately formed a hollow
square and gave three huzzas, which brought out
the garrison, and an inconsiderable skirmish
with cutlesses and bayonets ensued, in which a
small number of the enemy received some wounds.
The commanding officer soon came forth, Colonel
Easton claspped him upon the shoulder, told him
he was his prisoner, and demanded, In the name
of America, an instant surrender of the fort,
with all its contents to the American forces.
The officer was in great confusion, and expressed
himself to this effect —— Damn you, what ——
what —— does all this mean? Colonel Easton
again told him, that he and his garrison were
prisoners: The officer said, that he hoped he
should be treated with honour: Col. Easton re-
plyed, he should be treated with much more honour
than our people had met with from the British
troops. The officers then said he was all submission, and immediately ordered his soldiers
to deliver up all the arms, in number about 100
stands. As they gave up their arms, the prisoners were secured in the hollow square. The American forces having thus providently got possession of this important fortress, found in it
upward of one hundred pieces of cannon, several
mortars, and a considerable quantity of shot
stores and some powder. After this acquision, a
detachment of our troops were dispatched to take
possession od Crown-Point where there is a considerable number of Cannon.   Another detachment
was sent to Skenesborough, where they took Major
Skene and his family, with a number of soldiers,
and several pieces of Cannon."
   As the above account of that reduction of Ticonderoga, which from its complexion, I suppose
originated from that very modest gentleman Col.
Easton himself, is so replete with falsehood,
and is so great an imposition on the public,
that it is my duty, in order to undeceive the
public, and to do justice to modest merit, to
give you a candid detail of the whole matter,
for the truth in which I appeal to every officer
and private who were present, which is as follows:
   Some gentleman arrived in New-Hampshire grant

216

from Connecticut, with a design of seizing on
the fortress of Ticonderoga, were there, joined
by a number of men, among whom were Col. Allen
and Easton, the former, with the assistance of
Captain Warner, collected about 150 men, with
whom they marched to Castletown, 20 miles from
Tuconderoga where the left Col. Easton, and proceeded 10 miles towards Shoreham, the next day
Col. Arnold, arrived at Castletown from Cambridge
having concerted in similar plan, being commissioned by the Massachusetts Congress to raise a
regiment, he proceeded on to the party under the
command of Colonel Allen, ——— when Col. Arnold
made known his commission, &c. It was voted by
the officers present, that he should take a joint
command with Col. Allen (col. Easton not presuming to take any command.) When the party had
marched to Shoreham, two miles on the Lake below Ticonderoga. where they waited for Batteaus
to cross the Lake until midnight, and none arriving, Col. Arnold, with much difficulty, persuaded about 40 men to embark with him in a
batteau accidentally taken there, and landed
half a mile from the fort, and immediately sent
back the batteau, which by reason of a violent
storm of wind and rain did not return until
break of day with a small boat, and near 50 men
in both. It was then proposed by some gentlemen
to wait open day, and the arrival of the remainder of the men which amounted at that time to
near 100; This Col. Arnold strenuously opposed,
and urged to storm the fort immediately, declaring he would enter it alone, if no man had courage to follow him ——— this had the desired
effect, he with Col. Allen headed the party and
proceeded directly to the fort, when they came
within about 10 yards of the gate, the centry
discovered them and made a precipitate retreat,
he was pursued closely by Col. Arnold, who was
the first person that entered the fort, and Col.
Allen about 9 yards behind him ——— this I was
an eye witness of being only a few yards distant
——— Col. Arnold immediately order'd the men to
secure the doors of the barracks, and went himself with Col. Allen to the commanding officer,
Captain De la Place, and desired him to deliver

up his arms, and he might expect to be treated
like a gentleman, which he immediately complied
with, as did the whole garrison.

I do not recollect seeing Col. Easton until 9
o'clock, and was told he was the last man that
entered the fort, and that, and not till the soldiers and their arms were secured, he having
concealed himself in an old barrack near the
redoubt, under pretence of wiping and drying his
gun, which he said had got wet in crossing the
Lake. Since which I have often heard Colonel
Easton, in a base and cowardly manner abuse Col.
Arnold behind his back, though always very complacent before his face. Col. Arnold was soon
made acquainted with the liberty he had taken
with his character, and upon his refusing to give
proper satisfaction, I had the pleasure of seeing him heartily kicked by Colonel Arnold to the
great satisfaction of a number of gentlemen
present, although he (Easton) was armed with a
cutlass, and a pair of loaded pistols in his
pocket.   I am your humble servent,
                                   Vetritas.
Ticonderoga June 25, 1775.

N. B. The doughty hero, Easton, has been appointed to the command of a regiment in the
Massachusetts service.

NEW-YORK Aug. 3. Extract of a Letter from
Philadelphia dated 29th July.

I have a letter from London, dated May 31,
(by the Ship Rebecca, Captain Hazelwood, who
sailed the first of June) says "you will find by
the papers, that we have received an Account
from Salem of the defeat of Col. Smith, and the
precipitate Retreat of Lord Percy. This intelligence, so contrary to the Expectation of Government, who had daily denounced the American
Cowards, has panick-struck Administration, and
their Tory dependents, and has established the
Spirits of the Sons of America, in this Metropolis, and the Friends of Freedom, in the most
exalted Manner. It is impossible to describe
the countenances of North and his Tyrannical
Abetters; they are constrained to acknowledge
the Regulars were the aggressors, and equally
forced to admit the intrepidity of the Americans:

But what alarms them most, they expect every hour to hear General Gages's Army is cut off, or meanly sheltering themselves in the Castle, or on board the Men of War."

WILLIAMSBURG Aug. 4. Lord Dunmore received his 60 body-gaurdmen, lately arrived from St. Augustine, last Tuesday, at Gosport; and, we here, that he daily expects an additional reinforcement of 40 more soldiers, from the same place. His Lordship, it is said, as soon as they arrive, and when joined by the marines from the Mercury and Otter men of war, and a number of select friends in the different places, intends coming round to Yorktown; from whence, if not prevented, it is likely he will pay a visit in this City, although he cannot expect the same cordial reception as on former occasions, but will probably be received with such illuminations, &c. as may make him forget his way to the palace. The good People of Virginia now consider Lord Dunmore as their mortal enemy, and will no longer brook the many gross insults they have received from him, which are daily repeated; and the damn'd Shirtmen, as they are emphatically called by some of his minions, it is more than probable, will make some rue, before long, their blatant, base, and ungenerous conduct.

The men of war officers, we are credibly informed, have been guilty of many outrages, both in Norfolk and Portsmouth; which ungenteel behaviour lately exposed one of them to the resentment of a certain Mr. O'Shields, who drubbed him handsomely.

NEWBURN (N. Carolina) Aug. 5.   In Committee. From the late conduct of Governor Martin at Fort Johnston, an intelligence since received by the committee, it appears he intends erecting the King's Standards, & commencing hostilities against the people of this Province. It is therefore Resolved, That no person or persons whatsoever have any corespondence with him, either by personal communication or letter, on pain of being deemed an enemy to the liberties of America, and dealt with accordingly. And that no person or persons presume to remove him or themselves from hence to Core Sound, or any other

part of the province where the Governor resides,
without leave of this Committee, as he or they
will not be suffered to return here.

　　　　By Order,　　　　R. Cogdell, Chairman.

By a Gentleman just come to town from Cape
Fear, we have a certain account that the armed
force which lately went down to burn Fort Johnston, have affected the same by destroying all
the houses, and rendering the fortification entirely useless. Captain Collett, who commanded
that fort, 'tis said, had a number of slaves,
which he had instigated to revolt from their
masters, actually concealed in the fort, which
were again recovered by their several owners;
for this treachery they burnt his dwelling house
with all his furniture, and every thing valuable
he had not time to get on board the man of war.

WATERTOWN Aug. 7. Last Monday, near Charlestown Neck a warm Fire began between our advanced
Parties and those of the Enemy, attended with
cannonading from the Enemy's Works on Bunker's
Hill. We took two Marines Prisoners, and killed
several of the regulars, with the loss of one
Man, belonging to Marblehead, who was killed
with a Cannon Ball.

Parties of the Rifle Men, together with some
Indians are constantly harassing the Enemy advanced Guards, and say they have killed several
of the Regulars within a day or two past. One
of the Riflers which is missing, is a prisoner
in Boston Goal.

Friend Edes,　　　　　(Boston Gazette)
by inserting the following you will oblige many
of your Friends and Customers.

We the subscribers Testify and say that on the
29th Day of May, 1775, Capt. Linsey Commander
of a Ship of War, then at Tarpolen Cove, came
with a number of armed Men and landed on one of
the Elizabeth Islands called Reskatenash and
came to the place where the Men that owned part
of the Stock on said Island were shearing the
Sheep, and demanded their Sheep, saying and
promising that he would pay for them, and give
the full value of the Sheep, or words to that
purpose; but the owners of said Sheep told him
that they were unwilling to part with them, but

if he would take them they should not molest him, at most the Owners of the Sheep were of the people called Quakers and that they would not be concerned in defending themselves or their interest by force of arms, but would treat him with civility, but said Captain with his Men took said Sheep and carried them away, some of them shorne and many not shorne, the Sheep were hurried away in such a manner that we could not make an Account of the Numbers of them with exactness, but according to the best of our judgement the numbers and value of the Sheep are as follows, viz.

Took from Mr. Tucker and Bre's, 93 Sheep,
Took from Jeromiah Robinson, 17 Sheep,
Took from Messrs, William & Eliha Robinson,
24 Sheep,
Took from Mr. Ebenezer Meiggs, 72 Sheep.
Barnstable May 31st, 1775.

Jaromiah Robinson,
John Tucker,
Eliha Robinson,
Ebenezer Meiggs.

That the above named John Tucker, Jeromiah Robinson, and Eliha Robinson, being of the people called Quakers, affirmed to the truth of the above writing, by them subscribed: And the above named Ebenezer Meiggs made oath to the truth of the above written by him subscribed.

Before me Tho' Smith Just. of the Peace.

Charge of Horse hired and man, from the Island to Boston, 90 miles.

WARTERTOWN Aug. 7. Mr. Printer, Please to insert the following in your useful Paper, and it will oblige,   A Traveller.

Since I came out of Boston, where I left all my effects to the mercy of the lawless banditti, to amuse myself, have made several excursions into different parts of the country, and with pleasure have observed to firm, steady and resolute spirit which animates every individual. My last tour was to Portsmouth, where, to my astonishment, and I dare say to the astonishment of all America. I was informed that the committee for that town had voted to supply the Scarborough man of war lying in their river,

221

with 4 to 600 weight of fresh beef weekly. This
account, I must confess appear'd to be scarce
credible; but on making farther enquiry, found
it was true, and the reason assigned for this
conduct was owing to the threats of a paltry
sloop of war to deprive the inhabitants of fresh
fish, unless they afforded them such a quantity
of Beef. Too great a soul I hop'd animated the
breast of every American to submit to so insolent a demand; and instead of treating it with
the contempt such insolent deserv'd to the surprize of many of the worthy inhabitants, the
committee passe'd a vote to supply with privi-
sions those butchers of our countrymen who are
daily pilfering and destroying, by this unexampled instance, Submitting to their imperious
demands, and like suppliants, entreating their
favor. Such conduct at so important a crisis
cannot but wring tears from every well-wisher
to America. This Fact is of so important a nature, that it ought in justice to be made public:
And I hope it will so effect the minds of the
worthy inhabitants of that town, as to exclude
from all further service the timid members of a
committee who act in direct opposition to both
Constitutional and Province Congresses.

NEWPORT Aug. 7. On the evening of Saturday the
29th of July, leave was given for a number of
rifle-men, in the American camp, to reconnoitre
the enemy's entrenchments at the foot of Bunker
Hill; and the rifle-men lay concealed, a party
of the enemy coming out to relieve their guards,
they stumbled over them, when a fire ensued, and
the rifle-men killed 4 and brought off 2 prisoners, with the loss of one man only. The next
Day (Sunday) about 11 o'clock, A. M. the enemy were discovered making entrenchment between
the place where the Sun-Tavern Stood, and Penny
ferry, near the regulars advanced post, on the
Charlestown side, of which notice as dispatched
to General Green on Prospect Hill, who immediately got under arms with all his men, and sent
notice to the Generals Washington and Lee, who
sent orders for General's Green's men to return
to their tents; and leave was given for the
rifle-men to go down and try if they could make

any advantageous attack on them, which they did, but just as the came near enough to attack the Generals came down themselves and ordered them to retire and not make the attack, At 1 o'clock on Sunday morning a number of the enemy stole out by the way of Chelsea river and came down across the hills to the place where the Provincials piquet guards were, and fired on them at the distance of 6 rods, but neither killed nor wounded a man, and immediately ran off; at the same time about 400 of the enemy, near Roxbury, passed by the marshes between Roxbury and Cambridge; and come round upon the Provincials advanced guards near the George tavern, at Boston Neck and fired upon them, which compelled them to retire to the picquet guard with only one man wounded, and one deserted from the enemy; upon the junction of the advanced and piquet guards they returned the fire, upon which the enemy immediately set fire to a barn, which communicated to the George tavern, and ran off. Upon which a very heavy cannonading and bombarding began from the enemy's lines at Boston Neck, from 2 floating batteries up Cambridge river, a ship in Charlestown ferry way, and a floating battery in Chelsea river and at the lines on Boston Neck, and the ship in Charlestown ferry way; but continued in Chelsea river till one o'clock P. M.

The next day, notwithstanding all the cannonading, a few Americans went down to the enemy's advanced guard, killed 7 men, and brought off their firelocks, ammunition, hats, &c. among the firelocks was a very handsome officer's fuzee, from which it was judged that the officer of the post was killed. On Monday morning at 8 o'clock the enemy from Bunker hill began a very heavy cannonading, continued till 1 o'clock, but did no other damage than killing 2 men, owing too forward in catching the enemy's balls. On Sunday the 30th, afternoon 270 Americans from Roxbury went in whale boats, down the light house, to burn a house that was left standing there, and also to destroy the repairs which Gage's men had been making on the light house. When they arrived there they found 29 marines, commanded

by a Lieutenant, 10 carpenters and 9 Marshfield
Tories, with whom a skirmish ensued, when the
Americans killed the Lieutenamt and 3 marines
wounded 4 Tories badly, and brought off the rest
of the marines, carpenters, and Tories, prisoners (excepting 6 who took a small boat and got
away) and burnt 2 small schooners. The prisoners were carried to the camp last Monday at 3
o'clock P. M. and after examination sent off to
head quarters at Cambridge.

NEWPORT Aug. 7. Last Week came to town from
Connecticut, who exhibited several samples of
salt petre, of excellent quality made in that
colony, a number of works are erecting for making that useful article, and it is not doubted
but there will soon be a sufficient quantity
procured to supply the whole continent for making as much gun powder as will be wanted.

NORWICH Aug. 7. Yesterday forenoon we had intelligence of three Men of War and eleven transports plying in the Sound, opposit Fisher's Island. This advice arrived in the Time of Divine
Service, when the People immediately came out
of the Meeting and many of them set out for New-
London to the Assistance of their Brethren in
case of an Attack.

In the Afternoon they took a Sloop belonging
to New-London, filled her with Men and sent her
to Fisher's Island where she landed them. We
hear they have landed 1000 Troops on said Island.

They have taken one Yoke of Oxen and 30 Sheep
off Montiack Point, which is since guarded by
400 Provincial Troops. They are also 150 stationed on Oysterpond-Point to watch the motions
of the Fleet.

A Gentleman who left New-London this Day, informs us, that as he came away he saw two of the
Men of War beating up into the Harbour.

Since receiving the above we learn, that they
have taken 2000 Sheep and 100 Head of horned
Cattle from Fisher's Island. Also a Sloop belonging to New-Haven, loaded with live Stock,
and a vessel belonging to New-London with stores;
and that three Men of War, with a Number of
Transports, were gone somewhere else. The above

being only part of the Fleet from Boston.

HARTFORD Aug. 7, We hear from Middletown, that some time since, a number of respectable Senior gentlemen near 60, formed themselves into a company for attaining the military Art. They have met every Monday since, and have got to a great degree of perfection in the Art. and are resolved and determined to preserve the liberty of their country at the hazard of their lives. What is still more remarkable the drummer is upwards of 80 years of age, and as much engages, and alert as any young lad.

NEW-YORK Aug. 7. Committee-Chamber New-York 4th August 1775.

Whereas the Continental Congress by their resolve of the 27th of May last, ordered that no Provisions (except from the Colony of Massachusetts) from whence they were to be supplied with Provisions only for their internal use; and the said Congress deemed it of great Importance to North-America, that the British Fishery should not be furnished with Provisions from the Continent through Nantucket, did by their said Resolves earnestly recommended a vigilant Execution thereof by all the Committees and whereis it appears to the committee by the Confession of Abraham H. Van Vleck, of the City Merchant, and the Examination of George Coffin that the same Abraham H. Van Vleck being owner of the Sloop Henry, (whereof the said George Coffin was Master) and about the 23d of June last send from this port the said Sloop, laden with Provisions to Nantucket, on account and Risque of the said Abraham H. Van Vleck, and that the said George Coffin sold the same there for the use of the inhabitants. And whereas it also appears on the said Examination and Confession, that the said Abraham Van Vleck had again, during this present Week, laden the same Sloop at New-York with provisions, for a like voyage to Nantucket, and that the said Goerge Coffin was to proceed on the same as Master of the said Sloop, but was directed in such a design, and the voyage and cargo detained by this Committee.

Resolve 1st. That the Examination of the said George Coffin, and the confession of the said

Abraham H. Van Vleck be published in the several News-Papers of this Colony.

Resolve 2d. That the said Abraham H. Van Vleck and George Coffin have knowingly violated the before mentioned resolve of the Continental Congress, and the general Association entered into by the Inhabitants of the City and County.

Resolves therefore 3dly, that the said abraham H. Van Vleck and George Coffin, have severely acted inimically to, and been guilty of a high Infringement of the liberties of the associated American Colonies, by order of the Committee,

Henry Remsen, Dep. Chairman.

Gentlemen,

I Acknowledge to have bargained with George Coffin, about late end of May last, for the sloop Henry, of which I was owner; but as our Agreement fell through, I then, by Advice of the said George Coffin, concluded to load her for Nantucket with a Cargo of Provisions, and gave the Command of the Vessel to him: Soon after the resolve of the Hon. Continental Congress was made public, respecting the Non-Exportation of Provisions to said Place; notwithstanding which the Ignorance of the Consequences, and a strong imagination that it would not hurt the Cause of America. I very impudently proceeded to load the said Sloop for Nantucket, for which place the said George Coffin immediately went, and on his Arrival there was solicited by the Inhabitants to go to New-York and return as soon as possible with another Load, as they were in great want of Provisions, and she was nearly completed loaded with the said Cargo, on the same event as last Voyage at this Period. The Vessel and both Cargoes were owned entirely by me, and no person whatsoever either directly or indirectly, had any Share of Part to the same; and I likewise do most solemnly exculpate my Father Henry Van Vleck (who has been out of Town a long time) and every other Person from having my knowledge in this matter, and I will, if required, satisfy the same by an oath. Now Gentlemen, after having made this open Confession, I throw myself on the mercy of my Country, hoping that every indulgence will be allowed me, consistent with

the Interest of the Public: I can and do appeal
to my fellow Citizens, that I never did in any
one Instance transgress against the Liberties
of America; and had I have thought the Provisions shipped by the aforementioned Vessel would
have fell into the Hands of the King's Troops,
no Consideration whatever could have induced me
to have sent the same. I again beg Leave to crave
the Lenity of the Public, and am, Gentlemen,
                Your and their most devoted Servant,
                            Abraham H. Van Vleck.
   I further certify that Capt, George Coffin on
his Voyage to Nantucket, had Orders to sail out
of Sandy-Hook, and on the Voyage to avoid all
Vessels he should happen to meet or see, and not
to any Vessel whatever until he got to Nantucket,
in order to avoid his falling in the way of any
King's Vessels which might carry him into Boston.
                            Abraham H. Van Vleck.
         Committee Chamber.
   George Coffin says, That after the Account
received of the Congress not to ship Provisions
to Nantucket, the Examinest being Master of the
Sloop Henry, did take on board the said Sloop
at New-York, a Cargo, or Part of a Cargo of Provisions for Nantucket which belonged to Abraham
H. Van Vleck of this City. That the said Vessel
also belonged to him the said Van Vleck. That
the said Examinant sailed with the said Vessel
and Cargo to Nantucket, and there sold the Cargo
but had Liberty from said Van Vleck, to go to
the West-Indies if he thought fit. That the Cargo of Provisions now on board the said Sloop,
also belonged to the said Abraham Van Vleck,
and were shipped with intentions to go to Nantucket. That the Cargo first above mentioned
was sold for the Use of the Inhabitants of Nantucket. That he thinks he was about three days
taking in the first Cargo, and thinks that the
Vessel was cleared out immediately, or very soon
after the first Cargo was taken on board; and
thinks the Vessel sailed the next day after she
was cleared out. That when the Vessel sailed on
said Voyage the Examinant knew he was contravening the Order of the Continental Congress.
                            George Coffin.

PHILADELPHIA Aug. 7. We are credibly informed that General Burgoyne has lately shown every appearance of a deep settled melancholy, in continually walking the streets of Boston with his arms folded across his breast and talking to himself.

WORCESTER Aug. 9. Extract of a letter from a Gentleman in Cambridge, dated August 8th, to the Publisher hereof.   (Massachusetts Spy)

"Mr. Thomas I have seen Mr. P_____, who left Boston last Friday evening, who informs me it is very sickly both among the inhabitants and the soldiery; that many of the inhabitants die broken hearted; that the enemy have entirely dismantled Castle-William, undermined the walls and intended blowing them up; that several officers are embarked and sailed for England and he supposed, to give a true state of facts; that fewel is so much wanted, the enemy have broken open several cellars and took washing tubs, empty casks, and all the wood they could find to make fire to cook with, and tore all the rope walks down for the same purpose; and that strict orders are given, that no mechanic of any kind whatsoever should leave the town."

CAMBRIDGE Aug. 10. To the Hon. John Sullivan, Esq; Brigadier-General of the Continental Army.

Sir,

The Committee of Safety for the County of Hillsborough, in the Colony of New-Hampshire, having in contemplation the greatest service you lately rendered the County in your civil Capacity, and the great Abilities you then exerted at the bar, in their defence, at a Time when the People were most cruelly oppressed by the Tools of Government, pray Leave to address and congratulate you, on your Appointment to the Rank of Brigadier-General. An Appointment, which as it distinguishes your Merit so at the same Time it reflects Honour upon, and shews the penetrating Discernment of all those truly eminent Patriots, from whom you received it, one of whom composed the Continental Congress. Nor are we less sanguine in our Expectations, of the high Advantages, which must result (under God) to the Public, by your military Skill and Courage. As

You had been Indefatigable in attaining the first, and have given a recent Instance of the latter, to your great Honor and Reputation in the depriving our Enemies of the means of annoying us at Castle William and Mary, and at the same time furnishing us with Materials to defend our invaluable Rights and Privileges.

This Sir, must be ever had in Remembrance, and (amongst the Actions of others our Heroes of 1775) landed down to the latest posterity. That the Almighty may direct your Council, be with you in the Day of Battle, and that you may be preserved as a Patron of this People, for many Years to come, in our Servant Prayer.

July 19.   Per Order, Mathew Pattin, Chairman.

CAMBRIDGE Aug. 10. The Information given me (and inserted in our last) respecting the Expedition to the Light-House we have been since told was rather imperfect. Major Tupper commanded the Troops, consisting of 250 Men, they found on the Island 53 Persons, 33 of them Marines of whom a Lieutenant and two Prisoners, with three Tories, were killed on the Spot. Five of the Marines and several of the Tories, were wounded, among whom was the notorious Capt. White of Marshfield.

The whole Number besides the killed were made Prisoners, one of whom was the infamous Jonathan Hampton, the Master Carpenter from New-York.

The Army continues in high Spirits, ardently wishing for Action; and as the Needful is to be not wanting, we hope they will soon be gratified and tread under their feet every Son of Tyranny on this side of the Atlantic.

PORTHSMOUTH Aug. 10. We hear that four Gentlemen, late Captains in the Ministerial Army at Boston, have resigned their Commissions to General Gage, from a Conviction that the Service they were employed in, was derogatory to their Honour, disgraceful to Humanity, and subversive of common Rights of Mankind.

NEW-YORK Aug. 10. Last Tuesday the first division of Col. M'Dougall's battalion of provincial troops sailed, under the command of Lieut. Col. Ritzema, to join Maj. Gen. Schuyler, at Ticonderoga, they will soon be followed by the second, under Maj. Zedvoitz, and the Col. is preparing immediately to follow with the third and last division.

By accounts received (via Antigua) we are informed that the dispatches with Gen. Gage's account of the affair at Lexington, arrived in England on the 13th of June, 17 days they were sent from the inhabitants of Massachusetts, by Capt. Darby.

NEW-YORK Aug. 10. By a return Express, who left the Camp at Cambridge, last Friday Evening, we are informed that 6 Sail of Transports sailed from Boston under convoy of a Man of War, some Time ago, for the Eastward of Casco Bay, for Forage; that they landed a Number of Men for the Purpose; That while the Men from the Ships were landed, a Number of Men from Shore possessed themselves of 5 of the Ships, made the Seamen and Soldiers Prisoners, and secured the Ships out of reach of the Man of War.

Last Monday an Express arrived from East Hampton, with the following Intelligence, that several Vessels were seen crossing off Fisher's Island and Long Island, with an intent to carry off some of the Stock from the East end of Long Island and Gardner's Island for the use of the Army and Navy at Boston. That the Inhabitants were assembling under Arms, to oppose their landing, and to drive the Stock from those places, where they were most likely to be taken off. Our Provincial Congress immediately ordered four Companies of Gen. Wooster's Forces, in conjunction with the Men now raising in Suffolk County, for the Continental Service to repair thither, to the assistance of the Inhabitants. General Wooster moved accordingly from his Camp in Hearlem last Tuesday. By an Express which arrived on Tuesday we learn the number of Ships were thirteen.

Last Thursday Capt. Patrick Sinclair, Lieut. Governor and Superintendent at Michilimackinack who lately arrived from North Britain, at some Port in Maryland, and after passing through Pennsylvania and New-Jersey, was apprehended by Order of the Provincial Congress and sent to Suffolk County on Nasshau Island, there to reside on his giving his Promise of Parole on his

Honour, that he will not take any Part in the present unhappy Controversy between Great-Britain and the Colonies, without Permission of the Continental Congress, or of this, or some future Provincial Congress, until the present unhappy Controversy between Great-Britain and the Colonies shall be determined

In Provincial Congress New-York Aug. 9th, 1775

Whereas the Barge ordered to be built, to replace the one belonging to his Majesty's Ship Asia, lately destroyed, was when nearly finished sawed to pieces in the night, by some disorderly persons.

Resolved, That the Mayor and Magistrates of this City, be requested to procure another Barge to be built in this City, for the purpose aforesaid; and all persons are strictly enjoined not to obstruct the building pf the said Barge, or the delivery thereof to the Commander of his Majesty's said Ship, and those who shall give any obstruction thereto will be considered and treated as Enemies to their Country.

A true Copy from the Minutes

Robert Benson, Secretary.

Last Thursday at White Plains in Westchester county, one Nathaniel Adams, a Tory, shot and wounded desperately, John M'Donald, a recruit belonging to Col. Holmes's regiment, now raising in this Colony. The villain made his escape, but was secured, and is now under confinement.

NEW-LONDON Aug. 11. Last Lord's Day Morning, about 6 o'Clock, we discovered 9 Ships, 1 Brig, 1 Snow, 1 Schooner, beating up this Harbour, with the Wind at N. E. which greatly alarmed the Inhabitants of this Town, and they immediately sent off an Express to alarm the neighbouring Towns; that they, might get themselves in Readiness to march wherever they might be wanted; but in a few Hours it was discovered they were bound for Fisher's Island to take off the Stock, which they effected by the next morning: It Consisted of 1130 Sheep, 3 Milch Cows, 1 pair of working Oxen, and 25 Young Cattle, and 10 Hogs. (all the Beef that was fit for Market was carried off the day before.") As soon as they came to Anchor, an Express was sent off to

those Towns that had before been notified, to
let them know the Situation of the Fleet, and
to recommend their being in Readiness, as it was
uncertain where they would proceed next. On
Tuesday Morning they sailed for Gardiner's Island, and anchored on the East Side, and were
there Yesterday taking Stock.

The Inhabitants of the Town of New-London,
return their sincere Thanks to those Gentlemen
in the neighbouring Towns, who so readily came
to their Assistance, and if ever Occasion should
require it, will return the like favor.

WATERTOWN Aug. 14. Since Monday Morning last
eight Companies of Rifle Men, consisting of
100 Men each, from Virginia, Maryland, and Penn-
sylvanis, have arrived here. Four more are daily
expected. They are an excellent Body of Troops,
and appear, to a Man, healthy disposed to prosecute, with the utmost Resolution and Vigour,
the noble Cause in which they are engaged.

Col. Thompson, of the Pennsylvania Regiment
of Rifle Men, and a number of young Gentlemen
Volunteers, are also arrived at Head Quarters
from Philadelphia.

THe Rifle men commanded by Capt. Daniel Morgan,
of Frederick County in Virginia, which is about
600 Miles from this Place, arrived here in three
Weeks.

We hear from Cape-Ann, that a Vessel bound in
there from the West-Indies, being discovered off
the Harbour last Tuesday, several of the Inhabitants went off in a Boat to assist in bringing
her in. Soon after, about 30 Armed, from the Man
of War commanded by Capt. Lindzee, boarded and
took possession of the Vessel; but she running
aground in the Cape, was vigorously attacked by
a Number of Men from the Town of Glocester, who
soon obliged the Enemy to give up the Vessels
to their proper Owners, and to surrender themselves Prisoners. The whole Number was immediately sent to Ipswich Goal, in which 26 of them
were confined. The Rest (4 Or 5 in Number) were
discharged, it appearing that they had been
cruelly forced into the Enemy's Service. Lindzee
was so enraged that he fires several Cannon
Shot into the Town of Glocester but did little

Damage.

Friday last was conducted to this town by an escort commanded by Capt. Melcher, the officers and crew of the armed cutters Magaritta, Diligent, and their tender, taken at Machias, together with the Friend to Government Icahabod Jones, formerly of Boston, and a stanch friend to that infernal traitor to his country, Thomas Hutchinson. Capt. Moore of the Magaretta was killed in the engagement. Capt. Knight, Lieutenant Spry, five Midshipmen and Warrant Officers together with 17 Privates belonging to the above vessels, we hear are order'd to the more interior part of this colony.

We hear that last Thursday afternoon a number of Rifle men killed 2 or 3 of the Regulars as they were relieving the centries at Charlestown lines.

HARTFORD Aug. 14. Extract of a Letter from Ticonderoga, Dated Aug, 4, 1775.

"Two persons who have lately come from St. John's being examined under oath before the General, gives accounts that the King's troops are well fortified at St. John's, That they is at that place 470 regulars, and 110 at Chamblee about 12 miles distance, about 20 at Montreal, and one company at Quebec; 40 Indians at St. John's, Col. Guy Johnson and Col. Sloss with 500 Indians just arrived at Montreal and going to join the English Rebels against us. One of these men was from Montreal and saw Johnson and his Indians. They appear to be two senseble men and give a direct account. There is Two large strong vessels near finished at St. John's to carry about 14 or 16 carriage guns each, and they are every day in expectation of being joined by about 4000 regulars that are come into the river and them come against us; The Canadians are determined not to fight against us, unless forced by a formidable Army: About three weeks ago and attempt was made to force the Canadians to take up arms, and were about to hand some in every Parish, when the Canadians arose in a body of near three thousand men, disarmed the officer that was after recruits and made him flee, being determined to defend themselves in the best

manner they could by a full resistance, rather
than be forced to arms against the colonies.
The common people there cant bare to have the
old French laws take place again amongst them,
as they will be thereby plunged into enormous
taxes. We had a few days ago two men who went
down the lake with an Indian boy from Dr. Wheelock's college, intending to land him about 30
miles this side of St. John's, who are taken by
a scout of the enemy and held Prisoners."

A correspondent observed, "That our worthy
brethren of Farmington have been so vigilant to
perform their part of the grand resolve of the
hon. Continental Congress, concerning Minute-
Men, that they have already, compleat, three
companies, properly officered, and are ready to
march, Also wishes every town in this colony
would go and do likewise, as the Language of the
times is , Be ye also ready: for procrastination
is the thief of time."

Yesterday a company of Rifle-Men from Lancaster County Pennsylvania, together with two companies of recruits raised by the colony, passed
through this town, on their march for the continental army.

At a meeting of the committee of inspection
holden at Waterbury, Aug. 2d, 1775. William
Nichols of Waterbury aforesaid, being fuly notified to appear before said committee, to answer
some charges exhibited against him for violating
the association of the Continental Congress, by
treating the said committee in a contemptuous
manner, by refusing to treat with them as a committee, and by labouring on the last continental fast on the 20th of July last, with design
to bring the advice of said congress into contempt. And the said Nichols having refused to
make his appearance, or answer to said charges,
the committee after due consideration, are of
opinion, That the above said allegations are
fully proved and supported, and therefore resolve that the same be made public, to the end,
that such a determined foe to the right of British America may be properly known, and all persons are desired to break off all dealings and
commerce with said Nichols, agreeable to the

11th article of said association. By order of
Committee,   Timothy Junn, Chairman.
   Mr. Watson, (Connecticut Courant) Please insert the following.
   Notwithstanding I profess to be a friend to the
liberties of America, I confess I have spoken
words in anger tending to depreciate the authority of the continental congress, and to subvert
the foundation of the common liberties of the
colonies. I do therefore now in this public
manner, as well for the restoration of my Character as the satisfaction countrymen, freely
and voluntarily express my sorrow for my unwarrantable conduct herein, and expressly retract
the same, and for the future promise to behave
myself in all respects as becometh a friend to
his country.   Amasa Case.
   Dated Simsbury, 7th August, 1775.
   The above instrument being subscribed by Mr.
Amasa Case of Simsbury, at the instance and in
the presence of the committee of inspection for
said town was voted to be satisfactory, provided the same be made public.   Attest.
                  Elisa Barber Con. Clerk.
   PHILADELPHIA Aug. 14. Extract of a letter from
Cambridge aug. 5.
   "Since the riflemen arrived they have killed
6 or 8 officers of distinction on the lines at
Charlestown; a son of Lord Holland is Life dangerously wounded. We have the names of the officers in camp.
   For some days past Gen. Gage has been permitting the people to come out of Boston, stripped
of every thing, and what they call a pocket
serjeant to search every persons pockets, that
any man carries with him or her more than five
pounds. The inhabitants are extremely distressed,
and the troops almost as much. Almost all their
wounded at Bunker's Hill and elsewhere are dead,
and all the Provincials among them, is a more
probable charitable way of accounting for the
Death of the wounded. Certainly there never was
any poison balls used. Some of the Officers are
still very angry with the high and big, but the
more sensible men among them are dispirited,
and say that it is in vain to attempt any thing,

                        235

for if they should attempt our lines success is uncertain; and should they succeed, the enemy will rally again on the next hill, increased in number and in rage, and will harrass them to death; and those thay may happen to survive the conflict at the lines; that that they cannot do as in Europe, fight one or two battles in a season, and then lie still and quiet, and refresh on good provisions, forage, &c. and get recruited from the neighbourhood; here they cannot be succoured in the course of months.

"The troops are universally dishearted; both officers and men heartily cursing Mr. Gage and the Tories; not one of the latter dare be seen wanting them. It has been seriously talked of to plunder the town of Boston, and desert it. If they are not soon recruited, I shall not be surprise of the sight. Eight or ten of their men has lately deserted to us, and some hundreds will do the same the first opportunity. By deserters, inhabitants of Boston, &c. It is agreed that the enemy have not so many men now as the first of April. Their losses, killed and wounded have been great, and by sickness greater still. Those troops, who have been here three and four years, have not been so sickly, but those who have come lately have been very sickly, and now remain so; I believe most of them will be swept off by the sickness, if we sit and only look on, and keep them from fresh provisions."

WORCESTER Aug. 16. A correspondent at Gloucester, Cape-Ann has sent us the following authentic and particular account of the engagement there viz.   Gloucester Aug. 13.

Mr. Thomas,

"On the 9th inst. the Falcon sloop of war, Capt. Linzee hove in sight, and seemed to be in quest of two schooners from the West-Indies bound to Salem, one of which he soon brought too, the other taking the advantage of a fair wind, put into our harbour, but Linzee having made a prize of the first pursued the second into the harbour, and brought the first with him. He anchored and sent two barges with fifteen men in each, armed with muskets and swivels, these were attended with a whale boat, in which was the Lieutenant and six privates; their orders were to seize the loaded schooner and bring her under the Falcon's bow. The militia and other inhabitants were alarmed at this daring attempt, and prepared for a vigorous opposition: The Barge-men under the command of the Lieutenant, boarded the schooner at the cabbin windows which provoked a smart fire from our people on the shore, by which three of the enemy were killed, and the Lieutenant wounded in the thigh who thereupon returned to the man of war. Upon this Linzee sent the other schooner and a small cutter he had to attend him, well armed, with orders to fire upon the damn'd rebels wherever they could be seen, and that he would in the mean while cannonade the town: he immediately fired a broad-side upon the thickest settlement and stood himself with diabolical pleasure to see what havock his cannon might make, "Now, (said he) my boys, we will aim at the damned presbyterian church will my brave fellows, one shot more and the house of God will fall before you." While he was thus venting his hellish rage, at setting himself as it were against heaven, the almighty was on our side, not a ball struck or wounded an individual person, although they went through our houses in almost every direction when filled with women and children; under God, our little party at the water-side, performed wonders, for they soon made themselves masters of both the schooners, the cutter, the two barges the boat and every man in them, and all that pertained to them: In the Action which lasted several hours, we lost but one man, two others wounded, one of which is since dead, the other slightly wounded. We took the man of war's men thirty-five, several were wounded and one since dead; twenty four were sent to headquarters, the remaining being impressed from this and neighbouring towns, were permitted to return to their friends. Next day Capt. Linzee warped off with but half his men, never a prize, boat nor a Tender, except a small skiff the wounded Lieutenant returned in."

We are informed that among the prisoners taken at Cape-Ann, is one Budd, Gunner of the Falcon sloop of war, who was some time ago taken at Marchias with a number of others brought to this town, and and upon being released from close confinement, took an opportunity of running off with a few of our Tory gentry, and got on board the Falcon again. It is hoped, the fellow, if retaken will be better secured.

Last Friday at Mr. Peter Mumford, the Post-rider from Newport to Cambridge, was crossing Bristol ferry, he was taken with the Southern mail, by an armed boat belonging to one of the Pirate ships, which infest the seacoast of this and other governments.

How is the glory departed! Her Army which not long since was the terror of many nations, is now employed in cutting the throats of his Majesty's loyal subjects, and Sheep Stealing! —— Fellows indeed!

We are well informed that Gen. Gage has a now a packet-boat, which goes and returns weekly to a small town, New-Castle New-Hampshire, about three miles below Portsmouth, where some of his emissaries reside. A deligent watch for whom it ought to be kept, that if taken, their lives may in some measure atone to their injured country for their heinous crimes.

PHILADELPHIA Aug. 16. To the King your Excellent Majesty.

Most Gracious Sovereign,
We your Majesty's faithful Subjects of the Colonies of New-Hampshire, Massachusetts-Bay, Rhode-Island & Providence Plantation, Connecticut, New-York, New- Jersey, Pennsylvania and Counties of New-Castle, Kent, and Sussex on Delaware, Maryland, Virginia, North Carolina and South Carolina in behalf of ourselves, and the Inhabitants of these Colonies, who have deputed as to represent them in General Congress, entreat your Majesty's gracious Attention to this our humble Petition.

The Union between our Mother Country and these Colonies and the Energy of mild and just Government, produced Benefits so remarkably important, and afforded such an Assurance of their permanancy and increase, that the Wonder and Envy Of other Nations were excited, while they beheld

Great-Britain rising to a Power, the most extraordinary the World had ever known.

Her Rivals observing, that there was no probability of this happy Connection being broken
by civil Dissensions, and apprehending its future effects, if left any longer undisturbed,
resolved to prevent her receiving such continual
and formidable accession of Wealth and Strength,
by checking the growth of those Settlements
from which they were to be derived.

In the Prosecution of the Attempts, Events so
unfavorable to the Design took Place, that every
Friend to the Interest of Great-Britain and
these Colonies, entertained pleasing and reasonable Expectations immediately given to the Operations of the Union hitherto to experience, by
an Enlargement of the Dominions of the Crown,
and the removal of the ancient and warlike Enemies to a greater Distance.

At the conclusion of the last War, the most
glorious and advantageous that ever had been
carried on by British Arms, your loyal Colonist,
having contributed to its success, by such repeated and strenuous Exertions, as frequently
procure them the distinguished Approbation of
your Majesty, of the late King, and of Parliament, doubted not, but that they should be permitted, with the Rest of the Empire, to share
in the Blessing of Peace, and the Emoluments of
Victory and Conquest.

While these recent and honorable acknowledge-
ments of the Merits remained on Record in the
Journals and Acts of the August Legislature the
Parliament, underfaced by the Imputation or even
the suspicion of any Offence, they were alarmed
by a new System of Statutes and Regulations,
adopted for the Administration of the Colonies,
that filled their Minds with the most painful
fears and Jealousies; and to their Inexpressible
Astonishment, perceived the Danger of a foreign
Quarrel, quickly succeeded by domestic Danger
in their Judgement of a more dreadful kind.

Nor were these Anxieties alleviated by any
Tendercy in the System to promote the Welfare
of the Mother Country. For though its Effects
were more immediately felt by them, yet its

Influence appeared to be injurious to the commerce and Prosperity of Great Britain.

We shall decline the ungrateful Task of Describing the irksome Variety of Artifices, practiced by many of your Majesty's Ministers, the delusive pretences, fruitless Terrors, and of unavailing Severities, that has from Time to Time been dealt out by them, in their Attempts to execute this impolitic Plan, or of tracing through a Series of Years past the progress of unhappy Differences between Great-Britain and these Colonies, that have flowed from this fatal Source.

Your Majesty's Ministers, persevering in their Measures, and proceeding, on open Hostilities for enforcing them, have compelled us to move in our Defence, and have engaged us in a Controvercy so perculiary abhorted: to the Affections of your still faithful Colonies, that when we consider whom we must oppose in the Contest, and if it continues, what might be the Consequence, our own particular Misfortunes are accounted by us only as Part of our Distress.

Knowing to what violent Resentments and incurable Animosities, civil Disregards are apt to exasperate and inflame the contending Parties, we think ourselves requited by indispensable Obligations to Almighty God, to your Majesty, to our Fellow Subjects and to ourselves, immediately to use all the means in our Power, not incompatible with our Safety, for stopping the further Effusion of Blood, and for averting the Impending Calamities that threaten the British Empire.

Thus called upon to address your Majesty on Affairs of such moments to America, and probably to all your Dominions, we are earnestly desirous of preforming this Office, with the utmost Deference for your Majesty; as we therefore pray, that your Majesty's royal Magnanimity and Benevolence may make the most favorable Construction of our Expressions on so uncommon an Occasion. Could we represent in their full force the Sentiments that agitates the minds of us your dutiful Subjects, we are persuaded, your Majesty would ascribe any seeming deviation from

Reverence in our Language, and even in our Conduct, not to any reprehensible Intentions, but to the Impossibility of reconciling the usual Appearance of Respect with a just Attention to our own Preservation against those awful and cruel Enemies, who abuse your Royal Confidence and Authority, for the Purpose of effecting Destruction.

Attached to your Majesty's Person, Family and Government, with all Devotion that Principle and Affection can inspire, connected with Great-Britain by the strongest Ties that can unite Societies, and deploring every Event that tends to any Degree to weaken them: We solemnly assure your Majesty, that we, not only must ardently desire the former Harmony between Her and the Colonies, may be restored, but that a Concord may be established between them upon so firm a Basis as to pepetuate its Blessings uninterrupted by any future Dissentions, to succeeding Generations in both Countries, and to transmit your Majesty's Name to Posterity, adorned with that signal and lasting Glory that has attended the Memory of those Illustrious Personages, whose Virtues and Abilities have extricated States from dangerous Convulsions, and by securing Happiness to others, have erected the most noble and durable Monuments to their own Fame.

We beg leave further to assure your Majesty, that notwithstanding the Suffering of your loyal Colonists, during the Course of this present Controversy, our Breasts retain too tender a Regard for the Kingdom from which we drive our Origin, to request such a reconciliation, as might in any manner be inconsistent with her dignity or her Welfare. These related as we are to her, Honor and Duty, as well as Inclination, induce us to support and advance; and the apprehensions, that now oppress our Hearts with unspeakable Grief, being once removed, your Majesty will find your faithful Subjects on this Continent ready and willing at all times, as they have ever been, with their Lives and Fortunes, to assert and maintain the Rights and Interests of your Majesty, and our Mother Country.

We therefore beseech your Majesty, that your

Majesty, that your Royal Authority and Influence
may be graciously interposed to procure us relief from our afflicting Fears and Jealousies,
occasioned by the Systems before-mentioned, and
to settle Peace thro' every Part of your Dominions, with all Humility submitting to your Majesty's wise Consideration, whether it may not be
expedien for facilitating those important purposes, that your Majesty be pleased to direct some
Mode, by which the united Applications of your
faithful Colonists to the Throne, in presence
of their Common Councils, may be improved into
a happy and permanent Reconciliation; and that
in the mean Time measures may be taken from preventing the further Destruction of the Lives of
your Majesty's Subjects; and that such statutes
as more immediately Distressed any of your Majesty's Colonies may be repealed.

For by such Arrangements as your Majesty's
Wisdom can form for collecting the united sense
of your American People, who are convinced, your
Majesty would receive such satisfactory Proof
of Disposition of the Colonists towards their
Sovereign and the Parent State, that the wishes
for Opportunity would soon be restored to them,
of evincing the sincerity of their Professions,
by every Testimony of Devotion becoming the most
dutiful Subjects and the most affectionate Colonists.

That your Majesty may enjoy a long and Pros-
perous Reign, and that your Descendents may govern your Dominions, with Honor to themselves
and Happiness to their Subjects, is our sincere
and fervent Prayers.

CAMBRIDGE Aug. 17. The Hon. Continental Congress on the 2d Instant adjoined until the 5th
of September, then to be again convened at
Philadelphia, having several Committees to prepare some Matters of Importance against their
Meeting. Among other Things, they have taken the
Management of Indian Affairs out of the Hands
of the Crown Officers, and divided the Indian
Tribes into three Departments; the first taking
in the Six Nations, and all to the Northward of
them; the second, all the Tribes from the Six
Nations to the South Line of the Colony of

Virginia; and the third, all the Indians to the Southward of the South line of Virginia. They have appointed Commissioners for each of their Departments, with proper Presents. Talks, and Belts of Wampum, and the usual and necessary Articles of Trade for the several Nations. The Commissioners for the first and second Departments have already set out for the Places of their Destinations; and we are well assured, that such measures have been taken, and such satisfactory and authentic Accounts received by the Congress, that all Apprehensions of Danger from our Fellow Subjects in Canada, and the Indians, are entirely removed. The Congress appointed Messrs. Hillegas and Clymes, of Philadelphia, joint Treasurers of the United Colonies. They have also established a Post-Office from Georgia to New-Hampshire, and appointed Dr. Benjamin Franklin, sole Post-Master. No other Alteration hath been made in the Continental Association, than permitting all Vessels which shall bring Powder into the Colonies, to receive Provisions, or any Thing also to the amount thereof.

Since our last the Hon. John Hancock, the Hon. Thomas Cushing, Hon. John Adams, Hon. Samuel Adams, and the Hon. Robert Treat Paine Esqurs, the worthy Pepresentatives of this Colony in the Hon. Continental Congress, have returned to their respective Home from Philadelphia.

We hear from Virginia, That the Provincial Convention had stopped all Exports (except Tobacco) from the 5th Inst; That Lord Dunmore had seized a ship and 9000 Pounds, out of one of the Custom-House Treasury. &c.

We are informed that last Thursday Evening returned to Boston, after about 3 Weeks Cruize, twelve Transports (having on board about 1000 Ministerial Butchers) under convoy of three Men of War. During their Cruize they plunder'd and pillag'd about 1130 Sheep and 30 Head of Cattle off Fisher's and Gardner's Islands near New-London, though, 'tis said they were secured they tendered Payment. They also said they took and carried in with them an outward-bound Vessel with about 40 Head of Cattle, and 30 Sheep.

With these Trophies of Victory on their arrival at Boston, the Bells, we hear, were set to Musick, to the small Joy and Comfort of the poor, half-staved Tories.

NEW-YORK Aug. 17. Extract of a Letter from Philadelphia, dated Aug. 15, 1775.

"Yesterday a seizure was made of Major French, of the 22d regiment; Ensign Romer, and a cadet, Demot, who came passengers in a ship from Cork; and also 45 packages of baggage among which there is cloathing for 1500 Men. The whole is safe landed, and in store. These three gentlemen have given their parole of honour, not to act against the united colonies for one twelve month, unless exchanged. They are to be sent to General Washington's headquarters."

The following is the best account we are able to collect, of the late expeditions of the piratical regular traitors to the English Constitution, and the British colonies, in plundering Fisher's, Gardner's, Plum and Black Islands, of Stock, Provisions, &c.

The Design of the Regulars, to plunder these Islands, having been communicated to the Inhabitants and Proprietors by the Congress of New-York, and other Intelligence, as early as Tuesday the 8th, there was Time to have taken off all the Stock; and some was actually taken off: But some Differences having arisen between the Proprietors and the Committee concerning the Expence of the Business, before any Thing could be determined, the ships of the Enemy appeared in Sight. Dispatches were immediately sent to alarm and assemble the People on the Connecticut and Long Island Shores, who, notwithstanding the utmost haste they could then make, were too late to prevent the Execution of the Design of the Enemy, who on Friday the 11th approached Gardner's Island, with the following Vessels and forces, 7 Transport Ships, 2 Brigs, a Man of War, 7 Snows of 30 Guns, 2 armed Schooners of 17 Men and 200 Regulars, as reported by Sailors, landed on the Island and assisted by 10 villainous Tories From South-Head, &c. took off the following Stock, &c.

By Accounts of Banjamin Miller the Overseer,

100 Sheep, 30 Hogs, 13 Geese, 3 Calves, 1000 lb. Cheese, 7 tons Hay, were taken off, and much Damage done to Gardens, Fences, Fouls, &c. When they went away, they left on the Table Half a Guinea and a Pistareen.

Signed by Benjamin Miller,   And attested.

Besides the fore-mentioned Stock from Gardner's Island, we are informed that the same crew of Free Boaters, took from Fisher's Island 26 Fat Cattle, and about 1000 Sheep; also from Plum Island, 14 Fat Cattle: At this last Island they had only one Prize Wood Boat and a Transport Brig. On Their arrival and loading on one side of the Island they were fired upon by about 100 of Col. Wooster's Provincials, who had landed at the other side. But it being represented to the Commanding Officer, that the Island was nearly surrounded by a Number of the Enemy's armed Vessels, who would be likely to cut off their Retreat, they fired but one volley, which did not appear to have any execution, and then retired to the main Land, when the 14 Cattle were taken off.

It is the Opinion of good Judges, that only 200 Provincial Soldiers well posted on either of these Islands, would have repelled the Attack made upon it by Regulars.

The Number of Men who appeared to oppose these Depredations of the Regulars, is suppose exceed 2 thousand, with Whale Boats ready to have carried them to the scene of Action? But being deceived by false Intelligence, and turned back only one Company of about 40 went to Gardner's Island, where they arrived in Time to see the Enemy under sail, and in a few hours after their departure.

WATERTOWN Aug. 21. The Honorable Continental Congress, has appointed the honorable James Warren, Esq; Pay-Master General on the United Forces of North-America.

The honorable Council of this Colony have been pleased to appoint the Hon. Samuel Adams, Esq; Secretary, and Perez Norton, Esq; Deputy Secretary.

Yesterday another Company of Riflemen Commanded by Captain Michael Cressup, arrived in this

Town on their Way to join the Grand American Army. Some of this Company, we hear have travelled from the Missisippi.

NEW-LONDON Aug. 21. From the publick Press of Aug. 18, 1775.

The account of our last, a Treaty with the Six Nations of Indians is confirmed by Capt. Breed from Wyoming, who adds, that he (Capt. Breed) was desired by some of their Chiefs to give their Love, to the Great Man at the head of the Congress at Philadelphia, and desired that all future Messages from the Congress to the Six Nations might be communicated to them through the Medium of Capt. Butler: But the Congress being prorogued before Capt. Breed's Arrival at Philadelphia, prevented his delivering their message.

Since our last seven Companies of the last recruits raised by the Colony, have arrived in Town, They were on their March to join the Continental Army, when they received orders to rendezvous here.

Mr. Benjamin Mumford, Post Rider, between Newport and this Town, was last Friday in crossing Rhode-Island Ferry, ordered by Capt. Wallace, on board the Rose Man of War, where he was detained until Monday, and had his Mail, broke opened and examined.

HARTFORD Aug. 21. Committee of Observation New-Milford, June 28, 1775.

THe Committe of Observation of this town having had due process against Arthur Knowles and Henry Straight, both of this town, according to the association of the Continental Congress, and finding them absolutely fixed in full opposition to the spirit of said association hereby give notice thereof to the public, that they may be treated with all that neglect and contempt which is so justly their due, for their incorrigible enmity to, the rights of British America.

By order of the Committee,

Samuel Canfield, Clerk.

N. B. The two dispicable animals, above named; are so far below the contempt of Rationals, that the committee would never have honoured them with notice, had not their low practices become

intolerable in this respective neighbourhood.
'Tis now done with reluctance, as the committee
are sensible it will give those wretches a degree
of importance which otherwise they would never
acquire.

HARTFORD Aug. 21. We hear three Regiments of
Troops raised by the province of New-York, has
marched to Join Gen. Schuyler at Ticonderoga.
When all the forces ordered for the place should
arrive, the army will consist of about 7000 men,
and their destination is reported, is Canada.

WORCESTER Aug. 23. We hear from Westmoreland,
in the western Part of Connecticut, that last
Thursday Se'nnight about 50 Indians came in that
Place, and encamped at a small a distance from
the Settlement; the next Day they came in and
delivered a Message, which was this Purpose.
That they were very sorry to hear of the differences which subsisded between Great-Britain and
the Colonies. That they should not take up the
Hatchet on either side. That they meant to be at
peace with the English as long as the stream
ran down the Susquehannah River. that should
difference should arise between us and them,
they should try every gentle and healing Measure
to obtain redress of the Grievances. That as
Col. Guy Johnson had left his Habitation and are
destitute of a Superintendent they desire Col.
Butler to take upon him that trust; and that the
place for holding their future Congresses might
be Westmoreland.

Several deserters from the enemy at Boston,
have, during the course of this week past, come
over to our guards at Roxbury. One who seems to
be an intelligent person, asserts that they are
not above 5000 of the ministerial troops in
Boston, and on Bunker's Hill, which are able to
do duty, and that 3000 and upwards are now sick.

We are told that Gen. Gage's lady sailed for
England on Sunday last.

It is said for a certainty, that the enemy
have dismantled that part of Castle-William
which commands the Harbour of Boston, and blowed
up the walls.

We hear that Gen. Gage has seized the donation
stores in Boston, and placed a strong guard over

the same.

Mr. John Gill, late one of the publishers of the Boston Gazette, was seized by order of Gen. Gage, in Boston, and cruelly committed to gaol.

Last Saturday were brought through this town on their way to Northampton, the infamous Ichabod Jones, a well known Tory, several navy officers, together with one Budd, gunner of the Falcon sloop of war, mentioned in our last to have ran off from their place, and several other prisoners forty in the whole.

Cambridge Aug. 24. Last Week arrived, at the Camp in this Place Swashan the Chief, with four other Indians of the St. Francois Tribe, conducted hither by Mr. Reuben Colburn, who has been honorably recompenced for his Trouble. The above Indians came hither to offer their service to the Cause of American Liberty, have been kindly received, and enter'd the Service. Swashan says he will bring one half of his Tribe, and has engaged 4 or 5 other Tribes, if they should be wanted. He says the Indians of Canada in general, and also the French, are greatly in our Favor, and determined not to act against us.

In Consequence of a Vote of the Committee of Safety, for the Town of Portsmouth, that no Boats should pass or repass to and from the Scaborough Man of War in their Harbour, without a Permit ——— We are informed that Capt. Barclay of said Ship has stopped all their Shipping, either inward or outward bound.

Samuel B. Webb, Esq; of Whethersfield, Lieut. in Major Chester's Company, is appointed Aid de Camp to Major General Putnam.

Several Deserters from the Enemy have arrived at our Camp within a few Days past, from the Intelligence they brought, and some correspondences in the conduct of the enemy, it has been apprehended by some that they intended, this Week, to make an Attack on some of our Posts. Others conjecture that they are weary of Yankey Fighting, and will e'er long; in a fit of Madness evacuate the town; at least, that they will not dare to attempt to occupy it during the ensuing Winter.

It is constantly said, that General Gage has

lost since the 18th of April last, in the engagements that have happened, and by sickness and desertion, Two Thousand Five Hundred Men.

We are informed that the Negroes in Boston were lately summoned to meet at Faneail-Hall, for the purpose of chusing out of their Body a certain Number to be employed in the cleaning the Streets. The well known Cesar Merian opposed the Measure, for which he was committed to prison, and confined till the Streets were cleaned.

NEW-YORK Aug. 24.   To The Public.
I the subscriber, Abraham Van Vleck, of the city of New-York, merchant, knowing that I have committed a most Attrocious crime against my country, by Contravening one of the recommendations of the Honourable Continental Congress, in shipping provisions to Nantucket, and being heartily desirous of executing my crime by any means in my power (though I am convinced at the same time, that no pecuniary gift, or any Submissions whatever, on the part of an individual of the community, can atone for an offence committed against the same) I do hereby without the least compassion, make a free and voluntary gift of the sloop Henry, and her cargo, to Messr's Isaac Sears, Oliver Templeton, Edward Fleemimg, and Daniel Phenix, in trust, for the benefit and advantage of the poor of this city, giving and granting, to the said Gentlemen, full power, and authority to dispose of the same in any manner, as they may think best for the advantage of the poor; and if I can in any other manner give further satisfaction to the public, I shall gladly embrace the opportunity: I do not expect that my fellow citizens will take me immediately into favor, but that they would so far condescend, as to let me pass unmolested: As to my unhappy family, I hope the good people of New-York have to much humanity to punish the innocent with the guilty.

I am the public's Most afflicted servant, New-York Aug. 4, 1775.   Abraham H. Van Vleck.

The foregoing method of Recantation is thought to be the most effectual of any that has hitherto been practiced; and it is hoped that all recanting Gentlemen, in future, will not fail to imitate so good an example, and give Proof of their Sincerity equally substantial.

NEW-YORK Aug. 24. The Provincial Congress having resolved that the Cannon should be removed from the Battery, a Number of the Citizens collected for that purpose last Night; and, Part of the Provincial Artillery, under the Command of Capt. Lamb, were posted on the Battery, to prevent the Landing of any Party from the Asia Man of War, to annoy them while at Work. When they marched down, they observed one of the above Ship's Barges lying at some Distance from the Shore, where she continued for upwards of an hour; then she set under sail, and fired a Musket at the men that were posted on the Battery. This was immediately returned by a constant fire from the Artillery Men, and a number of Citizens, that was likewise posted there for the above purpose. Upon this the Asia fired more than 28 Times; some of their Cannon were loaded with Grape-Shot: But as far as we have learnt, without doing any further Mischief than damaging several Houses, and wounding two or three Men. But notwithstanding the Fire from the Asia, the Citizens effected their purpose, and carried off Twenty one Pieces of Cannon, that were mounted on their Carriages.

NEWPORT Aug. 28. Extract of a letter from Middletown, Connecticut Aug. 23, 1775.

"By Express last night to Hartford from Crown Point, we hear that all the Indians have left Johnson except thirty, and that 'tis expected our men are passed St. John's by this time, where all the regulars are posted; that they intended to be with them before they would get the vessels ready. I am in expectation we shall have Governor Carleton at Hartford soon."

HARTFORD Aug. 28. Extract of a letter from Crown-Point Aug. 14.

"Yesterday came in two Subalterns who had been down the Lake as far as Onion River, to procure all the water craft on the Lake. On their return one of them turn'd in to see one Gilliland, a Justice of the Peace, late a merchant in New-York, now settled about 30 miles down the Lake, a man of good interest, and our Zealous Friend.

They were Scarce seated, when one White-high
sheriff of Tryon county (at Sir William Johnson's) with two others, entered without ceremony
and inquired for Mr. Gilliland. After a few words
our men disarmed them. Soon after came up more
white men, with three Indians, who seeing the
situation of their friends, attempted to make
their escape, but were soon taken and safely
conducted to this place. The Indians say they
came to take Mr. Gilliland, and to carry him to
Canada, as White and his accomplices could stay
no longer at Tryon County, the people there were
so enraged against them. The Indians are dismissed with presents, but the others sentenced
to New Gate, in Sinsbury, who gloomy mansions
are judg'd a suitable abode for those sons of
darkness."

Mr. White, Sheriff of Tryon County, with his
Accomplices, mentioned in the foregoing letter,
is now a prisoner in Albany Goal.

Last Week about six Hundred Indians from the
Six Nations, arrived at Albany, where they are
to be met by a number of Gentlemen from this and
the neighbouring Colonies. We hear their business is to enquire into the Cause of the present
Controversy between Great-Britain and the Colonies.

HARTFORD Aug. 28. The following comes from the
New-Hampshire Gazette.

To the Printer,
It gave me mush Pleasure to read in your Gazette,
General Lee's Letter to General Burgoyne, and
his Answere thereto. The former Gentleman writes
like a Roman Senator, for while he expresses
the greatest Sympathy for his Friend, in the
most easy and polite Strain of Diction, he sup-
ports at the same Time the Justice of his Cause,
with the most conclusive Argument, and with a
Spirit of Firmness and Manliness, ever the Attendants on great Minds. General Burgoyne's
Answer is very polite and friendly and discovers
him to be a well bred Gentleman, altho' of opposite Principles, in Polotick's to General Lee:
What a Melancholy Consideration does this Difference of Sentiments produce. Here we see two
Gentlemen professing the most intire Friendship,

for each other to-day, ready to embrace, and
perhaps before the Morrow's Sun, has finished
its diurnal Round, one may lay breathless at the
others Feet, by the Uncertain Fate of War. And
for what? Mr. Lee tells you, That his Motive to
take up Arms in Defence of the charter'd Rights
of the Americans, invaded by Administration.
Mr. Burgoyne says, he is conscientiously bound
to protect the Supremacy of Parliament, over the
Colonies, against whom he supposes America re-
sists: If we examine the principles of these
Gentlemen, without prejudice and impartiality,
we shall soon be able to judge, who has the most
justification on his side, and of Consequence
can best satisfy his Conscience. Mr. Lee is well
acquainted with the intrigues of the Court and
of a Minister and his Sycophants; he wisely
Judges that the sole Support of Ministerial
Measures depends upon the Encrease of Revenue,
to multiply Dependants, and to procure a Majority in the House of Commons, with which he is
always sure of Indemnification, a Regular Plan
has been laid to flick a Revenue from America,
amd a sett of most miscreant Wretches, has been
found, of her own Sons, who have been so base
at not only to plan her Ruin, but even to carry
such Plans into Execution; they have sordidly,
meanly, and infamously accepted of Pensions and
Places as the Returns of their Villainy and the
Price of their Blood. They impose upon the Nation, and every Administration itself, with
their vile misrepresentations, against America
in so many flagrant instances that nothing but
Perfidy conceales them from the People in England
whose Delusion is the only Security to such
Wretched Lives. The Sons of America are attained
of Rebellion agains their liege Sovereign, only
for a manly Resistance to Measures taken in
Consequence of the Advice of their known, open
and avowed Enemies. Measures subversive not only
to the American Constitution, but which will
eventually involve the whole British Nation in
one great Desolation: Lord Chatham and Chamber-
land, those great and good Men, have warned
Britain of her fate, can we suppose that France
and Spain don't improve by Sentiments of these

252

great Politicians, whose council have formerly so afflicted those Nations? Yes! we may be assured they look on them as Conscripu Fathers of Britain, and will avail themselves of their Discretion. When we can cite those & many other Great Lords, as the Supporters of American Resistance, as even to Rejoice at It, we need do or say no more to prove the Justice of our Cause or bring any greater Authority to support it.

Mr. Burgoyne does not attempt to justify the Conduct of Administration, but tacitly winks out of sight the Severity of their Measures, with one general Charge and Supposition, that america is aiming at Independence. By this artful Stroke he Introduces a System of Policy adapted to his own Conception of the Supremacy of the British Parliament, and very roundly supposes Legislation and Taxation inseparable; but yet condescendently admits that Britain will never attempt to tax America after this Experiment. Such Reasoning is not Argumentum ad Hominem, for altho' Britain may not tax America again, yet that does not amount to a total surrender of the Right of doing it. We are not surprized that Mr. B---- Should entertain an Idea of American independency, because we are not certain that he has not yet thorough Knowledge of this People, and he has too implicitly believed the Misrepresentation of Americans Parricides, by whom he has been trepanned.

We believe they are scarcely ten in America who wish an Independency or an unconstitution with Great-Britain: The very Idea of such a State is amazingly absurd, and so very incompatible with her Interest, that she cannot exist without such a Connection, unless she is forced to form another with other State, which is equally abhorrent but thro' Extrmity of the Times: The Sovereignty of the King has never been denied, but repeatedly recognizes; and what greater hold would Great-Britain Have? than an acknowledgement, that her King and his Representatives shall controal all the municipal Laws in the Colonies, and make one Branch of the Legislature. This is an effectual Bar of Independency, & will always operate as such, besides it has been

always conceded on the Part or America, that no
Law shall be made by her incompatible or incon-
gruous with the Act of the British Parliament,
but if Parliament can controul the Legislature
of the American Colonies. Then legislation in
them ought to be at an end, for the Subject
ought act to be governed by two distinct Codes
of Laws, especially when they militate with each
other, and in many instances they are known to
do: That there is a Want of an American Constitution we do not deny, but let the Americans
have their Share in the proposal of the Plan,
but to be Dragooned into a Compliance with any
arbitrary Schemes, evidently tending to Slavery,
they never will consent 'till power overcomes
Right, and Death is swallowed up of Victory.

                                        Coloni.

NORWICH Aug. 28. Deserted from Ensign John
Summer of Ashford, belonging to Capt. Daniel
Lyon's Company of Woodstock, in Colonel Huntington's Regiment of Norwich, in Connecticut, one
who calls himself by the Name of William Daby,
a transient Person, about 5 Feet 10 inches high,
27 Years of Age, a slim Fellow, with brown hair,
and dark Eyes --- Had on when he went away a
blue Coat, Leather Breeches something old, a
pair of coarse white Tow Stockings, or a Pair
of mix'd coloured Worsted ditto which he stole,
is a Fiddler by Trade, and looks something wild
in his eyes. Whoever shall apprehend said Deserter, and return him to me the subscriber,
shall have Three Dollars Reward paid by

                        John Summer, Ensign.

BATLIMORE Aug. 29. By Capt. James Wood, who
was deputed by our Assembly to write the several
Tribes of Ohio Indians to a treaty, to be held
at Fort Pitt, on the 10th of next month, and who
returned last night, we learn, that he has visited the Delawares, Shawanese, Senacas, Tawans,
and Wiandots. That the Commanding Officer at
Detroit, and Deputy Agent for Indian Affairs,
and Monsieur Baubee, a Frebchman, had sent Belts
and Strings of Wampum in several Nations, including, those above-mentioned; informing them,
that unless they all united, the Virginians
would take their country from them; that they

purpose to attack them two different ways; one
by the Ohio, and the other by the Lakes; that
the Virginians would invite them to a Treaty,
but that they ought by no means go, as the (Virginians) were people not to be depended on. That
many other diabolical artificers had been used
by those tools of Government, to instigate these
Savages to attack our frontiers. Particularly
the Virginians were presented to them, as a distinct people, and their attacking them would
not be resented by the other Colonies.

Captain Wood had the account first from the
Delawares, who appeared friendly, and gave him
the Belt and String which had been sent them.
All the other Tribes confirm this account, and
promised to attend the Treaty. The Shawanese
assured him whatever they had received from Fort
Detroit they had buried in the ground never more
to rise, but that the foolish Tawixtawas and
Peats, had accepted the Belts.

Chenusaw one of the hostages who escaped from
Williamsburg sometime ago, arrived at the Sha-
eany Town the day before Captain Wood. He had
informed the Indians, that all the people of
Virginia were preparing for war, and determined
to attack the Indians, except the Governor, who
the people had obliged to go on board a man of
war. That the hostages had discovered they were
to be made slaves, and sent to some other country, which he assigned as a ransom for his escape. But on Captain Wood'd explaining the matter to the Indians, they appeared entirely satisfied.   Winchester Aug. 16, 1775.

PHILADELPHIA Aug. 30. Extract of a letter from
Charlestown, South Carolina, dated August 20.

"Every thing here is suspended but warlike
preperations. It is said that there are scarce
two hundred men in town not enrolled. The country is unanimous. Our Two regiments of foot are
every day training, and almost complete. About
a week ago a small sloop from this town boarded
a snow from England, in Augustine Bay, and carried her off between twelve and fourteen thousand pounds of powder, truly belonging to the
King. She had been boarded privately with 30
resolute men, well armed, by the committee,

in order to intercept the vessel on the sea but
was disappointed, being too late, for there were
forty thousand pounds landed, with 4 brass field
pieces the day before the sloop boarded her.
There were twelve soldiers sent from St. Augustine to protect and defend the snow, to whom our
people gave ten Guineas for helping them out
with the powder, being so modest as not to resist. A Man of War was in sight, bur fortunately aground the few hours our people stayed. We
spik'd up the snow's guns, and then went off
triumphant, altho' attacked by three boats full
of men. One got within 150 yards, it being quite
calm, but that moment a fresh gale springing up.
Our people brought the booty safe to Beaufort,
a town on the coast about 70 miles S. W. of this
place. It was reported they were pursued by the
armed vessels from Augustine, to which place,
on hearing of this, our council of safety dispatched fifteen artillery men and 15 grenadiers
by water, and a company of our provincials to
Beaufort, to ask the country people in the defence of the acquisition. We are putting the
town in a posture of defence, and are all determined to oppose whatever troops that may come
here."
    PHILADELPHIA Aug. 30. The Hon. Payton Randolph,
Richard Henry Lee, Benjamin Harrison, George
Wythe, Thomas Jefferson, Thomas Nelson, and
Francis Lightfoot, Esquires, were appointed Delegates, by the Virginia Provincial Congress, to
be held the fifth of next month.
        In the Committee of Safety of New-Jersey.
                Princeton August 31.
    Resolved, That the several officers and pri-
vates who embody themselves as minute men in
this province, be, and they hereby are directed,
for the sake of distinction and convenience, to
adopt, as their uniform, hunting frocks, as near
as may be similar to those of the Rifle Men now
in the Continental service.
        A true copy from the minutes,
                William Paterson, Sec'ry.
    Cambridge Aug. 31. Last Saturday Night about
2000 of the United Colonies entrenched on a Hill
in Charlestown, known by the Name of Plow'd Hill,

within point blank shot of the Enemy; and notwithstanding a continuous fire from them almost
all Day following, we had only two killed and
two wounded viz. Adjutant Muntore of Rhode Island, and a private killed, and Mr. Simpson, a
Volunteer of Pennsylvania, lost a Leg, and another man wounded. While our entrenchments were
carrying on upon the Hill, Parties of Rifle Men
were employed in firing upon the advanced Guards
on Charlestown Neck; but how many of the Enemy
were killed, we have not been able to learn; one
of their Officers and several Men were seen to
fall. Two of the Enemy's floating Batteries attempting to annoy our People at Work upon the
Hill, were silenced in Mistick River, and one
of them partly took by some of our Cannon placed
at Temple's Farm.

Bunker Hill, Plow'd Hill and Winter-Hill are
situated in a Range from East to West each of
them on or near Mistick River; Plow'd Hill is
in the Middle, and is the lowest of the three.
The summit of which is about half a Mile from
the Enemy's Works of Bunker Hill.

The Enemy finding but little Effect from their
firing last Sabbath, begin to relax on Monday;
they, however, at Times, still continue their
fire. Our Men are now well secured in their new
Posts, and are compleating their Works with
great Expedition.

The Hon. Continental Congress have appointed
Colonel Samuel Mott, Chief Engineer of the Army
under General Schuyler.

The Enemies to Liberty and America, headed by
Tom Gage, lately gave a notable Specimen of
their Hatred to the very Name of Liberty. A party of men, of whom one Job Williams was Ring-
leader, a few Days since, repaired to a Tree at
the South End of Boston, known by the Name of
the Liberty Tree, and, armed with Axes, &c. made
a furious Attack upon it, After a long spell of
lauguing, grunting, swearing, sweating and foam-
ing, they cut down the Tree, because it be the
Name of Liberty. But, be it known to this infamous band of Trators that the Grand American
Tree of Liberty, planted in the Center of the
United Colonies of North-America, now flourishes

with unrivalled, increasing beauty, and bids fair, in a short Time, to assure, under its wide spreading Branches, a safe and happy Retreat to all the Sons of Liberty, however numerous and dispersed.

We are told that a Captain and Lieutenant, both belonging to the Marines, in the ministerial Army, lately fought a Duel in Boston, occasioned by a political Dispute; in which the Captain was killed, and the Lieutenant badly wounded.

By a Gentleman from Dartmouth, we hear, that a few Days ago, as one of the piratical Ships of War (suppose to be the King Fisher) was passing up the Sound between Martha's Vineyard and the Elizabeth-Islands, she stood into Tarpolan Cove, close in with one of the Houses, where stood a Number of People without Arms, looking at the Ship; whom, without the least Provocation, they received a Number of Cannon Balls, and some Musket Shot, from the Ship, which obliged them to secure themselves: After which the Ship fired a Number of Cannon shot at the House, some of which went through the same, and damaged several barrels of Provisions, &c. but happily no Person was killed or wounded. As soon as this was done, the Ship immediately put about and came to Anchor in a considerable Distance from the Shore, and soon after made off.

It may be remembered, that the beginning of June last, on one of the Islands, a Number of poor People were robbed by Capt. Lindsey, in the Falkland Sloop of War, of more than 200 Sheep, besides other Stocks, for which they have received no Recompence. Surely, after such repeated Abuses, the Admiral and Commanders of the King's Ships cannot think it hard if they are not suffered to land in these Parts.

Massachusetts-Bay in Council, August 26, 1775. Ordered, That Mr. Richard Devens, Paymaster, be, and he is hereby empowered to pay to the Order of all the sick and wounded Soldiers, who are absent on Furlow, the advance Pay that is due to them. And to Pay to the Order of the Widows and Relations of such Men who were lost in Battle, or by Sickness in the Camp, and did not in their

Life Time receive their advanced Pay, upon their producing a Certificate from the Selectmen of the Town where they reside, that they have a right to receive it.

P. Morten, Deputy Secr'y.

CAMBRIDGE Aug. 31. From the London Gazette, Whitehall June 10, 1775.

Lieut. Dunn, of the Navy arrived this morning at Lord Dartmouth's and has brought letters from Gen. Gage, Lord Percy, and Lieut. Col. Smith, containing the following particulars of what passed on the 19th of April last, between a detachment of the King's troops in the province of Massachusetts-Bay, and several parties of rebel provincials. viz.

Gen. Gage having received intelligence of a large quantity of military stores being collected at Concord for the avowed purpose of supplying a body of troops to action opposing to his majesty's government, detached on the 18th of April at night, the grenadiers of his Army and the light infantry, under the command of Lieut. Col. Smith, of the 10th regiment, and Maj. Pitcaine of the marines, with orders to destroy the said stores; and the next morning eight companies of the fourth; the same number of the twenty-third and forty-ninth, and some marines, marched under the command of Lord Percy, to support the other detachments. Lieut. Col. Smith finding after he had advanced some miles on his march, that the country had been alarmed by the firing of guns, and ringing of bells, dispatched six companies of the light infantry in order to secure two bridges on the different roads beyond Concord, who, upon arrival at Lexington, found a body of the country people drawn up under arms on a green close to the road, and upon the King's troop marching up to them, in order to enquire the reason of their being thus assembled, they went off in great confusion, and several guns were fired at the King's troops from behind a stone wall, and also from the meeting-house and other houses, by which one man was wounded, and Maj. Pitcaine's horse was shot in two places. In consequence of this attack by the rebels, the troops returned the fire, and killed several

of them; after which the detachment marched on
to Concord, without any thing further happening
where they effected the purpose for which they
were sent, having knocked off the trunnions of
three pieces of iron ordinance, burnt some new
gun carriages, and a great number of carriage
wheels, and thrown into the river a considerable
quantity of flour, gun powder, musket balls, and
other articles. Whilst this service was performing, great numbers of rebels assembled in many
parts, and a considerable body of them attacked
the light infantry posted at one of the bridges,
on which an action ensued, and some few were
killed and wounded.

On the return of the troops from Concord they
were much annoyed, and had several men killed
and wounded, by the rebels firing behind walls,
ditches, trees, and other ambushes; but the brigade under the command of Lord Percy, having
joined them at Lexington with two pieces of cannon the rebels were for a while dispersed; but,
as soon as the troops resumed their march, they
began to fire upon them from behind stone walls
and houses, and kept up in that manner s scat-
tering fire during the whole of the march 15
miles, by which means several were killed and
wounded; and such was the cruelty and barbarity
of the rebels, that they scalped and cut off the
ears of some of the wounded men who fell in
their hands. It is not known what number of the
rebels were killed and wounded, but it is supposed that their loss was considerable.

Gen. Gage says too much praise cannot be given
to Lord Percy for his remarkable activity during
the whole day; and that Lieut. Col. Smith and
Major Pitcaine did every thing that men could
do, as did all the officers in general; and that
the men behaved with the usual intrepidity.

Total of the commission, non-commission officers, rank and file, killed, wounded and taken
prisoners, on the 19th of April 1775, in Civil
War, Commenced in Support of the Usurpation of
Parliament.

One Lieut. Col. killed. Two Lieut. Col. wounded. Two Captains wounded. Nine Lieuts. wounded.
One Lieutenant missing. Two Ensigns wounded.

One Serjeant killed, two missing. One Drummer
killed one wounded. Seventy-two rank and file
killed, one hundred and fifty-seven wounded,
twenty-four missing,

M. B. Lieut, Isaac Potter reported to be wounded and taken prisoner.

(signed)   Thomas Gage.

NEW-York Aug. 31. The following are copies of
Letters sent to the Mayor of this City by Capt.
Vandeput, of the Asia Man Of War, the first and
second day of the firing upon the City.

Asia, August 24, 1775.

"After the event of the last Night I think it
necessary to inform you, that having information
that it was intended by some people in New-York
to take away the guns from the battery, which,
as some belonging to the King, it was my duty
to protect. I sent a boat to lie near the shore,
to watch their motions; soon after 12, they begun to move the guns from the battery, which being observed by the officer in the boat, left
his station to come on board to inform me thereof but being perceived from shore, he was fired
upon by a great many musketry, by which one of
the men in the boat was shot dead. My duty called
upon me to repel and attack the fort, as well as
to defend the guns, which occasioned met to fire
upon the battery. I acquaint you with this, that
the people of the town may not imagine it my
intention to do them any hurt, which I wish as
much as possible to avoid; but if they will persist in behaving in such a manner as to make
their safety and my duty incompatible, the mis-
chiefs that may arise must lie at their door,
and not mine. An Answer is desired. I am Sir,

G. Vandeput."

"To the Mayor amd Magistrates of New-York."

"Gentlemen"   Asia, August 24, 1775.

"Whereas a boat belonging to his Majesty's
Ship Asia (under my command) was between 12 and
1 o'clock this morning fired upon by a number
of people, from the walls of the city, by which
firing one man in the said boat is dead. And
whereas his Malesty's cannon mounted upon the
walls, were about that time soon afterwards
taken off from thence; the perpetrators of which

are guilty of the crime expressed in the statement for such offences; this is to require at hands of the magistrates, due satisfaction for these high misdemeanors; as I must otherwise look upon these acts, not as acts of rioters, but as done by the whole community. I wrote a letter to you this Morning, to which I have not received any answer, I must therefore inform you that if you do not think proper to send me some answer to this, as soon as may be reasonable be expected, I shall take such measures as may seem necessary to me accordingly.   I am, &c.

G. Vandeput."

To the Mayor and principal Magistrates.

"Asia, N. River, August 25, 1775.

"Sir,

I received a letter from you last night, in which you said that you would this morning, send me an explicit answer to my former letters. As you certainly have had sufficient time to make every necessary inguiry, I am to desire you will send me your answer upon the Receipt of this.

I am, Sir your very humble Servant,

To W. Hicks, Esq;   G. Vandeput."

"Asia, N. River, August 25, 1775.

"Sir,

I have just now received Answers; in return which I am to reacquaint you that the Musket fired from our Boat, was fired as a signal towards the ship, and not on the battery, as the people in the boat will likewise make their affidavits of. You say you are at a loss to account how my duty could oblige me to fire upon the city, in defence of those guns, in the fear of civil government; and you add that you can neither account for my inducement, half an hour after to return of the boats and the removal of the cannon, for firing a broadside at the city at large. You surely cannot doubt its being my duty to defend every part of the King's stores, wherever they may be; For this purpose I fired upon the battery, as the only means to prevent the intention of the people employing in removing the guns. For a considerable time I thought they had deserted from their purpose. Their hazzuing and their firing from the walls upon

the ship, convinced me to the contrary; this
occasioned the broadside to be fired, not at the
city at large, but at the most effectual method
to prevent their persisting in their pursuit,
which it were impossible I could tell they had
effected. I have no more to add, and that I shall
persist in doing what I know to be my duty: in
doing which I shall, if possible, avoid to hurt
to any one.

I am Sir, your humble servant,
To W. Hicks, Esq;   G. Vandeput."

NEW-york Aug. 31. On Tuesday Intelligence was
received from General Washington and Wooster,
that a number of Transports, with some men of
war (20 sails in all) on the move from Boston
on a secret expedition supposed to be for fresh
provissions, and that it is probable they would
attempt a landing from the Sound, on Long-Island
about Montaug Point, or perhaps further down as
far as Queen's County, Huntington, Lloyd's Neck,
or Flushing, every place ought yo be on guard.

The King Fisher Sloop of War, with several
cutters was observed to be reconnoitering the
north side of Long-Island, and was followed by
a topsail vessel, who as they went through the
road fired a signal.

Capt. Jenkins who left Quebec the 21st of July
Informs, that the Canadians seemed well pleased
with the proceedings of the Colonies; that he
understood they had received and highly Approved
a Letter sent them by the Continental Congress.

Lieut. Joseph Hayward of Concord gives Notice,
That on the 19th of April last, in the flight he
took from the Regulars in Menotomy, a Horse and
Chaise; The Chaise was owned by Reuben Brown of
Concord; what remains on his Hands is a Mouse-
coloured Horse, about 15 Hands high, old, poor
and dull, a good Red Quilt, Tammy on both sides;
a good camblet Riding-hood brown colour; one
Pillow, and a Piece of Red-Tuck. The owner may
have them by telling the Marks and paying for
the charge of this Advertisement.

Joseph Hayward.

CAMBRIDGE Aug. 31. American Hospital Aug. 24,
All Persons who have furnished Necessaries to,
or have any Demands on the late General Hospital

for the Colony of Massachusetts-Bay, are desired
to bring or send their Accounts to the Subsrib-
ers, on or before the 14th of September next,
that they may be paid before the General Court
for a Settlement.

      Isaac Foster Jun. & John Warren, Surgeons.
  Camp at Cambridge, August 17, 1755.

Deserted, in Col. Sergent's Regiment, William
Turner, a short thick Fellow, about five Feet
high, mark'd with the Small-Pox, has very thick
Lips, mutters and swarls when he speaks, had on
when he went away a green Coat faced with black,
and yellow Buttons; carried with him a short
blue Jacket which he commonly wears. Whoever
will apprehend said Turner, and return him to
Capt. Hart, or Col. Sergent, shall receive Forty
Shillings Reward, by me,   Moses Hart Captain.

SEPTEMBER 1775

NEW-LONDON Sept. 1. Wednesday Morning a Tender chased two small Sloops into Stonington Habour, who had a number of People on board bound to Block Island, and they had but just Time to get on Shore before a Tender came in, and after making a tack they came close along side Captain Denison's Wharf, and discharged a full Broadside into the Stores, Houses, &c. and sailed out again, and in a little Time returned with the Rose Man of War, and another Tender, who were under Sail, and continued firing the whole Day, with very little intermission; during the Time a Flag was sent off from the Shore, asking Capt. Wallace, commander of the Rose, to let them know what he meant by firing on the Town? His answer was, that he did it in his own Desires. We have one Man mortally wounded, and the Houses, Stores, &c. very much shattered. Yesterday Morning they sailed out and anchored at the North Side of the West end of Fisher's Island, where they remain at this Publication. There were five of the People killed on board the Tenders by the Inhabitants who assembled with their Arms the whole Day.

NEW-LONDON Sept. 1. The Commissioners appointed by the Hon. the Continental Congress, for the Nothern District, were to meet the Chiefs and Attendants of the Iroquois (which Comprehend the five nations,) and the Oeaquegos, inhabiting near Lake Champlain, last Thursday at Albany. The names of the Commissioners are, Colonel Frenels, from Pennsylvania; General Shuyler, and Colonel Dowe, from New-York, Colonel Oliver Wolcott, from Connecticut; and Major Hanley from Massachusetts-Bay. It was expected that the above Chiefs and their Attendants would amount to near 500 men.

NEW-YORK Sept. 1.   Provincial Congress.

Whereas attempts may be made to promote dis-
cord among the Inhabitants of this colony, and
to assist and and the ministerial army and navy
in their endeavours to carry in execution the
cruel and oppressive acts of the Parliament
against the rights and liberties of the inhabitants of this continent. And as the immutable
laws of said defence and preservation justifies
every reasonable measure entered into to counteract or frustrate such attempts, therefore.

Resolved, That if any person or persons shall
be found guilty, before the committee of any
city or county, of attempting (after the date of
this resolution) to furnish the ministerial army or navy, with provisions or other necessaries, contrary to the resolution of the Continental or of this Congress, or of holding a corre-
pondence by letter or otherwise, for the purpose
of giving important information to the said army
or navy, of the measures pursued by the united
colonies, or any of them; or of advising expe-
diate which the said army or navy might or ougth
to pursue against the said colonies or any of
them; such person or persons, so found guilty,
shall be punished at the direcrtion of the ex-
aminer before whom he or they shall be found so
guilty, or at the discretion of the Congress or
committee of safety of this colony, so as the
punishment by them, and their discretion inflicted shall not exceed three months imprison-
ment, or other the punishments herein after mentioned, for the first offence.

Resolve, That if any person or persons shall
be found guilty, before the committee of any
city or county in this colony, of having furnished the ministerial army or navy (after the
date of this resolution) with provisions or any
necessaries, contrary to resolution of the Continental or of this Congress such person or persons found guilty thereof upon due proof, shall
be disarmed, and forfeit double the value of the
provision, or other necessaries so furnished:
to be applied to the public exigencies of the
colony in such a manner as the Congress or Committee of safety of this colony for the time

being, shall order and direct, And that such person or persons so found guilty, shall be put into and detained in close confinement, at his or their own expence and charge, until three months after he or they respectively shall have paid such forfeiture. And that every such person or persons who shall be found guilty of a second offence, of the same kind, shall be banished from this colony for the term of seven years, from the time of such second conviction.

Altho' this Congress has a tender regard to the freedom of speech, the rights of conscience, and personal liberty, as far as an indulgence in these particulars may be consistent with our general security; yet, for the public safety, by it, Resolved, That if any person or persons shall hereafter oppose or deny the authority of the Continental or of this Congress, or the committee of safety or the committee of the respective counties, cities, towns, manors, precinct, or districts in this colony, or dissuade any person or persons from obeying the recommendations of the Continental or this Congress, or the committee of safety or the committee abovesaid, and be therefore convicted, before the committee of the county, or any thirteen or more of their members, who shall or may meet upon a general call of the chairman of such committee where such person or persons may reside, that such committee shall cause such offenders to be disarmed; and for the second offence they shall be committed to close confinement, at their respective expence. And in case any of the said committee are unable to carry this, or any resolution into execution, they are hereby directed to apply to the next county committee, or commanding officer of the militia, or to the Congress, or committee of safety of this colony, for necessary assistance, as the case may require, But if it shall so happen that any violators of this resolution, shall reside in a county where there is no committee of the county, in that case the matter shall be triable before the committee of the next county: Provided that no person shall be tried before a general committee of the city or county of New-York, upon the resolutions herein contained, which the stated quorum be present; and in the city and county of Albany, unless they are present 25 members.

Resolve farther, That the respective committees; and the militia of the several counties, by order of the committees, or the commissioned officer of the militia then nearest; and hereby expressly enjoined to apprehend every inhabitant or resident of the colony, who now is or shall hereafter be discovered to be inlisted, or on arms against the liberties of America. and to confine such offenders or offenders in safe custody: And his or their punishment is received to the determination of this, or some future Provincial Congress. And the committee nearest to any person who shall be so inlisted, or have taken up arms against the liberties of America, are hereby directed to appoint some discreet person to take charge of the estate of both real and personal, of any such person or persons: Which person so appointed, shall be invested with such estate, and render on oath a just and true account thereof to this or some future Congress, or to commissioners by them to be appointed, and pay the issue and profits thereto to the treasurer appointed by Congress, for the use of the associated colonies.

Resolve, That if any person be taken upon suspicion of any of the crimes in the above resolution specified, he shall immediately taken before the committee of the city, town, manor, precinct, or district where the offender shall have been taken up; and if upon examination the suspicion shall appear to the said committee to be groundless, that he be discharged: Provided also, that no person charged to be an offender, shall be tried upon any of the foregoing resolves until the person to be judged of the offence, be first severely sworn to try and adjudge the person so charged, without partiality, favour, or affection, or hope of reward, according to evidence; and that every witness who shall be examined on such trial, shall have the charge distinctly and clearly stated to him, and he thereupon sworn to speak the truth, the whole truth, and nothing but the truth.

A true Copy of the minutes.

Robert Benson Secretary.

NORWICH Sept. 4. We hear from Stonington, that about seven o'Clock last Wednesday Morning, two Vessels, one of which had on board about 70 armed Men, destined to Block Island to defend the Stock there, were persued into the Bay by a Tender, who fired sundry Guns at the Town, upon which some of the People from the shore returned the fire. The Tender went off, but soon returned with the Rose Man of War and two other tenders. The Ship arrived, and, with the Tenders, began a very heavy Fire upon the Town. A Flag of peace was sent from the Shore, to Capt. Wallace, Commander of the Ship Rose, to enquire the occasion of their firing upon the Town. He returned for Answer, that he did it in his own Defence. That he and the People on shore had taken Turns firing, that if they would cease Hostilities, he should fire no more upon them, but, if they had a mind for more sport they should have it. He gave them an Half Hour to consider of it, upon which the Flag returned and was setting out again with an Answer, but the Time being elapsed, Wallace renewed the Fire, on which some of the Men on board the Flag fell overboard and swam ashore. They took four Vessels, two of which were loaded, one with Molasses, belonging to Providence, the other with Hay from the Jerseys. Though the Man of War and Tenders fired on the Town (with little intermission) the whole Day little Damage was done either to houses or to Stores.

It is with Pleasure we assure the Public that no lives were lost, and only one man wounded.

Yesterday the Vessel loaded with Hay, above-mentioned, was put into New-London with Hay, above-mentioned, was put into New-London in a Gale of Wind and retaken by the inhabitants

NEWPORT Sept. 4. A sloop was lately carried into Boston, with live-stock from Connecticut, which was taken by a cruiser which vessel and cargo was condemned in Boston as forfeited; the Captain of which left Boston last Tuesday, and informs, that ten regulars were carried into

Boston dead, the Sunday before, who had been killed by the rifle men belonging to the American army, on Saturday night, the 26th of last month; that it was very sickly among the inhabitants and the ministerial troops; and that there were but 2000 regulars in Boston, fit for duty, and the same number at Bunker's Hill.

HARTFORD Sept. 4. To the suppressed inhabitants of the united American Colonies.

Whereas I the subscriber have heretofore Tho't myself not obliged to pay any regard to the Association of the Hon. Constitutional Congress, which has had a tendency to raise opposition to the advice of said Congress and to make diversion in this town; for which I am sorry, and am now convinced that I ought to adhere to the advice of the said Congress, as being the only means to defend these colonies in the Possession of their Rights and Liberties, and request that my former opinion may be charitably overlooked, as I am determined not to contract the major part of my brethren in this and neighbouring colonies.   George Nichols.

The above is accepted and approved by the committee of Inspection, and ordered that copies be transmitted to the printers that they may be published in the Hartford and New Haven public papers.

     Test.   Timothy Judd, Chairman.
     A true copy of the minutes,
     Test. Joseph Hopkins Committee Clerk.

From Waterbury, dated Aug. 21, 1775.
To my brethren and fellow subjects in the american colonies.

Whereas I the Subscriber urged by a crowd of business and imagining I was not bound to observe the late Continental Fast on the 20th of July last, was induced to suffer people in my business to labour on said day, and am now convinced of my mistake, am sorry I have thus offended and ask your charitable forgiveness; and I have no intention to counteract the advice of the Hon. Continental Congress or the minds of the major part of my brethren, I am determined for the future to pay all proper respect to the advice of said Congress.   Samuel Peck.

The above is accepted by the committee of inspection and ordered a copy to be transmitted
that they may be published in the Connecticut
Courant.
               Test.   Timothy Judd, Chairman.
               A true copy of the minutes.
     Test. Joseph Hopkins, Committee Clerk.
                         Waterbury,   August 21, 1775.
     HARTFORD Sept. 4. Jonathan Pentabone Esq; Col.
of the 18th Regiment of Militia in this colony,
on receiving the advice of the Continental Congress recommending the inlisting of the fourth
part of the Militia to be in readiness on the
shortest Notice, for the public Service, gave
Orders to the Captains of the respective companies in the Regiment under his Command, immediately to muster their Companies for the purpose of inlisting their proportion of minute-
men; which being done, there appeared such a
generous Spirit in the Soldiery, and Willingness
to serve in their Country's Cause, that a Number
sufficient to form three Companies, to consist
of Sixty Eight Men, exclusive of Officers, were
immediately inlisted, and were accordingly formed
and led to the choice of their Officers, and are
preparing with all expectation, and will soon be
well equipt to march, wherever they may be ordered, on the shortest Notice.
     We hear a number of officer's ladies have
lately arrived at Boston from England, Ireland,
&c. and on this landing found they were to a
woman widows.
     HARTFORD Sept. 4.   (Connecticut Courant)
     Mr. Watson,
Please give the following a place in the Hartford Paper. General Burgoyne's Letter to General
Lee is a finished piece of Finesse and Sophism,
Treachery itself cannot exceed it. He designed
it should be received as a Testimony of pure and
ardent Affection; and is the height of seeming
Endearing to have given the fatal thrust. The
Ruin of Mr. Lee was conspired under the Pretext
of infuse Charity. And the Interview taken Place,
an effecacy of Burgoyne's hellish Sophistry
would have filled the dark Regions of Tyranny
with Acclamations of joy and Triumph. The

271

peculiar solicity of Mr. Lee's infatuation was
not hid from General Burgoyne. Hence the infernal Plot was concerted: and then under the sacred cloth of Friendship, the attempt was made
to rob him of what he held dearer than Life, the
Confidence of the People. A Man of less Ability
and Peroration than General Lee might might have
drank the poisonous Draughts; but in vain the
snare laid in flight of any Bird. His Acquaintance with History, human Nature, the stratagems
of War, and the Sickness of Burgoyne's Character, warned him of the Danger of the interview,
by which means he effected the snare of the
Fowler. Hannibul's Fate at _____ was doubtless
full of his view, and his knowledge in the Arts
of War secured him against an infernal Policy
of Burgoyne. In declining the conference he exhibited to the World a Specimen of his Abilities
as a General. —— baffled by the malicious efforts of his treacherous Friend, and shunned
the fatal Rock that ruined the Carthagenian.

Scipio.

NEW-YORK Thursday Evening a Boat being perceived coming from the Transport lying in North
River, in which two Negroes and two white-Men;
they were waited upon when they came on shore
by a Number of the Inhabitants to know upon what
Design they were on; but receiving but little
Satisfaction from them, they were all carried
before the Congress. The Negroes said they were
Freemen, and had been hired to carry two Women
on board the Transport, which they did, and then
searched these Men on Shore. The Negroes and one
of the white-Men were discharged, the other being a suspicious Fellow, and of a refractory
Temper, was committed in the Care of the Guard
in the Barracks, till further Examination. The
People that were on the Wharf, drew the Boat out
of the Water, and carried it to the Commons,
where they set it on Fire, and rendered it to
Ashes, amidst the Acclamations of Thousands.

We hear the Inhabitants of North-Carolina are
raising three Regiments of Foot, in Order to
defend themselves against any Arm troops that
may be made against the Province.

We are credibly informed the Hon. Provincial

Congress of New-Jersey, have passed a resolve
that, all Men capable of bearing Arms, who depart from the City of New-York, into that Province, in Times of Distress, shall be compelled
to return forthwith, and that the several Committees are enjoined to see the said resolve
carried into execution.

Friday Afternoon a Sloop with Dispatches from
General Gage, lying near the Man of War, sent
her Boat ashore with four Men and one Woman, who
being observed by some of our People, they were
all taken Prisoners, and carried to the Guard
house; the Woman was discharged, but the Men are
detained for further Examination. The Boat was
stove to pieces on the Beach near Greenwich, and
then burnt.

Tuesday a small Sloop came down the North-River
from a Place called Little Elopus, and anchored
along side the Asia Man of War, in order 'tis
supposed to supply that Ship with Necessaries:
A first Watch was kept on her from that day until Yesterday Morning, when she set Sail and
stood up the River attended by one of the armed
Sloop and some Boats from the Asia, but she was
immediately persued by a Number of Boats from
this City and soon taken.

By a Gentleman from Albany, we are informed,
that when he left the Place, seven hundred Indians of the Mohawks and Orandago Nations had
arrived there, and declared themselves to be in
our Interest in the present Contest: They say
they are connected by Marriage and otherwise
with the Canadian Indians, and do not despair
of bringing them over to our Side, Notwithstanding the unwearing Endeavours of Governor Carleton to the contrary.

NEW-YORK Sept. 4. Capt. Jenkins who left Que-
beck the 21st of July, informs us that the Canadians seem to be well pleased with the proceedings of the Colonies, and he likewise understood
they had received Letters from Congress which
were wery agreeable to them. Ship Bread was five
Dollars per CWT. Wheat six Shillings sterling
per Bushel. Six or seven Transports were loaded
with Provisions for Boston. the inhabitants were
very uneasy, being apprehensive of a Scarcity.

Wheat Bread Three pence Sterling per pound. The
Garrison is in a poor State of Defence, as there
were not more than twenty-five Regulars in it.
Governor Carleton had taken the greatest Part of
the Cannon from the Forts to mount on the floating Batteries at St. John's. By bad Information
he has not above 5 or 600 men with him; and that
he had 3 or 400 Canadians to Goal for refusing
to take up Arms against the Colonies: The only
Vessel of War there was the Gaspee Brig. A
Transport sailed with him loaded with Provisions
for General Gage, about 500 Tons Burthen. He saw
a Letter from a Serjeant of the Regulars at St.
John's, to his Wife in Quebec wherein he informed her, that he had not had his cloaths off
this fortnight past, being so busy in building
floating Batteries to go and retake the Forts
from the Yankies.

On Tuesday last the following was published
in a Hand-Bill through this City:

Oyster Ponds, 27th August 1775.

Sir,

"Your Favour of the 11th instant, come duly to
hand, and I should have sailed for Haerlem,
without Loss of Time, had I not received the
following important Intelligence from General
Washington, viz.

"Aug. 23, 1775, Yesterday I received Advice
from Boston, that a Number of Transports have
sailed on a second Expedition, for fresh Provisions: As they may they may continue the same
Course only advancing further, we think Montaug
Point, on Long-Island, a very probable Place for
their Landing: I have therfore thought best to
give you the earliest Intelligence; But I do not
mean to confine your Attention or Vigilance to
that Place; you will please to extend your Views
as far as the Mischief may be probably extended." Thus for the Intelligence. I will further
inform you, that the King's Fisher, last Wednesday went up the Sound with several small cutters, reconnoitring the north Side of the Island;
and Thursday there followed past the Place two
Top-sail Vessels, which I apprehended to be
Transports, as they fired two signal Guns when
they went through the Race. I would therefore

recommend to the Provincial Congress, to keep a
good Guard upon Queen's County, as I Imagine
their Design is to get Stock from Huntington,
Lloyd's Neck, and Flushing; and as we hope to
secure all the Stock upon this Part of the Island, you may expect the Boston Fleet will proceed further up the Sound.

I am Sir, your most obedient humble Setvant,
David Wooster.

WORCESTER Sept. 6. By a gentleman of undoubted veracity; from Boston, which place he left
very lately, we learn, that distresses of the
inhabitants daily increase; when he left the
town, twenty two hundred were sick, and great
numbers had died, he supposes near thirty in a
week for some time past, that such provisions
was scarcely ever seen and when they was for
sale, the price was so high that but few could
purchse it, that the inhabitants are destitute
of fewel, and had no prospect of obtaining any;
that when the cold season comes on, they must
be as complete a state of misery and distress
as perhaps people ever were, that notwithstanding the present and the prospect of a much
greater scene of misery, our Modern Pharoah,
(Gage) as if he was determined to be exceeded
by none, still persists in hardness of heart,
by refusing to let the people go; That the ill
usage of the inhabitants was in a great measure
owing to the influence some of the tory gentry
had over Gage, and seemed determined like their
masters Nort and the Devil, to reak their vengeance upon those unhappy people whether innocent or guilty; That many houses have been broken
open the furniture of some totally destroyed,
and others plundered of goods to a very great
amount.

Our Army continue duty at the work on Plough
Hill, and notwithstanding a heavy and almost
continuous fire from the Enemy on Bunker's Hill,
have never yet quitted the shot, but go on with
their work as if nothing molested them.

WORCESTER Sept. 6. The following may serve as
a specimen of the humanity of the ministerial
tools in Boston. A Soldier's wife was sick in a
house upon Noble's wharf and hired another

275

soldier's wife to tend her, to whom she gave her
two or three dollars, upon receiving which she
left the sick woman to tend herself, the neighbours knowing the woman lived there, and observing for several days that no person went in or
out of the house, they went in, to the great
Amazement they found the woman dead; some days,
a little tender infant with all the horrors of
death in its face sucking the dead mother's
breast the rats had eaten into the bowels of the
dead corpse; they applied to the Selectmen, but
as the affair was not their department, they
sent them to Gage, at first refused having any
thing to do with it, but after some time sent a
number of soldiers, who dug a hole by the first
door of the house, and flung in the body, hardly covering it with earth, which made such a
stench as caused another application from the
neighbours, when a coffin was made and the dead
body taken up and buried.

PHILADELPHIA Sept. 6. Yesterday arrived here
the Hon. John Hancock, Esq; and Lady, from Connecticut; and the Hon. Payton Randolph, Esq; and
Lady from Virginia.

The same day arrived several other of the Delegates from the southward, to attend the Congress.

Yesterday the Honourable Continental Congress
met agreeable to asjournment.

On the 22d day of July last, one hundred pounds
of current money of the province of Pennsylvania
was sent to William Henry Esq; Treasurer of the
County Committee of Lancaster, collected from
the inhabitants of Paxton, in said county, for
the relief of our greatly oppressed and suffering brethren in Boston, to be transmitted thither for the benevolent purpose of the donors.
The Township of Paxton has raised above fifty
Riflemen, who are gone with the Pennsylvania
Company to join the continental troops near
Boston; and they have yet in said township upwards of one hundred effective Men, fit for and
ready to enter on service, in support of our
constitutional rights and liberties.

CAMBRIDGE Sept. 7. The People of New-Hampshire
are building a strong Fort on Pierce's Island,

in Piscataqui River, in order to prevent their Capital, the Town of Portsmouth, from being attacked by the piratical Ships of War, which now infest this coast.

One of the Enemy's Serjeants, having returned out of a Gunnering, was taken Prisoner at Malden last Tuesday.

It is said the Enemy since we began our Works at Plow'd-Hill, have thrown from their several batteries above 300 Shells, and one of which has occasioned the least Hurt to a single Man in our Army.

A Party of the Enemy, who came out last Saturday, with a design to throw up a Battery or Intrenchment near where Mr. Brown's House lately stood, on Boston Neck, were drove back, with the Loss, we hear, of several killed. We also, it is said, had two men killed at the same Time.

The Provincial Congress of New-Hampshire have chose Col. Joshiah Bartlett of Kingston, a Delegate to represent that Colony in the Continental Congress, in room of General Sullivan, now serving his Country in the Continental Army.

In the late Exploit of the cutting down of the Liberty-Tree in Boston, by Gage's Men, a Soldier in attempting to dismantle it of the Branches, fell on the pavement, by which he was instantly killed.

Deserted from the Camp at Cambridge, James Adams of Stow, in Capt. Parish's Company, in Col. Prescot's Regiment. Whoever will take up the said Deserter and convey him to the said Company, shall have Two Dollars Reward, and necessary charges paid by Samuel Patch, Captain.

CAMBRIDGE Sept. 7. We hear that a young Gentleman lately from England, a Volunteer in Gen. Gage's Army, and one or two more were killed in the Enemy's floating Battery at Temple's Farm.

Governor Wentworth has left his Retreat at the Mouth of the Piscataqua River, and taken refuge in Boston.

NEW-york Sept. 7. From the Lloyd's Evening Post London. Political Observation.

In The course of anemadversion from upon our dispute with America, the principle "That wheresoever the supreme power of Legislation is vested,

there also centers the supreme power cf Taxation."
has been (it is thought) fully proved to the
conviction of every unbiased Reader; and indeed
the Americans themselves seem so thoroughly
convinced of it, as to have given up the distinction, not only between internal Taxation
but also the difference between the legislative
and the Taxing Power; with knowing that they who
can tax will rule, and those who can rule must
and will tax; the act of Taxation being an essential act of Stanchion and Sovereignty, without which the Government can subsist, or maintain its authority.

The rebellious Americans depend upon their
members, and distance from us; but we hope they
will be of but little service to them, for there
are other ways and means of distressing them,
besides our inducing them in the field. Their
wealth is the source of their rebellion; and our
Ministry have already wisely begun to reduce
them to reason by lessening it, and when they
find themselves so blocked up by sea, that nothing can go to or from them without falling into
our hands; or, if that will not do, that their
vessels and properties are seized, and, if occasion requires, their coasts plundered, &c.
poverty and distress will by degree break in
upon them; and though they have got a great army,
they will see their ruin daily approaching,
without being able to prevent it. If therefore,
they still persist in their rebellion, contrary
to their own interest, and contrary to all the
feelings of humanity for their fellow Subjects
but in a more particular manner, contrary to the
compassion they ought to have for their Wives
and Children, all the evils and calamities that
arise from it will, in the sight of God and Man,
will lie at their door; and even the cries of
the injured Orphans and Widows, that will go up
to heaven upon that account, will go up against
them."

NEW-YORK Sept. 7. Extract of a Letter from
Bermuda, dated August 23, 1775.

"Upwards of one hundred barrels of gun powder
has been taken out of our magazine: supposed by
a Sloop from Pennsylvania, and a Schooner from

South-Carolina: It was very easily accomplished, from the magazine being situated far distance from town, and no dwelling house near it."

NEW-YORK Sept. 7. The following is an Extract of a letter from an officer at Ticonderoga to a Gentleman in Connecticut, dated August 25, 1775.

"Our regiment is in a great state of health, we have not lost a man by death, since we left Connecticut. Col. Miaman's has not lost one since they inlisted, which I think something remarkable. I expect we shall go for St. John's within ten days, we have all the encouragement from the Canadians and Indians, that we can desire, and that they will assist and join us, if need be. I was at Crown-Point yesterday, and had the pleasure to see Major B------, who has lately been at Canada, as a spy, he said he was extreme-well used by the inhabitants in general, secreted from the enemy, and conveyed back from place to place. He has received letters since his return, which say, that if our army will come on they will join us with four thousand men. Major E. who has been at the point all summer, told me, that he should not doubt taking St. John's with 500 resolute men. By best account that we can get, there is about 700 Regular troops and Johnson is there with about 300 beggarly Scotch-men and a very few Indians. Our men are very fierce to push forward. We are about 2400 strong, and more coming daily. We hope to complete what we have to do, and be on our return in 8 weeks."

NEW-YORK Sept. 7. Since our last several vessels with provisions &c. has been stopped and detained by the man of war, who put his own price upon whatever he thought proper to take, on the other hand, several vessels which had benn on board the man of war, have been seized by our people, the men examined; some were discharged and others confined, and vessels destroyed, Twelve persons from one vessel were confined and still remain so.

Yesterday afternoon two Sloops Capt. Holley and Hazard, from New-Fields or Peguanock, loaded with grain, flour, provisions, and live Stock, came down the sound to this city, and having no clearance or other necessary papers to produce,

were taken into custody on suspicion of being
intended for Boston or to sail into the hands
of the men of war. In their defence they said,
that the committee of Fairfield knew and did not
disapprove their design; and that they could not
obtain them in Connecticut, by reason of an embargo there upon all vessels, and that they came
to New-York to clear out.

The same Evening, Information was given by two
Sailors, that the Sloop Hannah, Capt. Winn, lying here some time, but not entered, lately from
the West-Indies via Philadelphia, where it is
said he was not allowed to enter, had just sailed
with a West India Cargo for Boston. The Committee was immediately called, but we have not yet
heard the Results of their Deliberation.

Since our last, Capt. Goforth and his Company
and Capt. John Lamb's Company of Artillery embarked for Albany, to join our Army under Gen.
Schuyler, at Ticonderoga.

Committee Chambers, Norwalk, September 4th.

Whereas the removal of persons and families
into this town, who are inimical to the liberties and constitution of these colonies, (as the
same were delineated by the late Continental
Congress) will tend to disturb the peace of this
town, and obstruct our endeavours in defence of
our liberties thereof.

Resolve, That no person or family shall be
permitted to reside here, unless he or they,
shall produce a certificate from a Provincial
or County Congress, or from the Committee of
Observation, of the town or place, from whence
they removed; certifying that the are friends
of liberties of these colonies, and defenders
of the association recommended by the Continental Congress held at Philadelphia on the 5th day
of September last, and that this Resolve be
published in Mr. Holt's Journal.

By order of the Committee,

John Cannon, Chairman.

A true copy of the Minutes,

Attest.   Thaddeus Hetts, Clerk.

WILLIAMSBURG Sept. 8. The Provincial Convention of Virginia, have published a declaration
of the motives and necessity of their meeting

to exercise the powers of government, and deviating from the usual forms of proceeding. They have also appointed a committee of safety, with powers to appoint proper officers, to raise the military forces of the colony, provided for, and direct their operations on any emergency, and command payment from the treasury for all the necessary expences; also to remove the treasury and records, in case of danger.

HARTFORD Sept. 11. Deserted from Capt. Nagel's company, in the 2d regiment of foot in the Continental army, commanded by Col. William Thomson, the following persons, viz. Elias Ritger, a thick, well made man, about 5 feet 6 inches high, swarthy complexion, black hair, had on a hunting shirt and trowsers, and took with him a rifle and shot pouch. Michael Mayer, about 18 Years of age, 5 feet e inches high, swarthy complexion, short hair and on likewise a hunting shirt and trowsers; he took with him an Indian blanket, a good rifle, and shot pouch. they took with them other clothes, and may possibly change their dress.

Likewise is with them John Potter, of Captain Smith's company, about 5 feet 10 inches high, of a swarthy complexion, with a large crooked nose, took with him an Indian blanket, a hunting shirt and trowsers of an ash colour, a good rifle, powder horn and shot bag. Whoever apprehends the said deserters, and secures them, so they may be had again, shall receive a reward of thirty shillings, lawful money for each, and reasonable charges.   Geo. Nagel, Captain.

NEW-HAMPSHIRE. Sept. 12. Last Thursday began the march from Haverhill, Coos, Capt. Timothy Beedel with his three companies of Rangers, in order to join General Schuyler in his expedition against St. John's &c. Also marched at the same time part of a company under the command of Capt. Veal who is one of the Green-Mountain-Boys, inlisted by Lieutenant Allen and Scalley; said company consisted of men from these parts. Likewise marched this day an independent company of Volunteers, under the command of Major Israel Curtis of Hanover, which he raised on hearing that the troops were wanted to go to the

Westward; they were inlisted, equipped themselves, and marched in three days. This shows their warm zeal for their country's defence.

CAMBRIDGE Sept. 14. On Monday last a Regular Soldier, from the besieged Army in Boston, went off in a Canoe, with a Design as is supposed, of deserting; being discovered, a Serjeant and four Men Hastened in Pursuit of him; but he had reached so near Dorchester Point before they overtook him, and having an unwieldy Boat to manage, and the wind against them, they could not recover the Wharf again, Lieut, Sporrow, of Col. Cotton's Regiment, marched down with a small Party, and by his Dexterity soon got within Musket Shot, and threatening to fire in case they attempted to escape, they all surrendered themselves Prisoners. The Boats were immediately secured. The same Day the 6 Prisoners were all brought under Guard, to Head-Quarters in this Town.

The following List of Persons now confined in Boston Goal, for no other Crime then that of being the Friends of their Country, was brought out a few Days since.

Prisoners taken at Bunker's Hill, June 17, 1775.

Lieut.-Col. Parker	Chelmsford	Dead
Captain Benjamin Walker	Ditto	Dead
Lieut. William Scott	Petersburg	Alive
Lieut. Ameriah Fosset	Groton	Dead
Serjeant Robert Phelps	Lancaster	Dead
Oliver Stephens	Townsend	Dead
Daniel M'Grath	Unknown	Dead
John Perkins	New-Rutland	Alive
Jacob Frost	Tewksbury	Alive
Daniel Seffians	Andover	Alive
Jonathan Norton	Newbury-Port	Alive
Arnasa Fisk	Pepperrell	Dead
Philip Johnson Peck	Boston Mansfield	Alive
Benjamin Bigelow	Pecherfield	Alive
Benjamin Wilson	Bellrica	Alive
Archibald M'Intosh	Townsend	Dead
David Kemp	Groton	Dead
John Deland	Charlestown	Alive
Lawrence Sullivan	Wheathersfield	Alive
Timothy Kettle	Charlstown a Lad dismissed	
WilliaM Robinson	Unknown	Dead

```
John Lord            Unknown    Dead
James Milliken       Boston     Dead
Stephen Foster       Groton     Dead
Phineas Nervere      Windsor    Dead
     Dead 20      Alive 10    Dismissed 1.
              Rifle-Men Prisoners.
```
Walter Cruse   Taken York County Pennsylvania.
John Brown   Ditto   Ditto,
Cornelius Tunison deserted from American Camp
and confined for attempting to get back.

Prisoners, Inhabitants of Boston Sept. 2.
Master Lovell, Imprisoned 65 Days, charged with
being a Spy, and giving intelligence to the
Rebels.
Mr. Leech 65 Days charged with being a Spy, and
suspected of taking plans.
Mr. Peter Edes, Son of Benjamin Edes, Printer,
and Mr. William Starr, 75 Days each, for having
Fire Arms concealed in their Houses.
Mr. John Gill, Printer, 29 Days, for printing
Treason, Sedition and Rebellion.

NEW-YORK Sept. 14. Extract of a Letter dated
31st August 1775. from a Gentleman at Ticonderoga, to his Friend in New-York. (A Student of
the Law.)

" Col. Waterbury and Ritzema, under the command of General Montgomery, embarked on Monday
Night, with 1200 Men for the Isle Aux Noix, near
St. John's to stop our Enemimies strong Vessels
by pickets and Booms, till the Army and Artillery are ready. Your Country Men with united
Voices, cry aloud for your utmost Exertion in
this Time of Need, Pray to Arms, to Arms, my
Friend! Give your Country Testimony of your Attachment to the Cause in which we are engages,
Supineness and Lukewarmness, breathes Distrac-
tion to a free People. Our all is at Stake, I
have rather never again return from the Field,
than live and die a Slave.

"I am on the eave of Embarking with the remainder of the Army, and nine or ten Pieces of
Artillery; four Twelve Pounders are gone, you
will soon hear of very bloody Scenes. Hostilities are already commences in this Quarters. I
hope in five Days to be one of the Possessors
of Montreal.

"The Indians Convention will be very favourable to our Cause. Gage has got 1950 Carrels of Flour, from Philadelphia."

NEW-YORK Sept. 14. Extract of a letter from a Gentleman at Albany, September 2, 1775.

"By and express arrived last evening, we hear there have been a skirmish near St. John's between a reconeitring party and our men in a boat, and a boat of Regulars, Canadians and Indians. The General's letter on the occasion mentions, that the captain of our party was killed (one Baker) and a number of the whites, and two Indians of the enemy were slain; that General Montgomery, with 1200 men, set off the first of the week for St. John's, and were to muster on the Isle of Noix, until joined by Gen. Shuyler, who, with about as many more men, has by this time arrived, so that within a very few days it is possible the blow will be struck, which shall determine the fate of three provinces; and here I must wait an idle listner to news, merely because hard necessity ties me down, and our men cannot yet march from the want of their campaign equipage."

Extract from the same Gentleman, Septmber 5.

"Before you get this you will hear of the unhappy affair of Capt. Baker, near St. John's: It seems Baker had often been sent by General Shuyler, to make observations, but always with strict orders never to molest either Canadians or Indians. The last tour he made was without any orders from the General, and landing somewhere on the shore of the Lake, he indiscreetly or wickedly snapped his firelock at some indians he saw near him; immediately he was fired at and slain, on which his people returned the fire, and killed two of the savages. This matter was immediately represented in its true colours by the Commissioners, or Indian affairs, to the Six Nations, now on Congress in this City, who thanked them for their Candour, and in order to put out the flame which this unhappy affair could not help hiding, a Lieutenant set out today with four Mohawk Indians, and an Interpreter, to join General Shuyler, wherever he shall be, to endeavour to make up matters. This affair was prodigiously misrepresented here at first."

NEW-YORK Sept. 14. Extract of a letter from an officer in the army at Ticonderoga to his friend in this City, Aug. 25, 1775.

"I have now the pleasure to inform you, that we arrived here on the 19th ult. in good spirit, though we had a very fatiguing march, being obliged to go round by Skenesboro; as there were not a boat at Lake George to bring us over, Out of 4 companies we had 12 deserters from us on the road, and the most of those were old deserters from the Regulars. We held a court-martial at every other stage, and gave several of the unruly one Moses's law, I. B. thirty-nine; and now they begin to behave very well, being kept under as strict a discipline as any of the regulars. There is the greatest plenty of fresh and salt provisions here, the men have as much as they can use; a jill of rum and as much spruce beer as they can drink, every day, so that they have no occasion to drink the Lake water, It being reckoned very unhealthy. The number of troops here at present is 1700 men, and 700 at Crown-Point, about 14 miles from here. We expect this day 4 companies of the second battalion of New-York forces, the boats being already sent for them. We are ordered to be in readiness in 8 Days, to sail for St. John's, where we shall have a smart brush with the regulars; the battoes are now making with the greatest expedition, and I am afraid the rest of our regiment will not be here in time."

"The General talks a good deal of this being so dilatory in coming up, and seems to regret very much the being obliged to go without them."

There has been a French Gentleman here lately from Canada, who has put our men in great Spirits, by assuring us that the greatest part of the Canadians, would join us upon our arrival, but they dare not make themselves known to be our friends, till we are landed amongst them. The same gentleman, who is a person of great property there, declared that upon our arrival, he would kill five fat Oxen to make a treat for the Officers. As for my own part, there is nothing gives me the least uneasiness.

285

P. S. Since writing the above a Spy of ours arrived here from St. John's who says, they were two vessels already landed at that post, each mounting 16 guns, in order to take possession of the Lake, which would render it impossible for us, for some time, to get past, therefore we have received immediate orders to embark for that place and are to sail to morrow morning the 28th.

"Col. Waterbury's regiment of 1000 men, Capt. Mott's company of 100 men, and our own four companies, with 700 that are now at Crown-Point, and 500 of the mountain boys are to join us. Our Spy informs us that there were only 570 regulars at St. John's, and 50 Indians; so that I am in hopes we shall meet with very little resistance, if we do, we are pretty well prepared for them. We leave five companies of the second battalion of New-York forces here, and about 3 companies of the New-England troops. This is all the intelligence I can give you at the present."

WILLIAMSBURG Sept. 15. A Few days ago the King Fisher sloop, Capt. Montague arrived at Norfolk, with Lieutenant Graham on board, to take command of his Majesty's ship Mercury, Capt. M'Cartney being put under arrest (for disobedience of orders, it is said) as is to be sent to Boston, to be tried by a court-martial.

Lord Dunmore has received another reinforcement from St. Augustine, of no less than between 20 and 30 effective men, and soon expects to have his army augmented to 500; with which, we hear, he intends taking possession of his Palace in this city, that he lately abandoned, if not prevented by those he terms rebels.

From Hampton we learn that Captain Squire has fallen down the Hampton road, where he now lies, and has seized three passing boats with negroes in them by way of reprisal, he says, for the stores, &c. taken out of his tender, when driven ashore in the last storm; which boats and negroes, it is likely he intends taking into the king's service to send a pirating for hogs, fowls, &c. A very pretty occupation for the Captain of one of his Majesty's ships of war!

Newport Sept. 18. Several vessels, which had

286

been most unrighteously taken by the ships of war on this station, were last Monday stripped of every rag of sails, all their rigging except the shrouds, all their small stores, cables, and anchors, turned adrift, and drove ashore on Goat Island, &c. These vessels, we understand, belonged to poor, labourous people, the whole support of whose families depended on what they made by freighting wood, &c.

Last Monday the Swan sloop sailed to convoy several vessels to Boston, which had been taken in and off this port, viz. a sloop from Connecticut bound to the West Indies with horses, &c. a schooner from the West-Indies, taken out of Stonenington; and a large sloop from Jamaica, which had been to New-York, sailed from thence under pretence of going to England and Pretended to put in here for a mast; [the sloop here meant, is Capt. Wynn's] and another sloop, with salt and some sugar, from the West-Indies.

WATERTOWN Sept. 18. The Committee of Inspection for the Town of Londondarry has done themselves great Honour by the assiduity, in collecting a Quantity of Wearing Apparel and some Household Furniture, which was taken from the unhappy sufferers on the Day of the Battle of Charlestown. Said Goods are in the keeping of Mr. Richard Davens at Watertown; an inventory of them will be published as soon as the General Court shall direct some Person to deliver them. It is hoped that other Towns will copy after this Example.

WATERTOWN Sept. 18. By a Vessel arrived from Cape Francois, we learn that about 7 weeks ago a Vessel arrived there from Bordeaux, after 52 days passage. The Master of which says, that he saw in the French News-Paper, which he read, that the English Ministry had made an offer of Canada to the French King, if he would engage not to assist the English Colonies in the present dispute; but that the French King replied, 'that he would not accept it as a present, as he could take Canada when he pleased.' He also read in the French papers that the English ministry had offered West Florida to the spaniards, on condition that they would not assist the

Colonies, but the Spaniards had rejected the offer, bidding the British Ambassador to remenber the conduct of the English when the Seven Provinces of Holland revolted from Spain.

BOSTON Sept. 21. Colonel Gorham, lately arrived from England, has almost compleated his Battalion here, which is called, the Royal Sencible Americans.

Several other Corps are actually raising in the Northern Provinces with great Success; and many deluded People have left the Rebels to enter therein.

We have a certain Person of Weight among the Rebels, hath offered to return to his Allegiance on Condition of being pardoned and provided for; What Encouragement he has received, remains a Secret.

CAMBRIDGE Sept. 21. We hear that Colony Troops destined for Canada, under the command of Col. Arnold, sailed from Newburyport last Tuesday morning.

We hear that some arrived at the Eastward, in a few Days from Canada, and inform, that the Canadians, hearing reports that our Troops had taken St. John's immediately took Possession of the City of Quebec.

Extract of a Letter from Richmond in the County of Berkshire.

"A Number of Men in this and the neighbouring Towns having refused to sign the Non-Importation Agreement, were forbid by the Sons of Liberty, to pass or repass the Streets with any Carriage, whatsoever, until they had made public acknowlegement of their Fault to the Committee. Quere, is it not just those who are advocates of Slavery, should be denied the privileges of Freemen."

HARTFORD Sept. 18. Extract of a letter from Ticonderoga, Aug. 28, 1775.

"This day Col. Waterbury's regiment, and a regiment from New-York, containing in the whole about 1100 men, embarked for the Isle Aux Noix, about 14 miles this side of St. John's, with a view to fortify there for the purpose of Commanding the Lake, so that the enemy cannot pass by. Another detachment is to set out in a few days: General Montgomery goes with the first detachment and General Shuyler with the second; in the whole I suppose there will go forward about 3000 men. Col. Allen has gone forward in the first detachment. Col. Warner has got his regiment almost full, who is expected forward soon. Our troops here are in high spirits, much engaged to go forward; we hope that with a blessing, we shall soon be masters of St. John's and Montreal. The York forces are daily coming forward, for that we are not likely to be in want of men here. The number already here, with these expected soon to arrive, it is supposed will make about 7000 men in this department. We have plenty of provisions, fresh half the time, so that we live well, and feel contented."

By the latest accounts from Ticonderoga we learn that the army that went down the Lake under the command of General Shuyler, landed the 9th inst. on the island of Noix 15 miles this side of St. John's. Each side of the island is within gun-shot of its opposite shore, by which means it commands the whole Lake. From hence a brigade of 800 men were sent to parade themselves within sight of the fortifications at St. John's but were attacked by a number Regulars and Indians, who had formed an ambuscade, at the distance of about one mile and a half from the Fort. Five of our men were killed on the spot by the first shot from the enemy, and eight more wounded, three of which are since dead. Major Hobby, and one Captain are among the slain or wounded. The enemy were soon routed and forced to quit the ground, leaving behind them six of their dead Indians. What other loss they sustained is not yet known. We are also informed that Col. Allen, with 400 men, had cut off all communication between St. John's and Montreal. Mr. Lassingwell from Albany, who passed this town last Saturday with the above intellegence further says, that Gen. Schuyler went on board to go down the Lake, sick with the fever and ague, that three large battoes were furnished weekly, and sent after the army with military stores, provisions, &c. and that the roads from Albany were lined with invalids returning from the army.

PHILADELPHIA Sept. 20. Intelligence received
by Congress from General Shuyler, Sept. 18.
"General Montgomery, from information received
on the 25th of August, being apprehensive that
the enemy's armed vessels might get into the
Lake, unless an immediate movement was made to
the Isle Aux Noix, resolved to proceed with what
force he could carry, of which he advised General Shuyler, who was at Albany, attending the
Indian treaty. General Shuyler upon receipt of
this immediately left Albany, and on the 30th
arrived, very much indisposed, at Ticonderoga,
which place he left the 31st, after having giv-
en proper orders for bringing up the artillery,
&c. &c. On the 4th of September, General Shuyler
joined General Montgomery at Isle Aux Motte, On
the same day both moved on, and arrived at the
Isle Aux Noix. On the 5th, General Shuyler drew
up a declaration, which he sent among the Canadians, and as it was judged going in St. John's,
weak as he was, his numbers not exceeding 1000,
might have a good effect on the Canadians, and
encouraged them to join, he resolved upon the
measure, and accordingly early on the 6th embarked, and without any obstruction proceeded
towards St. John's. When he arrive in sight of
the enemy's work, and at the distance of about
2 miles, the enemy began to fire from the fortress but without doing any damage: he approached
half a mile nearer, and then landed, without
opposition, in a close deep swamp. After being
formed, his army marched in the best order they
could thro' grounds, marshes and cover'd with
woods in order to approach and reconneitre the
fortress. Major Hobby and Capt. Mead and the
Connecticut forces being on the left, and a little advanced, was attacked in crossing a creek
by a party of Indians, from whom they received
a heavy fire, but our troops gallantly pressing
on them, they soon gave way, and left us the
ground. In this encounter we lost a serjeant, a
corporal and three privates killed, one missing
and eight wounded, three of whom are since dead.
Besides Major Hobby was shot through the thigh,
but not dangerously, and Capt. Mead received a
slight wound through the shoulder, as did Lieut.

Brown in the Hand. The surviving wounded are in a fair way of recovery.

Night now come on, our Generals drew their men together and cut up a small entrenchment to defend themselves, in case of attack in the night.

In the evening General Shuyler received certain intelligence, that the enemy's fortification were complete, and plentifully furnished with cannon; that one of their vessels was launched, and would be ready to sail in three days, and is to carry 16 guns.

He also learned, that in the afternoon's engagement five Indians were killed, and four badly wounded, besides several others, the condition of whose wounds were not known; that Capt. Tyce, of Johnston was wounded in the belly.

On the 7th, in the morning (having been undisturbed through the night, excepting by a few shells, which did no other damage than slightly wounding Lieut. Mills) it was thought most advisable return to the Isle Aux Noix, throw a boom across the channel, erect the proper works for its defence, and prevent the enemy's vessels from entering the lake.

Upon this General Schuyler ordered the troops to embark, and he returned to the Isle Aux Noix without any molestation, where, when the express came away, he was erecting proper works to secure the entrance into the lake, and to be in readiness, on the arrival of further reinforcements, which were expected, to take the advantage of any event that happens in Canada.

Published by Order of the Congress.

Charles Thomson, Secretary.

CAMBRIDGE Sept. 21. We hear the besieged Army of Boston have pulled down a Number of Houses between the Hay Market and the fortification; but whether from the want of fuel or to make room for erecting new Works of defence, or digging a canal, we have not been able to learn.

Five or Six impressed Seamen, we are informed, had the good fortune to make their Escape from the Enemy last Monday Night. One of them inform that the Sailors on board the Men of War, are very sickly, and almost all of them very feeble and greatly emaciated, owing to bad provisions.

A Gentleman who lately travelled through Connecticut, met with an old Gentlewoman who told
him, that she had fitted out and sent five Sons
and eleven Grandsons to Boston, when she heard
of the engagement between the provincials and
regulars. The Gentleman asked her, if she did
not shead a tear at parting with them? But Supposed (said the gentleman) they had all been
killed; "I had rather (said the noble matron)
this had been the case, then that one of them
had come home a coward."

NEW-YORK Sept. 21. Isle-Aux Noix (12 Miles from
St. John's) Sept. 8, 1775.

We embarked on Monday the 28th of August, and
proceeded from Ticonderoga to Crown-point; there
we encamped until Wednesday; from thence down
the Lake to a place called Willsborough, where
we tarries that Night: In the Morning proceeded
on our passage to a place near that, called Four
Brothers; from thence to the Isle Aux Mottes,
where we remained until the second Division came
up. From the Isle Aux Mottes we proceeded to the
Isle-Aux-Noix: having staid there one Day went
to St. John's, and kindly saluted with Bombs and
Cannon from the Fortification. We immediately
landed to entrench ourselves within about a mile
and a half of the Fort. But no sooner had we
landed, that we were attacked by a Body of Indians and Regulars who lay ambush for us: We
lost four Soldiers on the Spot, three more were
mortally wounded, who died, in about four hours.
Seven others were wounded, among whom are two
Officers, Major Hobby and Capt. Mead. We drove
the Enemy off, and thought it prudent to return
to the Isle Aux Noix, until the Artillery could
come up. We are determined to Attack shortly,
and a bloody Engagement must ensue, as they are
very strongly fortified, and a Number of Johnson's Indians are among them: We have a few with
us.

Another Letter from the same Place says, that
the Officer who cpmmanded the Party of the King's
Troops, was either killed or wounded.

Whereas it is currently reported, that several
Persons in this City and Province have advanced
the Price of their goods, contrary to the 9th

Resolve of the Continental Association in Congress; Notice has hereby given, to all Persons who apprehends they have been imposed on by Paying such an advanced Price, that will enter a regular Complaint before the Committee and prove their Charges, they will not only obtain Redress, but proper Measures will be taken with the Delinquents to deter them from the like iniquitous Practice for the Future.

NEW-YORK Sept. 21. It is said that his Excellency Governor Tryon acquainted the Mayor of this city, on Tuesday last that he had received a letter from Lord Dartmouth informing him, that orders had been given to the commanders of his Majesty's Ships in America, that in case of any more troops should be raised or any fortifications erected, or any of his Majesty's stores taken, that the commanders of the ships of war should consider such cities or places in a state of war.

On Tuesday Evening the Amboy Stage Boat in returning to this City with Passengers, was brought to, by the Asia Man of War's Boat, and Captain Tiley an Officer belonging to General Wooster's Regiment, taken out and carried on board the Man of War, with a Box of Papers in his Custody, also 3 Guns which were on board the Stage Boat. The pretence of this felonious piratical outrage, is said to be the detention of a suspected Person, who is on his Parole of Honour in Gen. Wooster's Camp. The Person having been observed to follow at a Distance, a load of Powder on its way to the Camp at Cambridge, was taken into Custody by the Rifle Men and carried to General Washington who not finding any Evidence against hin, sent him to General Wooster, who at his request, permitted Captain Tiley to go for him to Borden Town for a Box of Papers, which he said would clear his Character, and prove him to be a true Friend to the Liberties of America. It is imagined, that on his Intelligence, Captain Tiley was detained. If, so it will be but Justice to retaliate on him any Ill Usage Tiley may receive.

NEWBURN (North Carolina) Sept. 22. This week will ever be remembered as the most remarkable

epocha in the annals of this country, for the
discovery of the grand repository and dark de-
positum of Governor Martin's magazine, which,
with cool deliberation, he intended to deal out
in missive weapons of death to the good people
of this province. In the palace garden, and under a fine bed of cabbage, was discovered and
dug up a barrel containing about three bushels
of gun powder; in the palace cellar was also dug
up, two quarter casks of the same commodity,
the casks quite new, and Marked R. B. In the
palace garden was also dug up, about 1000 weight
of musket balls, lately cast, about 500 weight
of iron swivel balls, a large quantity of small
shot, lead, iron worms, for the cannon, with
swabbs, rammers, artillery boxes, matches, and
the whole apparatus for his park of artillery,
which he would certainly have mounted at that
place, had not the appearance of the people of
the town of Newburn, on his attempting to move
the palace guns, driven him from the trenches
before he had made them quite tenable. 'Tis said
his Excellency, the night before he took his
precipitate flight from the palace, buried these
engines of death, as they might remain in places of safety till he or his creatures might have
an opportunity to use them. The palace cannon,
'tis said, were spiked up after his Excellency
left the palace, by a person who no doubt will
be obliged to answer for his conduct. As 'tis
improbable the Governor could procure these
deadly weapons without assistance; the Committee
of this town and county are using their utmost
diligence to discover the authors of so black a
treachery.

Committee Chamber Newbern August 22.
The following letter was wrote by his Excellency
Governor Martin, to the Hon. Lewis Henry de
Rossett, Esq; in answer to an information given
him of his being charged with giving encouragement to the slaves to revolt from their masters.
As the substance of this letter is truly alarming, his Excellency therein publicly avowing
the measure of arming the slaves, against their
masters, when every other means to preserve the
King's government should prove ineffectual, the

294

Committee have orders the said letter to be published, and an alarm to the people of this province against the horrid and barbarous designs of the enemies, not only to their internal peace and safety, but to their lives, liberties, and properties and every human blessing.

Sir,   Fort Johnston, June 24, 1775
I beg leave to make you my acknowledgement for your communication of the false, malicious, and scandalous report that has been propargated of me in this part of the province; of having given encouragement to the Negroes to revolt against their masters; and as I persuade myself you hardly intended thereby to give me an opportunity to confute so infamous a charge, I eagerly embrace this occasion, most solemnly to assure you, that I never conceived a thought of that nature. And I will add my opinion, that nothing could ever justify the design falsely imputed to me giving encouragement to the Negroes, "But the actual and declared rebellion of the King's subjects, and the failure of all other means to maintain the King's Government."

Permit me, therefore Sir, to request the favour of you, to take the most effected means to prevent the circulation of this most cruel slander, and to assure every body with whom you shall communicate on this subject, that so far from entertaining so horrid a design. I shall be ever ready and heartily disposed to concur in my measure. "That may be consistent with prudence." to keep the Negroes in order and subjection, and for the maintenance of peace and good order throughout the Province.

I am with great respect, Sir,
Your most obedient humble Servant
Jo. Martin.
The Hon. Lewis H. De Rossett, Esq;

Resolved unanimously, That his Excellency Governor Martin by the whole tenor of his conduct since the unhappy difference between Great Britain, and her Colonies, has manifested himself an enemy to American liberties, and the rights and blessings of free people; and that by his many wanton exertions of power as Governor of this province, his hostile and dangerous

letters to the Ministry and General Gage, replete with falsities, and misrepresentations of
the true state of this province, he has proved
himself to hold principled abhorrent to the
rights of humanity, and justly forfeited all
confidence with the people of this government.
Resolved unanimously, That notwithstanding the
very great pains that have been taken by those
who call themselves friends to the government,
and their favourable explanation of the emphat-
ical words between turncommas in the body of the
above letter, to make them speak a language
different from their true import, they certain,
in plain English, and in every construction of
language, a justification of the design of en-
couraging the slaves to revolt, when ever other
means should fail, to preserve the King's government from from open and declared rebellion.
And the public avowal of a crime of so horrid
and truly black in complexion, could only ori-
ginate in a soul loss in every sense of the
feeling of humanity, and long hackneyed in the
detestable and wicked purpose of subjugating
these Colonies to the most abject Slavery.
By Order, of Goodell, Chairman.
Committee Chamber, Newberg August 10,
The following letters have fallen into the
hands of the Committee. This alarming tendency
sufficiently apologizes for their publications.
As Governor Martin stands singly, as a Provincial Governor, in his unremitting ardor to com-
mence hostilities against the province, are
ministerial orders to him different, or his of-
ficious zeal to injure the people of his government prompted by any malevolent principle?
North-Carolina, Cape Fear, June 13, 1775.
My Dear Sir,
I Take the liberty to enclose herewith a letter
to Mr. Martin, whose safe arrival I am most anxious to hear, the wind having been easterly ever
since her departure.
I shall be extremely obliged to you if you can
send me with the royal standard I mentioned to
you some time ago, or without it, if that is not
to be had, a good tent and Marquis, of the size
of the Colonel's tent in the army, with tent bed

to fit the boot of it, and furniture, viz.
matrass, bolster and pillow, to be sent by my
vessel bound to Cape Fear river, or in default
thereof, to Newbery, directed to care of Mr.
Cornell.

I should rejoice to set a prospect of a happy
termination of the deplorable times, that more
or less threaten the happiness of every man
throughout the British dominions.

My Complements and warmest wishes atend you
and Mrs. White, and all your family, I am,
                    Dear Sir ever yours,   Jo. Martin.
                    The Hon. Henry White Esq;

I forebear to give you your due addition to
the outside of my letter, to obviate private
curiosity.

Cruizer Sloop of War, Cape-Fear, River July 21.
    Sir,
I have received your letter of the 15th inst.
by Mr. Conningham; and highly approve your proper and spirited conduct; while I cannot sufficiently express my Indignation and contempt of
the proceedings of Capt. General Spencer, and
his unworthy confederates.

You, and the other friends of government have
only to stand your ground firmely, and unite
against the seditious, as they do against you,
in firm assurance that you will be soon and effectually supported. I wait here to forward the
proposes of the friends of government, or I
would have been among you. At a proper season
you may demand I shall render myself among you,
and in the mean time let nothing discourage you.

The spirit of rebellion has lately received a
most severe check in New-England, and I have
not the least doubt that all the country is, by
this time, entirely reduced by the Majesty's
army, which, by my latest advices, were carrying on its operations with the utmost vigour.

Major Shead may be assured of my attention to
all his wishes at a proper time.

I beg my compliments may be presented to Col.
M'Donald, and am Sir, Your most humble Servant.
                                        Jo. Martin.
    Lieut. Col. James Cotton, Anson County.

WATERTOWN Sept. 23. The Committee appointed to receive cloathing for the Army, hereby give public Notice, that they cannot receive any more Summer Breeches, the season being so far advanced that the Army will not receive them.

Abraham Watson, Junr. per Order.

WILLIAMSBURG Sept. 23. It is said the King-fisher remains at Norfolk, and the Otter at New-port-News. We hear they make a practice of stop-ping passage boats, &c. take the people on board put them in irons, and otherwise insult and abuse them before they are suffered to depart. One hundred volunteers from the camp are sta-tioned at Hampton to watch the motions of the tenders, and prevent their committing any out-rages at or near the place.

Thursday last arrived here Patrick Henry Esq; Commander in Chief of the Virginia Forces. He was met and escorted to town by the whole body of volunteers, who paid him every mark of re-spect and distinction in their power, in tes-timony of their approbation of so worthy a Gen-tleman to the appointment of that important trust, which the Convention has been pleased to repose in him.

The Number of regulars with Lord Denmore, which lately composed the garrison of St. Augustine (being part of the 14th regiment, under the com-mand of Lieutenant Colonel William Dalrymple) does not exceed 80 effective men; the other part we have reason the believe is at Boston, where, in all probability their assistance is, or will be, so absolutely required that we need not be under apprehension they will be sent to this Colony.

WILLIAMSBURG Sept. 23. To Mathew Squire Esq; Commander of his Majesty's ship Otter, lying in Hampton Road.

Sir, Hampton Sept. 16, 1775. Your's of the 10th instant, directed to the committee of the town of Hampton, reciting "that a sloop tender on his Majesty's service was on the 2d instant cast on shore near this place, having on board some of the King's stores, which you say were seized by the inhabitants, and de-manding an immediate return of the same, or that

the people of Hampton will answer the consequences of such outrage," was laid before them;
who knowing the above recital to be injurious
and untrue, think proper here to mention the
facts relating to the matter. The sloop we apprehended, was not in his Majesty's service, as
we are well assured that you were on pillage or
pleasuring party; and although it gave us pain
to use indelicate expressions, yet the treatment
received from your calls for a state of facts
in the simple language of truth, however harsh
it may sound. To your own heart we appeal for
the candour with which we have stated them; to
that heart which drove you into the woods in the
most tempestuous weather, in one of the darkest
nights, to avoid the much injured and innocent
inhabitants of this county, who had never threatened or ill used you: and who would, at that
time, have received you, we are assured, with
humanity and civility, had you made yourselves
and situation known to them. Neither the vessel
or stores were seized by the inhabitants of
Hampton; the gunner, one Mr. Gray, and the pilot,
one Mr. Ruth, who were employed by you on this
party, are men, we hope, who will still assert
the truth. From them divers of our members were
informed, that the vessel and stores, together
with a good seine (which you, without cause, so
hastily deserted) were given up as irrecoverably
lost, by the officers and some of the proprietors, to one Finn, near whose house you were
drove on shore, as a reward for his entertaining
you, &c. with respect and decency.

The threat of a person whose conduct hath
evinced that he was not only capable, but desirous of doing us, in our then defenceless
state, the greatest injustice, we confess, were
somewhat alarming; but, with the greatest pleasure, we can inform you our apprehensions are
now removed.

Although we know we cannot legally be called
to account for that which you are pleased to
style as outrage, and notwithstanding we have
hitherto by you been treated with iniquity, we
well, as far as in our power lies, do right upon just and equitable terms.

First. We on behalf of this community, require from you the restitution of a certain Joseph Harris, the property of a gentleman of our town, and all other of our slaves whom you may have on board; which said Harris as well as other slaves, hath been long harboured, and often employed, with your knowledge (as appeared to us by the confession of Ruth and others, and as is well known to all your men) in piliging us, under cover of night, of our sheep and other live stock.

Secondly. We require that you will send on shore all boats with their hands, and every other thing you have detained on this occasion.

And Thirdly. That you shall not, by your own arbitrary authority, undertake to insult, molest, intercept, or detain, the persons or property to any one passing to and from this town, as you have frequently done some time past.

Upon complying with those requisitions, we will endeavour to procure every article left on shore, and shall be ready to deliver them to your pilot and gunner, of whose good behaviour we have had proofs. We are &c.

The Committee of Elizabeth City.
County and town of Hampton.

WATERTOWN Sept. 25. Extract of a Letter from a Gentleman dated Edgerton (Martha's Vineyard) Sept. 18, 1775.

On the 16th instant his Majesty's Ship Swan, Capt. James Ascough, lay by Homer's Hole to Anchor, with a Tender. Said Tender being observed to take on board a number of Marines from the ship, and pursue several boats as they passed, and frequently running backward and forward by the Point of said Harbour, the people with about twelve Men, to watch their Motions, said Tender discovering three leaning on a fence near my house, they stood for the shore, as near as they could, and instantly fired two guns about 2 pounders, with Grape Shot, which was followed immediately with several volleys of small Arms from the Marines, which put the women and children in great confusion. Said Guard running direct for the shore, the Tender instantly stood off, and before they could get to the shore by

300

reason of a pond, she was out of shot, altho'
the shot flew very thick, a small number of Wom-
en and Children escaped without hurt.

The effect of Military Law, or
Who would not live in Boston?

A few weeks past, as some of the light horse
who were now in Boston, who passing towards
their stable at Mr. Inche's rope walk at New-
Boston, when they were opposite Mr. Lewis Gray's
house, (Son of the notorious Harrison Gray, late
treasurer,) there felt a shower of rain, one of
them dismounted and led his horse into the kitch-
en, but nor liking that very well, he led him
in to the sitting room; Mr. Gray who was above
stairs and hearing a noise, called to his maid
to know what was the matter, the fellow damn'd
her heartily; as soon as it ceased raining, led
his horse through the entry and out of the front
door, and went about his business. This may be
depended on as a fact.

NEW-YORK Sept. 25. In Committee of Safety for
the Colony of New-York, September 23d, 1775.

Resolve,
That any Soldier belonging to the Continental
Army, who shall be absent from his Corps in this
Colony without a Furlough or Discharge from the
Commanding Officer of the Regiment or Company
in which he belong, shall be deemed a Deserter;
And the Committee of every County, City, Town
and Precinct within the Colony, are hereby respectively directed to cause each and every such
Soldier, who shall be found in their respective
Districts, to be apprehended and sent to his or
their Regiments or Company. But if they cannot
be informed to what Corps such Soldier belongs,
they are to publish his Name and the Place where
he shall be apprehended, in the News-Papers; to
the End, that the Captain from whom he deserted,
may be informed where he may be found. And the
Committee aforementioned are also directed to
transmit to the Congress, of the Committee of
Safety of the Colony, for the Time being, without Delay, an Account of the Expences incured
in apprehending, securing and sending such Soldier to his Corps.

Resolved, That if any Person in the Colony

shall knowingly harbour or conceal any Soldier
belonging to the Continental Army, without his
having a Furlough or Discharge from the Commanding Officer, or neglect to inform the Committee
of the District where he resides, or the appearance of such Soldier in it; he shall be deemed
and treated as an Enemy to his Country, and be
subject to pay all Expences that shall accrue
in apprehending, and sending such Soldier to his
Corps.   A true Copy from the Minutes,
                    Robert Benson, Secretary.
    CAMBRIDGE Sept. 28. The following Address will
be published in Canada, on the Arrival there of
Col. Arnold, with the Troops under his Command.
    By His Excellency George Washington, Esq;
Commander in Chief of the Army of the United
Colonies of North-America.
To the INHABITANTS of CANADA
    Friends and Brethren,
The unnatural Contest between the English Colonies and Great Britain, has now risen to such a
Height, that Arms alone must decide it. The
Colonies, confiding in the Justice of the Cause,
and the purity of their intentions, have reluctantly appealed to that being, in whose Hands
are all human events. He has hitherto smiled
upon their virtuous Efforts. The Hand of Tyranny
has been arrested in its Ravages, and the British Arms which have Shone with so much splendor
in every Part of the Globe, are now tarnished
with Disgrace and Disappointment. Generals of
approved Experience, who boasted of subduing
this great Continent, find themselves circum-
scribed within the Limits of a single City and
its Suburbs, suffering all the Shame and Distress
of a siege. While the freeborn Sons of America,
animated by the genuine Principles of Liberty
and Love of their Country, with increasing Union,
Firmness and Discipline repel every Attack, and
despise every Danger.
    Above all, we rejoice, that our Enemies have
been deceived with Regard to you, they have
perswaded themselves, they have even dared to
say, that the Canadians were not capable of
distinguishing between the blessing of Liberty,
and the Wretchedness of Slavery; that gratifying

the Vanity of a little Circle of Nobility, would blind the Eyes of the People of Canada. By such Artifices they hoped to bend you to their Views, but they have been deceived, instead of finding in you what Poverty of Soul, and Baseness of Spirit, they see with a Chagrin equal to our joy, that you are enlightened, generous and virtuous, that you will not renounce your own Rights, or serve as Instruments to deprive your fellow Subjects of theirs. Come then, my Brethren, unite with us in an indissoluble Union, let us run together to the same Goal. We have taken up Arms in Defence of our Liberty. our Property, our Wives, and our Children, we are determined to preserve them, or die. We look forward with Pleasure to that Day not to far remote (we hope) when the Inhabitants of America shall have one Sentiment, and, the full Enjoyment of the Blessings of a free Government.

Incited by the Motives, and encouragement by the Advice of many Friends of Liberty among you, the Grand American Congress have sent an Army into your Province, under the Command of General Shuyler; not to plunder, but to protect you; to animate, and bring forth into Action those Sentiments of Freedom you have disclosed, and which the Tools of Depotism would extinguish through the whole Creation. To co-operate in the Design and to frustrate those cruel and perfidious schemes, which would deluge our Frontiers with the Blood of Women and Children; I have detached Colonel Arnold into the Country, with a part of the Army under my command. I have enjoined upon him, and I am certain that he will consider himself, and act as in the Country of his Patrons, and best Friends. Necessaries and Accommodations of every kind which you may furnish, he will thankfully receive, and render the full Value. I write you therefore as Friend and Brethren, to provide him with such Supplies your Country affords; and I pledge myself not only for your Safety and Security, but for ample Compensation. Let no Man desert his Habitation. Let no one flee as before an Enemy. The Cause of America, and of Liberty, is the Cause of every virtuous American Citizen; whatever may be his Religion or his Descent, the United Colonies know no distinction but such as Slavery, Corruption and arbitrary Domination may create. Come then ye generous Citizens, range yourselves under the Standard of general Liberty, against which all the Force and artifices of Tyranny will never be able to prevail.   G. Washington.

CAMBRIDGE Sept. 28. The Authority of Portsmouth in New-Hampshire, a few Days since disarmed all those people in the Town called Tories, (including Crown Officers) who would not declare their Readiness to use their Arms, in the present Contest in Favour of the United Colonies. The Sandemanians urged their Religious Principles is excuse for their not taking up Arms, which, as tending to effect a Revolution, the could not conscientiously do; but declared their intentions of peaceably submitting to whatever Form of Governmental might be established.

CAMBRIDGE Sept. 28. The miserable tools of Tyranny in Boston appear now to be somewhat conscious of their infimy in burning Charlestown, and are, with the assistance of the father liar, devising methods to clear up their characters. One Of them in Mr. Draper's paper, asserts, that the provincials, on the 17th of June, after firing out of the houses upon the King's troops, set the buildings on fire. This, doubtless, is as true as that the provincials fired first upon the King's troops at Lexington. Both equally false, and well known to be as palpable lies as ever uttered. The propagation of them are, however, perfectly consistent with their perfidy, cowardice and barbarity of Gage and his detestable understrappers.

NEW-YORK Sept. 28. Extract of a Letter dated the Carrying Place, near Ticonderoga, Sept. 14, 1775, from an Officer in the New-York Forces.

"I have the pleasure to inform you that I have at length reached this place, with all my people having been so fortunate as not to be left by one of them on the way. They are a parcel of hearty lads, and from some circumstances that have occurred, I flatter myself they will not turn their noses from the smell of gun powder,

in the day of trial, which is near at hand, as
we intend setting off tomorrow morning on our
way to the Isle Aux Noix where I understand they
are impatiently waiting our coming, in order to
make an attack on the fort which the regulars
have erected at St. John's. We are so much wanted there, that the boats are ordered to be in
readiness to receive the company under my command in preference to all others. We have met
with nothing but difficulty and embarrassments
at every post on our way. The troops have been
much retarded for want of Boats &c. &c. and some
still detained on that account. I am in perfect
good health, which I pray God to continue, till
I can give a good account of the defeat of Carleton and his bloody backs. I call them so, not
so much for the colour of their cloth, as for
their base and savage conduct of suffering the
head of brave Capt. Baker, to be severed from
his body and fixed upon a pole at St. John's
where it now remains, as a monument of their
savage temper, and an incentive to us, bravely
to revenge his death, or fall in the glorious
attempt. I have nothing new to communicate except that a small skirmish have lately happened
near St. Johm's, occasioned by a party of about
50 of our men, going out to reconnoitre; they
were surprised (it is said) by a party of regulars, Canadians, and Savages, who lay in ambush,
concealed in the sedge or very high grass; we
had 5 or 6 men killed, and several wounded, 4
or 5 of whom have since died of their wounds:
Major Hobby, and Capt. Mead of Connecticut are
slighty wounded. The enemy had several killed
and wounded, among the former a certain Capt.
Tice of John's Town, in Tryon County, a native
of New-Jersey; who was formerly a Captain in the
service of that province, and an old acquaintance of mine, but it is now appears that he was
a rank tory, I am very happy to think he met the
fate which I hope every rascal like him will
share before the matter is ended.

"The above is the best account I could obtain,
and I believe it is a pretty just one.

"I have only to add my compliments to all my
Friends, and request they will be kind enough

to excuse my writing to them severally, as I have this moment received orders to embark and every minute of my time will necessarily be taken up in preparing for my departure from hence."

Extract of another letter from Mr. Walter Livingston, Dep. Commissary General, dated at Albany, the 20th or the 21st instant September, 1775, to a gentleman in New-York.

"General Montgomery is by this, either in possession of St. Johm's or defeated; he embarked with 11 or 1200 men and a party of Canadians, who came to the Isle Aux Noix to join our army, the number is not mentioned. Mr. Livingston of Montreal with a party of Canadians attacked the King's troops, killed 12, and drove off the remainder; He has sent for some men to Isle Aux Noix, and, they are granted him."

NEW-YORK Sept. 28. Extract of a Letter from an Officer at Isle Aux Noix, to his Friend at New-York, dated Sept. 17. 1775.

"I have just time to acquaint you, that to-morrow we intend to strike a decisive blow at St. John's. We have already had two skirmishes; in the first we lost 7 men, besides 6 or 7 wounded. Our enemy had 9 Indians killed on the spot, with twice as many wounded, as we are informed. The savages appear barbarous to the last degree, not content with scalping, they dug up our dead, mangled them in the most shocking manner: I had the pleasure to see two of them scalped as a retaliation for their barbarity. This happened after our last action in which none of us were hurt. An armed boat, which threw shells and grape shot briskly at us for some time, tho' without doing mischief, was fortunately divided by a salute from a 12 pounder from one of our gondolas. It is said there were 30 regulars in the boat, who all perished, either by the shot or the lake.. The chief obstacle we shall meet with to-morrow, will be a strong schooner, which we are determined to board; she mounts 18 9 pounders, and was launched but two days before we took possession of this Island. How this enterprize will succeed, God only knows, but I shall have hopes to see you and all my friends once more at New-Year."

WORCESTER Sept. 29. We learn by the last Boston Paper, that the grand Rebel to his God, his Country and his King, Thomas Gage, and his despicable Band of Traitors and military Butchers, intend raising a Regiment of "Loyal Sensible Americans," the command of which is already given to one Gorham who served last war in America: We are told that some hard Tories, a few negroes, and some Scotch Rebels and convicts, have already inlisted. Whether a regiment of such being can be called, "Loyal, Sensible Americans," the world can judge. We are likewise informed by the said Boston Paper, that regiments similar to the above are forming in the other colonies: —— Yes ye Judases, for your, concolation we would inform you, that (exclusive of our army in camp) regiments of truly "Loyal Sensible Americans," are now raising in all the Colonies from Nova-Scotia to the Floridas, who are determined to defend their liberties and properties; and to Resist, while life lasts, the Tyranny of your master the Devil, whose chief vicegerents in the British dominions are Bute and North. Rebels, remember that American reveres their King while he governs righteously, they love their country and are ready to bleed for its behalf: But ye, ye butchers! disgrace your King and Millions, yet unborn, will Curse your Memory!

NEW-LONDON Sept. 29. We hear that a Post who left Ticonderoga Yesterday se'nnight, arrived at His Honor Governor Trumbull's last Wednesday: It is said he brings Intelligence that an Express had arrived at Ticonderoga, from our forces at Isle Aux Noix, with Intelligence that a Detachment of 150 Men had been sent from our Forces there, to Chamblee (lying between St, John's and Montreal,) with a view to cut off the communication between those two Places; and that upon their arrival at Chamblee they were joined by 300 Canadians in Arms.

PHILADELPHIA Sept. 29. The following Letters are published by order of the Honourable Continental Congress.

Head-Quarters, Cambridge, Aug, 11, 1775.
Sir,
I understand that the officers engaged in the

307

cause of Liberty and this country, who by the
fortune of war have fallen into your hands, have
been thrown in discriminately in the common jail,
appropriated for felons. That no consideration
has been had for those of the most respectable
rank when languishing with wounds and sickness,
that some of them have been even amputated in
this unworthy situation.

Let your opinion Sir, of the principle which
actuates them be what it may, they suppose they
act from the noblest of all principles, a love
of freedom and their Country. But political opinions, I conceive, are foreign to this point. The
obligations arising from the right of humanity,
and claims of rank, are universally binding and
extensive, (except in case of retaliation)
These, I should have hoped, would have dictated
more tender treatment of those individuals, when
chance of war had put in your power. Nor can I
forebear suggesting its fated tendency to widen
that unhappy breach, which you and those Ministers under whom you act, have repeatedly declared you wish to see for ever closed.

My duty now makes it necessary to apprize you,
that for the future I shall regulate my conduct
towards those gentlemen, who are, or may be in
our possessions, exactly by the rule you shall
observe in your custody.

If severity and hardship mark the line of your
conduct, (painful as it may be to me) your prisoners will fell its effects, but if kindness
and humanity are shown to ours, I shall with
pleasure to comforter those in our hands only
as unfortunate, and they shall receive from me
that treatment to which the unfortunate are
ever intitled.

I beg to be favoured with an answer, as soon
as possible, and am Sir, your very humble
Servant,   George Washington.
To His Excellency, George Gage.

Boston Aug. 13, 1775.

Sir,
To the glory of civilized nations, humanity and
war has been compatible; and compassion to the
subdued is become almost a general System.

Britons, ever pre-eminent in mercy, have outgone

common examples and overlooked the criminal in the captives. Upon these principles your prisoners, whose lives by the laws of the land are destined to the gord, have hitherto been treated with care and kindness, and more comfortably lodged than the King's troops in the hospitals; indiscriminately it is true, for I acknowledge no rank, that is not derived from the King.

My intelligence from your Army would justify severe recrimination. I understand there are of the King's faithful subjects, taken some time since by the rebels, labouring like Negro slaves to gain their daily subsistence, or reduced to the wretched alternative, to perish by famine, or takes arms against their King and country. Those, who have made the treatment of the prisoners in my hands, or your friends in Boston, a pretence for such measures, found barbarity upon falsehood.

I would willingly hope, but, that the sentiments of liberality, which I have always believed you to possess, will be opened to correct those misdoings. Be temperate in political disquisition; give free operation in truth, and punish those who deceive and misrepresent, and not only the effects, but the cause of the unhappy conflict will be removed.

Should those under whose usurped authority you act, controul such a disposition; and dare to call severity retaliation, to God who knows all hearts, be the appeal for the dreadful consequences. I trust that British Soldiers, asserting the Rights of the state, the laws of the land, the being of the conditions, will meet all events with becoming fortitude. They will cort victory, with the spirit their cause inspires, and from the same motive will find the patience or martyrs under misfortune.

Till I read your insinuations in regard to Ministers, I conceive that I had acted under the King; whose wishes, it is true, as well as those of his Ministers, and of every honest man, have been to see this unhappy breach for ever closed; but unfortunately for both countries those, who long since projected the present crisis and influence the councils of America, have views very distant from accommodation.

I am, Sir, your most obedient, humble servant,
Thomas Gage

To George Washington, Esq;

Head-quarters, Cambridge Aug. 19, 1775.

Sir,

I addressed you on the elevent instant in terms
which gave the fairest scope for the excuse of
that humanity and politeness, which were supposed to find a part of your character. I remonstrated with you on the unworthy treatment
shown to the officers and citizens of America,
whom the fortune of war, chance or mistaken
confidence, had thrown into your hands.

Whether British or American mercy, fortitude,
and patience, are most pre-eminent, whether our
virtuous citizens, whom the hand of tyranny has
forced into arms, to defend their wives, their
children, and their property, or the mercenary
instruments of lawless discrimination, avarice
and revenge, best deserve the application of
rebels, and the punishment of that cord, which
your affected clemancy have foreborn to inflict;
whether the authority under which I act, is
usurped, be founded upon genuine principles of
liberty, were altogether foreign to the subject.
I purposely avoided all political disquisition;
nor shall I avail myself of those advantages,
which the sacred cause and country, or liberty,
and human nature give me over you, much less
shall I stoop to retort any invective. But the
intelligence you say you have received from our
army requires a reply. I have taken time, Sir,
to make a strict inquire, and find it has not
the least foundation in truth. Not only your
officers and soldiers have been treated with
tenderness due to fellow citizens and brethren,
but even those execrable parricides, whose councils and aid have deluged their country with
blood, have been protected from the fury of a
justly enraged people. Far from compelling or
permitting their assistance, I am embarrassed
with the number that crowd to our camp, animated
with the purest principles of virtue, and love
of their country. You advise me to give free
condition to truth, to punish misrepresentation

and falsehood. If experience stamps value upon counsel, yours must have a weight, which few can claim. You best can tell how far the convulsion, which has brought such ruin on both countries, and shaken the mighty empire of Britain to its foundation, may be traced to these malignant causes.

You affect, Sir, to despise all ranks not derived from the same source with your own. I cannot conceive one more honorable that that which flows from the uncorrupted choice of a brave and free people, the purest source, and original fountain of all power. Far from making it a plea for cruelty, a mind of true magnanimity and enlarged ideas would comprehend and respect it.

What may have been the ministerial views, which have precipitated the present crisis, Lexington, Concord, and Charlestown can best declare. May that God of whom you then appeal, judge between America and you. Under his providence these, who influence the Councils of America, and all the other inhabitants of the United Colonies, at the hazard of their lives, are determined to hand down to posterity those just and invaluable privileges which they received from their ancestors.

I shall now, Sir close my correspondence with you perhaps forever. If your officers, our prisoners, receive treatment from me, different from what I wished to show them, they and you will remember the occasion of it.

> I am, Sir, your very humble servant.
> G. Washington.

___To General Gage._____

PHILADELPHIA, Dateline Sept. 22. 1775. Extract of a letter from London, july 8, 1775.

"In a few months should there be not submission on your side (which God grant there may be) they will call home Gage and let you alone for a while, as they cannot get men to go on so wild an errand. The officers hear that the minute men intend to kill them only, which is most disconsolate news, as it not only discourages the officers but make the soldiers think well of the Americans, as they hate their officers and will

certainly desert if they have the opportunity.
It is not England, but eight Ministers of State
which the King and his tools of Parliament,
that are fighting against you, and use every
unfair means to deceive the people of England.
I understand Fort Ticonderoga is to be re-taken
by Carleton, who has 1000 Scotch Highlanders
gone over to him, commanded by Col. Murray, with
1000 more who are now inlisting in Scotland:
This you may depend on.

"No status can be made to put arms into the
hands of the Roman Catholics, and, in consequence, if you could procure proof that General
Carleton has done this, and convey that evidence
to this city, you would find the great cause
brought to home here in a few month, sat verbum!
Your salvation depends on your firmness and assiduity, if you submit, sixty of you is to be
hanged in Philadelphia and the same number in
New-York; 500 pounds is offered for Captain
Sear's head in particular in a secret order."

WATERTOWN Oct. 2. Captain James Wood's information to the Committee of Pittsburg August 10,
1775.

Mr. Wood informs the committee that at Cushoc-
tou, a Delaware town on the 22d of July, he delivered a speech to the Chiefs of that place,
inviting them to a treaty to be held at Pittsburg the 10th of Sept. likewise he informed them
that he understood that the Wiondots and French
had lately been in council with them, that they
made a speech, and delivered a belt to them, and
that he expected from the friendship that has
for a long time sustained between them and their
elder brothers, the Virginians, that they would
inform him what had passed between them. On the
23d of July, Newcommer, and some other Delaware
Chiefs, delivered him a speech or answer to his
of yesterday, in substance as follows:

"Thanking him for his speech, and that they
would cheerfully meet the Virginians at the
treaty: and to convince their brothers that they
desire to live in the strictest friendship with
them, they delivered to him a belt and string
that was sent to them by an Englishman and a
Frenchman from Detroit, with a message informing them, that the people of Virginia are determined to strike them, and they would come on
them two ways, the one by way of the Lakes, and
the other by way of Ohio, and that the Vergin-
ians are determined to drive them off and take
their lands from them, and that they must constantly be on their guard, and not pay any regard to what the Virginians should say to them,
as they were a people not to be depended on; and
that the Virginians would invite them to a treaty, that they must not go by any means, and to
take particular notice of the advice which they

gave.

That he arrived at the Senaca town the twenty fifth of July, and found Logan there, with some of the Mingoes that were prisoners at Fort Pitt. They all appeared very desirous to know his business, he called them together, and made the same speech to them that he did to the Delawares: they made no other answer than, that, they would acquaint the rest of their nation with what he had said. These Indians appeared very angry, and behaved with great insolence to him. That on the twenty-seventh he delivered a speech to the Indians at the Wiondots town, which was as follows:

"Brothers, the Wiondots and Tarwaas,

"Your Brethren of Virginia, in their great council, are desirous of brightening the chain of friendship between you and them; they have appointed commissioners to meet the Chiefs of different nations of Indians on the Ohio and the Lakes, at Fort Pitt, in forty six days from this time; and have ordered me to come to this place, to assure you that their hearts is good towards you, and that they hope to agree upon a peace with all the Indians so that their Children and ours may hereafter be in the greatest friendship, and give you a kind invitation to their council fire, and that they will give you a hearty welcome. Brethren it is with great concern I have lately heard that some people, whom I consider to be enemies as well to you as well as us, have endeavoured to make you believe that the people of Virginia intends to strike your nation; this you may depend upon is the greatest falsity, as I can, with truth, assure you that they desire to live in strict friendship with all Indians, while they continue to live peaceably with us."

Brothers, the Tarwaas,

"It is with great pleasure I take this opportunity of speaking to you in the name of my countrymen, to return you thanks for the kind treatment given by your nation to one of our young brothers, who was delivered into your hands, last summer, by the Shawanese, and to assure you that if any of your people should ever

314

fall into our hands, they will meet with friendly treatment."

To which the War Post returned the following
answer.

"Brethren, the Big Knife,
"We have heard what you have said, and desire
them to consider of it, when we will meet you
in the Council House, at the time mentioned;"

The War Post, with six others, came to his
camp. They came to talk to him as friends; that
they always understood the English had but one
King, who lived over the great river, that they
were much surprized lately to hear that we were
at War with ourselves, and that we had several
engagements at Boston, where a great many men
were killed on both sides; and as they had heard
many different stories, they would be glad to
hear and know the truth. Capt. Wood then explained to them the nature to the dispute, and
acquainted them of the general union of all the
colonies, and undeceived them in an error he
found the Wiondots had been led into, viz. that
the Virginians were a people distinct from the
other colonies.

At the appointed time the War Post delivered
the following answer to Capt. Wood's speech of
yesterday,

"Brother, the Big Knife,
"You tell us you were sent to our towns by the
great men of Virginia, to let us know there is
a large council fire kindling at Fort Pitt; That
it would be ready in forty-six days, and that
we should hear them and there every thing that
was good. Brothers, we have listened, to every
thing you have said with great attention, and
considered it well. We think it is good and will
send immediately over the Lakes to our Chiefs,
and will be ruled in our determination by them.
Brothers, I have nothing further to say, than
that it has always been a custom with us, that
whatever news we hear, we immediately sent it
to our Headmen, as we shall on this occasion."

He arrived at the Shawanese Towns the 31st. He
desired the Headman to call the Headmen of the
different Towns together as soon as possible,
that he had something to say to them from the

Headman of Virginia. The Headmen then informed
him that Chinecsaw, or the Judge, had returned
home the night before; that he brought alarming
accounts from Virginia, that all the people,
except the Englishmen, were determined on war
with the Indians that the Governor was for peace,
but was obliged to fly on board a ship; That
the hostages found that they were to be made
slaves, and sent to some other country, that the
white people were all preparing for war, and
that they showed him many Indian scalps amonst
which was the Wolf knew his Brothers; upon which
they determined, if possible, to make their escape, and accordingly set off all together in
the night; that the next day, he, being behind
the others at some distance was seized by three
men; that he heard them say they would kill him,
and one of them began to load his gun; while the
other two, before the gun was loaded, held him
by the arm, he found means to disengage himself
and made his escape, leavin his gun and every
thing else he had behind him; soon after he heard
several guns go off, and was sure that Cuttonwa
and Newa were killed, as he had been sixty days
travelling and had not heard nothing of them.
  Capt. Wood told the Headman that the most of
what Chinecsaw, or the Judge told him was false;
and that he would be glad he would send for him,
which he did. As soon as he came, Capt. Wood
explained the whole matter to him and many more
Indians, and informed them Cuttonwa and Neva
were both well, and on the road; and that they
were bringing his clothes, and what other things
he left behind him; and that it was very unlucky
for him he did not turn back, as the others did,
and have a horse and saddle to ride home as the
others had. That on the first of August he enquired sundry squaws concerning the speeches
and belts sent to the Shawanese from the French
at Detroit. They all gave the same account he
had received before, with the addition, that the
Post and Twigiwees had returned the belts, but
that the Shawanese had dug a hole in the ground,
and burned them never to use again.
  The second of August he delivered a speech to
the Shawanese the same substance to what he had

316

delivered to other nations. He explained the nature of the dispute with Lord Dunmore, and convinced them that Chinecsaw had not told them the truth and likewise explained to them the nature of the dispute with Great-Britain. The Headman returned them the following answer.

"Brother, the Big Knife,

"I am very thankful, as well as all my Friends, who are now present for your good speech this day delivered to us at our council fire. It gives us great pleasure to think that our brothers, the big Knife, have not forgot us; and that we still have an opportunity of talking to them in friendship, at the time you mention. We are much obliged to out brother the Big Knife, for their care in directing all their people to let our brother Chinecsaw come to us. His coming away in the manner he did, proceeded from a mistake. We are fully satisfied with what you have told us, and hope you will not think hard of us for his bad behaviour."

NEWPORT Oct. 2. Last Saturday arrive here, from Boston, the Viper ship of 12 guns, and a brig of 6 guns, with two large transports, supposed to be in quest of live stock; it is said these vessels attempted to take stock off the Vineyard, but were disappointed by the assembling of a number of armed men.

On Friday the Nautilus, with 2 tenders, sailed, to convoy 4 brigs to Boston; the next day one of the brigs, Capt. Benj. Bowers, being near the shore off Dartmouth, was boarded by a number of Provincials, and carried into Bedford. after she was boarded, one of the ships tenders came up, fired two broadsides, and grappled her; the people on board lying close till the tender was fast, when they rose and fired a number of small-arms into her, which 'twas thought killed and wounded a number of the people; upon which the tender cut her fasts and made off.

CAMBRIDGE Oct. 5. On Wednesday Morning, last Week Major Tupper, with 200 Men, embarked on board a number of Whale-Boats at Dorchester, and proceeded to Governor's Island, within three quarters of a Mile N. E. of Castle-William, and within two Miles S. E. of Boston. They landed

317

on the Island without opposition, and brought off twelve Head of meat Cattle, and two fine horses, belonging to the Enemy; and burnt a large valuable Pleasure Boat just ready for launching. The Major and his Men returned safe to their Quarters, with the Bounty, without sustaining any Lose.

The Brig Dolphin, from Quebec, with Cattle and Sheep, sent as a present from Gov. Carleton, to Gage. She sailed from Quebec with 62 Head of Cattle, besides Sheep 17 of the former were lost by bad weather; the remaining 45, together with 65 Sheep, was safe landed at Cape Ann.

We hear General Howe, a besieged Officer in Boston, was on Sunday last proclaimed Governor of the whole Province of Massachusetts-Bay. The immaculate Gage, Howe's Predecessor in this mighty Command, is ordered to return to England forthwith. Howe also succeeds to the Command of all of the King's Troops in America.

The Enemy are now preparing to send off from Boston several Men of War, and a Number of Troops, supposed to be on some plundering, robbing Expedition.

Last Monday arrived in Piscataqua River a Ship from England, intended for Boston. It appears that the Day before her arrival she was in company with the Raven Man of War, bound to the same Place but parted with her in the Night. Meeting with a Fisherman to the Eastward of Cape Ann the crew requested some Directions, what course to bear for Boston; the Fisherman, pointing towards Piscataqua River, told them, there is Boston. The Crew shape their Course accordingly, and soon very luckily found themselves, with their Ship and Cargo, under the Guns of a Battery lately built by the People of New-Hampshire. The Commander of the Battery, with a Number of Men, very humanely goes on board to their Assistance, and offer the pilot the Ship up to Portsmouth. I can't go there, says the Captain of the Ship, I am Bound for Boston. But you must, replied the other: And immediately ordered her to get under Way, and soon carried her safe into a Wharf, where she was taken proper care of by the People of Portsmouth. She had been out 12

Weeks from Bristol in England, and had on board 1800 Barrels and 400 half Barrels of Flour for the use of the besieged Army at Boston.

We are informed that three or four of our good Friends, lately confined in Boston, in order to regain their Liberty, pretended they were converts to Toryism: On which they were permitted to embark on board a Vessel, and to sail from Boston, in Company with two real Tories. When they had got off to a convenient Distance from that seat of Despotism, our Friends above mentioned obliged their two Tory Companions to accompany them into Salem, where the Vessel arrived last Tuesday.

CAMBRIDGE Oct. 5. The following letters were lately intercepted in the Ship Dolphin, Captain Wallace, from Quebec to Boston, and are now published by Authority, to show that the brave and enlightened Canadians are fully sensible of the Blessings of a free Government as their Southern Brethren, and will doubtless soon join the great Union now formed for the Defence and preservation of American Liberty.

Quebec Sept. 6th 1775.

Sir,

I have the Honour to inform Your Excellency, that by General Carliton's Orders I have taken up a Vessel to transport a Quantity of Cattle, Sheep, &c. present from the Province of Quebec to the sick and wounded Soldiers of his Majesty's Forces in Boston; Bills of lading for which together with the Charter Party, I have enclosed to Major Sheriff.

I still Continue to send (by order of General Carleton) as many bollocks and Sheep as the Deck of each Transport will Contain which I hope meets Your Excellency's Approbation; Could wish the Cattle were better; but in General they are very Poor and small in this Country, General Criston had given out Direction to comtract for some Forage, in order to be in readiness to load the Transports he expects you will send to Quebec this Fall; and I am in hopes I shall be able to procure a Quantity of Oats & Hay time enough to dispatch these Transports you may think proper to send.

I hope you will Pardon me for reminding You of my situation; my Length of Service, and pretensions as an Officer, I took the Liberty to set forth in a Memorial I transferred to Your Excellency by the last Transport that sail'd; and I shall only add, that when a proper opportunity offers I hope you will take the Prayer of it into consideration; and Grant me Either the purchase of a Company; or one in a new Corps; which ever Your Excellency shall think most proper.

No prospect Yet of the Militia being Embodied here; nor do I think they will; Gen. Carleton I am apt to think is afraid to give the order least they should refuse to obey; and I believe this Year will Pass over without the Canadians doing any thing in favor of Government; this day's Past has brought an Account that the Rebels have taken Post at Point O'Fare with a Body of Troops; if so they may have thought of advancing into the Province; two small Vessels of ours were launched at St. John's Yesterday; we are told here that Mr. Shuyler is building four at Ticonderoga; in short Sir You must look for no Diversion in favor of the Army Immediately under Your Excellency's Command, this Year from Canada; the language here being only to defend the Province; in its Generally thought here that if the Rebels were to push forward a Body of four or five thousand men the Canadians would lay down their Arms; and fire not a shot; I hope you will Pardon my thus writing so frankly; and not impute it to Presumption; as it is merely intended to let your Excellency into a true State of Facts; as from many Quarters You may have interesting Accounts.

I have the honor to be with the utmost Respect,
Your Excellency's Most Obedient humble Servant
Tho. Gamble.

To his Excellency Geo. Gage.

Quebec September 6th, 1775.

Dear Sir.

I enclose your Charter Party for the vessel taken up by order of Major General Carleton to Transport Some live Stock Purchased by a contribution of this Province; for the Use of the Sick

and Wounded Soldiers of His Majesty's Forces at
Boston, also bills of lading.

The Vessel belongs to John Dunn Your old friend,
Tho' Chartered by Mr. Grant, and I am to beg you
will do every Office in your Power to the Master; Either Employing the Vessel, or (should he
return this Fall to Quebec) by Assisting him to
get out of the Port of Boston with a little Pitch
and Tar with some Wine, Candles and some other
Articles that are much wanted here. The Freight
Mr. Dunn begs you will be paid in Boston as Pre-
agreement with Mr. Grant, to Enable the Master
to Purchase a Cargo at Your Port; as it was the
hopes of making something by the Profit of her
Cargo back that induced Dunn & Grant to let me
have her; and it makes no Difference to the
Crown whether it is paid at Boston or by me here;
in short Dunn writes to you on the Subject, and
to his letter I refer you.

The Rebels have Taken Post at Point O'Fare;
and no invasion of the Province is Expected;
should that take Place I am apt to think the
Canadians will lay down their Arms, and not fire
a shot, their Minds are all poisin'd by Emissaries from New-England and the damn'd Rascals of
Merchants here and at Montreal; Gen. Carleton
is I believe is afraid to order out the militia
least they sho'd refuse to obey in short the
Quebec bill is of no use on the Contrary the
Canadians talk of that Deviled Abused Word
liberty.

Remember me to all with you and believe me Yours
very Sincerely.   Tho. Gamble.
To Major Sheriff. D.Q,M.G.

NEW-YORK Oct. 5. By a gentleman from Albany
we have a conformation of the report of the provincial forces having cut off the communication,
between St. John's and Montreal, and of Mr.
Livingston's being attacked and defeated a part
of the regulars; and a further account that Gen.
Montgomery, had summoned the commanding officer,
at St. John's, present, to surrender, which he
for the present had declined.

A gentleman arrived here yesterday morning
from the camp at the Isle Aux Noix, which place
he departed from the 16th ult. where he left

General Montgomery with about 3000 men, who intended the next day to make an attack on St.
John's, which is defended by Col. Templer and
about 600 regulars with some Indians: He says a
large Schooner of 12 guns lay waiting half a
mile from the fort, out that she could not get
into the Lake so as to annoy the troops by reason of a large boom being laid from the Isle Aux
Noix to the opposite shore; that Colonel Allen
and Brown had got into Canada, where they were
joined by 500 men from La Praire and Chamblee,
and had cut off an escort of thirteen waggon
loads of provisions intended for St. John's and
were determined to prevent any supplies being
sent to that post; that in the first skirmish
our people were up to their waist in water, but
being animated by their brave General, and other
worthy officers who exposed themselves much on
the occasion, they soon made the enemy retreat,
with the loss of their commander Matthias Johnson; that in the boat which was sunk by the Gon-
dola there was a number of gentlemen from Quebec
and Montreal, who all perished.
    WILLIAMSBURG Oct. 7. Last week a vessel from
the West Indies, with a cargo of rum, Sugar, &c.
consigned to Capt. Phrior, of Norfolk, was
seized by the Ministerial pirates, and sent to
Boston, for the use of their Brethren in great
distress there; who now begin to stand in need
of artificial spirits, to support their droop-
ing courage.
    And on Saturday between two and three o'clock
in the afternoon, an officer with twelve or
thirteen soldiers, and a few sailors, landed at
county wharf in Norfolk, under cover of the man
of war, (who made every appearance of firing
upon the town, should the party is molested)
and marched up the main-street to Mr. Holt's
Printing Office, from whereon, without the smallest opposition or resistance (although there
were some hundred spectators) they deliberately
carried off the Type, and sundry other printing
implements, with two of the workmen, and after
getting to the waterside with their booty gave
three huzzas, in which they were joined by a
crowd of Negroes. A few spirited gentlemen

in Norfolk, justly incensed at so flagrant a breech of good order and the constitution, and highly resenting the conduct of Lord Dunmore and the Navy Gentry, (who have now commenced downright pirates and Banditti) ordered the drums to beat to arms, but were joined by few or none; so that it appears Norfolk is at present a very insecure place for the life or property of any individual, and is consequently deserted daily by members of the inhabitants with all their effects.

We hear that Lord Dunmore is exceedingly offended with the Virginia Printers, for presuming to furnish the public with a faithful relation of occurrences, and news and that making a few stricture's of his Lordship's own conduct, as well as some of them of his distinguished associates, such as Duby Squire and titled white headed Montigue. Some of their actions have certainly deserved the severest reprehension, to say no worse; for which the printers appeal to the whole world, with Fredy North himself, and the immaculate John Bute. It seems his Lordship has it much at heart to destroy every channel of public intelligence that is inimical to his design upon the liberties of the country, alleging that they have poisoned the minds of the people; or, in other words, had open to them the Tyrannical design of a weak, and wicked Ministry, which have been supported, in character, by most of their slavish dependents. It is to be hoped, however that neither his Lordship. nor any other person (however distinguished) will have it in his power to proceed in so diabolical a scheme, only fit to be accomplished among the Turks, and never could have been devised but by a person of the most unfriendly principles to the liberties of mankind.

We hear that a Press is to be set up on board the ship, which Lord Dunmore lately seized from Messrs Eilbert, Ross, and Co. under his Lordship's immediate inspection, with proper assistance, so that we may soon expect to see the Gosport Chronicle published by authority, which, it is said, is to contain, occasionally, the commentaries of a certain illustrious chief's war in Vandilia, some curious anecdotes, diverting stories, and a number of the valuable and interesting particulars, which no doubt will insure to this new publication a very extensive circuit, and consequently resolved to their credit and interest of its noble Proprietor.

Newport Oct. 9. By the motions of some of the men of war and transports, in this harbour, last Monday, it was suspected they intended to take off live stock from the farms on the south part of the island, called Brenton's Neck, the ensuing night; whereupon a number of persons went down in the evening and brought off about 1000 sheep and between 40 and 50 head of horned cattle from the several farms: But there still remained a considerable number of cattle, sheep and hogs, on two farms belonging to J. Jobleel and Benjamin Brenton, a great part of which 'tis supposed were by them there collected for and sold to the men of war, to be sent to Boston, for the express purpose of supplying our inveterate enemies. The next day the ships took off from Benton's farms farms, about 25 heads of cattle and 150 sheep; on Wednesday they took 5 or 6 more cattle. There being still left on the farm of James Jobleel and Benjamin Brenton, between 60 and 70 head of cattle. On Wednesday and Thursday morning, about 300 Minute-men arrived here from the county of Providence, Tiverton and Campton, under the command of Colonel E. Hopkins and William Richmond Esqrs; and as soon as they refresed themselves, they marched into the neck, and brought off 66 horned cattle, some sheep, hogs, and poultry, the ships the same time being within gun shot, and discharged several cannon at them, but without effect.

The town having been threatened to be fired on from the men of war, on account of the armed forces which made its appearance here, a great many of the inhabitants moved part of all their effects out; and many families have left the town. The carts, chaises, riding chairs, and trucks, were so numerous that the streets and roads were almost blocked up with them. Thursday and Friday being rainy and muddy, the poor women and children were much exposed in looking out for some place of safety; the people continued moving out very fast all Saturday, and yesterday, with their effects.

Saturday afternoon the Ship Rose, Glasgow and Swan, a brig with 6 guns, and 1 or 2 small kind of bomb-mortars, 3 or 4 tenders, 2 transports, and several wood vessels, &c. making in all 15 sail, weighed anchor and went up the river entered the harbour of Bristol, and demanded three hundred sheep, which not being complied with, between 8 and 9 o'clock, they began a heavy fire on the town; in which time, a number of shot went through the houses of William Bradford, Esq; Capt. Ingraham, damaged the church a little, and several shops, stables, &c. The women and children in great distress, (dark and rainy as it was) were obliged to leave their habitation and seek shelter in the adjoining country. Between 9 and 10 o'clock, a committee was appointed to go on board, who settled the matter by giving or selling 40 sheep. In the small defenceless town of Bristol, were near 100 persons very sick, and dead, at the time of the firing, and we are assured two sick people really died of fright.

HARTFORD Oct. 9. By an Express from Ticonderoga which came to Town last Night we have certain intelligence.

That our people are in possession of Montreal. That they have taken a Quantity of Provisions going to the Enemy at St. John's. intercepted a Letter from the Commander of the Fort to Gen. Careleton informing that they had not more than three weeks Provisions, and must speedily give up, unless some relief could be had. We further advised, that our People had intrenched near the Fort, were about to attack it, and that articles of Capitulation had been proposed by the Enemy, but rejected by Gen. Montgomery.

NEW-YORK Oct. 9. Extract of a Letter from Schenectady, September 26, 1775.

This Afternoon an Express arrived at Albany from our Army, which mentions they have met with great success, had taken a Schooner well manned and armed, killed all the people on board, and possessed themselves of a Twelve Pounder. The

Companies of New-England Men landed at St. John's and engaged a Party of Regulars going to the Fort with Carts, Cattle and Provisions, which they took and defeated the Regulars; Capt. Yates commander of a Company of Germans; and one Lieut. Van Slyk, of this Town have greatly distinguished themselves, which has recommended them to the Notice of Gen. Montgomery. Five Hundred Canadians have voluntarily joined our Army.

Extract of a Letter from General Shuyler to the Provincial Congress of New-York, dated Ticonderoga, September 29, 1775.

"I am still confined with the remains of an inverterate Disorder. I have this moment received a Line from General Montgomery: he holds St. John's besieged. The Canadians are friendly to us, and join us in great numbers. We have taken Fifteen Prisoners, Seven of which are soldiers, and the rest unfriendly Canadians and Scotchmen in service of the Ministry."

By Capt. Little, in eleven days from Charlestown, South Carolina, we are informed that on the 15th of September, the Commander of his Majesty's Ship Tamer, and another armed vessel pressed two of Capt. Little's Men, and two Passengers, likewise Hands out of all the vessels they could come at, on purpose to assist them in taking the Cannon from Fort Johnston, and but could not effect the Design; the Tamer's barge with a Number of armed Men, went on Shore, Spiked up some cannon and threw the carriages over the Walls, next morning before Day about 500 of the Militia took Possession of the Fort and in a few Hours had several of the Guns mounted again; The Fort is in good Repair; the Tamer and the armed Vessel very prudently withdrew from the Reach of the Cannon, and fell further down the Harbour where they lie. The Governor is on board of one of them.

We are informed from undoubted authority, that Lord William Campbell, Governor of South-Carolina, has fled with utmost Precipitation, on board the Man of War in the Harbour. The Committee of Charlestown having very fortunately discovered that his Excellency had employed one Cameron, and Indian Commissary in the interior

Parts of the Province, to enrage the Indians in
the Ministerial Service who had actually inlisted 600 of them, and furnished them with every
Necessary in order to Butcher the back Inhabitants. This plan was discovered by a Gentleman
who siezed the Express on his Way from the said
Cameron to the Governor, who he knew to be disaffected to the American Cause, and conveyed
the Dispatches to the Provincial Committee. The
above Gentleman disguised himself in a Drover's
habit and attended the Express to the Governor's
House, and heard the Conversation between them,
and then discovered the whole plot to the Committee.

We hear Capt. Wallace has made a Demand from
the Inhabitants at Newport, of all the live Stock
they could spare from the island, the Inhabitants had only three Days to consider of the
matter.

We understand from North-Castle, that in last
Saturday Night, Abraham Hetfield, Esq; of the
White Plains, and Lieutenant William Lourens-
bury, of Mamaroneck, were discovered in the very
act of indeavouring to cut down a Liberty Pole,
which was strongly fortified with Iron that it
occasioned their bring find out, and for that
time disappointed in their loyal Attempt.

CAMBRIDGE Oct. 12. Last Tuesday one of the
privateers from Beverly, having been on a cruise
in the Bay, was followed on her return into the
port, by the Nautilus man of war. The privateer
ran aground in a cove a little without Beverly
harbour, where the people speedily assembled,
stripped her, and carried her guns &c. ashore.
The man of war was soon within gunshot, when she
also got aground, she however let go an anchor,
and bringing her broadside to bear, began to
fire upon the privateer. The people of Salem and
Beverly soon returned the compliment from a number of cannon on shore, keeping up a warm and
well directed fire on the man of war for two or
three hours, and it is supposed did her consi-
erable damage and probably killed and wounded
some of her men; but before they could board
her, which they were preparing to do the tide
arose about eight in the evening, when she cut

327

her cable and got off. Some of her shot struck one or two buildings in Beverly, but no lives were lost on our side, and the privateer damaged very little if any.

NEW-YORK Extract of a letter of a Sea Captain in Boston to his wife in Philadelphia. Sept. 26.

"I should be glad if you would move into the country, as there are 4 sail of men of war going to your port and I am informed, and have got on board materials for destroying the town, There are no signs here of matters being made up."

Extract of a letter from Hartford.

"It is reported that General Washington a few Days ago sent a Flag of Truce to Boston, proposing an Exchange of Prisoners: Major French for Colonel ——— , Lieutenant Knight, of the Navy, for Capt. Scott; and his Excellency Governor Skeen, for Corporal Cruise, of Capt. Dirile's Company of Riflemen: The two former were accepted with readiness; but the last exchange General Gage rejected with scorn, as an insult to his understanding; so that in all probability we shall have the Honour of his Excellency Governor Skeen's residing among us, God knows how long."

Monday came to town a number of Paxton Boys, dressed and painted in the Indian fashion, being part of a body of 200 Volunteers, who are on their way to General Washington's army at Cambridge. Several of these we hear are young gentlemen of fortune.

We hear from St. John's. that Capt. Prescot, commander of the Fort, sent word to Gen. Montgomery, that he would deliver it up to him, if he would permit him and the King's troops to march to Quebec, with their arms, stores, and artillery, but the General refused to comply with his request. Governor Carleton, it is said, has bought up the powder from the merchants at Quebec, and stored it there, the whole of which amounts to upward of 10,000 barrels.

WILLIAMSBURG Oct. 12. Some time last week Lord Dunmore was alarmed with information that 19 pieces of cannon were fitted up, and would be soon placed on the wharves, &c. in Norfolk to annoy the ships of war, and that a number of men were daily expected from Williamsburg, who were to fire them from behind hogsheads fitted with sand. Yesterday se'nnight, in consequence of the above intelligence, his Lordship sent ashore a party of soldiers, under command of two officers, who marched through Norfolk to the place where the cannon were, distroyed 17 of them, and carried off two off for their own use, without any molestation. The above cannon, we are confident were never intended for such a purpose; on the contrary, they belonged to sundry private Gentlemen, who had removed them for safety.

A large Sloop from St. Eustatia mounting 16 six pounders and a number of swivels is said to be gone up the bay with a large quantity of gunpowder. Mr. Goodrich at Portsmouth, whose vessel Lord Dunmore suspected of having brought in a supply of that article lately, in confined in irons on board a man of war.

PHILADELPHIA Oct. 13. On Friday last a discovery was made of some letters sending by Christopher Carter, who had taken his passage on board the snow Patty for London, the vessel was pursued to Chester, where the letters were found on Carter, were concerned in writing the most infamous lies their malice could invent, to spirit up the ministry against this city and province, to indite them to send troops here, and that Carter was the carrier, and was instructed to tell a great deal which they were afraid to trust to paper. In consequence of the above discovery, Keersley, Brooks, and Snowden were taken up on Friday night and put under a strong guard, and Carter who had been suffered to go from Chester, after the delivery of the first letters, was pursued by order of the committee; taken from on board the snow at Ready-Island, and brought back. They have all been since examined by the committee of safety; in which examination such a scene of villainy was opened, that it was thought proper to keep them confined from the fury of the populace till they shall think of a proper punishment for such enemies to this country.

WILLIAMSBURG Oct. 14. The following Address was presented to Lord Dunmore, by the corporation of Norfolk in consequence of Mr. Holt,

Printer of that Borough, being robbed of his
Printing materials and his servants carried off
by order of his Lordship.

To his Excellency the Right Hon. John, Earl of
Dunmore, his Majesty's Lieutenant and Governor
General of the colony and dominion of Virgina &c.

We his Majesty's faithful subjects, the Mayor,
Alderman, and Common Council of the Borough of
Norfolk, in Common hall assembled beg leave to
represent to your Lordship, that on this day a
party of men under the command of Capt. Squire,
of the Otter sloop of war, lying in this harbor,
landed, in the most public part of the borough,
in the most daring manner, and in open violation
of the peace and good order seized on the printing utensils belonging to an inhabitant of this
town, as well as the persons of two of his family.

We beg leave also to represent to your Lordship, that this act is both illegal and riotous,
and that, together with a musket ball fired into
the town yesterday, from aboard the King Fisher,
had greatly alarmed and incensed the inhabitants, and has occasioned a great number of the
women and children to abandon this borough, and
that, if these arbitrary proceedings pass unno-
ticed by your Lordship, as chief magistrate of
this colony, that none of the inhabitants are
safe from insults and abuse. We therefore, as
our duty, represent this matter to your Lordship, for your interposition.

We, my Lord, as men, and as a common hall,
have ever preserved the peace of this town, and
have never prevented the ships of war, and others
from being supplied with provisions, or any other necessaries, and have carefully avoided offering any insult to any of his Majesty's servants. We had therefore hoped, that the inhabitants would never have been doubted in their
lawful business. We are sorry however to have
it in our power to state this fact to your Lordship; which we must, and do think, a gross violation of all that men and freemen can hold dear.

Allow us to observe to your Lordship, that if
the inhabitants had been disposed to repel insult, they were sufficiently able either to have

cut off, or taken prisoners, the small party that came on shore, and this, we hope, is another proof of their peaceable intentions.

We the Mayor, Aldermen, and Common Council of the Borough of Norfolk, do most earnestly entreat your Lordship that the Captains of the men of war may not reduce the inhabitants to the dreadful alternative of defending their persons, or tamely suffering themselves to be abused; and request that your Lordship will interpose your authority to put a stop to such violent infringements of our rights and to order the persons seized on by Captain Squire, to be immediately put on shore, and the property to be replaced from whence it was taken.

To the Mayor, Alberman, and Common Council, of the Borough of Norfolk.

"Gentleman,
I was an eye-witness to a party, belonging to the Otter sloop of war, landing at the hour and place you mention, and I did see them bring off two servants, belonging to the Printer, together with his Printing utensils; and I do really think they could not have rendered the Borough of Norfolk, or the country adjacent to it, a more essential service, that by depriving them of their means of poisoning the minds of the people, and exciting in them a spirit of rebellion and sedition, and by that means drawing inevitable ruin and destruction on themselves and country. As to the Illegality of the act, I am afraid some of you, in this very Common Hall assembled ought to blush when you make use of the Expression: as I know you cannot but be conscious that you have, by every means in your power, totally subverted the laws and conditions, and have been advisers and abettors in throwing off all allegiance to that Majesty's crown and the government to whom you profess yourselves faithful subjects. As to the musket ball being fired into the town, I do believe there is not a man in it that is not satisfied it was an accident; and such as one as, I hope will not happen again. But with regard to you having ever preserved the peace in your town, there is a recent proof of the contrary. As to you not repelling

the insult as you call it, or taking prisoners
the small party that was on shore, I impute it
to some other reason (from your drums beating
to arms during greatest part of the time that
the party was on shore) that to your peaceable
intentions. As to your last requisition, I do
assure you that every means in my power shall be
employed, both with the Navy and Army to preserve the peace and good order, and happiness
of the inhabitants of the Borough of Norfolk so
long as they behave themselves as faithful subjects to his Majesty. I expect at the same time,
that if any individual shall behave himself as
your Printer has done, by aspersing the characters of his Majesty's servants, and others, in
the most scurrilous, false and scandalous manner, and by being the instigator of treason and
rebellion against his Majesty's Crown and government, and you do not take such steps as the law
directs to restrain such offenders.

I do then expect you will not be surprised if
the military power interposed to prevent the
total dissolution of all decency, order and government. But I promise the Printer, on my Honour, if he will put himself and servants under
my protection, that they shall not meet with the
least insults, and they shall be permitted to
print every occurence that happens during these
unhappy disputes between the Mother Country and
her Colonies, he only confining himself to truth,
and representing matters in a fair, candid impartial manner at both sides.

This I hope will convince you that I had nothing more in view, when I requested Capt. Squire
to seize the types, than that unhappy deluded
public might no longer remains in the dark,
concerning the present contest, but that they
should be furnished with a fair representation
of facts, which I know never can happen whilst
the press remains under the controul of the
present dictator.   Dunmore.

To the Righr Hon. the Earl of Denmore.
My Lord,
The representation and remonstrance of the gentle men of Norfolk upon your answer thereto,
demands the notice of the public, and call forth

the following Address.

A strict adherence to truth is ever necessary to give weight to assertion. The facts relate here, and not testified by your answer to the gentlemen of Norfolk, will find their support in your history, recent in the minds of many, or recorded in the annals of this colony. I was really at a loss to discover what act of the unhappy printer had rendered him so obnoxious to you, until I looked into the Norfolk Gazette of the preceeding week, and there I find your genealogy described, which I confess reflects but little honour on your family; yet, as we presume it to be truth, the recital could not justify subject the bare retailer to such violence and oppression. The disgrace of your ancestors could have little effected you, had your character been free from guilt; but when the blood flows contaminated, it is not difficult to investigate the rise and cause of perfidy. Had not this observation had its full force, your revenge could not have been so violent. But, my Lord, you tell us you did it for the good of the people. In one instant, then, you become the asserter of arbitrary power and despotic rule; and, having avowed the hostile act, must await the public judgement.

You have robbed forcibly two men of their freedom, without hearing a trial; and you have deprived the public of a free press, the property of a free man, and one of the criterions of a happy constitution.

The attempt, atrocious as it is, has been made in Britain; and had your Lordship been capable of deriving wisdom from experience, you would surely have declined the commission of a crime against the public, still more wicked and unwarrantable. Perhaps your renowned Gardian* unable to establish this species of slavery amongst the people of England, has through you begun the execution here. The Stings and scourges of his machinations have, indeed, involved us in misfortune; but assure yourself my Lord, deep and diabolical as they are, this country will rise and triumphant over them all.

You have often said, you condemned the man,

why then will you imitate his vice? Can you so blind your understanding as to seriously to think, what you affect to believe, that you have rendered a service to the borough of Norfolk and the people adjacent? Although not remarkable for penetration or sagacity, you cannot so far impose upon yourself as to believe man's happiness is to be promoted by slavery or ignorance, both which must be the effects of your proceeding. You must know, by our law, the persons or men, and property of the Printer, were sacred. How then could you dare invade the privilege of the one. or the property of the other, and thereby deprive the public of a press, by which their wrongs are known, and through all knowledge is conveyed.

Most Genius then bow the neck, and court the smiles of Nero, while fair science fits melancholy, deploring her happy state?

Do you my Lord, to whom nature has denied the first of these blessings, and who remains unimproved by the letter, supposed they can be subservient to a control like yours, guided by passion, and dictated by folly? Banish the thought, and at least relinquish part of your depredation.

Can you vainly suppose, my Lord, such acts as these will pass away with impunity? Not content with the mischief your debauchery and impudence have brought on this country, added by your false and disgraceful official letters, you now wish to complete your administration by rapine and despotism. Having banished your favorite, by deception, you singly stalk the destroyer of peace and good order.

And yet, as if the measures of your guilt were not full, you have provoked the gentlemen of Norfolk to acts of violence, by upbraiding them with cowardice, that you might have an opportunity of venting your farther rage upon them by fire and sword, To drive them still farther to desperation, you have audaciously declared you will interfere with the military, and call in aid of the naval power, wherever you think proper to seize any person who shall cast contrary to your opinion.

The charge, indeed in grating; but your threat

is intolerable, Who is there would hold his liberty on the precarious tenure of your Lordship tyrannical mandate? Your cruelty, exercised on those who have unhappily fallen under your hands, would have made the state more than wretched; yet, under all this despotism, you, falsely assert yourself a friend to his Majesty and government. Is then the end of government perverted so far from its original intention as to make the misery instead as the good of mankind, its ultimate view? If it is, your Lordship's is the character best adapted to complete and execute the purpose; for it may be truly said, that your administration here has changed a happy people into a contrary state, and widen the breech which every friend to his country meant to heal. Thus far have you executed, not the desire, I hope, of our prince, but certainly the design of an abandoned ministry.

The scope of your answer, and character, might carry me farther; but as you have long narratives I will reserve my further animadversions to a future paper, and subscribe myself, Your's &c. C.
* Lord Mansfield.

WATERTOWN Oct. 16. The following is a Copy of a Letter from a principal Officer of the New-Hampshire Troops. Camped near St. John's dated 23d September 1775.

Gentlemen,
We are now encamp'd within a Mile of St. John's, the Enemy every day throwing Shells or Balls at our Intrenchments, but without success. We shall have our Batteries ready to play upon them Tomorrow or the next Day at further. Our Men are all in good Spirits. We arrived at the Isle Aux Noix the 4th, and next Day we came within a Mile and half of the Enemy, who saluted us with shells; no damage was done; we lay upon our Arms all Night, and in the Morning I was detached with a Party of Men to reinforce Major Brown, who had taken 8 Waggons from the Enemy loaded with stores. Before we could get up to them he was engaged, and obliged to retreat, but saved his Booty. They upon our Approach saluted us very warm with Grape-Shot; we did not lose one Man; what the Enemy lost I cannot tell, but we found

some Blood on the Ground; they retreated to the
Fort, and we kept Possession of the Ground, and
we have a considerable Intrenchment. Major Brown
has took twelve Waggons more loaded with Wine,
Rum, Pork, &c. Every Thing seems to prosper well.
I have nothing more particular, only a Party
was fired on at Capt. Hogan's House. We had
three Canadians wounded.

I have the Command of the Green Mountain boys,
and a Detachment of Col. Henman's Regiment.

I am, &c.   T.B.

WATERTOWN Oct. 16. The Committee of Inspection
for the Town of Weston, being applied to by complaint sundry Times, and by sundry persons,
against Eliazer Bradshaw of Waltham, of being
inimical to his country and who has for some
time past employed himself to going to Albany,
under pretence of purchasing furr, and also purchased a quantity of Tea. Whereupon the committee of Waltham, with the committee of Newton,
Watertown, Weston and Sudbury being met on the
second Day of October instant, to examine into
the matter, and having sent a messenger for said
Bradshaw, he appeared and frankly confessed he
had purchased and sold a quantity of Tea, and
had signified to one of said committee that he
would do as he tho't fit in spite of the said
committee or any other person whatever, and
would be the death of any person that should
molest him. Therefore determined by this joint
committee, the Eliazer Bradshaw, by his conduct
and behaviour, has proved himself inimical to
his country; and that all persons be cautioned
to with-hold commerce and dealing with said
Bradshaw until there appears a reformation in
said Bradshaw.

The above to be published in the Watertown
and Cambridge Papers.   By Order,
        Jonathan Parmenter, Chairman.

I David Townsand, by the desire of the Wife
of Dr. Clark, of Newton to buy some Tea for her
and I applied to Eliazer Bradshaw, at Waltham
and had six Pounds, which I sold to said Clark's
Wife, and others, which I am hearty sorry for
that I had any thing to do with said Tea, and I
hope the Public will forgive me, for I did it

without consideration; and I promise to have no
more to do with Tea till allowed on by the Continental Congress.
This is to the acceptance of the Committee,
David Townsand.
NEWPORT Oct. 16. The present time will convince the Americans of the necessity of building their sea-port towns as far up the river as
they most conveniently can, so as not be liable
to the threats and insults of piratical ships
of war.
From good authority we learn Tom. Gage is highly condemned in England for his conduct, and
particularly for burning Charlestown, for which,
'tis not improbable, if there is any justice in
Britain, he may lose his head soon after he ar-
rives there; such a savage wretch.
NEWPORT Oct. 16. Within 4 days past the men of
war have taken out, and cut away, the masts,
bowsprits, &c, of a number of small sloops and
ferry boats.
Last Friday in the afternoon a barge with a
number of hands from one of the ships in the
harbour, landed at the N. W. part of this town,
took a boat which lay haled up on the shore; and
was carrying her off, when the owner got his
musket, ran down to the shore, and fired upon
the barge, but did no execution, upon which the
Glasgow, and one of the tenders, fired several
shot at the owner of the said boat but missed
him. A 9 pound shot from the Glasgow, entered one
side of Mr. Matthew Lawton's house on the point,
carried away part of a beam inside, and fell
down, without hurting any person.
The Swan and several tenders and transports
are this morning getting ready to sail for Boston.
NEW-YORK Oct. 16. Extract of a letter from
Cambridge.
"Dr. Church (surgeon-General of the army, and
Chairman of the Committee at Watertown) having
been found guilty of traiterous practices in
corresponding with the enemy. is put under an
arrest."
We are informed that Dr. Church in confined
in a house opposite to the head quarters, in
Cambridge. His correspondence it is said, was

337

carried on in cyphers with a field officer in General Gage's army in Boston.

We are informed that General Gage, with all the expedition to Lexington and Concord, have been ordered to return home; that a man of war was to sail with them on Saturday last for England, and that the government and command of the army would be confered on General Howe.

PHILADELPHIA Oct. 16. Extract of a letter from Charlestown, South Carolina dated September 12.

"We are not altogether without our fears from the Indian enemy, but our Negroes are quite quiet since the execution of one of the most sensible and most daring of them, named Jemmy a free Negro, who was found guilty of having endeavoured to cause an insurrection. It is a general received opinion that we shall have troops here in the winter, and all preparations are making to oppose them; many people have all their valuable goods and furniture packed, and stores are building in the country to lodge them in."

We have certain intelligence from Newcastle County, that on Friday last Brigadier General MacKinley's battalion of Militia was received near Wilmington, when about five hundred men appeared under arms, and chiefly in uniform, who went through their exercise, evolutions, various firings and maneuvers with great exactness, regularity and alertness, so as to obtain very high applause from a great number of Military Gentlemen who were spectators.

CAMBRIDGE Oct. 19. Since our last arrived in town; the honourable Benjamin Franklin, Thomas Lynch, and Benjamin Harrison, esquires, from Philadelphia, a committee from the Continental Congress; the Honourable Matthew G----wold, Esq; Deputy Governor, and ------ Wales, Esq; of Connecticut; the honourable Nicholas Cooke, Esq; Deputy Governor and Commander in Chief of Rhode Island; and the honourable John Wentworth, Esq; President of the Provincial Congress of New Hampshire. At the present time for which the present army is raised will all expire in two or three months, these gentlemen, with the members of the honourable Council of this colony, are appointed to meet and confer with his Excellency

George Washington of the subject of forming and establishing another Continental Army, for the defence of the invaded rights of the united Colonies.

NEW-YORK Oct. 19. Copy of a letter from Governor Tryon, to Whitebrad Hicks, Esq; Mayor of this city.

From undoubted authority from the city of Philadelphia the Continental Congress have recommended it to the Provincial Congress, to seize or take up officers of this government, and particularly myself by name: I am therefore to desire you would inform the corperation, and the citizens of this city, I place my security here in the protection, that when that confidence is withdrawn by seizure of my person, the commander of his Majesty's ships of war in the harbour will demand that the inhabitants deliver me on board the fleet, and on refusal enforce the demand with their whole power; therefore, anxious to prevent if possable, so great a calamity, to the city, as well as in consequence to myself, I am ready, should the voice of the citizens be unfavourable to me staying among them, immediately to embark on board the Asia, requesting that the citizens will defeat every attempt that may be made to hinder my removal domesticks and effects should that be their wish; Since I returned to this province, with every honourable intention to serve them, consistent with my branden duty to my Sovereign."

We are informed that several gentlemen in Ulster county, have lately received letters, (one of which is from and officer of note, dated the 4th instant) from our Capt. Prescot, the commanding officer at St. John's had sent out a flag to General Montgomery, offering to surrender the fort, and being allowed to march out with the honours of war, and artillery; but that the General had returned for an answer, that the possession of the garrison was not his principal object, and that he could not capitulate on any terms but their surrendering as prisoners of war.

The letters also mention, that 4 or 500 Canadians had joined our Army, that great numbers of others were employed in providing necessaries for it, and that the people in general appeared very friendly, and ready to promote our Design.

We have heard from several credible persons that there was no truth in the reports which was current last week, that Col. Allen and his party or any of them had been taken prisoners, in Canada.

By accounts, dated the fourth of October, we are informed, that General Montgomery was carrying on his approaches towards Fort St. John's with the utmost vigour; and that the officers and men bear the severities of the climate with great firmness and fortitude.

NEW-YORK Oct. 22.   (From the Pennsylvania Mercury) published in Philidelphia.

Copy from an Address generally agreed to by the privates of upwards of thirty companies, belonging to this city and district, and presented to the Officers by the General Committee of the privates of said companies, being in consequence of an application from the officers to know those reasons for refusing to sign the Military articles delivered out by the Committee of Safety, which address was presented by the Officers on the 27th ult. in the Honourable House of Assembly.

Gentlemen,

At this time of difficulty and danger when our privileges are attacked by a powerful enemy, and the best blood on the continent is daily spilling in there defence deem any attempt to weaken or destroy the principles on which we have associated to be subversive of our liberties, and unbecoming any well-wishers to America, and are determined to the utmost of our power to oppose it. We therefore beg leave to assure you, that the objections we make to signing the rules of the committee of safety proceed from no such principle, but from a sincere desire to promote and encourage the association.

We conceive it to be contrary to the true end and intention of legislation, for any body of men, claiming legislative authority, to make any laws which shall, under heavy penalties, oblige

one part of the community to the performance of
duties of the utmost difficulty and danger, while
it exempts another part of the said community
from the performance of them, though the party
exempted is to reap equal advantage by the performance with those who are obliged to perform
them. This principle we conceive is destructive
of the end and design of civil society.

For we have been thought to believe, that in
a free state, no man is above the laws, but that
even the King of free countries are as much under the dominion of the laws as the treatment
of their subjects. And the true distinction between the liberty and despotism, consist in
this, that in a free state, every member thereof
is subject to every law of the land, but in
despotic states, one part is bound whilst the
other is free, and by this means the party bound
is always considered as slaves to the party which
is free.

We conclude therefore, that the laws which
equally binds every member of the community, be
it ever to severe has its origin in freedom, and
may safely be submitted to by freedom; but the
law which bears hard upon or blinds one part of
the community to the performance of difficulty
and danger services, while it exempts another
part, though both are to be equally benefited
by said services; has its origin in despotism,
and ought never to be submitted to by freemen.

The being promised, we proceed to lay before
you our objection against the present article
drawn up by the committee of safety.

1st Because as the Continental Congress has
recommended that a general association of all
able bodied effective men; between sixteen and
fifty years of age in each colony, should take
place, so we judge it very imprudent to sign any
military laws until that measure is come into.
And we cannot help hinting, that the attempting
to have such laws signed before the order takes
place, looks as if there was a design to make
the present associators a kind of regular army
of defence of the whole province, as the gentlemen who made the rules seem to claim to themselves the right of calling out any or all the

present association, and of putting then on pay, which, if once submitted to, the rules will enable them to keep up in their condition as long as they please, or subject us to martial law in case of refusal. This we apprehend has a direct tendency to prevent a general association, as the present association, if the rules are once signed must march forth, and as long as they can stand, defend the whole province. Let a general association take place according to the resolve of the congress and then we pledge ourselves, that we will show a sufficient degree of tenderness to join our brethren in every measure necessary for the repelling every hostile invader, and establishing our inestimable privileges on the most lasting foundation.

2d Because we look upon standing armies as dangerous to the liberties of mankind, we refuse to subscribe any laws which may put it henceforth in the power of any number of men to make use of us as such. Nevertheless, tho' we have expressed our dislike to standing armies, and are unwilling to put the province to any needless expence, yet as the present stoppage of trade will necessarily throw many poor people out of their bread, and as we are bound on duty and humanity to provide for such, we should think the most decent and useful way of doing it would be to enlist such on pay for six months as would voluntarily offer at the end of which they may be retained or discharged, as the state of our affairs may make it expedient, provided the persons, so enlisted and continued, have liberty at the end of each year to renew their enlistments, or demand their discharge, which shall be granted, unless they at the time are commanded, or have notice to hold themselves in readiness against a common enemy.

3d Because we know of no right which our assembly has to invest any body of men with legislative authority, the being an unalienable essential right belonging to the whole body of the freemen of which society is constituted. We therefore conceive it to be a new and unheard of exertion of power, inconsistent with the trust reposed in them by their constituents, and erecting a dangerous precedent if submitted to, as the body thus invested it not subject to the controul of, or liable to be called to an account by the people.

4th Because if any emergency we should permit our representatives to exercise such a power while confined to their own body, yet we conceit that they have no right to invest any one of their body with such a trust, unless by the express direction of the freemen at large.

5th Because no representative body has a right to make, nor will we ever submit to the operation of any military law made by our Assembly, but such as equally extends to every inhabitant of the whole province, except on the following conditions, viz.

"If at any time an exception from the operation of any law be judged proper and necessary, let the term of exception be fairly and fully expressed, let the mulct or fine, if any thereby, be proportioned to each man's property, and then let every man have the liberty to submit to the law, or by paying according to the terms of excemption be free of its operation."

Thus far we apprehend the partiality of the articles has constrained as to object, and we should most certainly be wanting to ourselves, and to the rights of mankind in general, if we did not with honesty, freedom and security, exhibit our utmost sentiments to the present legislature of Pennsylvania, men who, we trust, will ever rejoice to hear the voice of their constituents.

PHILADELPHIA Oct. 22. Extract of a Letter from Ticonderoga, Oct. 5, 1775.

"Our last account from St. John's, inform us, that Col. Allen, with about 30 of our Men and 40 Canadians made an attempt to take possession of Montreal, but that Governor Carleton (at half johanas each man) had prevailed on a number of the inhabitants to assist some few regulars; who beat off our party, took Col. Allen prisoner, with some others; and as many killed and wounded. The party that came out of Montreal were more worsted than our men, had many killed; amongst which it is supposed, several principal inhabitants of the city.

"The expedition was a thing of Col. Allen's own head, without orders from the General; and from whom (as well as others) he received much censure. If they had been apprized of it, they could have put him in a situation to have succeeded without danger. But Allen in a high flying genius, persued every scheme on its first impression, without consideration, and much less judgement. It is with the utmost difficulty, and through the greatest entreaty, that General Shuyler permitted him to go with the army, knowing his natural disposition; and indeed his fears having proved not groundless; and tho' trifling our loss, and the detachment, yet it gives a check to our progress.

"General Montgomery writes, they have got a battery of two twelve pounders and two mortars open on our enemy; our shells are thrown into the fort: they, on their part do little damage to us. I think but two men have been killed, one by cannon ball, and the other by a shell."

We hear 30 Ministerial troops at St. John's had deserted from the fort and joined General Montgomery, who commands the Continental troops, and they report that as many more will desert as soon as the opportunity offers.

WATERTOWN Oct. 23. Extract of an intercepted letter to an officer in the navy, to his father in Great-Britain, dated August 24, 1775.

"I think it my duty to inform you at every opportunity which offers, where, and how I am situated. We find the country (as much as we can view of it from the mast head of our ship) to be very inviting, but the people are so strenuous in support of their rights and liberties that there is no venturing among them; no lad of 16 without his musket, and every man has in proportion; with ammunition in great plenty. I know not what you think of the Americans, but it so generally thought that their pretensions are in such measures founded of just principles, and we hear they wish for peace: They are determined to stand out to the last, and are so warlike that they oblige us to keep a good look out all day, and to be under arms all night,

expecting hourly some attack to be made; it is
tho't possible for them to destroy us if they
please, being the only man of war at or near
this place, and as affairs are at present carried on so much against them, I make no doubt
but they will attempt it before long."

WATERTOWN Oct. 23. We have seen an address to
Gen. Gage on his departure for England, dated
6th October, 1775; signed by 93 of the tory
faction in Boston, with the General's answer.
Also an address from his new fanglee council,
without any signers,, and the General's answer
thereto. And an address from the refugees in
Boston, signed by 76 of them, with the General's
answer; all which being so lenghthy we could
not give them a place in this day's paper.

Thom. Gage before his departure, issued a commission appointing Glenn Brush "Receiver of all
such goods, chattles, and effects as may be voluntarily delivered, into his charge, by the owners of such goods, or the person or persons
whose care they may be left in, and to give a
receipt for the same; and he is to take care and
deliver said goods when call'd upon, to those
whom he shall give a receipt for the same."
Faneuil-Hall is provided for the reception of
such goods in order that they may be as compact
as possible in case of plunder:

Bostoneans !!! Have you forgot your arms were
most shamefully deposited there?

Thom. Gage on the Third Instant, (5 or 6 Days
before his Departure for England) issued a Proclamation, offering a reward of Ten Guineas, to
any one who shall discover the Thief or Thieves,
that some Time in the Month of September last
stole from the Council Chamber in Boston, the
Public Seal, his private Seal, and the Seal of
the Supreme Court of Probate of the Province.
Quere. Whether as he carried his Secretary. T.
Flucker, with him, 'tis not as likely that he
might have carried them off as any one else?

HARTFORD Oct. 23. Extract of a letter from an
officer at St. John's.

"On the 16th of September we left the Isle of
aux Noix, in order to lay seige to St. John's
as we had before sent a party of 100 to Chamblee,

who hearing that some regulars were transporting some provisions to St. John's attacked them took 2 prisoners, and a considerable prize, and then began to fortify about 2 miles from St. John's in order to cut off communications, expecting soon reinforcements from our army. But being discovered by the enemy at St. John's, a party of 200 regulars sallied out with field pieces, and our men being but half their number, and poorly fortified, were obliged to retreat to the camp. In the Action Capt. John Watson, in Col. Hinman's regiment, was badly wounded, but is likely to recover. We were then on our march thro' the woods for their relief, but too late! when we came to the place where the battle was fought, we found the enemy in possession of our breast work. They gave us a very heavy fire, and then retreated back to the fort. Col. Allen with a party hath since had a battle near Montreal, and is taken prisoner with 14 more. We have shut up St. John's, and expect soon to be in possession of that Place. We are constantly playing on them with our cannon and bombs. The Canadians are chiefly on our side, the Indians are for us."

Our intelligence from St. John's is as late as the 10th instant, when our army were bombarding that place, and it was expected the enemy would soon surrender.

NEWPORT Oct. 23. A letter from a gentleman at Bristol Oct. 12, 1775.

"Dear Sir,
Having observed the Newport Mercury, an inperfect account relating to the conduct of his majesty's ships, under the command of Capt. Wallace at Bristol, last Saturday night, I embrace this opportunity to give you a true particular detail of facts, that took place, from their anchoring in the harbour till they left town. On Saturday the 7th Instant P. m. appeared in sight of the harbour, a very formidable fleet, consisting of 16 sail, viz. three men of war, one bomb ketch, and other vessels all which, excepting the Glasgow (who was ashore at Paquash point) drew up in a line for battle, from one end of the town to the other: soon after they had moored, a barge came from the Rose, to the head of the wharf,

with the lieutenant, who asking if there were any gentlemen on the wharf? William Bradford being present, answered yes; whereupon the Lieutenant informed him, Captain Wallace had a demand to make on the town, and desired that two or three of the principal men, of magistrates of the town would go on board his ship, within an hour, and hear his proposals, otherwise hostilities would be commenced against the town: the above gentleman replied as a magistrate, that, in his opinion Captain Wallace was under a greater obligation to come on shore, and make his demands known to the town, than for the magistrates to go on board his ship to hear them; and added, that if Capt. Wallace would come to the head of the wharf the next morning, he would be treated as a gentleman, and the town would consider of his demands; with this answer the Lieutenant returned on board the Rose. The inhabitants being made acquainted with the above conversation, repaired to the wharf, and waited with the utmost impatience, for a reply from Captain Wallace till an hour had expired, when the whole fleet began a most heavy cannonading, and the bomb vessel to bombard, and heavy shells and carcases into the town, which continued, without interruption an hour and a half.

In the mean time Col. Potter in the height of the fire, went upon the head of the wharf, and hailed the Rose, went on board and requested a cessation of hostilities, till the inhabitants might choose a committee to go on board to meet with Capt. Wallace; which request was complied with; and for six hours were allowed for the above purpose. Col. Potter returned and made report to the committee of inspection, who chose a select committee to hear Capt. Wallace's demands, which after they had gone on board Capt. Wallace informed them were a supply of 200 sheep and 30 fat cattle. The demands, the committee replied, it was impossible to comply with, for the country people had come in and drove off their stock, leaving a few sheep and some milch cows.

After some hours had expired during the negotiation, without coming to any agreement, Capt.

Wallace told them. I have this proposal to make "if you will promise to supply me with 40 sheep at or before 12 o'clock, I will assure you that another gun shall not be discharged." The committee seeing themselves reduced to the distressing alternative, either to supply their most inveterate enemy with provisions, or devote to the flames of the town, with all the goods, besides many 100 sick persons, who could not be removed without the most hazard to their lives. I say, seeing themselves reduced to the dreadful dilemma of two evils reluctantly chose the least, by agreeing to supply them with 40 sheep at the time appointed. which was mutually preformed.

The Rev. Mr. John Butt having been confined to his house by the camp distemper, when the cannonading begun left his habitation, to seek some place of safety, and the next day was found dead in a neighbouring field. It is conjectured that being overcome with fear and fatigue fell down and was unable to rise himself up, and so expired; A child also of Captain Timothy Ingraham having been removed in the rain, died the next day.

What equally challenges our administration, and gratitude to God is, that no more than five were lost, or persons hurt, by such an incessant and hot fire; the street being full of men, women and children, the whole time; the shricks of the women, the cries of the children, the groans of the sick, would have extorted tears of even the eyes of Nero. --- But I forebear --- words can't describe the dreadful scene.

After the ships had received their supply, and stole about 90 cheeses, and some poultry, from Papaquash Point; weighed anchor, and moored at Papaquash Point; the next day (being Tuesday) they went into Bristol ferry and fired a number of shot at the houses and people on each shore, where three of them got aground, but the tide rising towards evening, they left us, and have not molested us since.

A great number of the dwelling houses, &c. were shot through; but suffered very little damage. A cannon ball entered a distill-house, then passed through three hogsheads and barrels of rum, and spilt all their contents."

NORWICH Oct. 23. Lately received form London, dated July 27, 1775.

The following is said to be the plan which will be put in execution for reducing America.

Ten thousand Hanoverians are to be taken into British pay, the expences to be defrayed out of duties to be laid by Parliament, and levied in America. This body of men are to be stationed in several parts of the continent, and to be kept foot in peace as well as war. Fortresses are to be built in the provinces of New-England, New York, Pennsylvania, and Virginia, in which those foreign mercenaries are to be stationed, and accommodated with barracks, firing, &c. at the expence of the several colonies, in which they shall happen to be quartered. Besides this. a fleet of five ships of the line and twenty frigates are always to be stationed in that service, both to prevent smuggling, and in case of any disturbance to be ready to co-operate in reducing the rebellious or disaffected to obedience. Every Hanoverian soldier, who shall have served seven years with the approbation of his superior officer or officers shall have a portion of ground, not more than fifty, nor less than twenty acres, rent free, for ever. The expence of raising a proper habitation furnishing the same, purchasing implements of husbandry &c. to be provided in like manner, that is to say 50 pounds for every soldier, and 100 pounds for each trooper, rating his horse at 50 pounds and himself at as much more.

This mercenary army is to consist of thirty battalions of infantry, of 300 men each, and four regiments of calvary,twenty battalions and two regiments of which are always to be stationed in the four New-England provinces; and the remaining ten battalions and two regiments at New York Pennsylvania, and Williamsburg in Virginia, and their neighbourhood. On the whole, as the Germans are known to be very prolific people, it is supposed that by the beginning of the year 1800. there will be no less than a million of that nation, including their offspring' within the four New-England provinces alone.

NORWICH Oct. 23. Last Saturday Evening Donald Saffard arrived here from the American Camp, near St. John's, which place he left the 7th instant. He employed by the Connecticut troops to go Post alternately between Ticonderoga and this Town, but happening to be at the former Place when orders were received for the Army to proceed to Canada, and lay seige to St. John's, went along with them to see the Issue. He kept a journal of the proceedings of both Armies as far as lay within the Circumference of his ability; and has favoured us with the following Extracts viz.

Sept. 17. We embarked for St. John's, arrived the same day, and that night received five shot from the enemy.

Sept. 18. The enemy threw eight bomb shells, and fired 30 cannon, without doing us the least damage, we returned forty-four shot (12 poundders) struck a batteau, and an armed schooner several times. Received an intelligence that Major Brown had an engagement with the enemy, and had taken 8 waggons loaded with provisions.

Sept. 19. Both sides quit:

Sept. 20. A Batteau was sent out by the enemy as a spy, and drove back by Capt. Douglas, who fired a twelve pounder at her, one of which took effect: three head of horned cattle and 40 sheep taken by our troops at Chamblee: Three women took one of the enemy's serjeants, who was going through the country as a spy (in disguise) and brought him in a horse cart to our army: between 10 and 11 at night a smart fire was received from the enemy.

Sept. 21. The fire from the enemy last night was occasioned by a party of troops being repulsed who went to take same cattle and hogs, near Major Brown's encampment; 11 o'clook three French tories and one of the enemy serjeants, taken prisoners and brought into our camp; information received that one of the scouting parties have taken 16 waggon loads with provisions, rum, brandy, &c. At 2 o'clock the enemy renewed their fire and we kept exchanging shot with them till night.

Sept. 22. The enemy kept firing alternately till sunset without doing us any damage, began a heavy fire at 7 o'clock with balls, grape shot, and bombs, one of our men killed.

Sept. 23. They kept up a brisk fire all day and threw between 30 and 40 shells; no damage done except one man slightly wounded; in the evening seven prisoners were brought into camp.

Sept. 24. The enemy began to fire at sun-rise, and continued all day without doing any damage.

Sept. 25. They began their usual music this morning and continued all day: At five o'clock we fired four cannon, two shot of which went through their armed schooner, and 'tis supposed would have sunk her, if they had not been immediately wharped on shore.

Sept. 26. At 4 o'clock, in the afternoon we fired 4 cannon, received a like complement from the enemy, suffered no damage.

Sept. 27. A brisk fire on both sides the whole day, one of our gunners killed by a cannon ball from the enemy.

Sept. 28. Intelligence is receive that Col. Allen with 20 men had engaged a body of 200 of the enemy, about two miles from Montreal, that Col. Allen was either killed or taken prisoner, together with his men.

Sept. 29. The enemy fired a few shot this morning, and about 9 o'clock at night a smart fire began on both sides, which continued till ten.

Sept. 30. No firing on either side.

Oct 1st, 2d, and 3d. The enemy fired a few shot.

Oct. 4. A party of French, who act in concert with our army, began entrenchment on the east side of the Lake, which the enemy perceiving, sent an armed sloop with troops on board to drive them off; but the French gave them so warm a reception, that they were obliged to make a precipitate retreat back to St. John's, with the loss of about 20 men. The French had one man slightly wounded.

Oct. 5. No material occurrence.

Oct. 6. In the night we threw 6 bomb shells into St. John's, and had 31 in return without doing any damage.

Oct. 7. The enemy were playing their cannon on our troops this morning, when I came away.

Mr. Safford informs, that it is generally believed Col. Allen is alive. That the account of the armed schooner being taken is without foundation, that St. John's is surrounded and must soon surrender and it is thought, Their stock of provisions is nearly exhausted and that the Canadians are much in our favor.

The Cambridge post, who arrived here on Saturday informs; That on the Night of Tuesday last, that three Floating Batteries went from our army to the bottom of Boston common, and began a smart fire on the encampment of the Ministerial Army; they had not played long before one of the Cannon burst, killed one man and wounded nine, and set fire to the stock of powder, by means of which unlucky accident they were obliged to return. That some young men, who came out of Boston the Day following (with permission) to catch fish, informed that if our Troops had made a general Attack that Night, they might have easily taken the Town; for the Officers were at a Ball, and more intent to please the Ladies than defending themselves.

PHILADELPHIA Oct. 25. On Monday morning, the 18th instant before day, a transport ship Capt. Hastings, was stranded on Brigantine Beach, on the New-Jersey Coast. She had on Board, Captain Duncan Campbell, Lieut. Sims, two Serjeants, and twenty-one privates bound from Boston to New-York, as a recruiting party. The Captain and Lieutenant, got off the Beach the next day in a small boat, went towards New-York, in order to get on board the Asia Man of War, but were prevented by the zeal and activity of Lieutenant Loveland, off Egg Harbour, who, after a pursuit of 3 hours, took them on board a small vessel at Cranberry Inlet, assisted by Lieutenant Cook with six men from the adjacent county. Captain Hasting, and three of the soldiers, were brought to this city last Saturday evening, under guard; the rest of the soldiers, with the Captain and brought here yesterday. Before they quitted the ship they threw overboard several pieces of cannon belonging to the vessel, 60 muskets and

two and a half barrels of powder. The vessel
left Boston the 5th of October, in company with
a twenty gun ship, and one transport with some
troops bound to Halifax. No other ship of war or
troops had sailed. General Gage was to sail in a
day or two in a merchant ship of 16 guns. The
48th and 59th regiments being greatly reduced,
the privates are Incorporated into other regiments, and their officers going home. The object
of Col. Arnold's expedition was not known at
Boston, but supposed to be determined against
Halifax.

PHILADELPHIA Oct. 25. Extract of a letter from
Quebec, dated 18th Sept.

"The 17th instant, at the request of Lieut.
Governor, the British and Canadian inhabitants
assembled on the Parade, the latter were formed
into eleven companies the former into six. The
British and Canadian Militia of this place, will
consist of about 1100 men, many of whom neglect,
and others think the duty hard, and the greater
part are dissatisfied with the conduct of the
Government, and every day convinces them that
they are deceived. The snow Field of Whitby is
taken into Government service, to be commanded
by Capt. Napier, it is said she is to carry 18
six and nine pounders; The ship Charlotte, being engaged to Mr. Roach of Rhode Island; likewise a sloop schooner of this place; can't inform
you what force they will carry; they have also
a small vessel that is sent express to Boston.
Our militia amount guards from nine to nine in
the morning; and yet they have not received any
ammunition, except four rounds in the evening,
which gives reason to believe the Government is
afraid to trust them with a large quantity. The
public in general are dissatisfied with Government for not letting them know the true state
of the province, which may be supposed much worse
than is represented, for the Governor ordering
his Lady to England; she has taken her passage
in the Ship Lydia, Capt. Deane, who is said on
Friday next; there are many other Ladies who are
preparing to leave the province; Likewise some
men who are conscious that their conduct does
not deserve civil treatment from the Provincials,

should they come into the province. It is constantly reported here, that Mr. Livingston and
Jerry Dugan, had raised 190 Canadians, the former with the title of L. Colonel, the latter
with Major, who were near taking Lord Pitt and
General Carleton, on the river Chamblee. ————
Government reports that on General Carleton's
publishing a pardon for those that should come
in at a certain time,that.a great number of them
had abandoned their Officers."

PHILADELPHIA Oct. 25. Last Sunday died of an
appoplectic stroke, in the fifty third year of
his age, The Honourable Peyton Randolph, Esq;
of Virginia, late President of the Continental
Congress, and Speaker of the House of Burgesses
of Virginia.

PHILADELPHIA Oct. 25. Extract of a letter from
Quebec, Sept. 17, 1775.

"We have accounts from St. John's where the
King's troop are in garrison, that the continental troops were lying seige of it. The confusion
this has thrown every thing into, is inexpressible. Proper persons were immediately employed
in collecting what Canadians they could, in order
to take up arms, and I have the pleasure to assure you, they met with little or no success.
Was a vigorous effort to be made on your side,
this country would be your own. The tools of
government are in such employment, some in observing the conduct of the Canadians, and others
in watching the motion and actions of the English
Americans, who can neither speak or stir without
it being known."

CAMBRIDGE 26. Last Tuesday se'nnight, about
two hours before night, arrived before the town
of Falmouth, Casco-Bay, from Boston, the Canceaux, ship of war, Capt. Mowat, with four other
armed vessels. Mowat, who was the commandore,
sent a flag of truce ashore, informing the inhabitants that he should destroy the town in two
hours, unless they complied with certain proposals he should make. The people immediately assembled at the court-house and chose Brigadier
Preble, Dr. Coffin, and Mr. Pagan, a committee
to go on board the Canceaux, where Mowat read
his orders to them, which were in substance;

that, as a rebellion now existed in the american
colonies, unless the town would deliver up their
arms and ammunition, acknowledge the supremacy
of Parliament, and give up four hostages as security for their future good behaviour, he must
begin to cannonade and bombard the town within
two hours. On the committee's signifying that
they would not comply with his proposal, and
remonstrating to him the cruelty of not giving
the inhabitants time to remove their families
and effects, he consented as it was just night,
in their delivering to him eight arms, not to
fire on the town till eight o'clock the next
morning. The arms were procured and sent on board
and the inhabitants proceeded in removing the
women, children and effects, assisted by the
people from the country. In the morning the committee persuaded the barbarian to lenghten the
time half an hour, and on another application
prevailed upon him not to fire till nine o'clock.
In one minute after this time, the execrable
monster, with his infernal crew, began their
hellish work. Under protection of their cannon
and mortars, they landed about 100 men, who
plundered the houses, and set the town on fire
in several places, and in other parts the buildings were fire by shells and carcasses. They
continued their firing till after dark. Great
numbers of the inhabitants with many from the
country, continued in the town the whole day,
removing their effects notwithstanding the incessant fire of the enemy from five vessels.
Some of the people attacked and drove off the
party who landed, killing and wounding several
of them. But, by the goodness of providence,
not one of our men were killed, and but one
slightly wounded. The number of dwelling houses
destroyed, we are told, is 139, and 278 stores
and other buildings, which last being mostly
built near the water, were more immediately exposed. Mr. Mowat, on being asked why that town
was singled out, said, all the places, within
reach of their cannon, from thence to South-
Carolina, were to have the same fate. May heaven
protect an innocent, distressed people; and may
their implacable, cruel enemies perish in the

fire they are kindling for others.

NEW-YORK Oct. 26. Extract of a letter from
Ireland to an acquaintance at New-York.

"Though most of the people here wish well to
the cause in which you are engaged, and would
rejoice to have you continue firm and steadfast,
yet it is the prevailing opinion, of specially
among the friends to government, (so called)
that you will be at last frightened into submission to the ministerial measures. They are
raising recruits through this kingdom. The men
are told they are only going to Edinburg, to
learn military discipline, and then to return.
The common people are industriously kept from
the knowledge of public affairs. They know nothing but what the great people please to let them.
Newspapers, since the stamp act are so high, the
poor and middling people cannot purchase them,
nor even an almanack, not any to be found within
60 miles, except among the great folks; however,
so few are sold, that it is thought there will
be no more printed unless the act is repealed,
which is expected next session.

"It is most grievous to hear the innumerable
burden they have imposed on the people here. It
is intended to send Bishops to America, one at
least to every city, with salaries of 400 pounds
sterling each, to be paid by the people where
they are stationed.

It is expected that New-York will be the first
to submit to any terms that shall be offered,
and great pains have been taken to spread a general belief, that the people in all the colonies
are all cowards, ready to run at the sight of an
army. The news papers that are most circulated
are filled with such words, but not a word of
any thing spirited on your part, so that our
people are altogether ignorant of the true state
of affairs with you.

Dear Countrymen & Fellow Sufferers, who have
been so happy as to have your lot in a land of
Liberty, though now persecuted and your rights
invaded, suffer not your most precious Inheri-
tance, your Liberty and property, your noble
constitution, to be torn from you.

You are contesting for what is of more value to

life, fear not to give your lives freely in defence of it. Keep your presses free that the
people may know all that concerns them. By every
means on your power keep everyone from influenc-
ing any of your offices of public trust, you
cannot possibly be too much guarded against this
terrible evil, which has almost undone us here.
Let not arbitrary power and despotism have any
footing among you. Many in the country who groan
under it would be gland to give their utmost
assistance, and hope to be over with you before
the contest is ended.

It is my opinion, that if you continue firm,
you will without doubt, succeed in your glorious
struggle; justice will give strength to your
arms, and weaken those of your enemies. God himself is on your side, and will cause them to
fall before you. Mean while, let me caution you
against the appearance of submission; you can
hardly conceive the ill effects of every thing
that may feed the hopes of your enemies, even
bare complisance, in this case is criminal, for
like drowning men they are ready to catch at
straws, and, if possible interpret every thing
you say or do, in favor of their own designs,
whereby they are encouraged to continue their
efforts to subdue you; it Behoves you, therefore, to be resolute, plain and absolute in your
refusal of every treaty proposal that implies
giving up one one title of your rights and liberties, or might bring them into the least
danger; and resist every attempt against them,
with all your might. The least slackness or compliance on your part will embolden them to proceed in their endeavours to enforce their laws,
to tax and enslave you. May God guide and protect you Amen.

I am a sincere friend to the natural rights
and liberty of mankind, and yours, &c. M. W.

P. S. It is reported that Charles Stuwart is
preparing to make an attempt, to obtain the
crown of Scotland. I wait for further Intelligence.

WORCESTER Oct. 26. We are informed, that a
vessel arrived at Norwich landing, last Monday
morning, which left New-York five days before,

the master of which informs, that certain intelligence was received in New-York before he sailed, of a large ship, being cast away on Barnegat, the inhabitants of New-Jersey had secured every person on board; the ship was said to be high and dry; the Master could not ascertain whether the ship had soldiers on board or King's stores.

PHILADELPHIA Oct. 27. Extract from the Votes of the House of Representatives, Wednesday Oct. 18, 1775.

A Member presented at the table a letter from the Continental Congress to the Committee of Safety for this province, inclosing certain resolves of the said Congress, passed the ninth and twelfth of this instant, which were read by order, and are as they respectively follow, viz.

Congress Chamber, Oct, 12, 1775.

"Gentlemen,

"The present situation of affairs renders it absolutely necessary in the opinion of the Congress, for the protection of our liberties, and safety of our lives, to raise several new battalions, and therefore the Congress have come into the inclosed Resolutions, which I am ordered to transmit to you.

The Congress have the firmest confidence, that from your experienced Zeal in the great cause, you will exert your utmost endeavours to carry into execution the said Resolutions, and raise the battalion recommended to be raised with all possible expedion.

"The commissions I will fill up with the names of the persons you determine upon, immediately on the receipt of the list.

"I am Gentlemen.
"Your most obedient servant,
John Hancock, President."

To the Gentlemen of the committee of safety for Pennsylvania. Congress October 9, 1775.

"On Motion made,

"Resolve, That it is recommended to the convention of New-Jersey, that they immediately raise, at the expence of the Continent, two battalions, consisting of eight companies each, and each company of sixty eight privates, and officered with one Captain, one Lieutenant, one Ensign four Serjeants, and four Corporals.

"That the privates be enlisted for a year, at the rate of Five Dollars per calender month, liable to be discharged at any time, on allowing them one month's pay extraordinary.

"That each of the privates be allowed, instead of a bounty, a felt hat, a pair of shoes, a pair of yarn stockings; the men to find their own arms.

That the pay of the officers for the present be the same as that of the officers in the present Continental Army, and in case the pay of the officers is augmented to pay of the officers in these battalions shall in like manner be augmented from the time of their engaging in the service.

OCTOBER 12, 1775.

"Resolved,

"That each Captain and other commissioned officers, while on the recruiting service of this Continent or on their march to join the army, shall be allowed Two Dollars and Two Thirds of a Dollar per week, for their subsistence; and that the men who enlist, shall each of them, while in quarters, be allowed One Dollar per week, and One Dollar and One Third of a Dollar when on their march to join the Army for the same purpose.

"That the President transmit to the Convention of New-Jersey, blank commissions to be filled up by the Convention, to the Captains and Subaltern officers in the said two battalions and that the appointment of the field officers be for the present suspended untill Congress shall order on that matter.

The form of the enlistment to be in the following words, Viz.

I ------ -------, have this day voluntarily enlisted myself as a soldier in the American Continental Army for one year, unless sooner discharged, and do bind myself to conform in all instances to such rules and regulations as are, or shall be established for the government of said Army."

Resolved, That a similar recommendation issue

359

to the Assembly, or Committee of Safety of Pennsylvania, to raise one battalion on the same terms as those ordered to be raised in New-Jersey, and to be officered in like manner.

Resolve, That the men enlisted be furnished with a hunting shirt, not exceeding in value One Dollar and a Third of a Dollar, and a blanket, provided they can be procured, but not to be made part of the term of enlistment.

Ordered to lie on the table,
John Hancock, President.
A copy from the minutes
Charles Thomson, Secretary.

WILLIAMSBURG Oct. 8. After Lord Dunmore, with his troops and the navy, had been for several weeks seizing the persons and properties of his Majesty's peaceable subjects in this colony, on Wednesday night last a party from an armed tender, landed near Hampton, and took away a valuable negro man slave and a sail from the owner. Next morning there appeared off the mouth of Hampton river, a large armed schooner, a sloop, and three tenders, with soldiers on board; and a message was received at Hampton from Captain Squire, on board the schooner, that he would that day land and burn the town. On which a company of regulars, and a company of minute men; who had been places there in consequence of former treats denounced against that place made the best disposition to prevent their landing, aided by a body of militia, who were suddenly called together on the occasion. The enemy accordingly attempted to land, but were retarded by some boats sunk across the channel for that purpose. Upon this they fired several small cannon at the Provincials, without effect, who in return, discharged their small arms so effectually, as to make the enemy move off with the lost of several men, as it is believed; but they had, in the mean time burnt down a house belonging to Mr. Cooper on that river.

On the intelligence reaching Williamsburg, about nine at night a company of the rifle men were dispatched to the aid of Hampton, and the Colonel of the second regiment sent to the command of the whole, who, with company, arrived

about eight o'clock next morning. The enemy had
in the night cut through the boats sunk, and
made a passage for their vessels, which were
drawn up close to the town, and began to fire
upon it soon after the arrival of the party from
Williamsburg; but as soon as our men were so
disposed as to give them a few shot, they went
off so hastily, that our people took a small
tender with 5 white men a woman, and 2 slaves,
6 swivels, 7 muskets, some small arms, and other
things, a sword, pistol, and several papers belonging to a Lieutenant Wright, who made his
escape by jumping overboard, and swimming away
with Mr. King's negro man, who are on shore and
a pursuit it is hoped may overtake them. There
were in the vessel, two men mortally wounded,
one is since dead and the other near his end;
besides which, we are informed, nine men were
to be thrown overboard from one of the vessels.
We had not a man even wounded. The vessels went
over to Norfolk, and we are informed the whole
force from thence is intending to visit Hampton
to day. If they come, we hope our brave troops
are prepared for them, as we can with pleasure
assure the public, that every part of them, behaved with spirit and bravery and are wishing
for another skirmish.

NEWPORT Oct. 30. Last Wednesday arrived here
his Majesty's Viper sloop of war having taken 2
brigs, loaded with salt, and a larger sloop,
loaded with rum and sugar, from antigua; all
belonging to New-York. One of the brigs, Capt.
Liburn arrived here a few hours after the Viper.
The sloop had a Midshipman, and 7 hands put on
board; one of whom, belonging to Bristol in the
colony, was to pilot her into this harbour; instead of which he carried her up near Howland's
ferry, where she was taken possession of by some
of the troops stationed on this island, and the
people taken prisoners. The other brig, above
mentioned arrived here yesterday.

Extract of a letter from Charlestown, South
Carolina, to a gentleman in this town dated
Sept. 13, 1775.

"A post is now established, and I cheerfully
pay the expence of a letter, now and then, that

I may have the pleasure of hearing from you. I want much to know what station you are in at Newport, whether you are in danger of having your town destroyed from the man of war or who have come to terms with them? I hope they will not do any thing they may bring them into disgrace with the other colonies; people here in general seem fully determined at present not to let any troops that may be sent here land, at the risk of their lives properties, and every thing that is dear to them. We have an exceeding well regulated militia in town, consisting of 13 volunteer companies, all in uniform, and two more raising besides 1500 Provincial troops in pay, and for their maintenance have ordered a million of paper money to be made."

HARTFORD Oct. 30. Last Friday were conducted to this Place, 18 Prisoners of the 26th Regiment of Ministerial Troops, taken by a Party from the American Army near St. John's.

NEW-YORK Oct. 30. The following is the substance of the Examination of Elijah Cable, of Fairfield, in Connecticut, taken on Friday last before the Provincial Congress, viz.

That he left St. John's on Friday the 13th, that there is about 4000 Men at that Place; General Montgomery is on the South Side, and the Canadians on the East Side; the Bomb Battery is 66 or 67 Rods from the Fort, that they has set one Barrack on fire in the Fort, with the great Mortar commonly called Old Sow. On Saturday the 14th, when he was at the Isle aux Noix, a very heavy firing began early in the morning, and continued until Night, and then began the next morning, and continued until ten o'clock, when firing ceased; what was the Event of this action he cannot tell, the wind being fair he set sail. He met General Wooster near Ticonderoga; our People had taken from the Regulars some Blanket Coats, Stockings and Shoes, four hogsheads of Rum, and some Wine; that a party of the Regulars went out in a Floating Battery to drive off our Canadians, about 500 in Number, who were at work on the East Battery, but were repulsed three days successively. Saw several Indians when he came away. Our People lie on the North side about

Three Quarters of a Mile from the Fort, and often
go up and kill the Centinels. Provisions plenty
and the Men in good Spirit. Our Army had lately
received a reinforcement of 600 Men, a Sloop, a
Schooner, and two Row-Gallie, each has a twelve
Pounder, and eight to nine Swivels; A Boom is
across at Isle aux Noix. Our People shot several
holes through the King's vessel after she was
hauled up. No snow when we left St. John's.

Saturday last Capt. Quakenboss arrived here
from the Camp at St. John's: He confirms the
above account, with this addition, that Battery
last constructed would rake the Parade in the
Fort at St. John's.

FAIRWEATHER, Thomas 68
FARMER, Nathaniel 25
FARRAR, Jonathan 49
FARRIS, Zaheriah 124
FELT, Jusha 26
FERGERSON, Thomas 138
FERRIS, Joseph Jr 123-124
   Zackeriah 123
FESSENDEN, Thomas 47 Thos
   48
FINNEY, Lt 185
FISK, Arnasa 282
FITZGERALD, Apt 184
FLEEMIMG, Edward 249
FLINT, William 25
FLOYD, Richard 54
FLUCKER, Thos 122
FOOT, Mr 125
FOSSET, Ameriah 282
FOSTER, Capt 79 Col 9 Dr
   114 Isaac 264 Stephen
   283
FRANKLIN, Benj 40
   Benjamin 156 243 338
   Dr 63
FRASER, Malcom 70
FREEMAN, Sam 147 Samuel
   37 64-65 88 94 113 129
   161 171 181
FRENCH, Maj 244 328
FRENELS, Col 265
FROST, Jacob 282 Samuel
   26 114
FULLER, Capt 185 Maj 161
FULSON, Nathaniel 126
G----WOLD, Matthew 338
GADSDEN, Christopher 33
GAGE, 123 223 275-276 284
   304 318 G 97 Gen 5 13
   15-16 19 24-25 27 37-
   39 52 57 59 62-63 65
   73-74 78 91 95 118 127
   133 136 162 167 178-
   179 185-186 195 199-
   200 203 229-230 235
   238 247-248 259-260
   273-274 277 296 311
   328 338 345 353

GAGE (cont.)
   Geo 320 George 308 Mr 236
   Tho 200 Thom 345 Thomas
   119 126 134 147 172 261
   307 310 Thos 122 Tom 186
   257 337
GAGES, Gen 219
GAINE, Mr 206
GAMBLE, Tho 320
GARDINER, 212
GARDNER, Col 17-18 132 137
   Isaac 25 Lt 185 Mr 142
   Thomas 156
GARFIELD, Abraham 48
GARNDER, John 172
GATES, Horatio 171 Huratio
   157
GAY, Martin 178
GILBERT, Thomas Peres 37
   Thos 37
GILDARD, Mr 192
GILL, John 248 283
GILLILAND, 250 Mr 251
GLAKEESEY, Capt 184
GLOVER, Col 199
GOFORTH, Capt 280 William
   191
GOLD, Lt 78
GOLDTHWAIT, Ebenezer 25
GOODELL, 296
GOODRICH, Mr 329
GORDON, William 99
GORHAM, 307 Col 288
   Nathaniel 53
GOULD, Edward Thornton 52-53
   Lt 26 108-109 185 Mr 29
   William 199
GRAHAM, Lt 286
GRAMAN, Samuel 18
GRAME, Ens 185
GRANT, Col 15 196 Francis
   200 Mr 321
GRAVES, Adm 93 Capt 69
GRAY, Danield 18 Edward 68
   George 155 Harrison 301
   Lewis 301 Mr 299
GREATON, Col 202 John 37
GREEN, 37 Gen 222 Isaac 45

NEVINS, David 1 5 Mr 3
NICHOLS, George 270
    William 234
NIXON, Col 84 John 149
NORTH, 110 198 307 Fredy
    323
NORTON, Jonathan 282
    Perez 245
NOYES, Mrs 18
O'SHIELDS, Mr 219
OBORNE, James 123
OLSWOLD, Capt 90
OSBORNE, James 124
OSWELL, Mr 83
OSWORLD, Capt 91
P----, Mr 228
PAGAN, Mr 354
PAGE, Engineer 185 John
    33
PAGETT, 37
PAINE, Robert Treat 26
    243 Robert-treat 40
    Timothy 80-81
PALFREY, William 185
PALMER, Capt 105 Pearse
    187 T 9
PARISH, Capt 277
PARKER, 108 Capt 43 47
    Col 148 201 Ebenezer
    45 John 43-46 Jonas 25
    Lt Col 282
PARKS, Isaac 48
PARMENTER, Jonathan 336
PARRY, Thomas 113
PARSON, Capt 29 76 Capts
    29 Col 73 132
PARSONS, Capt 76 109 184
    James 138 Samuel 5
PATCH, Samuel 277
PATERSON, William 256
PATTIN, Mathew 229
PAXTON, Lt 185
PECK, John 114 Philip
    Johnson 282 Samuel 270
PEIRCE, Nathan 49
PENDLETON, Edward 33
PENN, John 21
PENTABONE, Jonathan 271

PERCY, Earl 30 Lord 14 17 28
    77 102 109 212 218 259-260
PERKINS, Asa 207 John 282
    Robert 207
PETTIGREW, Lt 184
PHELPS, Noah 67 Robert 282
PHENIX, Daniel 249
PHIPP, 23
PHRIOR, Capt 322
PICKNEY, Charles 138
PIERCE, Benjamin 25 Col 29
    Solomon 25 45
PIERCY, Earl 24 38
PITCAINE, Maj 259-260
PITCAIRN, Col 148 Maj 74-75
    77-78 103-104 106-107 135
    180
PITECAIRN, Maj 185
PITT, Lord 354
PLICAIRN, Lt 185
POLLY, William 25
POMEROY, Gen 141
PORTER, Azeal 25
POTTER, Col 347 Isaac 261
    John 280 Lt 26 113
PREBLE, Brig 354
PRESCOT, Capt 328 339 Col
    277
PRESTON, 180 Daniel 114
    George 200
PUTNAM, Brig Gen 113
    Brigadier 73 Capt 199 Col
    84 Gen 78 94 114 116-117
    137 141 Henry 25 Israel 4
    7 157 Maj Gen 193 204 248
    Nathan 26 Perley 25
QUAKENBOS, John 191
QUAKENBOSS, Capt 363
RAMSDELL, Abadage 25
RANDOLPH, Payton 33 84 256
    276 Peyton 144 354
RAY, Lt 185
RECHWICH, Lt 184
REED, George 25 Joseph 149
    Joshua 45 Josua Jr 45 Mr
    25 Nathan 45
REID, George 33
REILY, Richard 156

372

REMSEN, Henry 226
REVERE, Mr 13 Paul 16 105
 148
REYNOLDS, Capt 69
RICHARDSON, Edward 49
 Moses 40
RICHMOND, William 324
RIGHARDSON, Lt 184
RITGER, Elias 280
RITZEMA, Col 191 283 Lt
 Col 229
ROACH, Mr 353
ROBBINS, John 25
ROBERDEAU, Daniel 149 156
ROBERSON, Lt 184
ROBERTS, Owen 138
ROBINS, John 44
ROBINSON, Bradberry 51
 Col 115 Eliha 221
 Jaromiah 221 Jeromiah
 221 William 221 282
RODNEY, Ceasor 33
ROMANS, Mr 90
ROME, George 95
ROMER, Ens 244
ROSS, George 156 Mr 323
ROSSETT, Lewis Henry 294
ROWLAND, Andrew 18
RUSMAND, John 25
RUSSEL, James 68 Jason 25
 Philip 44 Seth 26 114
RUTGERS, Capt 54
RUTH, Mr 299
RUTLEDGE, Edward 33 John
 33
RUTTER, John 191
SAFFORD, Mr 352
SANDERS, Capt 172
SANDERSON, Elijah 41-42
SAVAGE, Thomas 138
SAYBROOK, W 149
SCALLEY, Lt 281
SCHEEN, Maj 55 57
SCHEENE, Maj 67 81
SCHUYLER, 149 Gen 247 280
 289 291 Maj Gen 198
 229 Philip 157
SCIPIO, 272

SCOLEY, John 68
SCOTT, Capt 328 William 282
SEAR, Capt 312
SEARLE, Nathaniel Jr 143
SEARS, Isaac 249
SEAVER, Elijah 114
SEFFIANS, Daniel 282
SERENT, Ens 184
SERGEANT, Col 172
SERGENT, Col 264
SHARP, Thomas 113
SHARYST, Capt 185
SHAW, Mr 127
SHEA, Lt 185
SHEAD, Maj 297
SHERIFF, Maj 180 319
SHERMAN, Roger 41
SHUTWORTH, Lt 185
SHUYLER, Gen 191 265 284
 289-291 303 326 344 Maj
 Gen 203 Mr 320 Philip 54
SIMONDS, Joseph 45 Joshua
 107
SIMPSON, Mr 257
SIMS, Lt 352
SINCLAIR, Capt 185 Patrick
 230
SKEEN, Gov 328
SKENE, Maj 127 216
SLO--, Capt 81
SLOSS, Col 233
SMELT, Malor 185
SMITH, Archibald 172 Capt
 185 281 Col 52 65 76-78 96
 107 218 John 45 Lt Col 9
 23 28 74 259-260 Phinias
 45 Tho 221 Timothy 46-47
SNOW, Simeon 45
SNOWDEN, 329
SOUNDERSON, Samuel 45-46
SOUTER, Capt 128
SOUTHWICK, George 25
SPENCER, Capt Gen 297 Gen
 204
SPENDLOVE, Maj 184-185
SPORROW, Lt 282
SPRING, Samuel 51
SPRY, Lt 233

WARREN (cont.)
    Joseph 37 64-65 67 88
    94 Maj Gen 148
WASHINGTON, Col 63 137 G
    304 311 Gen 133 149
    180 183 222 244 263
    274 328 George 33 150
    157 160 302 308 310
    339
WATERBURY, Col 203 283
    286 288
WATSON, Abraham 298 John
    346 Mr 123 172 204 235
    271
WAYNE, Anthony 156
WEBB, Jothan 25 Samuel
    204 Samuel B 248
WEBSTER, Grant 69
WEISSENVELT, John 191
WENDALL, Oliver 115
WENTWORTH, Gov 182 277
    John 338
WEST, Capt 184
WHARTEN, Thomas Jr 156
WHEELER, Adam 199 Francis
    49 Peter 49
WHEELOCK, Dr 234
WHITE, Capt 229 Henry 297
    Mr 251 Mrs 297 Robert
    156
WHITEHEAD, John 48
WILCOX, Gidion 143

WILLARD, Lt 185 Thomas Price
    42
WILLET, Capt 191
WILLIAMS, Col 180 E 4
    Ebenezer 8 Job 257 John 68
    Maj 185 Mr 115
WILLING, Thomas 156
WILLINGTON, Enoch 45
WILSON, 200 Benjamin 282
    John 178 Jonathan 25
WINKOOP, Henry 156
WINN, Capt 280
WINSHIP, 106 John 25 Simon
    42-43 105 Thomas 25
WINSHOP, Thomas 45
WOLCOTT, Oliver 265
WOOD, Capt 255 315-316 David
    275 James 254 313
WOOSTER, 263 Col 245 Gen 136
    147 230 293 362 Maj 84
WORMELEY, Ralph 33
WRIGHT, Lt 361
WUNSHIP, John 45
WYLLY, Samuel 68
WYMAN, Jabez 25 James 45
    Nathaniel 25
WYNN, Capt 287
WYTHE, George 256
YATES, Capt 326
YOUNG, Capt 37-38
ZABLY, Dr 184
ZEDVOITZ, Maj 229